Get the eBooks FREE!

(PDF, ePub, Kindle, and liveBook all included)

We believe that once you buy a book from us, you should be able to read it in any format we have available. To get electronic versions of this book at no additional cost to you, purchase and then register this book at the Manning website.

Go to https://www.manning.com/freebook and follow the instructions to complete your pBook registration.

That's it!
Thanks from Manning!

Secure by Design

DAN BERGH JOHNSSON
DANIEL DEOGUN
DANIEL SAWANO

Foreword by Daniel Terhorst-North

MANNING
SHELTER ISLAND

For online information and ordering of this and other Manning books, please visit www.manning.com. The publisher offers discounts on this book when ordered in quantity.

For more information, please contact

Special Sales Department
Manning Publications Co.
20 Baldwin Road
PO Box 761
Shelter Island, NY 11964
Email: orders@manning.com

©2019 by Manning Publications Co. All rights reserved.

No part of this publication may be reproduced, stored in a retrieval system, or transmitted, in any form or by means electronic, mechanical, photocopying, or otherwise, without prior written permission of the publisher.

Many of the designations used by manufacturers and sellers to distinguish their products are claimed as trademarks. Where those designations appear in the book, and Manning Publications was aware of a trademark claim, the designations have been printed in initial caps or all caps.

♾ Recognizing the importance of preserving what has been written, it is Manning's policy to have the books we publish printed on acid-free paper, and we exert our best efforts to that end. Recognizing also our responsibility to conserve the resources of our planet, Manning books are printed on paper that is at least 15 percent recycled and processed without the use of elemental chlorine.

Manning Publications Co.
20 Baldwin Road
PO Box 761
Shelter Island, NY 11964

Development editor:	Jennifer Stout
Technical development editor:	Luis Atencio
Review editor:	Aleks Dragosavljević
Production editor:	David Novak
Copy editor:	Frances Buran
Proofreader:	Carl Quesnel
Technical proofreader:	John Guthrie
Typesetter:	Happenstance Type-O-Rama
Cover designer:	Marija Tudor

ISBN 9781617294358

Printed in the United States of America

To our families
　　　　—Dan Bergh Johnsson, Daniel Deogun, and Daniel Sawano

brief contents

v

contents

foreword

In the early 1990s I was in my first graduate job in the middle of a recession, and they were having a tough round of layoffs. Someone noticed that each victim's UNIX account was being locked out just before the friendly HR person came to tap them on the shoulder and escort them from the building. They wrote a small script to monitor differences in the user password file and display the names of users whose accounts were being locked. We suddenly had a magic tool that would identify the next target just before the hatchet fell...and an enormous security and privacy breach.

In my second job, as a programmer at a marketing firm, there were lots of password-protected Microsoft Word documents flying around, often with sensitive commercial information in them. I pointed out how weak the encryption was on these files, and how easy it was to read them using a freely available tool that was making the rounds on Usenet (your grandparents' Google Groups). No one listened until I started emailing the files back to the senders with the encryption removed.

Then I figured most people's login passwords were probably too weak as well. I got the same lack of response until I wrote a script that ran a simple password-cracking tool on a regular basis, and emailed people their login passwords. There was a pretty high hit rate. At that stage I didn't know anything about information theory, Shannon entropy, attack surface areas, asymmetric cryptography—I was just a kid with a password-cracking tool. But I became the company's *de facto* InfoSec Officer. Those were simpler times!

Over a decade later, as a developer at ThoughtWorks building a large-scale energy trading platform, I received what is still my favorite ever bug report. One of our testers noticed that a password field didn't have a check for password length, which should have been 30 characters. However, she didn't log the bug as "30 character password limit isn't being checked." Instead, she thought "I wonder how much text I could shove into that password field?" By a process of trial and error, the final bug report was "If you enter more than 32,000 characters in the password field, *then the application crashes.*" She had turned a simple validation error into a denial-of-service security exploit, crashing the entire application server just by entering a suitably crafted password. (Some years later I was at a software testing conference where they decided to use iPads for conference registration, using an app they had written themselves. I learned you should never do this with software testers, when a tester friend tried registering as "Julie undefined" and brought the whole system to its knees. Testers are evil.)

Fast-forward another decade or so to the present day, and I watch in dismay as nearly every week yet another data security breach of a high-profile company appears in the news. I could cite some recent ones, but they will be ancient history by the time you read this, and newer, bigger, more worrying data hauls of passwords, phone numbers, credit card details, social security numbers, and other sensitive personal and financial data will have appeared on the dark web, only to be discovered and reported months or years later to an increasingly desensitized and vulnerable public.

Why is this picture so bleak? In a world of free multifactor authentication, biometric security, physical tokens, password suites like 1Password (https://1password.com/) and LastPass (https://www.lastpass.com/), and notification services like Have I Been Pwned (https://haveibeenpwned.com), you could be forgiven for thinking we've got security covered. But as Dan, Daniel, and Daniel point out in the introduction (I felt obliged to write this foreword on the basis there weren't enough people called Daniel involved), there is no point having strong locks and heavy doors if a malicious actor can just lift the doors off their metaphorical hinges and walk off with the prize.

There is no such thing as a secure system, at least not in absolute terms. All security is relative to a perceived threat model, and all systems are more or less secure with respect to that model. The goal of this book, and the reason its content has never been more urgent or relevant, is to demonstrate that *security is first and foremost a design consideration.* It isn't something you can graft on at the end, however well-intentioned you are.

Security is in the data types you choose, and how you represent them in code. Security is in the domain terms you use, and how faithfully you model domain concepts and business rules. Security is in reducing the cognitive distance between the business domain and the tools you build to address customer needs in that domain.

As the authors demonstrate again and again throughout this book, reducing this cognitive distance eliminates entire classes of security risk. The easier we can make it for domain experts to recognize concepts and processes in the way we model a solution, and in the corresponding code, tests, and other technical artifacts, the more likely they are to spot problems. They can call out the discrepancies, inconsistencies, assumptions, and all the other myriad ways we build systems that don't reflect the real world: online bookstores where you can buy a negative number of books, password fields that allow you to submit a decent-sized sonnet, and sensitive account information that can be viewed by casual snoopers.

Secure by Design is my favorite kind of book for two reasons. First, it weaves together two of my favorite fields: Application and Information Security—in which I am an enthusiastic amateur—and Domain-Driven Design—in which I hope I can claim some kind of proficiency. Second, it is a practical, actionable handbook. It isn't just a call to arms about treating security seriously as a design activity, which would be a worthy goal in its own right, it also provides a raft of real examples, worked through from design considerations to actual code listings, that put meat on the bones of *security by design*.

I want to note a couple of standout examples, though there are many. One is the treatment of "shallow design," exemplified by using primitive types like integers and strings to represent rich business concepts. This exposes you to risks like the password exploit (a Password type would be self-validating for length, say, in a way a string isn't), or the negative books (a BookCount type wouldn't allow negative values like an integer does). Reading this section, as someone who has been writing software professionally for over 30 years, I wanted to reach back through time and hit my younger programming self on the head with this book, or at least leave it mysteriously on his desk with an *Alice in Wonderland*-style *Read Me* label on it.

Another exemplar is the topic of poor error handling, which is a huge source of potential security violations. Most modern programming languages have two types of code paths: the ones where things go OK, and the ones where bad things happen. The latter mostly live in a twilight zone of catch-blocks and exception handlers, or half-hearted guard clauses. As programmers, our cognitive biases conspire to convince us we have covered all the cases. We even have the hubris to write comments like `// this can't happen`. We are wrong again and again.

The late Joe Armstrong, an amazing systems engineer and inventor of the Erlang language, used to say that the only reliable way to handle an error is to "Let it crash!" The contortions we go through to avoid "letting it crash" range from the "billion-dollar mistake" of null pointers and their tricksy exceptions, through nested if-else stacks and the will-they-won't-they fall-through logic of switch blocks, to leaning on our IDEs to generate the arcane boilerplate code for interpolating strings or evaluating equality.

We know smaller components are easier to test than larger ones. They have exponentially fewer places for bugs to hide, and it is therefore easier to reason about their security. However, we are only beginning to understand the security implications of running a system of hundreds or thousands of small components—microservices or serverless architectures—and the fledgling domains of Observability and Chaos Engineering are starting to gain mindshare in a way DevOps and Continuous Delivery did before them.

I see *Secure by Design* as an important contribution to this trajectory, but focusing on the very heart of the development cycle, in the domain-modeling activities that DDD folks refer to as *knowledge crunching*, and leveraging the ideas of *ubiquitous language* and *bounded contexts* to bring security to the fore in programming, testing, deployment, and runtime. Shallow modeling and *post hoc* security audits don't cut it anymore.

We can't all be security experts. We *can* all be mindful of good Domain-Driven Design and its consequent impact on security.

Daniel Terhorst-North, Security Amateur, London, July 2019

preface

As developers, good design feels natural to us. Even before we met, all three of us enjoyed good code: code that speaks its intention, that captures the ideas of its creators in ways that are easy to understand, and that's intuitive to work with. We assume you also like good code. We also share a common interest in security, realizing both how important and how hard that work is. The digitization of our world is a marvelous thing, but bad security is one of the things that can undermine it.

Over the years, we've met and worked with lots of people. We've discussed code and design in general, and security in particular. The idea that high-quality programming practices can reduce the number of security-related mistakes gradually took hold and grew. If programmers could have that kind of support at their fingertips, it could have a tremendous impact, making our world a little bit more stable. This is the idea that later became *secure by design* and this book. Independently, we've tried and tested that idea in various forms, most of which never got a name, and we've met and exchanged ideas with many people. Some of these exchanges have left a somewhat bigger imprint and deserve mentioning—at the risk of not mentioning other important exchanges.

Some important influences came from Eric Evans. His ideas about Domain-Driven Design (DDD) provided a terminology to talk about how code should capture meaning. In 2008, security researcher John Wilander and DDD enthusiast Dan Bergh Johnsson began to work together, and security entered the mix. The ideas from DDD came to form the platform for their discussions about security and code. Together, they coined the phrase Domain-Driven Security in 2009, which was one of the first-named front-runners to secure by design. Upon presenting at the OWASP European conference in 2010, they realized that Erlend Oftedal in Oslo had been playing with similar ideas, and the discussion broadened. These discussions led to a deeper understanding of how to mitigate risks such as injection flaws and cross-site scripting (XSS). In 2011, Daniel Deogun and Daniel Sawano joined the team, which started an era of increased industry practice. We evolved ideas on using design for improved security and tried them out in practice on a large scale, and, to our delight, they worked surprisingly well. For example, a client of ours secretly ordered a security audit to test one of our projects, and it came out with only one solitary security remark, where a comparable project received a list of 3,000 remarks!

Spreading our thoughts and findings through projects, blog posts, and conference presentations, we put more and more ideas under the umbrella of using design to avoid security weaknesses, until Daniel Deogun was approached by Manning in 2015 with a proposal to put these kinds of ideas into the form of a book. At the time of writing these lines in 2019, we've covered a lot of ground, and the book has become both thicker and denser than we had intended. But we've tried to only include material we think is important for security. We've also taken care to ensure that the book isn't too dependent on specific languages or frameworks. We hope that the ideas of secure by design transcend languages and frameworks and won't be outdated soon. We're glad you picked up a copy of this book, and hope you'll find it useful to make this wonderful digital world somewhat better, somewhat more stable, and somewhat more secure—to make it *secure by design.*

acknowledgments

We want to thank the wonderful community of software professionals that we have the honor to be part of. Thanks for all the conference discussions, thanks for all the blog posts, thanks for all the code. Without you, all our professional lives would be much duller.

We also want to thank those who have brought this book to life. Thanks to our patient editors—Cynthia Kane, Toni Arritola, and Jennifer Stout—who have given us excellent feedback on content and style. Thanks to our wonderful copy editor, Rachel Head, who has polished our rough, nonnative English to the shiny phrasings you read on these pages. And thanks to the Manning production team, who helped turn the manuscript into the book you're reading. Much appreciation goes to Daniel Terhorst-North for contributing the foreword and for his helpful feedback while writing it. Thanks to Gojko Adzic, Erlend Oftedal, Peter Magnusson, Jimmy Nilsson, Luis Atencio, and John Guthrie for technical reviews and feedback. To all the reviewers: Adrian Citu, Alexander Zenger, Andrea Barisone, Arnaldo Gabriel Ayala Meyer, Christoffer Fink, Daut Morina, David Raymond, Doug Sparling, Eros Pedrini, Henrik Gering, Jan Goyvaerts, Jeremy Lange, Jim Amrhein, John Kasiewicz, Jonathan Sharley, Joseph Preston, Pietro Maffi, Richard Vaughan, Robert Kielty, Steve Eckmann, and Zorodzayi Mukuya, your suggestions helped make this a better book. Thanks to the publisher, who believed in us and the book's topic. We also want to thank everyone else involved in creating this book, but whom we've not interacted with directly. It's amazing how much goes into creating a book like this.

Dan Bergh Johnsson: First, and above all, I want to thank my lovely wife, Fia, and my wonderful sons, Karl and Anton. Thanks for all the tea and support. You are the light of my eyes. On a more professional note, I'd like to thank Cons Åhs, who taught me programming; Eric Evans, for showing me the rigor of Domain-Driven Design; and John Wilander, who helped me understand the connection between good programming and good security. Thanks to the security professionals who can't be named. And finally, thanks to the spirit that lives in the computer.

Daniel Deogun: I'd like to thank my beautiful wife, Ida, and my beloved children, Lucas and Isac. Thank you for all your support, love, and understanding during the so-often stressful times while writing this book. This wouldn't have been possible without you—thank you. I'd also like to thank everyone who's challenged my ideas over the years; all the questions, comments, and interesting discussions have truly been helpful while working on this book.

Daniel Sawano: I want to thank my wonderful wife, Elin, and my beloved children, Alvin and Oliver, for the patience with all the late nights and long hours spent on writing this book—thank you for all your love and support. I also want to thank everyone I've had the opportunity to work with during my career (none mentioned, none forgotten). Thank you for the inspiring discussions, debates, and knowledge-sharing. You've all played a part in shaping the ideas that are expressed in this book.

about this book

Secure by Design is a book about security that comes with a different twist than regular security books. Instead of taking the classical approach, where security is the main focus, it makes software design its primary concern. This might sound a bit odd at first, but when you realize that security flaws are often caused by poor design, then the approach of looking at security from a design perspective becomes much more appealing. Because, what if a fair amount of security vulnerabilities could be avoided using good design and best practices? Then it would certainly revolutionize how we look at software development and justify why you need to make certain design choices.

Exploring how software design relates to software security is therefore the main objective of this book. This, in turn, means that you won't find discussions about classical security topics like buffer overflows, weaknesses in cryptographic hash functions, or which authentication method to use. Instead, you'll learn why certain design choices matter for security and how to use them to craft secure software from the inside out.

Who should read this book

Secure by Design is a book primarily written for software developers, but it can be read by anyone with a technical background and interest in security. What's important when reading this book is that you feel comfortable reading C-like syntax and have basic programming skills in a language such as Java or C#. Examples and best practices are all presented in a way that makes them relevant, regardless of your experience level, because learning how to design secure code is important to everyone, no matter if you're a junior developer or an experienced architect. Reading *Secure by Design* is therefore a good idea if you want to improve your overall programming skills or need to make an existing codebase more secure. The book is also suitable as lecture material at universities or to be read in study groups.

How this book is organized: A roadmap

This book is divided into three parts and 14 chapters. The first two parts end with an intermission that tells a story about security flaws that could have been avoided using the concepts in this book. The intermissions are based on real cases we've worked on during our careers and serve as mini-case studies, as well as being a good read.

Part 1 introduces you to the concepts of this book and why we believe they are an effective approach to creating secure software.

- Chapter 1—Teaches you how design can drive software security and how it can enable you to create secure software with ease. It also contains an appetizing example of how a security flaw can be prevented through a secure by design mindset.
- Chapter 2—Is an intermission about how a weak software design caused significant economic loss. The security weaknesses in this case study could have been avoided if the concepts presented in part 2 had been utilized.

Part 2 is about the fundamental concepts that makes up the foundation of secure by design. The chapters are roughly laid out so that they start with concepts close to the code and then move up to higher abstraction levels. Some chapters build on previous ones, so it makes sense to read them in the order presented. You're free to read these in any order you want, of course, but if you run into concepts or terms you don't really understand, you might want to go back to previous chapters to read up on them.

- Chapter 3—Teaches you some of the core concepts of Domain-Driven Design (DDD). The concepts discussed are essential for understanding many of the ideas of secure by design. The ideas and the terminology you learn in this chapter are used extensively throughout the book, so if you're not well-versed in DDD, we recommend you start with this chapter.
- Chapter 4—Introduces you to some code constructs that are important for security. It talks about the benefits of immutability and failing fast and how you can perform data validation in a secure way.
- Chapter 5—Discusses domain primitives and how they form the foundation of secure code. It also teaches you about the benefits of read-once objects and how domain primitives are the foundation for creating secure entities.
- Chapter 6—Talks about the basics of creating secure entities: how you can ensure that entities are consistent upon creation and how to protect the integrity of entities during their life cycle.
- Chapter 7—Continues with the topic of entities and teaches you different approaches to handle the inherent complexity that comes with them.

- Chapter 8—Shows you how you can use your delivery pipeline to enhance and verify the security of software. It also discusses some of the challenges when automating security testing.
- Chapter 9—Teaches you how to deal with failures and errors without compromising security. In addition to that, you'll also explore some ways to mitigate failures through design.
- Chapter 10—Describes how popular design principles used in cloud environments can be used to increase the security of your systems, even though the design principles were originally developed for other purposes.
- Chapter 11—Another intermission, relating how a system built with a service-oriented architecture ended up being broken even though none of the individual services were. The story is a real-life example of the unique security challenges that you'll face when building a system of systems. These challenges are discussed further in part 3 of the book.

Part 3 discusses how to apply what you've learned in part 2. You'll learn how to spot common security issues and how you can use secure by design concepts to address them.

- Chapter 12—Looks at design patterns and code constructs that are problematic from a security perspective and that are common in legacy code. You'll learn how to spot them and how to fix them.
- Chapter 13—Goes into the (sometimes subtle) challenges that come with microservice architectures and how they can be addressed using secure software design.
- Chapter 14—Discusses the importance of explicitly thinking about security every now and then. It also gives you some hints about important areas to address when creating secure software systems.

About the code

The concepts in this book are language agnostic, but we've chosen to use Java as the programming language for all code examples, partly because it's one of the most commonly used programming languages, but also because its C-style syntax should be readable by any developer. The purpose of the code is to showcase certain concepts, not to be fully runnable examples. We've tried to make the code look as close as possible to what you'd write in real life. At the same time, there's always a need to remove any distractions that could interfere with the teaching. This means we've sometimes omitted parts of methods and classes to improve clarity.

Another convention used in this book is that names of test methods (as in JUnit @Test annotated methods) are always written in snake case. The reason for this is readability. When using a behavior-driven development (BDD) style to express tests (as we often like to do), the names of the test methods tend to become long sentences—using proper grammar and being understandable by others than just developers. Very long method names become almost unreadable when using camel case. Snake case solves that problem. All other method and class names use camel case, which is the standard naming convention in Java.

This book contains many examples of source code, both in numbered listings and in line with normal text. In both cases, source code is formatted in a `fixed-width font like this` to separate it from ordinary text.

In many cases, the original source code has been reformatted; we've added line breaks and reworked indentation to accommodate the available page space in the book. Additionally, comments in the source code have often been removed from the listings when the code is described in the text. Code annotations accompany many of the listings, highlighting important concepts.

The code for the examples in this book is available for download from the Manning website at https://www.manning.com/books/secure-by-design.

liveBook discussion forum

Purchase of *Secure by Design* includes free access to a private web forum run by Manning Publications where you can make comments about the book, ask technical questions, and receive help from the authors and from other users. To access the forum, go to https://livebook.manning.com/#!/book/secure-by-design/discussion. You can also learn more about Manning's forums and the rules of conduct at https://livebook.manning.com/#!/discussion.

Manning's commitment to our readers is to provide a venue where a meaningful dialogue between individual readers and between readers and the authors can take place. It is not a commitment to any specific amount of participation on the part of the authors, whose contribution to the forum remains voluntary (and unpaid). We suggest you try asking the authors some challenging questions lest their interest stray! The forum and the archives of previous discussions will be accessible from the publisher's website as long as the book is in print.

about the authors

The authors from left to right: Dan Bergh Johnsson, Daniel Deogun, and Daniel Sawano

Dan Bergh Johnsson, Daniel Deogun, and Daniel Sawano have collectively been working with security and development for several decades. They are developers at heart, and understand that security is often a side-concern. They've also evolved work habits that enable them to develop systems in a way that promotes security while focusing on high-quality design habits—something that's easier for developers to keep in mind during their daily work. All three are established international speakers and often present at conferences on topics regarding high-quality development, as well as security.

about the cover illustration

Typically, the cover of a software security book signals values such as strength, defense, armor, or other signs of war. Even the terminology in the software security field is a bit like that, with terms like *attackers* and *attack vectors*. Because *Secure by Design* is about creating, rather than destroying, and about building instead of breaking software, it is appropriate that the illustration we've chosen conveys values such as creativity and nurturing.

The figure on the cover of *Secure by Design* is a "Sultana, or Kaddin," which means "wife" in Turkish. The illustration is taken from a collection of costumes of the Ottoman Empire published on January 1, 1802, by William Miller of Old Bond Street, London. The title page is missing from the collection and we have been unable to track it down to date. The book's table of contents identifies the figures in both English and French, and each illustration bears the names of two artists who worked on it, both of whom would no doubt be surprised to find their art gracing the front cover of a computer programming book...two hundred years later.

The collection was purchased by a Manning editor at an antiquarian flea market in the "Garage" on West 26th Street in Manhattan. The seller was an American based in Ankara, Turkey, and the transaction took place just as he was packing up his stand for the day. The Manning editor didn't have on his person the substantial amount of cash that was required for the purchase, and a credit card and check were both politely turned down. With the seller flying back to Ankara that evening, the situation was getting hopeless. What was the solution? It turned out to be nothing more than an old-fashioned verbal agreement sealed with a handshake. The seller simply proposed that the money be transferred to him by wire, and the editor walked out with the bank information on a piece of paper and the portfolio of images under his arm. Needless to say, we transferred the funds the next day, and we remain grateful and impressed by this unknown person's trust in one of us. It recalls something that might have happened a long time ago.

The pictures from the Ottoman collection, like the other illustrations that appear on our covers, bring to life the richness and variety of dress customs of two centuries ago. They recall the sense of isolation and distance of that period—and of every other historic period except our own hyperkinetic present. Dress codes have changed since then and the diversity by region, so rich at the time, has faded away. It is now often hard to tell the inhabitant of one continent from another. Perhaps, trying to view it optimistically, we have traded a cultural and visual diversity for a more varied personal life. Or a more varied and interesting intellectual and technical life.

We at Manning celebrate the inventiveness, the initiative, and, yes, the fun of the computer business with book covers based on the rich diversity of regional life of two centuries ago, brought back to life by the pictures from this collection.

Part 1

Introduction

In this first part, we set the stage for this book. We present how we think about security, development, and how they fit together. We analyze where problems tend to occur and what we think can be done about it. The opening chapter covers these aspects, together with an example of what we mean by secure by design.

We finish this part with an intermission chapter that is more of a light read. Here, we introduce some of the ideas of the next part through a case study from a client we've worked with. So, let's get started with how security and development fit together, and the basic ideas behind secure by design.

Why design matters for security

This chapter covers

- Viewing security as concerns, not features
- Design and why it's important for security
- Building in lots of security by focusing on good design
- Addressing the Billion Laughs attack

Imagine yourself setting up a typical software project. You assemble a team of developers, testers, and domain experts and start outlining the key requirements. With input from stakeholders, you come up with a list of important attributes: performance, security, maintainability, and usability. As with many software projects, quality takes top priority, time to market is of the essence, and you need to stay within budget. You decide to be proactive and add security features to your backlog, and some of the other team members come up with a good list of security libraries you can use in your code. After the initial planning, you get the project up and running and start implementing features and business functionality. The team is motivated and delivers features at a good pace.

Although you know you should *think security* all the time, it gets in the way of other tasks you're focused on. In addition to that, most of the time you aren't working on internet-facing code anyway, so those web security libraries you thought about using don't really fit. Plus, the security-related tasks in the backlog keep getting lower priority compared to the business functionality. After all, time is tight, and it doesn't matter if the system is secure if the features the users need aren't there. Business functionality is where the money is, and no user is going to thank you for putting CSRF tokens in your login form.[1] Besides, you can always go back and deal with lower priority tasks later.

As a developer, you feel the responsibility of security is a burden you'd rather not have on your shoulders. You think it'd be better if the company brought in a security expert on a permanent basis as part of the development team. Developers are experts at crafting good code, building scalable architectures, and using continuous delivery, not waving magic wands to cast spells that can defend against evil hackers in black hoodies. You have never understood why security has to be so secretive in the first place, and it's much more fulfilling to create than it is to destroy. The project must move forward, so you keep your focus on the top of the backlog and implementing features.

After some time, your software is ready to go into production. Your project's future can now play out in a couple of different ways. One way is that you conduct a security audit and a *penetration test*.[2] But the security review report finds vulnerabilities that are considered to be severe enough that you must address them before deploying to production. This sets your project back a couple of weeks, or maybe even months, with lost revenue as a consequence. If you're unlucky, solving the issues involves rewriting the entire program from scratch, so the stakeholders decide to scrap the project, and it never makes it into production.

Another scenario is that a security review is never conducted, and you deploy into production. Users start to use your service, and all is well, until one day you find your service has made it into the news after being hacked and having all its user data leaked. Those hard-earned users are now abandoning your service quicker than rats leaving a sinking ship.

Although this is a fictional story, it's not that far from reality. During our careers, we've seen similar scenarios play out more than once. A couple of interesting things are at play here, and some questions arise:

- Why is it that security tasks always get lower priority compared to other tasks?
- Why are developers in general so seemingly uninterested in security?
- Experts keep telling developers to think more about security, so why isn't everyone doing it?
- Why don't managers realize they need to include security experts in the team just as they put testers in the team?

Literature and experts have been telling us to focus more on security for a long time. Alas, we keep seeing news about systems being hacked every so often. Something is clearly not working.

IMPORTANT In order to efficiently and effortlessly create secure software, you need to have a mindset different from what you might be used to.

---

[1] For more about CSRF tokens, see https://en.wikipedia.org/wiki/Cross-site_request_forgery.
[2] A penetration test is a test performed on a system to uncover possible security weaknesses.

What if there were a different way to approach software security that allowed you to avoid many of the problems we see in our industry today? We believe that in order to efficiently and effortlessly create secure software, you need to have a mindset that might be different from what you're used to—a mindset where you focus more on design rather than on security.

This might sound counterintuitive at first, but in this chapter, we'll explain what we mean by the word *design* and why it's important for security. We'll discuss some of the shortcomings of the traditional approach to software security and show you how you can use design to overcome those issues. We'll also provide a couple of examples of how to apply these ideas in the real world in order to give you a first taste of some of the concepts covered in the upcoming chapters.

1.1   Security is a concern, not a feature

A productive way to view security is as a concern—as in, "we're concerned about security." But it's not uncommon to come across situations where security is described as a set of features. The difference is that even when security features address a specific security problem, your concern about security may not have been met. To illustrate how security is a concern rather than a feature, let's start with a historical example. Let's go back in time to one of the first recorded bank robberies in history to see how security features like high-quality locks don't matter if hinges are weak. In the example, the features implemented didn't prevent the robbery, so the concern for security wasn't met.

1.1.1   The robbery of Öst-Götha Bank, 1854

It is the night of March 25, 1854, and the Swedish Öst-Götha Bank is soon to be robbed. A military corporal and former farmer, Nils Strid, walks silently up to the bank with his companion, the blacksmith, Lars Ekström. The outer door to the bank office is locked, but the key hangs outside on a nail if you know where to look. The bank has also invested in high-quality locks for the vault—more or less impossible to pick. But for blacksmith Lars, it's not a big job to splinter the hinges and open the vault door backward. The two perpetrators walk away with the entire treasury of the bank: 900,000 riksdaler, the official Swedish currency at the time.[3]

For years, this was one of the largest heists in history. Not until the great train robbery in Buckinghamshire, England, at Bridego Railway Bridge in 1963, would the loot be of a similar size. In Sweden, the burglars left behind a single three-riksdaler banknote,[4] together with a message with a silly rhyming verse:

> *Vi länsat haver Östgötha Bank och mången rik knös torde blivit pank. Vi lämna dock en tredaler kvar ty hundar pissar på den som inget har.*

> *We now have plundered Östgötha Bank, and many moneybags will become broke. However, we leave a three-daler behind, because dogs piss on those who have naught.*

---

[3]   Comparing this to the value of money nowadays is hard, but a comparable sum would be in the range of 5 to 10 million dollars.

[4]   Yes, there actually were notes with the denomination of three.

Apart from being an interesting historical event, the robbery is also interesting from a security point of view in two different ways: one legal and one technical. From a legal perspective, the robbery resulted in new laws mandating a certain level of bank security. These laws forced the banks at that time to adhere to some level of security awareness and practices. The first, passed in the following year, 1855, was one of the earliest examples of regulatory security. From a technical perspective, the robbers consistently attacked the bank's weak spots: the office door was locked, but the key was poorly hidden; the vault locks were of high quality, but the hinges could be broken.

What this story spotlights is how security can be viewed as a set of features—locks and hinges. In our example, using high-quality locks gave the perception of security, but security wasn't implemented by that feature as such. Having high-quality locks isn't sufficient if the key hangs on a nail or if the vault door hinges are weak. Rather than treating security as a set of features, it's more fruitful to understand it as a concern that should be met.

Had the bank viewed security as a concern, it would have asked, "How do we stop people from walking away with the bank's money?" The answer wouldn't have been with a lock; it should have included keeping the office key elsewhere or checking if there were other ways to force the vault door. The bank's owners might have come up with novel ideas about alarms. They might have invented some of the theft-deterring mechanisms that emerged during the coming century, but they wouldn't have relied on just having a lock on the door.

Now let's return from nineteenth-century banking to the contemporary world of software development. It's time to see how the idea of security as a feature or a concern applies to your projects today. In the next section, we'll show you how you can turn from specifying security as a feature to identifying security as a concern.

1.1.2   *Security features and concerns*

Software is often described in the language of features (or what you can do with the product). For example, this is an app that lets you share a shopping list; this is a site where you can upload photos for others to see and comment on; this is a program for creating presentation slideware. Software is also described in this way in formal contexts.

Many methodologies have their primary focus on what the system should do—the functional side. The Rational Unified Process (RUP), which still influences a lot of software development, puts the major focus on the functionality in the form of *use cases*. Other considerations like response time or capacity required are put in a peripheral section called supplementary specifications. In the agile community, the dominating format for describing what's to be done in the next sprint (or comparable) is a *user story* in a format along the lines of "As a such-and-such user, I'd like this feature so that I reap this benefit." With this focus on features (what the system does), it's no surprise that often security is described in the same way: we need a login page; we must have a fraud detection module; there should be logging.

Security experts John Wilander and Jens Gustavsson researched how security was described and specified. They studied a selection of major software initiatives that were financed through public funding. When security was mentioned, they found that 78% could be directly classified as security features.[5]

Of course, there exist security features that add value, both visible and invisible. A visible example can be a high-quality authentication mechanism that allows customers to trust that their access and communications are safe.[6] The problem is that describing security through features often misses the point. Let's try to phrase a security story to see how you can turn from a *feature focus* to a *concern focus*.

Let's look at an example of user authentication at a photo-storing website. If you try to squeeze this into the format of a function-focused user story, you might end up with something like this: "As a user, I want a login page so that I can access my uploaded pictures."

Although phrased as a *feature*, most probably the stakeholder is airing a *concern* about security. If you implement only this functionality, then you've met the objectives of the login page story. But the mere existence of a login page as such doesn't provide the security you're after. It might seem obvious that nobody really wants a login page like this, but we've seen this kind of feature-focused user story about security many times.

Imagine that you and your team implement a login page. After logging in, the user is redirected to a listing of their pictures, and among them is a really-embarrasing-pose.jpg. The user can click a link to get a download of the picture as well. To complicate things, imagine further that another user happens to have the direct download link and is also able to download that embarrassing photo (figure 1.1). How does that feel? You have implemented the story, because you have a login page with the described functionality, but you've subtly missed the point, have you not?

Taking a step back, we realize that the purpose of the story wasn't the login page as such. The purpose was rather that only the owner of the pictures should be able to see their pictures and download them—no one else. The login page is just there to uphold that rule. There should be no way for a user to get to the pictures without going through the login page.

You can now propose a better phrasing for the story: "As a user, I want access to my uploaded pictures to pass through a login page so that my pictures stay confidential." This phrasing better catches the concern the stakeholder was airing when initially talking about the login page.

An even better phrasing is not to mention the login page at all: "As a user, I want all access to my uploaded pictures to be protected by authentication so that my pictures stay confidential."

The point of the user story wasn't to have a security feature, it was to address a security concern; in this case, a concern about *confidentiality* (keeping things secret). The tricky part here is that when implementing such a story, it doesn't suffice to change the code along one path to the pictures. Instead, *all* paths leading to the pictures must be guarded, and it's enough to miss just one of them for the concern to not be met.

---

[5] See Wilander, J., and Gustavsson, J., "Security Requirements—A Field Study of Current Practice," http://johnwilander.se/research_publications/paper_sreis2005_wilander_gustavsson.pdf.

[6] The Swedish certificate-based authentication system BankID is one example that has become a de facto standard, beginning with financial institutions and governmental agencies but now encompassing lots of industries.

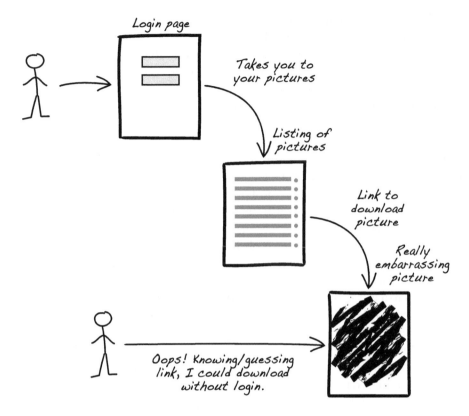

Figure 1.1 Having only a login page doesn't help much.

To get real security, you need to get away from thinking about security as a set of features. You must think about security as a cross-cutting concern—a concern that cuts across the functionality.

1.1.3 *Categorizing security concerns: CIA-T*

We've mentioned confidentiality as a security concern. But security is more than keeping things secret, and in this book, we'll talk about other aspects of security as well. To begin, let's provide some terminology around security concerns.

Classical information security usually talks about the security concern triad: confidentiality, integrity, and availability (or CIA as a mnemonic):

- *Confidentiality*—Most often associated with talking about security, is about keeping things secret that shouldn't be made known to the public. Your healthcare record is one of the best examples of confidential information.
- *Integrity*—Refers to when it's important that the information doesn't change or is only allowed to change in specific, authorized ways. An example of integrity is counting election results. Security in this context means that the votes haven't been manipulated.

- *Availability*—Means data is at hand in a timely manner. The fire department needs to know about the location of a fire, and they need that information immediately. If they get the location later, it might be too late, and the need for security can't be met.

All three factors might be important for any piece of data, but most often there's some kind of profile for the concern of how much you suffer from a breach. Take your health record, for example. If some data is revealed (breached confidentiality), you'll be irritated and angry. If there are errors in the data (breached integrity), things might get confused and dangerous. If the data isn't there when needed in the emergency room (breached availability), you might end up dead.

On the other hand, let's think about your bank record. If you can't see your balance (availability) when trying to pay your bills, it's irritating. If your balance is revealed publicly (confidentiality), you'll most probably be angry. But if your pension fund is suddenly wiped out (integrity), it's a catastrophe.

Later added to the CIA triad was the letter *T* for *traceability*, which captures the need for knowing who changed or accessed what data when. After some scandals, this became important in the financial sector and in healthcare. This kind of audit logging is also an important part of the European Union directive, GDPR (General Data Protection Regulation), which went into effect in 2018. For example, GDPR specifies that when personal data is accessed, the access should be traced and saved to a persistent audit log. We'll refer to confidentiality, integrity, availability, and traceability in the rest of this book when we want to be a little bit more specific about what kind of security is at stake.

Focusing on security concerns instead of security features does a lot for the quality of the system, but it also puts developers in a difficult position: how do you ensure security in the software you write? It's hard to make sure there are no security mistakes anywhere. Ensuring this would require developers to actively think about security all the time while working. But there's another way—embed security into the way you work and the way you design.

1.2 Defining design

Writing software is by no means a trivial task. As a developer, you're required to have skills within a wide range of disciplines. You're expected to be knowledgeable in areas ranging from programming languages and algorithms to system architecture and agile methodologies. Although these software development disciplines span various fields of knowledge and can be quite different from one another, one term that keeps occurring when discussing almost all the different disciplines is *design*. But what do people mean when they use the word *design*?

Our view, in general, is that the word *design* is used quite loosely and takes on a different meaning depending on whom you talk to and in what context it's being used. We believe that design is an extremely important concept in software development, so important that we even put the word in the title of this book. As such, it's only appropriate to start by defining our view of the term *design* and how it's used throughout this book. Understanding the meaning of the word will help you understand the discussions and concepts being conveyed in this book.

When developing software, you constantly make decisions on how to write the code that solves the problems at hand. You decide what syntax to use, what constructs and algorithms to apply, how to structure the code, and how to steer the flow of execution. If you're using an object-oriented approach, you'll make decisions on what your object model should look like and the interactions between the objects within that model. If you're applying a functional style of programming, you'll make decisions on what behavior to pass in as functions, making sure you're creating pure functions without side effects.[7] All these decisions can be viewed as part of the design process.

When you write code, you pay careful attention to how to represent your business logic, which is the functionality that makes your software unique. You'll think about how you'll implement that logic and how to make it explicit and easy to maintain. If you're involved in activities around modeling your business domain, you'll spend a considerable amount of time evolving and refining your domain model and how it'll be represented in code. Even when you're implementing simple logic such as a straightforward conditional statement, you're making an active choice. For example, you might consider aspects such as readability or performance, and, based on your preferences, you'll make a decision on how you're going to write the code in that statement. You're drawing from your experience and knowledge to actively make choices appropriate to the software you're creating. These choices are part of what determines the design of the software.

As your codebase evolves, you'll put effort into structuring your code into packages or modules to make it more understandable and easier to work with, while at the same time achieving desirable properties like high cohesion and low coupling. You might apply techniques and concepts like the use of interfaces, the Dependency Inversion Principle,[8] and immutability, while making sure you're not violating the Liskov Substitution Principle.[9] You might also think about breaking out and isolating certain functionality within the code in order to make it more explicit or to allow it to be easily testable. What you're doing is writing and refactoring your code in order to give it a better design.

If your software is interacting with other software (say, for example, you're developing a service in a microservices architecture), then you're going to need to think about how to define the public API for your service in order for it to be cohesive and easy to consume and be versioned. You'll also need to consider how it'll interact with other services in order to be resilient and responsive, and to provide acceptable uptime. On a higher level, you're probably going to have to take into account that your service also needs to fit into the overall system architecture. You're making decisions that, albeit quite diverse, are all part of shaping the overall design of the software.

---

[7] A pure function is a function that always returns the same result for a given argument and has no side effects.

[8] See Martin, R. C., "The Dependency Inversion Principle," C++ Report 8 (May, 1996).

[9] See Liskov, B., "Keynote Address—Data Abstraction and Hierarchy," OOPSLA '87 Addendum to the Proceedings on Object-Oriented Programming Systems, Languages and Applications (1987).

All of the activities that we've discussed so far are related to writing code. We've stated that they are all part of the design process, but if you think about them for a moment, which would you say are design activities and which are not?

- Are API design and taking system architecture into account typical examples of design activities?
- Can domain modeling also count as a design activity?
- Is the choice between making the declaration of an object's field final or non-final a design activity?

If you ask 10 people what activities in software development count as design, then you're probably going to end up with 10 different answers. Many will probably answer that domain modeling, API design, applying design patterns, and system architecture are clearly examples of design activities, partly because this is the more traditional view of what design is. Whereas only a few, if any, will say that thinking hard about how to write an `if` statement or `for` loop qualifies as part of the software design process.

The answer to the question of which activities are design activities is that everything involved in software development is part of the design process. A system or piece of software won't reach a point of stable design (stable as in *functioning*, not as in having stopped evolving) until it has been written and put into production. That means that domain models, software modules, APIs, and design patterns are just as important to the design of the software as are field declarations, `if` statements, hash tables, and method declarations. All of these contribute to the stability of the design.

One thing that all these activities have in common is that they involve conscious decision-making. Any activity that involves active decision-making should be considered part of the software design process and can thus be referred to as design. This, in turn, means that design is the guiding principle for how a system is built and is applicable on all levels, from code to architecture.

> **NOTE** Design is the guiding principle for how a system is built and is applicable on all levels, from code to architecture. It includes any activity that involves active decision-making.

In this section, you've learned how to view software design and what the word *design* means when used in this book. Next, we'll take a look at the traditional software security approach and some of its shortcomings.

1.3 The traditional approach to software security and its shortcomings

From our observation of the software industry, a common view when attempting to mitigate security vulnerabilities is that security should be a top priority when developing and writing code. Everyone involved in the process should be trained and experienced in software security. Let's refer to this view as the *traditional approach* to software security. This approach typically includes specific tasks and actions developers need to adhere to (figure 1.2).

Figure 1.2   Traditionally, software security is viewed as explicit activities and concepts.

Developers should know about things like cross-site scripting (XSS) attacks, be aware of vulnerabilities in low-level protocols, and know the OWASP Top 10 like the backs of their hands.[10] Testers should be trained in basic penetration testing techniques, and business domain experts should be capable of having discussions and making decisions concerning software security.

The weakness in this approach is that, for a number of reasons, it struggles to create software that's secure enough to withstand the harsh reality of production environments. If it had been successful, software security vulnerabilities wouldn't be as common as they are today, and we wouldn't see the same vulnerabilities responsible for massive security breaches over and over again. Let's take a closer look at some of the shortcomings of this approach to better understand why this approach struggles and why we think a different approach can be more successful.

As an example, say you have a simple domain object that represents a user in a typical web application, where the username is displayed on some page. The user object is quite simple and holds only an ID and a username. It's a simplified example but, in our experience, it's quite representative of code one might see. The implementation of the user object can be seen in the following listing.

Listing 1.1   Simple `User` class

```
public class User {
   private final Long id;
   private final String username;

   public User(final Long id, final String username) {
      this.id = id;
      this.username = username;          ◄──── Possible XSS vulnerability
   }

   // ...
}
```

---

[10] See the Open Web Application Security Project (OWASP) Top 10, https://www.owasp.org/index.php/Category:OWASP_Top_Ten_Project.

If you take a look at this representation of a user, you can see that there are possible security issues in this code. One issue is that because you're accepting any string value as a username, the username could be used for performing XSS attacks. An *XSS attack* occurs when an attacker uses a web application to send malicious code to a different user. The malicious code could, for example, be in the form of client-side JavaScript. If the attacker enters something like `<script>alert(42);</script>` as the username when registering for the service, later, when the user's username is displayed on some web page in the application, it could lead to an alert box being displayed in the browser showing the number 42.[11]

If you want to mitigate this security vulnerability using the traditional approach, you could introduce explicit, security-focused input data validation. The data validation could, for example, be implemented as web application filters that validate all posted form data in the web application and check that it doesn't contain any malicious XSS code. Or the validation could occur right in the domain class. If you chose to introduce input validation in the User class, it could look something like that shown in the following listing.

> **Listing 1.2   User class with input validation**

```
import static com.example.xss.ValidationUtils.validateForXSS;
import static org.apache.commons.lang3.Validate.notNull;

public class User {
   private final Long id;
   private final String username;

   public User(final Long id, final String username) {
      notNull(id);
      notNull(username);                          Checks that parameters aren't null

      this.id = notNull(id);
      this.username = validateForXSS(username);   Validates input with
   }                                              an (imaginary) external
   // ...                                         library, ValidationUtils
}
```

You can see in the listing how you're pulling in an (imaginary) security library that provides functionality to validate a string for possible XSS attacks. You also decided to check that none of the constructor parameters are `null` to further improve the validation. This way of handling security in software is common, but it's also problematic for several reasons, some being:

- The developer needs to explicitly think about security vulnerabilities, while at the same time focusing on solving business functionality.
- It requires every developer to be a security expert.
- It assumes that the person writing the code can think of every potential vulnerability that might occur now or in the future.

---

[11] In a real attack, the executed script would most likely perform something a bit more evil than simply showing this number!

Let's take a look at each one of these issues and see why they're problematic.

1.3.1   *Explicitly thinking about security*

The first issue, thinking explicitly about security, is problematic, because when you as a developer are writing code, your main focus will always be the functionality you're trying to implement. Saying that you also need to actively think about security while coding is going to conflict with that focus. When that conflict occurs, security will always come in second to the priority of the business functionality. Security always gets a lower priority for a couple of reasons, and we'll look into those in more depth in section 1.4.2.

1.3.2   *Everyone is a security expert*

The next issue, requiring every developer to be a security expert, is also problematic because not everyone can be or wants to be such an expert, in the same way as everyone can't be an expert on JVM performance or UX design. And if the developers aren't highly skilled in security, then the software they create is only going to reflect the level of security that the developers are capable of.

Perhaps sometime in the future, all developers will need to have a thorough understanding of software security similar to the more or less mandatory knowledge nowadays of how to write good unit tests. But this isn't what the current state in the industry looks like, so it's somewhat of an unrealistic expectation.

1.3.3   *Knowing all and the unknowable*

Even if you have a team of security experts writing your software, you'd still face the fact that you can only write countermeasures for the vulnerabilities that you already know about. Not only do you need to know a lot about the many different types of attack vectors that you're familiar with, but you also need to know about the attacks that you currently are unaware of. You need to know the unknowable, so to speak. Once you realize this dilemma, it becomes obvious that the third issue also has its shortcomings in creating secure software.

The approach of creating secure software by making security the top priority has been around for as long as anyone can remember, and we've all tried it. Sometimes it has gotten the job done, but many times we've felt that there was something missing and that there should be a better way of creating secure software. We believe that software design is the enabler for successfully creating truly secure code. And by focusing on design, you avoid many of the shortcomings posed by the approach we've discussed in this section.

1.4   *Driving security through design*

We're not arguing that security isn't important or that you don't have to be aware of security when developing software. But we believe that, instead of adhering to the traditional approach to software security, there's an alternative approach that achieves the same or even better results when it comes to how secure your finished software will be (figure 1.3).

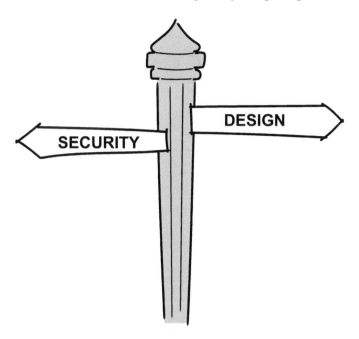

Figure 1.3 A focus on design rather than on security avoids issues with the traditional approach to security.

Rather than having security be one of the main focuses when you're developing software, you can choose to focus on software design instead—focusing on design in the sense that you're always aiming toward the highest possible standards with what you create. By shifting the focus to design, you'll be able to achieve a high degree of software security without the need to constantly and explicitly think about security.

1.4.1 *Making the user secure by design*

Let's go back to the example of the User class from the previous section and see how you'd approach it instead by focusing on good design. First, you'll discuss with your domain experts what the meaning of a username is in the context of the current application (figure 1.4).

You twist and turn on the concept and finally come to the conclusion that a username can only contain the characters [A-Za-z0-9_-] and must be at least 4 characters long, but no longer than 40. This is because that's what's considered to be a normal username in the application you're creating. You're not excluding characters like < or > because they might be part of an XSS attack in the event of the username being rendered in a web browser. Rather, you address the question, "In this context, what's a username supposed to look like?" In this case, you decide < or > isn't part of a valid username and shouldn't be included.

Figure 1.4   Exploring concepts with domain experts to gain deeper insight into the domain

This little exploration exercise with your domain experts has given you a deeper insight into the current domain that, in turn, allows you to create a more precise definition of a username. The following listing shows the new User class.

Listing 1.3   `User` class with domain constraints

```
import static org.apache.commons.lang3.Validate.*;

public class User {
   private static final int USERNAME_MINIMUM_LENGTH = 4;
   private static final int USERNAME_MAXIMUM_LENGTH = 40;
   private static final String USERNAME_VALID_CHARACTERS =
         "[A-Za-z0-9_-]+";

   private final Long id;
   private final String username;

   public User(final Long id, final String username) {
      notNull(id);
      notBlank(username);
```

```
        final String trimmed = username.trim();
        inclusiveBetween(USERNAME_MINIMUM_LENGTH,
                         USERNAME_MAXIMUM_LENGTH,
                         trimmed.length());
        matchesPattern(trimmed,
                       USERNAME_VALID_CHARACTERS,
                       "Allowed characters are: %s",
                       USERNAME_VALID_CHARACTERS);

        this.id = id;
        this.username = trimmed;
    }

    // ...
}
```

Using domain invariants validates input at the time of creation.

Looking at the User class now, you can see that there's a lot of logic concerning the username of a user. This, together with the fact that you discussed it extensively with your domain experts, is a sign that the username should be represented explicitly in the domain model. That's partly because it seems to be an important concept, but also because extracting the logic would follow the principle of high cohesion.

With that insight, you can go ahead and extract the logic into its own Username class that encapsulates all the knowledge about a username. The new class also enforces all domain rules at the time of creation. This new object is called a *domain primitive* (you'll learn more about them in chapter 5). The following listing shows what your User class will look like once you've extracted the new Username class.

Listing 1.4   User class with domain value object

```
import static org.apache.commons.lang3.Validate.*;

public class Username {
    private static final int MINIMUM_LENGTH = 4;
    private static final int MAXIMUM_LENGTH = 40;
    private static final String VALID_CHARACTERS = "[A-Za-z0-9_-]+";

    private final String value;

    public Username(final String value) {
        notBlank(value);

        final String trimmed = value.trim();
        inclusiveBetween(MINIMUM_LENGTH,
                         MAXIMUM_LENGTH,
                         trimmed.length());
        matchesPattern(trimmed,
                       VALID_CHARACTERS,
                       "Allowed characters are: %s", VALID_CHARACTERS);
        this.value = trimmed;
    }
```

The value object that upholds the domain invariants for a username

```
      public String value() {
         return value;
      }
   }

   public class User {                          ┌─────────────────────────────────
      private final Long id;                    │ The User object now uses the Username
      private final Username username; ◄────────┤ domain primitive, knowing that a
                                                 │ username is always valid if one exists.
      public User(final Long id, final Username username) {
         this.id = notNull(id);
         this.username = notNull(username);
      }

      // ...
   }
```

By focusing on design, you were able to find out more about the details surrounding a user and a username. This, in turn, let you create a more precise domain model. You also paid close attention to when concepts within the current domain became so important that they should be extracted into their own objects. In the end, you gained a deeper knowledge about your domain and, at the same time, protected yourself against the XSS vulnerability we discussed earlier; attempting to input `<script>alert(42);</script>` as a username becomes impossible because it's not a valid username anymore. And you haven't even started to think about security yet! If you were to consider security in your design choices, then you could probably tighten the restrictions on a username even more, hardening the code further, but still keeping the focus on good design.

> **NOTE** A strong design focus lets you create code that's more secure when compared to the traditional approach to software security.

So far, you've learned about the shortcomings of the traditional approach, and you've seen how to use design to your advantage to create secure software. Some of the concepts that we've briefly touched on in this section will be explained in detail in chapter 3. There, you'll learn core concepts about Domain-Driven Design relevant for this book. Then, in chapters 4 and 5, we'll explain fundamental code constructs that promote security. Now, let's take a look at the advantages of driving security through design and why we believe this approach succeeds better than the traditional approach to software security.

1.4.2   *The advantages of the design approach*

In the simple User example, we showed you how to use design to drive security in your development process. We also stated that by focusing on design, you can achieve a level of software security that's on par with, or even better than, the traditional approach. But on what grounds do we make the claim that this approach succeeds better than the traditional one?

We believe that if the main focus when developing software centers on design, security can become a natural part of the development process instead of being perceived as a forced requirement. We also believe that this overcomes or avoids many of the shortcomings of the traditional approach and that it brings its own advantages. The main reasons for this follow:

- Software design is central to the interest and competence of most developers, which makes secure by design concepts easy to adapt.
- By focusing on design, business and security concerns gain equal priority in the view of both business experts and developers.
- By choosing good design constructs, nonsecurity experts are able to write secure code.
- By focusing on the domain, many security bugs are solved implicitly.

Let's take a closer look at the reasoning behind these advantages and why we believe the design approach succeeds better than the traditional approach.

DESIGN IS A NATURAL PART OF SOFTWARE DEVELOPMENT

As software developers, you're taught from early on the importance of good design. You study it and you take pride in creating good designs that serve their purpose well. This makes design a natural part of creating software.

Many developers feel like it's hard to understand all the details around intricate software vulnerabilities, classifying themselves as people who don't do security—security is something that's best left to someone else. But because most developers understand and appreciate software design, if you can use design to achieve security, then suddenly everyone can create secure software.

When you focus on design, security becomes the concern and interest of everyone, not only the experts. It also means that there's no longer a conflict between business functionality and security concerns because the distinction between them no longer exists. This reduces the cognitive load on the developer and avoids one of the shortcomings of the traditional approach.

BUSINESS CONCERNS AND SECURITY CONCERNS BECOME OF EQUAL PRIORITY

One issue with the traditional approach is that it treats security as a separate activity. This forces security to compete with all the other important aspects you're trying to address, such as business functionality, scalability, testability, maintainability, and so on. Security-related tasks are added to the backlog and prioritized against everything else that needs to be done.

When you determine the priority of the different tasks, there's nothing that says security should automatically get the fast lane in the backlog. But what we often see is that security tends to consistently get too low of a priority. Here are some of the reasons for this:

- Security isn't well understood by either the business side or the development side of the organization.

- Developers tend to think security isn't their concern because of the reasons we discussed earlier.
- Even if security is understood, it's easy to think of it as less important than user features, and something that can therefore be added at a later time.

The caveat with the notion of adding security later is that it might not be possible if the security aspects needed imply a fundamentally different design. This is similar to why it's usually hard or impossible to add scalability or statelessness late in the software cycle.

By focusing on design and domain knowledge (as you did in the previous example with the User), you're removing several of the situations where it's necessary to prioritize security against other tasks in the backlog. It's no longer a question about whether to implement a security feature or a business feature. Now it's about implementing functionality relevant to your domain.

Finally, the design focus also makes security more accessible to all stakeholders, not only the experts. This is because it's easier to reason about, see the value in, and prioritize tasks that are related to your domain rather than specific security vulnerabilities.

NON-SECURITY EXPERTS NATURALLY WRITE SECURE CODE

Another interesting benefit of using a secure by design approach is that non-security experts can now naturally write secure code. This isn't because they consider attack vectors and how malicious data might affect the system, but rather because the design implicitly avoids insecure constructs. To illustrate this, consider the Username class in listing 1.4, where invariants ensure only valid usernames are accepted. How do we justify using this complex type instead of a simple string?

As it turns out, when talking to domain experts, most developers realize the importance of representing business concepts as precisely as possible. A username isn't an unbounded random sequence of characters; it's a well-defined concept with a precise meaning and purpose in the domain. Representing this by the standard String class isn't only a poor design decision, it's completely wrong—an insight that makes preciseness and correctness the natural choice for any developer, regardless of interest in security or experience level.

DOMAIN FOCUS SOLVES SECURITY BUGS IMPLICITLY

Security issues are often perceived as scary and complicated, but when using the design approach, the complexity suddenly disappears. This is primarily because the distinction between security bugs and ordinary bugs is erased when focus is placed on the domain rather than on which countermeasure to use.

If you look at Username in listing 1.4, the main reason for applying strict invariants isn't to protect a username from injection attacks, but rather to ensure the true meaning of a username is captured. As a consequence, every malicious input not satisfying the definition is rejected, and a username becomes secure by focusing on the domain rather than by thinking about security. The domain focus reduces the risk of security bugs in your code and, in some cases, it can also protect you against security bugs in third-party code.

1.4.3 *Staying eclectic*

As we mentioned earlier, if you complement your focus on design with a more traditional and explicit security awareness, then the resulting code becomes even more secure. This is an important note to point out, because the design focus gives you a high level of security but never covers all the security needs a system has (nor is that the intention). There's always a need to perform tasks like penetration testing and to actively think about specific attack vectors and vulnerabilities when creating software systems.[12] Even if the domain focus makes `Username` in the example secure, you still have to remember to perform proper output encoding when displaying it on a web page. By keeping the focus on design and at the same time taking an eclectic approach to software security, you can create truly secure software.

We've gone through quite a lot of material so far, but we believe it's important to understand the *why* before looking at the *how*. You've learned the meaning of design and the fundamental thinking behind the idea that a strong design focus can drive security in software development. You've also seen a simple example of how this can work. In the next section, we'll take a look at a slightly more complex scenario to give you another example of how design can improve security.

1.5 *Dealing with strings, XML, and a billion laughs*

When designing software, you're often faced with the decision of how to represent data. Unfortunately, there's a tendency towards using data types that are too generic for the purpose. For example, representing a phone number as a string can seem convenient at first, but from a security perspective, it's devastating, because a string can represent almost any kind of data—not just what you'd expect. Still, developers tend to favor strings, and often the protection against invalid input is enforced by *name typing* as seen in the next listing. The method `register` expects a phone number, but the argument is a `String`, which means it could be anything!

> **Listing 1.5 A `String` argument protected by name typing**

```
public void register(String phoneNumber) {
...
}
```
◄──── **phoneNumber can contain any character sequence because it's a String.**

Obviously, preventing invalid input this way doesn't work. The solution is to use strict domain types with rules, as you saw with `User` and `Username` earlier. But using strict types is only half of the story.

If you dissect `Username`, you see that the validation logic in the constructor contains a `notBlank` and a length check before applying the regular expression. This turns out to be

---

[12] We'll discuss some of the other aspects important for software security in more depth in chapter 14.

extremely important from a security perspective, and we'll further discuss why this is in chapter 4. So, for now, accept that validation should be executed in the following order:

- *Length check*—Is the input length within the expected boundaries?
- *Lexical content check*—Does the input contain the right characters and encoding?
- *Syntax check*—Is the input format right?

Up to this point, we've only touched on simple examples using validation, but that doesn't mean validation can't be used in more complex situations as well. To illustrate, we'll walk you through an example where you'll learn how to process XML securely. This seems quite remote from the previous examples, but when applying the same validation principles, you'll see that the parsing complexity is reduced to an ordinary input validation problem. So let's proceed with some XML.

1.5.1 Extensible Markup Language (XML)

XML is similar to a string in the sense that it can represent almost any kind of data.[13] Because of this, XML is often used as an intermediate data representation when communicating between systems. Unfortunately, not many realize there's a lot more to XML than just representing data on a normalized form.

   XML is really a complete language derived from SGML (Standard Generalized Markup Language), which means there are probably features supported by XML that most developers don't care about. Consequently, many security weaknesses are introduced in software because of how XML is used. And to illustrate, we'll use the *Billion Laughs attack* (which exploits the expandability property of XML entities during the parsing process) as a foundation when learning how to process XML securely. But before we dive into details, let's take a quick refresher on how internal XML entities work.

1.5.2 Internal XML entities in a nutshell

Internal XML entities are powerful constructs that allow you to create simple abbreviations in XML. They're defined in the Document Type Definition (DTD) and written in the form `<!ENTITY name "value">`. The following listing shows a simple example of an entity that's an abbreviation of *Secure by Design*.

Listing 1.6   Defining an entity and referencing it in XML

```
<?xml version="1.0" encoding="UTF-8" standalone="yes"?>
<!DOCTYPE example [
<!ELEMENT example (#PCDATA)>
<!ENTITY title "Secure by Design">
]>                                        | References the title entity
<example>&title;</example>        ◄───────┘
```

When the XML parser encounters the `title` entity, it expands the abbreviation and replaces it with the value found in the DTD. This, in turn, leads to a rich XML block without abbreviations, as seen in the next listing.

---

[13] For more, see W3C, https://www.w3.org/XML/.

Listing 1.7   XML after entity expansion

```
<?xml version="1.0" encoding="UTF-8" standalone="yes"?>
<!DOCTYPE example [
<!ELEMENT example (#PCDATA)>
<!ENTITY title "Secure by Design">        Replaces the title entity with
]>                                        the string Secure by Design
<example>Secure by Design</example>   ◄
```

Allowing entity expansion is handy indeed, but, unfortunately, it also opens up the possibility of entity expansion attacks. Let's see how the Billion Laughs attack exploits this behavior.

1.5.3   The Billion Laughs attack

The Billion Laughs attack is as simple as it is effective. The main idea is to exploit the expandability property of XML entities by defining recursive definitions that expand into a huge memory footprint. Listing 1.8 shows an example of the attack that's defined by a small XML block, less than 1 KB in size. This allows the block to pass most validation checks that rely on size or length. When the XML is loaded by the parser, lol9 expands into 10 lol8s, which then expands into 100 lol7s, and so on. This finally results in a billion lol strings that consume several gigabytes of memory.

Listing 1.8   XML expanding to a billion "lol"s

```
<?xml version="1.0" encoding="UTF-8" standalone="yes"?>
<!DOCTYPE lolz [
<!ELEMENT lolz (#PCDATA)>
<!ENTITY lol "lol">
<!ENTITY lol1 "&lol;&lol;&lol;&lol;&lol;&lol;&lol;&lol;&lol;&lol;">
<!ENTITY lol2 "&lol1;&lol1;&lol1;&lol1;&lol1;&lol1;&lol1;&lol1;&lol1;&lol1;">
<!ENTITY lol3 "&lol2;&lol2;&lol2;&lol2;&lol2;&lol2;&lol2;&lol2;&lol2;&lol2;">
<!ENTITY lol4 "&lol3;&lol3;&lol3;&lol3;&lol3;&lol3;&lol3;&lol3;&lol3;&lol3;">
<!ENTITY lol5 "&lol4;&lol4;&lol4;&lol4;&lol4;&lol4;&lol4;&lol4;&lol4;&lol4;">
<!ENTITY lol6 "&lol5;&lol5;&lol5;&lol5;&lol5;&lol5;&lol5;&lol5;&lol5;&lol5;">
<!ENTITY lol7 "&lol6;&lol6;&lol6;&lol6;&lol6;&lol6;&lol6;&lol6;&lol6;&lol6;">
<!ENTITY lol8 "&lol7;&lol7;&lol7;&lol7;&lol7;&lol7;&lol7;&lol7;&lol7;&lol7;">
<!ENTITY lol9 "&lol8;&lol8;&lol8;&lol8;&lol8;&lol8;&lol8;&lol8;&lol8;&lol8;">
]>
<lolz>&lol9;</lolz>      ◄       lol9 expands into 10 lol8s, which then
                                 expands into 100 lol7s, and so on.
```

Obviously, this violates the intended behavior of entities, but the mere fact that entities are part of the XML language makes every parser vulnerable to expansion attacks. From our experience, the best way to address this is to use a design that combines parser configuration with a lexical content check. Let's start this process by configuring the parser.

1.5.4   Configuring the XML parser

To disallow entity expansion, you need to figure out which settings control entity behavior in the parsing process. Surprisingly, this becomes a challenge without fully understanding the underlying parser implementation, because every parser can behave differently. To get a solid foundation, a good starting point is to use external resources such as OWASP (the Open Web Application Security Project) as a guide.

Listing 1.9 provides an example of a parser configuration based on OWASP's recommendations that attempts to avoid entity expansion.[14] The selected features are quite invasive because almost everything regarding entities is disabled. For example, disallowing doctype does indeed make it difficult to do an entity attack, but at the same time, it affects overall usability. In these situations, security concerns are often compared against business needs, and if it's decided to weaken the configuration, it's important to understand what the risks are.

Listing 1.9   XML parser configuration suggested by OWASP

```
import static javax.xml.XMLConstants.FEATURE_SECURE_PROCESSING;

public final class XMLParser {
  static final String DISALLOW_DOCTYPE =
         "http://apache.org/xml/features/disallow-doctype-decl";
  static final String ALLOW_EXT_GEN_ENTITIES =
         "http://xml.org/sax/features/external-general-entities";
  static final String ALLOW_EXT_PARAM_ENTITIES =
         "http://xml.org/sax/features/external-parameter-entities";
  static final String ALLOW_EXTERNAL_DTD =
         "http://apache.org/xml/features/nonvalidating/load-external-dtd";

  public static Document parse(final InputStream input)
                               throws SAXException, IOException {
    try {
      final DocumentBuilderFactory factory =
                          DocumentBuilderFactory.newInstance();

      factory.setExpandEntityReferences(false);       ◄──── Disables entity reference expansion
      factory.setFeature(FEATURE_SECURE_PROCESSING,
                                     true);
      factory.setFeature(DISALLOW_DOCTYPE, true);     ◄──── Disallows DTDs in XML
      factory.setFeature(ALLOW_EXT_GEN_ENTITIES,      ◄
                                    false);            Disallows external general entities
      factory.setFeature(ALLOW_EXT_PARAM_ENTITIES,    ◄
                                    false);            Disallows external parameter entities
      factory.setFeature(ALLOW_EXTERNAL_DTD, false);  ◄──── Disallows loading external DTDs
      return factory.newDocumentBuilder().parse(input);
    } catch(ParserConfigurationException e) {
          throw new IllegalStateException("Configuration Error", e);
    }
  }
}
```

Instructs the parser to process XML securely (points to setExpandEntityReferences / setFeature FEATURE_SECURE_PROCESSING)

Even though relying on the parser configuration is recommended, it feels as if there's a lot of risk to it. For example, what happens if the underlying parser implementation changes or a feature is forgotten? These concerns are valid, and to address them, we recommend applying another layer of security—design.

---

[14] See the "XML External Entity (XXE) Prevention Cheat Sheet," https://github.com/OWASP/CheatSheetSeries/blob/master/cheatsheets/.

TIP To detect entity expansion, add a test in your build pipeline with a recursive entity definition. If the entity is expanded and the XML is accepted, then the test should fail because the parser might be vulnerable to expansion attacks.

1.5.5 Applying a design mindset

Before approaching the Billion Laughs problem from a design perspective, we think it's important to let go of the idea that the root cause lies in how entities are expanded. This is because the expansion is in accordance with the XML specification and not the result of a faulty parser implementation. This implies that the problem shouldn't be treated as a structural problem of XML, but rather as an input validation problem in the receiving system. This, in turn, means that a malicious XML block (such as the Billion Laughs XML) must be rejected by the receiving system without parsing it—this certainly sounds appealing, but is it a viable solution? It definitely is, and the answer lies in the second step of the validation order presented earlier—to run a lexical content scan. It can seem like a complex operation at first, but running a lexical content scan isn't that difficult. It's simply the process of converting a stream of characters into a sequence of tokens without analyzing their order or meaning (because that's the job of the parser).

There are many ways to implement a lexical content scan. In listing 1.10, you see an example of using a SAX parser (Simple API for XML) to scan XML. It's somewhat counterintuitive to use a parser as a lexical content scanner, but a SAX parser is in fact quite suitable because it emits an event for each token that's identified in the data stream. These events can then be used to analyze contents, which would be done if using it as a parser or, as in this example, to reject XML with entities. The `startEntity` method of the `ElementHandler` in the example achieves this by throwing an exception to abort the scan as soon as an entity is detected.

Listing 1.10   Simple lexical scanner that detects entities

```
import static org.apache.commons.lang3.Validate.notNull;

public class LexicalScanner {
    private static final String LEXICAL_HANDLER =
            "http://xml.org/sax/properties/lexical-handler";

    public static boolean isValid(final InputStream data)
                                                throws Exception {
        notNull(data);

        final SAXParser saxParser = SAXParserFactory
                        .newInstance().newSAXParser();
        final ElementHandler handler = new ElementHandler();

        saxParser.getXMLReader().setProperty(LEXICAL_HANDLER, handler);
        try {
            saxParser.parse(data, handler);
            return true;
```

Annotations:
- **Creates a SAX parser** (pointing to `final SAXParser saxParser = SAXParserFactory.newInstance().newSAXParser();`)
- **Creates a lexical element handler to detect entities** (pointing to `final ElementHandler handler = new ElementHandler();`)
- **Registers the handler to listen to lexical events** (pointing to `saxParser.getXMLReader().setProperty(LEXICAL_HANDLER, handler);`)
- **Scans the XML for entities** (pointing to `saxParser.parse(data, handler);`)

```
        }
        catch(IllegalArgumentException e) {
            return false;
        }
    }

    public static final class ElementHandler extends
                                  org.xml.sax.ext.DefaultHandler2 {
        @Override
        public void startEntity(final String name) throws SAXException {
            throw new IllegalArgumentException("Entities are illegal");  ◄──────┐
        }
    }
}
```

Aborts the scan if an entity is found

The scanner does indeed meet the expectations, but the main objective of the lexical scan is greater than just rejecting entities. A lexical scan should also ensure that all required elements exist in the XML; otherwise, it doesn't make sense to parse it. To illustrate, assume there's a customer object with exactly one phone number, email, and address represented in XML, as shown in listing 1.11. The phone number and address are required elements, whereas the email is optional. The only time it makes sense to pass the customer XML to the parser is when it contains all the required elements. All other element combinations are invalid from a business perspective and should be rejected by the scan—similar to how invalid input was rejected in the Username example earlier.

Listing 1.11   XML example representing a customer object

```
<customer>
    <phone>212-111-2222</phone>
    <email>jane.doe@example.com</email>
    <address>
        <street>Fifth Ave</street>
        <city>New York</city>
        <country>USA</country>
    </address>
</customer>
```

To ensure the customer XML contains all required elements, a richer design of the ElementHandler is needed. But before diving into details, it's important to remember that a lexical scan only cares about the existence of elements, not the meaning, the order, or if the elements exist multiple times. This allows for a structurally incorrect customer XML block (for example, with multiple phone numbers or address elements) to pass a lexical scan. Even though this seems like a flaw, the behavior is exactly as intended. Because as soon as semantic analysis is added to a lexical scan, it turns into a parsing process, and that brings everything back to square one.

With this in mind, let's turn back to the updated ElementHandler in listing 1.12. The implementation shows a couple of interesting details worth pointing out. First, all of the required elements are stored in a collection that's consulted in the startElement method each time an element is found. This looks straightforward, but there's a subtle trick to this that's easy to miss. Because the lexical scan only cares about the existence of elements, it needs a mechanism to determine if all required elements are present at least once in the XML. This is achieved by trying to remove each detected element from the required elements collection. It doesn't matter if a detected element is required or not, it only matters that it doesn't exist in the collection after the remove operation. This is because when reaching the end of the data stream, the scanner needs to ensure that all required elements have been found, which is verified by checking that the collection is empty in the endDocument method.

Listing 1.12 Element handler with required elements check

```
import static org.apache.commons.lang3.Validate.isTrue;
import static org.apache.commons.lang3.Validate.notNull;

private static final class ElementHandler extends
                                org.xml.sax.ext.DefaultHandler2 {

    private final Set<String> requiredElements = new HashSet<>();

    public ElementHandler() {
        requiredElements.add("customer");
        requiredElements.add("phone");
        requiredElements.add("address");
        requiredElements.add("street");                  All required elements
        requiredElements.add("city");
        requiredElements.add("country");
    }

    @Override
    public void startElement(final String uri,
                             final String localName,
                             final String name,
                             final Attributes attributes)
                             throws SAXException {
        notNull(name);
        final String element = name.toLowerCase();
        requiredElements.remove(element);         Removes the element from the collection if and only if it exists
        isTrue(!requiredElements.contains(element));   Ensures the element doesn't exist in the collection
    }

    @Override
    public void endDocument() throws SAXException {    Verifies that all required elements have been encountered
        isTrue(requiredElements.isEmpty());
    }

    @Override
    public void startEntity(final String name) throws SAXException {
        throw new IllegalArgumentException("Entities are illegal");
    }
}
```

Normalizes the element name to lowercase

The second detail worth mentioning is the choice of using a liberal scanning strategy to ignore all nonrequired elements. This can seem like a potential weakness because it accepts customer XML that fails the parser requirements, but the choice is carefully made. When communicating between systems, Postel's Law and the Tolerant Reader pattern state that an implementation should be liberal when receiving data and conservative when sending data.[15] This makes system integration less painful because changes to data fields ignored by the receiving system becomes seamless to the overall integration. As a result, choosing to ignore all nonrequired elements makes the lexical scan resilient against less important data changes, such as updating an optional element in the customer XML.

This certainly makes it difficult to inject a Billion Laughs XML block, but what if entities are required? Wouldn't that render the lexical scan obsolete? Or is there a way to accept entities and prevent expansion attacks at the same time? There is, but to see how, we need to approach this from a different angle.

1.5.6   *Applying operational constraints*

Both the lexical scan and the parser configuration address expansion attacks by blindly rejecting XML with entities, regardless if they're malicious or not. This has the downside of working only when entities are illegal. All other situations call for a different solution. It's therefore interesting to revisit the Billion Laughs XML and try to understand where the real danger lies.

The primary suspect is the entity expansion, but that in itself isn't what makes entities unsafe to parse. Instead, it's the resulting memory footprint that's dangerous. This implies that parsing XML with entities isn't dangerous per se, but rather the actual size of the resulting XML. A viable solution is therefore to allow entity expansion but with operational constraints on the parser process (such as memory limits or quotas) to prevent runaway resource consumption.

Choosing this approach, however, doesn't automatically protect against resource depletion. Even if a single parser process is prevented from consuming too much resources (because it's killed when exceeding the limits), running processes in parallel can result in a similar situation as with the Billion Laughs attack. For example, assume there are parser processes running in parallel, where each process consumes the maximum amount of resources. The total amount of resources used is then proportional to the number of processes, which creates a significant resource consumption footprint. Consequently, any other part of the system that relies on the same resources (for example, CPU or memory) will be affected. This calls for a design where parsing is done in isolation because it reduces the risk of cascading failures. We'll elaborate more on this when discussing bulkheads in chapter 9.

Relying on operational constraints does indeed seem like a viable solution, but it doesn't render the use of a lexical scan or parser configuration obsolete. In fact, choosing a design where all strategies are applied makes the system even more resilient against expansion attacks, which brings us to the next topic—achieving security in depth.

1.5.7   *Achieving security in depth*

Most developers have a tendency to address entity expansion attacks using parser configuration only. This isn't flawed per se, but it's like building a fence around a house

---

[15] See RFC 760 for Postel's Law at https://tools.ietf.org/html/rfc760, and for the Tolerant Reader pattern, see https://martinfowler.com/bliki/TolerantReader.html.

without locking the doors. No one is able to enter the house as long as the fence holds, but if it's breached, access is granted. This really isn't desirable. The obvious solution is to lock the doors and perhaps add an alarm on the inside. This is what security in depth is all about. With multiple layers of security, it becomes a lot harder for an attack to be successful even if a single protection mechanism is breached.[16]

If we look at the design for dealing with the Billion Laughs XML and correlate it to the house metaphor, it becomes easy to see how it achieves security in depth. By configuring the parser, a strong fence is built around the house. Sometimes this is too strict, and you can't reject all types of entities. In those situations, it's important not to remove the entire fence, but rather to understand what type of entities are needed. It might be possible to weaken the configuration to only accept certain types of entities (for example, only internal entities), which isn't perfect, but it's still a fence around the house.

The lexical scan process made sure that only XML with required elements was passed to the parser. This is similar to only letting people with keys into the house. That way, the set of XML blocks that need parsing is significantly reduced to those that might meet the business requirements. In turn, this makes it a lot harder to exploit the parser because the attack vector is now reduced to XML blocks with required elements. But what about entities? What if you need to accept them?

This is where the last layer of protection comes in. By applying operational constraints on the parser process, it's acceptable to weaken the lexical scan and pass XML with entities to the parser—similar to having a window open on the second floor. The operational constraints then make sure the parsing process never consumes too much resources—like a watchdog inside the house.

All in all, by applying parser configuration, lexical scan, and operational constraints together, it becomes significantly harder to do an expansion attack. And this is what secure by design is all about: using design as the primary tool and mindset for creating secure software. In the next chapter, we'll dive into a real-world case story that shows how brittle design and a lack of domain knowledge caused significant economic loss for a big global company, a situation that could have been avoided using secure by design principles.

Summary

- It's better to view security as a concern to be met than to view it as a set of features to implement.
- It's impractical to achieve security by keeping it at the top of your mind all the time while developing. A better way is to find design practices that guide you to more secure solutions.
- Any activity involving active decision-making should be considered part of the software design process and can thus be referred to as design.
- Design is the guiding principle for how a system is built and is applicable on all levels, from code to architecture.

---

[16] See "Defense in Depth," https://www.us-cert.gov/bsi/articles/knowledge/principles/defense-in-depth.

- The traditional approach to software security struggles because it relies on the developer to explicitly think about security vulnerabilities while at the same time trying to focus on implementing business functionality. It requires every developer to be a security expert and assumes that the person writing the code can think of every potential vulnerability that can occur now or in the future.
- By shifting the focus to design, you're able to achieve a high degree of software security without the need to constantly and explicitly think about security.
- A strong design focus lets you create code that's more secure compared to the traditional approach to software security.
- Every XML parser is implicitly vulnerable to entity attacks because entities are part of the XML language.
- Using generic types to represent specific data is a potential door opener for security weaknesses.
- Choosing the XML parser configuration is difficult without understanding the underlying parser implementation.
- Secure by design promotes security in-depth by adding several layers of security.

Intermission:
The anti-Hamlet

This is a real story about how negative numbers can cause severe economic loss. It's based on a case we worked on with a client, but to be able to share the details, we've obfuscated the context. Most importantly, we've changed what the business sold. We can assure you that it wasn't books. Interestingly enough, there are other examples that actually did involve books. Amazon had a similar bug around the year 2000.[1] But for those cases, we don't know the under-the-hood details.

This is also a story about how a serious security problem persisted in production for a long time without being detected and without anything being broken—at least, not in the technical sense. Nevertheless, it still caused money to bleed from the enterprise. Although the company could have uncovered who benefited unfairly, for practical reasons it wasn't possible for it to recoup its losses.

---

[1] Described, for example, in Gojko Adzic's book *Humans vs Computers* (Neuri Consulting Llp, 2017).

Finally, this story is about how an international retail business accidentally gave its customers do-it-yourself discount vouchers in its online store. We'll show how its loss was the result of a shallow design with incomplete or missing modeling, something we often encounter.[2] And we'll discuss how an explicit and conscious modeling effort makes a difference.

This online store is nothing unusual; it's the typical kind of business where the customer puts books in a basket, checks out, and pays with a credit card, and the books ship (figure 2.1). The store has been in production for a while, with ongoing development since its initial release. The retail business brings in a security team to do some auditing and testing. Specifically, the team audits how the system is set up in production as well as in the codebase. They also do tests where they try to manipulate the system from the outside to find security flaws. The team has a pretty open mandate to follow up on anything strange they find.

The infrastructure seems solid as the security team pokes around. They probe the firewalls. They scan for open operating system ports. They throw malicious packages at the web server. Still, everything works fine. This isn't a big surprise. Nowadays, security problems are seldom the result of broken infrastructure. We've learned that things that shouldn't be exposed to the public should be cut off from the public.

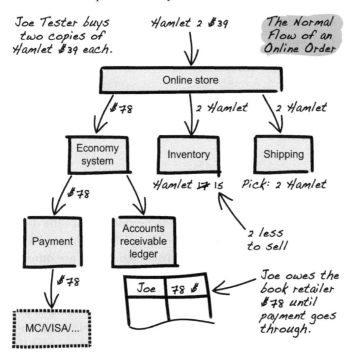

Figure 2.1   The normal flow when Joe buys two copies of *Hamlet* at $39 each

---

[2]   In this case study, we discuss modeling only briefly. We'll discuss it in more depth in chapter 3.

At the same time, other members of the team investigate the online store application from a technical perspective. They search for ways to circumvent the login. They see whether they can kidnap an open customer session. They try to poison the cookies. Same thing here—no success. These things would also be OK if the web server had been properly configured and, in this example, someone had obviously made the effort to read the documentation to implement the configuration.

A breakthrough comes when one of the team members, Joe Tester, gets curious about the Quantity field (where you specify how many books you want) on the order form. He passes in a JavaScript snippet to see if it executes, but nothing happens. Then he attempts to provoke a SQL injection—still nothing.[3] Finally, he gets curious and enters -1 as the quantity for a copy of *Hamlet* priced at $39. Phrased in another way, Joe Tester tries to buy a negative *Hamlet*—an anti-*Hamlet*.

Joe's surprised that he receives no error message. The store accepts the order, and it goes all the way through the order flow. He checks out with a credit card and gets an email confirmation that the order is accepted. "Strange," he thinks, makes a comment in his notebook, and continues working. The next afternoon, there's a knock on the security team's door. A lady hesitantly enters.

> "I'm from accounting," she presents herself, "and I wonder if any of you know anything about a person named Joe Tester." To clarify, she adds, "Because I asked around, and someone said you might know."
>
> "Yes, that's our test customer," the team answers. "What about him?"
>
> The lady from accounting continues: "I was running the accounts receivable ledger, and the system issued a credit invoice to him for $39. But when we were going to mail the book to him, we noticed a strange thing about his customer address; it's the same as our address here at headquarters. That's why I got suspicious and started asking around."

The system tried to pay real money to Joe Tester—not good.

2.1 *An online bookstore with business integrity issues*

Let's step back from the case for a moment to see what happened. It's definitely strange that the online store accepted an order of -1 copy of *Hamlet*. But now that this has happened, let's think about the logical consequences.

If someone buys a book that costs $39, then the value of the order is $39, and it makes sense that the customer pays $39 to the store. In this case, the customer, Joe Tester, didn't buy a copy of *Hamlet*, he bought a negative copy, so the value of the order is -$39 (figure 2.2). He should pay -$39 to the store, or the store should pay him $39. But a store isn't meant to pay out money in this fashion. Perhaps Joe Tester should give the store a copy of *Hamlet*.

---

[3] In SQL injection, the attacker tries to send commands to the database through the application. For more, see https://www.owasp.org/index.php/Top_10_2013-A1-Injection.

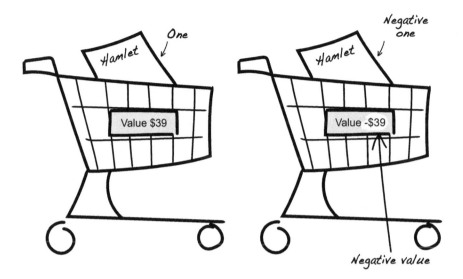

Figure 2.2   The "to pay" value of a negative book in a shopping cart

From a security perspective, this is a *security breach*. One aspect of security talks about the integrity of data, which roughly means that data hasn't changed or isn't generated in an unauthorized manner. Most often, you think about integrity in a technical way—providing checksums and cryptographic signatures to ensure data only changes according to the rules. In this case, the rules aren't technical rules but business rules. It's not sound business for a store to send customers money for anti-books. What we have is a breach of business integrity.

Suspicions raised, the security team starts investigating what's really going on. It turns out that the online store system calculates the "to pay" value for the order to be -$39, which is logical, although weird. The amount of -$39 passes through several online store systems, one after another (figure 2.3).

An interesting aspect of this story is that the security problem can't be understood without understanding each of these systems and how they react and interact. We'll start with two of them: the billing system and the accounts receivable ledger.

The purpose of the billing system is to collect payments from customers. If a customer sets the payment preference to a credit card and checks out an order worth $347, then that sum is charged to the customer's credit card. Customers can have other payment preferences too; for example, invoice, accumulated invoicing, or gift cards. Some customers have different payment methods for different amounts. Large amounts might be paid directly, whereas small amounts are accumulated into an end-of-month invoice.

When Joe Tester takes his order of -$39 to checkout, that amount is sent to the billing system. But the credit card module of the billing system doesn't know how to handle negative amounts. From the perspective of the billing system, a negative amount means there's no payment to collect. The payment task drops through without action.

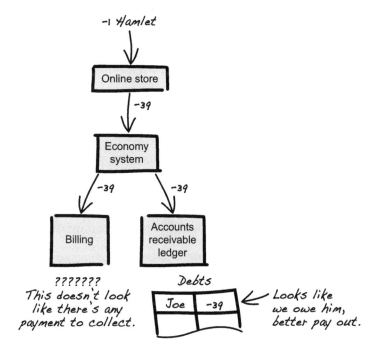

Figure 2.3 Online store sending -$39 to billing and to the accounts receivable ledger

2.1.1 *The inner workings of the accounts receivable ledger*

Now let's turn to the accounts receivable ledger. Part of the accounting system, the ledger keeps track of customers who owe the company money, which is the case when they've bought books but the company has yet to receive payment. In short, the accounts receivable ledger handles the balance of each customer. For example, if someone checks out an order of $347 and selects pay by invoice, then $347 is added onto that customer's balance. Later, when the company receives the payment, the balance in the ledger is cleared. Sometimes people pay too much, perhaps $350 in this case. The balance then drops to a negative, -$3, meaning that the company owes money to the customer. For a bank, it's often normal that a company owes money to the customer, even in the long run. But for an online bookstore, such a situation is only acceptable as a temporary condition. If it arises, the store should try to clear its debt as soon as possible.[4]

The normal procedure for the online book company is to pay out money owed to customers by sending a credit invoice. Those checks run as a batch job, which was what the lady from accounting referred to when she said, "I was running the accounts receivable ledger...." When Joe Tester makes his *anti-purchase*, the online store system sends a payment amount of -$39 to the accounts receivable ledger, which immediately puts him at an advantage to the company. The next night, the job runs and finds this outstanding debt, so it creates a credit invoice to be sent to him to clear the ledger, effectively

---

[4] A deeper explanation of accounts receivable is beyond the scope of this book, but see https://en .wikipedia.org/wiki/Accounts_receivable if you'd like to know more.

sending our tester a payment (figure 2.4). This is the invoice that a perceptive lady in accounting catches as suspicious and starts asking around about.

As these tests are done in production, it's obvious that the production system has had this flaw for a while. The only reason this particular case was caught was that the strange address raised suspicion. But there may have been similar cases earlier.

A financial investigation is started to see how big the problem is. Operations and the security team join forces to do a cross-check of all credit invoices that have been issued. Sieving away credit invoices to suppliers and partners leaves the customer-facing credit invoices. Most of those are valid credits issued for damaged goods or other legitimate reasons. Only a small portion is left, so the problem turns out not to be particularly big—or so it seems at the time. Still, it's strange that sending out money for nothing has gone undetected. The technical investigation continues to unveil the entire scope of what happens when someone orders an anti-book. And two more important systems are involved: inventory and shipping.

Figure 2.4   Accounts receivable ledger sending a credit invoice and clearing the ledger

2.1.2   *How the inventory system tracks books in the store*

The inventory system for the store keeps track of how many books of each kind the store has in stock and can sell from the warehouse. A good starting point for that is how many books of each kind are on the shelves in the warehouse, but, unfortunately, it's not quite that straightforward. For example, say that there are 17 copies of *Hamlet* in the warehouse. A customer has bought two of them, but those two haven't yet been picked from the shelf and shipped to the customer. These two copies shouldn't be counted, because they aren't sellable, and they don't belong to the store any more. The inventory of *Hamlet* should be 15 copies, not 17.

Another situation might be that the shelf for *Pride and Prejudice* is empty. The retailer has bought another 100 copies from the publisher, but those copies are still on a truck that hasn't yet arrived at the warehouse. As the copies are in the possession of the store, they are sellable and should be included in the inventory. The inventory of *Pride and Prejudice* should be 100 copies, not 0. There's lots of other strange situations that might occur as well. The inventory system is a complicated piece of logic in and of itself.

If the online store sells three copies of *Hamlet*, it sends a message to the inventory system, decreasing the inventory level of *Hamlet* from 15 to 12. But what happens if instead Joe Tester buys -1 copy of that book? The inventory level of *Hamlet* was 15 and should now be reduced by -1, resulting in an inventory level of 16 (figure 2.5). Selling one anti-*Hamlet* increases the inventory level by one!

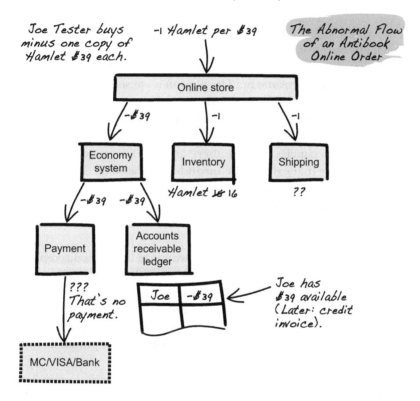

Figure 2.5   Joe Tester ordering -1 *Hamlet*

2.1.3   *Shipping anti-books*

The shipping system ensures the books are shipped to the customers. When an order arrives from the online store, the shipping system iterates through the order lines and compiles pick lists for the warehouse workers to pack the boxes. This is a complicated system that tries to minimize the work for the warehouse workers by letting workers pick books for several orders simultaneously, for example. The system handles that optimization well.

What the shipping system doesn't handle well is a negative number of books. Such an order line causes a runtime exception that's logged to the system log, together with a multitude of other messages. Unfortunately, no one ever looks at that log. In effect, the order line is discarded.

2.1.4   *Systems living the same lie*

Here dawns an interesting realization. From a financial perspective, the IT systems are consistent with each other. The billing system and shipping system are of less importance, as they don't change their state. The more interesting systems are the inventory system and the accounts receivable ledger.

- The inventory system falsely believes the inventory of *Hamlet* is 16 when it should be 15.
- The accounts receivable ledger falsely believes the retailer owes money to someone else.

From a financial perspective, this balances out: instead of having 15 books and owing nothing, the retailer has 16 books and has a debt of the value of one book. Both systems live a lie, but they live the same lie. The illusion is consistent.

Because the systems are consistent, the regular reports won't show any discrepancies. As a matter of fact, there are reports that run every night. More comprehensive reports are also run each quarter as part of the financial reporting. And none of these have reported any discrepancies because there are no discrepancies between the IT systems. The discrepancy that exists is the inconsistency between the inventory system (16 books) and what's actually in the warehouse (15 books). But that won't be noticed until the end-of-year inventory, when the inventory of the warehouse is counted manually and fed into the bookkeeping system. Then, and only then, will the missing book be noticed.

At the end-of-year inventory, there's nothing strange in finding a discrepancy. Books are physical objects, and things happen at a warehouse. A delivery from a supplier might arrive that should contain 134 books but only contains 133. Not all boxes are counted, and sometimes there's a mistake in counting. A book might be dropped, damaged, and discarded. This should be noted, but sometimes people are in a hurry and forget to do so. And sometimes, there's theft. All wrapped together, this is reported by finance as a loss-on-warehouse, and a certain level is expected.

As a matter of fact, the end-of-year inventory a few months earlier reported a higher level of loss-on-warehouse than usual. Management's analysis was that there was a motivational problem with the people at the warehouse: either they had gotten less careful and damaged more books or they had started stealing books. As a result, management sent them on a day retreat with a motivational coach to get their values more aligned with the company's ethics. The folks at the warehouse were confused and not happy.

2.1.5   *A do-it-yourself discount voucher*

On further study of the discrepancies, things turn out to be worse than they initially seemed. The inventory difference in the warehouse is much larger than the total number of credit invoices. But there's something more going on.

Realizing that the usual reports can't be trusted, the team starts a deeper investigation. It turns out that getting a credit invoice wasn't the most usual way the flaw had been exploited. A much more popular version was to give yourself a discount by ending your shopping trip in the e-store with some negative books to reduce the total amount of your order before paying (figure 2.6). The rumor about this strange feature had obviously spread, because quite a lot of customers used it.

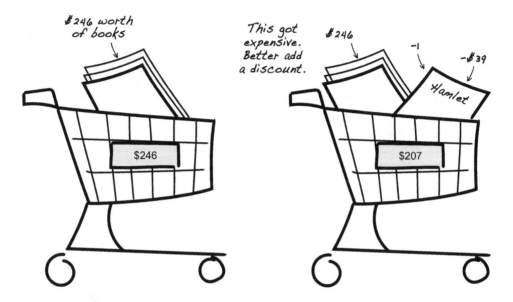

Figure 2.6 Do-it-yourself discounting—add an anti-*Hamlet*

The investigation shows that the company has lost a significant amount of money through this loophole. Now it's time to decide what to do.

The technical flaw will be addressed, and we'll return to that soon. But what about all the money customers owe the business because they've given themselves discounts? In the end, it's the board of directors that gets the call to decide what to do. After careful consideration, they decide to let things be. Chasing down customers, many of them returning and frequent customers, would generate more ill will and would hurt the company more than simply accepting the loss, patching the hole, and moving forward.

This continuous breach of business integrity had been going on for months without anything being technically broken. And it most probably would have continued unnoticed had it not been for the curious lady in accounting and a security tester with an interest in how the business worked—the domain of book sales. We're convinced that, throughout the world today, there are many similar flaws in existence, being continuously exploited without triggering any alarms.

2.2   *Shallow modeling*

A company leaking money this way obviously has a security problem. How could this occur? And, more importantly, how could it have been avoided? Our observation is that this kind of situation is often the result of modeling that stops short at the first model that seems to fit, without digging deeper or questioning and without planning or consideration. Let's refer to this ad hoc style as *shallow modeling* (in contrast to deep modeling).

Let's start by asking the question, "How could things go wrong this way?" Looking at it after the fact, it seems obvious that a quantity can't be an integer without restrictions. But why did someone design it that way? As we mentioned in chapter 1, *design* consists of all the active decisions you make when developing software. In this case, the design included the (active) choice to make a quantity an unrestricted integer. It might not have been a decision that was well thought through, but it was a decision nevertheless.

Let's look at the rest of the concepts in the design— and there are lots of concepts in the domain of online sales. Some of these are more important and some less. When designing, someone chooses some concepts to be the most crucial: order, order line, book, and quantity, for example. We often see designs where the main focus seems to be on answering the question, "How can I represent this?" With this mindset, design is about finding a way to code it. When you find a way to code it, you're done. And, in this case, the shortest distance between business and code is achieved if you can represent things using the language primitives: integers, floats, booleans, and strings (figure 2.7).[5]

Different things are represented in different ways in the domain, some explicit and some implicit. For example, the model contains *order* as a concept, and an order has a monetary value. An order also consists of order lines, each with a book and a quantity. A book

Figure 2.7   The how-can-I-code-this mindset at work

has a title, an ISBN, and a price. Order, order line, and book are *explicit* concepts in the domain. Quantity, title, ISBN, and price are *implicit* concepts, represented by integers, strings, and so forth. Rephrased, a quantity is an integer without restrictions. Looking at it this way, it seems strange that order, order line, and book are all well elaborated, but quantity is left as an integer without consideration. How did it become this way?

---

5   Well, in Java, strings are technically not primitives but are so fundamental that we can consider them as primitives for the sake of this discussion.

2.2.1 *How shallow models emerge*

We think many of these mistakes boil down to the modeling being incomplete or even missing. Imagine a conversation in the early stages of the project between a sales person, Sal Esperson, and a developer, Deve Loper. The discussion might go something along these lines:

"And then you can add books to the order," says Sal.

"So, how do we describe a book?" questions Deve.

"We show a title and a price," answers Sal.

"What can the price be? Is it always a whole number?" asks Deve.

"Well no, a book can be priced $19.50, tax excluded," clarifies Sal.

Deve thinks, "So a book has a title and a price as attributes. The title is a string. The price is not an int, it's a float."

> **WARNING** Never, ever, ever represent money as a float! See "No double money" in chapter 12 to find out why.

And Deve asks, "Is that all there is to a book?"

"Nah," answers Sal, "it's also important that it has an ISBN, so we can keep hardbacks and paperbacks separate."

"OK. And then we add books to the order," says Deve. "For example, *Moby Dick, Pride and Prejudice, Hamlet, Moby Dick* again, *1984*, and *Moby Dick* again?"

"Well, almost. We would say three *Moby Dick* books, as we don't care about what order you buy them in."

"OK," Deve thinks. "It isn't a float, it's an integer."

> **WARNING** Beware of leaving modeling as "It's an integer"!

Later on, this discussion is turned into code. Deve creates a class `Book` that gets the attributes `title`, `isbn`, and `price`. The `Order` class gets a new method, `addOrder-Line(Book book, int quantity)`. Because order, order line, and book get explicit representations, those each become classes. The type system enforces that these are used at the proper places in the code. If you try to pass anything else where a `Book` is expected, you'll get a compilation error.

On the other hand, quantity is implicitly represented by the primitive type `int`. But using quantity isn't enforced by the type system and compiler. You can accidentally pass in some other integer, such as the temperature outside, without getting a compiler error. The only hint that a quantity is expected is the parameter name `quantity`, as shown in the following:

```
class Book {
    String title;
    String isbn;
    double price;
    ...
}
```

```
class Order {
    void addOrderLine(Book book, int quantity) {
        ...
    }
}
```

In the conversation, note that Deve asks no further questions about what a title is or about the ISBN, jumping to the conclusion that they are simply text, and he represents them using `Strings` in the code. But, most probably, a title can't be any string, and an ISBN certainly can't.

Deve isn't incompetent when it comes to modeling. He does ask an interesting question about the nature of price ("Is it always a whole number?") but leaves it there. Also, he completely misses the hint that prices might be more complicated when Sal answers, "…tax excluded." The drive for Deve seems to be "Can I represent this in code?" and not "Do I understand how this works?"

We've seen that shallow modeling like this leads to having interesting business concepts represented as primitives: int, float/double, string, boolean, and so forth. Our experience is that these kinds of implicit representations are common. We often see systems where almost everything is represented by strings, integers, and floats. Unfortunately, this has several drawbacks.

2.2.2 *The dangers of implicit concepts*

You've seen that something as simple as leaving quantity as a primitive integer can cause severe security problems. This type doesn't capture the crucial restrictions. In the same way, having the title and ISBN as unrestricted strings provides too much leeway. Strange things can happen when a system assumes some data is formatted as a proper ISBN when it's not.

> **WARNING** Any integer between -2 billion and 2 billion is seldom a good representation of anything.

Credit card numbers and Social Security numbers (SSNs) are two other examples that we often see as implicit concepts represented by strings. Obviously, this risks having data that's not a valid credit card number or SSN, and it might not even have the right format. But worse is the risk that you might not treat it properly.

Both credit card numbers and SSNs have strong restrictions on how they can be revealed, put into logs, and so on. If they are represented as strings, there's a risk that they'll be accidentally put into logs or shown. Later, we'll see how representing these things as domain classes can avoid such mistakes; for example, by using read-once objects (we cover this in chapter 5).

Back to our implicit concepts represented by language primitives, such representations also create very funky code. Ponder the following method signature:

```
void addCust(String name, String phone, String fax, int creditStatus,
    int vipLevel, String contact, String contactPhone, boolean partner)
```

This code has only eight parameters, but if you accidentally swap two of them, then the customer might get a credit status or a VIP level they shouldn't have. As both the `creditStatus` and `vipLevel` are `int`s, the compiler won't catch that you've sent them in the wrong order. These kinds of mistakes can lead to subtle and hard-to-find bugs, sometimes with security connotations. And eight parameters isn't a long list. We've seen parameter lists with tens of parameters, all strings. Constructors especially seem to be at risk for this specific problem.

Shallow modeling and the resulting implicit concepts lead to a high risk of buggy and insecure code. The alternative is a more conscious approach with deep modeling and explicit concepts. Now let's turn to what this story would look like if the modeling had been a conscious effort to implement a deep model.

2.3 Deep modeling

To understand deep modeling, you must first acknowledge that any model you come up with is a choice. In any domain, there are uncountably many different models possible. When you design, you choose what set of concepts to build your design around, and what meaning you load into those words. Using the terminology from Domain-Driven Design, this particular choice makes up the *domain model,* the chosen distillation of the domain. In our work with security and design, we've gotten lots of inspiration from Domain-Driven Design and its focus on understanding and modeling the domain in a strict way.[6]

Making a conscious effort when modeling means that you actively search for ways to understand the domain. The drive isn't "How do I code this concept?" but rather "How can I understand this concept?" This leads to much deeper dialogues when modeling and often to an iterative process of discussions and coding. The result is that you unveil more concepts that need to be represented explicitly to capture the full understanding of your model.

2.3.1 How deep models emerge

Let's go back to the discussion between Deve Loper and Sal Esperson to see how it might evolve with a mindset of deep modeling:

"And then you can add books to the order," says Sal.

"So, how do we describe a book?" questions Deve.

"We show a title and a price," answers Sal.

"What can the price be? Is it always a whole number?" asks Deve.

"Well no, a book can be priced $19.50, tax excluded," clarifies Sal.

Deve thinks, "So, a book has title and price as attributes. And price seems to be a complicated issue in itself because you mentioned tax. I'll need to dive into those later," and asks, "Is that all there is to a book?"

---

[6] Eric Evans coined the term and wrote the seminal book *Domain-Driven Design: Tackling Complexity in the Heart of Software* (Addison-Wesley Professional, 2004). Read it, preferably a few times.

"Nah," answers Sal, "it's also important that it has an ISBN so we keep hardbacks and paperbacks separate."

"OK. And then we add books to the order," says Deve. "For example, *Moby Dick*, *Pride and Prejudice*, *Hamlet*, *Moby Dick* again, *1984*, and *Moby Dick* again?"

"Well, almost. We would say you have a quantity of three *Moby Dick* books, as we don't care about what order you buy them in," says Sal.

"Can you buy half a *Moby Dick*?" asks Deve.

"Of course not, silly."

"You used the word quantity," Deve says. "I want to understand that better. What happens if you have a quantity of three *Moby Dick* books and then they're removed? Do you then have a quantity of zero *Moby Dick* books?"

"Eehhh, not really. I mean, a quantity of zero isn't really a quantity at all. We'd say no quantity," Sal clarifies.

"This quantity seems to have some rules around it," Deve says. "So, how big can a quantity be? Two billion books?"

"Haha. Well, certainly not. Seriously, I think we're limited by the through-store logistics flow, and it can't handle orders bigger than a total quantity of 240."

"The through-store flow?" asks Deve.

"Yep, that's what they call it. It's how the orders from the online store are handled at the warehouse; it's about box sizes, packing stations, and stuff. Orders bigger than that must go to the warehouse bulk flow. But we can't use that from the online store," Sal explains.

"What is the total quantity of an order? Can you give me an example?"

"That's simply adding the quantity of all books. If you have three *Hamlet*s, four *Pride and Prejudice*s, and one *Moby Dick*, then you have a total quantity of eight," Sal says.

TIP When modeling, discuss upper limits—that always yields interesting information.

Deve makes a note that a single quantity can't be larger than 240, and the same goes for the total quantity of an order. Later on, this knowledge is captured as code:

```
class Book {              ◄────
    BookTitle title;            | Book has a class of its own
                                | (an explicit representation).
    ISBN isbn;
    Money price;
    ...
}
                                     The Quantity class contains restrictions
                                     on how small or large a quantity might
class Quantity {  ◄──────────        be (business insight captured as code).
```

```
    ...
    Quantity(int quantityOfBooks) {
        isTrue(0 < quantityOfBooks, "Quantity must be positive");
        isTrue(quantityOfBooks <= 240,
          "Quantity must fit in through-store flow, which is limited to 240");
        ...
    }
}

class Order {
    void addOrderLine(Book book,
                       Quantity quantity) {
        ...
    }

    Quantity totalQuantity() {
        ...
    }
}
```

There's no risk of someone sending in an illegal quantity; the compiler won't allow it.

NOTE Code is *encoded* knowledge, thus its name.

In a later chapter, we'll dig deeper into code like this. Chapter 4 covers contracts such as isTrue(0 < quantityOfBooks.... The class Quantity is an example of a domain primitive, to which chapter 5 is dedicated. Creating entities such as the Order class is the subject of chapters 6 and 7.

2.3.2 *Make the implicit explicit*

With deep modeling, you can find lots more concepts that are interesting—too interesting to be left implicit. Our standard advice is to make implicit concepts explicit. When you find an implicit concept like "quantity" in your story, take a few minutes to discuss it a little bit more deeply. If it seems interesting enough, make it into an explicit concept instead—spell it out as a part of the design. Later on in the code, quantity will show up as a class of its own and will uphold its own constraints. Using the concept of quantity also makes the rest of the code more expressive.

A common objection is that making all these concepts explicit creates a lot of classes. We'd like to point out that the code in those classes is necessary in any case: all the interesting business rules have to be caught in code, or else you're creating a worse system. Having explicit concepts as classes makes a difference in how your code is organized. Extracting interesting concepts into classes of their own makes them easier to find than if the same code is spread out into service methods in large service classes.[7]

TIP When modeling, make implicit concepts explicit.

---

[7] An architectural style Martin Fowler refers to as *Transaction Scripts*; see http://martinfowler.com/eaaCatalog/transactionScript.html.

Shallow modeling is a missed opportunity for learning. As you've seen, it's also a potential source of security vulnerabilities. To grab the opportunity would be to ask, "What do you mean by quantity? Can there be variants? Are there restrictions?" Most probably, you'd learn that a quantity of books can never be a negative value. Perhaps you'd even learn that it can't be zero because "We only use the word quantity with a number if there are books; otherwise, we say there's no quantity."

Discussing the lower bound might lead to a discussion about an upper bound. Is it sensible to be able to order 2,147,483,647 books? Asking about such an order might lead the domain expert to start explaining how logistics work, how books are loaded on pallets, and so on. Such a discussion will again give you a deeper understanding and, yet again, reduce the risk of business integrity problems.

A design like this is much more expressive, much more robust, and much less prone to contain security vulnerabilities. We'll spend the following chapters elaborating on how to achieve this and what design guidelines we've found most effective to avoid security flaws. We'll start by looking at some of the concepts of Domain-Driven Design we've found most useful.

Summary

- Incomplete, missing, or shallow modeling leads to a design with security flaws.
- A security flaw in the form of broken business integrity can live in production for a long time, bleeding money from your enterprise.
- Conscious, explicit design results in a much more robust solution.

Part 2

Fundamentals

The second part of this book is the longest and also the most important. This is where you'll learn the design principles, ideas, and concepts that make up the foundation of the secure by design approach of creating software.

We wanted to include many topics in this part, but those that made it into the book are the ones we believe are the most valuable. First, these topics will equip you with a set of tools and concepts that you can start to apply immediately in your daily coding. Second, and perhaps most important, they'll teach you the mindset of secure by design—a mindset that'll enable you to expand on the ideas in this book and perhaps come up with your own secure design practices. Once you understand the secure by design ideas and start seeing the connection between software design and software security, you'll probably view software development in a whole new light.

Core concepts of
Domain-Driven Design

This chapter covers

- The parts of Domain-Driven Design (DDD) most important for security
- Models as strict simplifications of the domain
- Value objects, entities, and aggregates
- Domain models as ubiquitous language
- Bounded contexts and semantic boundaries

During the years that we've been developing software, we've found inspiration from many sources—some different, some shared. One of the biggest sources of inspiration we have in common is *Domain-Driven Design*, often abbreviated as DDD.

DDD sets the bar a little higher in regards to most system development. We've seen a lot of system development where the attitude "just make it work" has been the guiding principle. When a bug was found, the solution was to just add an `if` clause. Although seldom a local programming mistake, the problem was poorly understood, and the solution was built on a model that was incomplete or inconsistent.

Domain-Driven Design is an approach to the development of complex software in which we:

1 *Focus on the core domain.*

2 *Explore models in a creative collaboration of domain practitioners and software practitioners.*

3 *Speak a ubiquitous language within an explicitly bounded context.*

—Eric Evans, Domain-Driven Design Reference (Dog Ear Publishing, 2014)

DDD says we don't just want our systems to work, we want to truly understand what we're building. Let's stress the word *what* in this context. What DDD emphasizes is a deep understanding of the problem domain, not just an understanding of the solution. The beauty we see in DDD is that it also insists on capturing that understanding in code—it makes the code speak the language of the problem you're solving. We find that a focus on deep understanding helps us become better developers. It was much later that we realized this approach also has a profound effect on security.

This chapter is about DDD, but not all aspects of it. DDD is in itself a huge and multifaceted subject. It spans from crafting code to system integration, from requirement analysis to testing. It links into other agile-minded methodologies and processes. You'll find multiple books and an overwhelming number of articles about DDD, so covering it comprehensively in one chapter would be impossible. We'll instead focus on those parts of DDD that we've found can drive security.

If you're unfamiliar with DDD, this chapter gives you the understanding of DDD that we'll use in later chapters. This chapter is also here as a reference. In later chapters, we use parts of DDD to promote security, so come back here when you need a refresher about value objects, aggregates, context maps, or any other DDD concept.

As a side note, we recommend you dig deeper into this subject, as there is a lot more to it beside the security aspects. The mini-book *Domain-Driven Design Quickly* is a good starting point.[1] *Patterns, Principles, and Practices of Domain-Driven Design* (Wrox, 2015), by Scott Millett, is also an easygoing start. If you want to dig deeply into the subject, then Eric Evans's seminal book *Domain-Driven Design: Tackling Complexity in the Heart of Software* (Addison-Wesley, 2003) is the definitive read.

If you're somewhat familiar with DDD, read this chapter as a refresher. If you're a proficient Domain-Driven Designer, read this chapter anyway, as there are some aspects we want to stress—those aspects that we'll use later for promoting security. Also, be aware that we might express some ideas in a somewhat compressed fashion, and they might seem somewhat distorted. We're not aiming for completeness, but for an understanding that's enough to talk about its relationship to security.

We'll cover *domain models*, which form the foundation of system development à la DDD. Domain models provide an unambiguous, strict foundation for what the system does. From a security perspective, this is interesting. When you define what the system should do, it also gives you a powerful tool to say what the system shouldn't do.

---

[1] *Domain-Driven Design Quickly* (InfoQ, 2006) can be downloaded freely as a PDF at https://www.infoq .com/minibooks/domain-driven-design-quickly.

When modeling, and implementing that model as code, it's handy to have some building blocks. Domain models are usually based on value objects and entities. Larger structures are usually represented through aggregates. Using these elements makes the code more precise and less prone to vulnerabilities.

When zooming out from a single system to the integration level, DDD gives you the tools of bounded contexts and context mappings. These tools give you a better possibility to ensure that integration between systems is tight so that it's easier to hold up security across several systems. As DDD is founded on domain models, let's start with creating strict models to capture a deep understanding about the problems you can solve with your software.

3.1　Models as tools for deeper insight

Let's start with explaining what DDD models mean, as they are at the center of DDD. In system development, the word *model* is used for many things: flow diagrams in UML, how data is laid out in the tables of a database, and more. In DDD, the model explains how you've captured your essential understanding of the business-at-hand as a selected set of concepts. Why do you need such models, and what should they look like?

We all know that there are no silver bullets, and DDD is no exception. To stay intellectually honest, it's important to point out when a technique or methodology *doesn't* yield a significant benefit, as well as under what circumstances it has its sweet spot. If you're designing a network router or a baggage-handling system, the circumstances differ wildly. DDD won't help much in the first case, but will help you in the second case.

In the case of a network router, the most important problem is technical: getting high enough I/O throughput and low enough network latency, which is a really complex problem. Should you fail to master this complexity, you'll get a product that no one wants to buy. Network performance is the critical complexity for your router. DDD can aid you in modeling the package queues and routing tables, but it won't address the throughput and latency.

In contrast, let's think about the case of the baggage system that handles checked-in baggage at an airport. In its technical implementation, it will use the same databases, message queues, and GUI frameworks as most other systems. There will be a lot of complexity to handle, but this is probably not the critical problem. For the baggage system, you need to represent how baggage is routed from check-in counters to airplanes via conveyor belts and loading trucks. If the representation is flawed, then the bags might not make it in time for the right flight or might end up on the wrong one. Passengers will be angry, and the business will lose goodwill, confidence, and money. Even worse, there are important security aspects at stake. For obvious security reasons, a bag is only allowed on the plane if the passenger is on the plane. If a bag is checked, but the passenger doesn't show up at the gate, then the baggage system must ensure the baggage is unloaded. If the system isn't properly crafted, it might be possible to trick it into loading a bag onto a specific flight or not unloading it—something that could have severe security consequences.

If you fail to capture a deep and precise understanding of baggage handling, you'll build a flawed system. But the greater risk is that it's harmful to the business and potentially dangerous to the customers. It might even be so bad it makes the system meaningless. The airport might be better off closed with such a flawed system in place. This isn't a hypothetical example; the opening of the Denver Airport in the 1990s was delayed a year-and-a-half because of deficiencies in the baggage system, resulting in heavy economic loss.[2] In cases like this, understanding and modeling the domain of baggage handling should be the focus of your work. Spending time on optimizing your database connection pool would be a bad choice. The critical complexity is the domain.

DDD is at its best when your system handles a problem domain that's hard to understand. In these cases, the most critical problem is understanding the complexity of the domain. Then understanding and modeling that domain should be your main focus. If you fail to master the complexity of various technical aspects, you get a system that's less useful. But, if you fail to master the complexity of the domain, you get a system that's doing the wrong thing. In that regard, the domain is the *critical complexity*. In our experience, most business applications fall into this category. Understanding the domain and crafting a purposeful model targets the core of solving the business logic problems.

It might be tempting to think that the domain isn't technical. However, that would be a mistake. Sometimes the critical complexity is understanding the domain, but the domain is technical. Consider writing an optimizing compiler. It transforms source code to highly optimized machine code that can be executed and, in doing so, applies peephole optimizations, performs dead-code elimination, evaluates subexpressions at compile time, and so on. The tricky part isn't the read/write performance of files, it's ensuring that all these optimizations result in a program that does the same thing as defined by the source code. The main effort should be to represent the source code and all transformations in a strict way that enables the optimizations but still guarantees that the resulting program is the same. Here it's the domain that's the critical complexity, but the domain is technical!

Now the connection to security. It's hard to capture enough understanding to make a system that behaves well in all possible cases. It's hard enough to do it for benevolent, normal data with all the weird cases that can occur. It's even harder to do it in a way that's resistant to malevolent data. Someone might try to attack your system by sending bizarre data to it, manipulating it into doing something unpleasant. The system still needs to respond in a sound and safe way. We saw an example of this in the case study of the online bookstore in chapter 2. No normal business procedure results in an anti-book (quantity -1) being placed in a shopping cart. Still, a dishonest customer might do so to manipulate the system (in that example, to avoid paying the full price for an order).

We've found that for security, it's essential to focus on building domain models. A lot of security problems are avoided as a side effect, especially business integrity problems. Domain models to a certain extent also shield your code from some technical attacks.

---

[2]   Denver is not alone. For example, Heathrow Airport, terminal 5, in Longford, England, has had similar problems.

What you need are domain models that support development in a stable and secure way. For a domain model to be effective, it needs to

- Be simple so you focus on the essentials
- Be strict so it can be a foundation for writing code
- Capture deep understanding to make the system truly useful and helpful
- Be the best choice from a pragmatic viewpoint
- Provide you with a language you can use when you talk about the system

DDD isn't a silver bullet; its value depends on the context. There are situations where a main focus on modeling the domain isn't the right choice. For example, if you write software for a network router, then I/O throughput will be the most critical thing. Your critical complexity is technical in this case. But even here, you should consider whether a sloppy domain model might be a security issue.

TIP There's always a critical complexity. Be aware of whether it's a technical aspect or the domain.

In our opinion, the main benefit of domain modeling is that it works as a vehicle for learning at a deeper level—and learning at that level is crucial. It's not hard to "catch the lingo" of businesspeople, and you can use that same language to write a requirements document that looks good. But without deep learning, such a document will contain subtle misunderstandings, inconsistencies, and logical loopholes. These flaws make it impossible to build a solid system that does the right thing in tricky situations, with security vulnerabilities as the worst consequence. Working in collaboration with domain experts to create a domain model fuels that learning.

3.1.1 Models are simplifications

A model is a simplified version of reality where you've removed irrelevant parts. For example, when you check in a bag at the airport, there's no need for the system to represent your shoe size. On the other hand, it's probably relevant to represent how heavy the bag is. To make it easier to understand and code the system, you create a model that contains the weight of the bag (but not the shoe size of the passenger), keeping just the details you think are relevant.

To be clear, models aren't diagrams. In many other contexts, *model* means a specific diagram type, like an entity-relationship model often used for database design or the class diagram from UML. These diagrams are representations of the model, but the model *itself* is the conceptual understanding of how our simplified view of reality works.

NOTE The model isn't a diagram. The model is a chosen set of abstractions.

The use of "model" in DDD is closer to another use of the word, as in the phrase "model train." When building model trains, the builders put much effort into keeping some aspects of reality, while totally ignoring others (figure 3.1). Knowing what details to keep and what details to distort is key to building train models, as well as domain models.

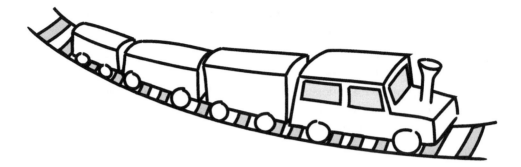

Figure 3.1   A model train looks like the real, original train.

Figure 3.1 shows a model train. It looks like a train and moves around on rails, but it's not a real train. We consider it a model because it has kept some important attributes while disregarding others. Let's list some attributes the model has in common with real trains:

- *Color*—We think that the model of a specific train should have the same colors as the original train.
- *Relative size*—We expect the proportions to be maintained. If the doors are twice as high as they are wide in reality, we expect the same ratio on the model train.
- *Shape*—We expect the model train and its details to have the same shape, such as the curvature of the front window.
- *Movement*—We expect the model train to move along rails in the same way as a real train does.

Let's also list some attributes where the model differs from reality and where we think the difference is fine:

- *Material*—It's OK that the model train is made out of plastic or tin when the original is built from other materials.
- *Absolute size*—If the real cars were 30 meters long, it's fine that they are much smaller in the model.
- *Weight*—The model is much lighter, which is OK.
- *Method of propulsion*—The model doesn't have a steam engine; it runs on electricity.
- *Rail curvature*—The curves in the model are much tighter than in reality, which we accept.

Strangely enough, it's easier to find differences between the model train and a real train than it is to find things they have in common. Still, we have a firm opinion that this is a proper model of a train. Clearly this specific model has managed to capture the essentials of our understanding of a train.

It seems like color, relative size, and movement are enough for us to understand that the model is a train. These three attributes are necessary; if the model doesn't fulfill these attributes, we won't play along and pretend it's a train. And these three are sufficient. If the model fails to fulfill some other expectation, such as material, we'll still play along and pretend it's a train.

NOTE A *model* is a simplification of reality, a simplification we still accept as a valid representation of the real thing.

We'll now leave the realm of toys and take with us the idea that a model is a simplified understanding of the real thing. This goes for the models you use in system development as well. If you model a person, you might choose to grab onto a few attributes: a person has a name, is of a certain age, has a specific shoe size, and optionally has a pet. Agreed, this is a crude model, but a model nevertheless (figure 3.2).

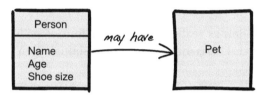

Figure 3.2   One possible model of people and pets

A model is a simplification, but it must still be general enough so that you can capture some variations that you think are interesting. In our example, we want to allow different names, different ages, and different shoe sizes, and we allow people to have pets or not. All these differences we allow to show up in the model. We don't make any distinctions between people of different height or pay any attention to their hairdo (figure 3.3).

You can represent this model in many different ways. You can use plain text to explain what you mean. You can use different kinds of diagrams to illustrate it (for example,

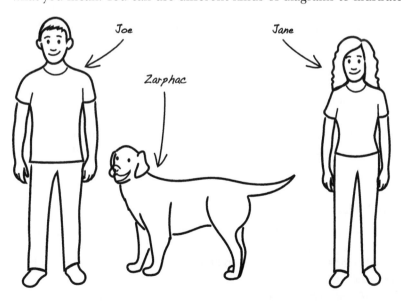

Figure 3.3   Joe, age 34, shoe size 9, and his dog Zarphac, together with Jane, age 28, shoe size 6, no pet

OO 896 5158

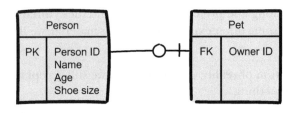

Figure 3.4   The same model as before, but another representation

compare figures 3.2 and 3.4). You can use code (pseudocode or actual code from a programming language). The important point here is that none of these representations is the model. Class diagrams in particular are often confused with being the model, but the model, as such, isn't any of the representations. The model is the conceptual understanding of what you consider as essential in your modeling—in this case, name, age, shoe size, and pet.

The main benefit of keeping models as really simplified versions of reality is that simple models are easier to make strict. This is something that's essential when you later build software from them.

3.1.2   *Models are strict*

The domain model isn't just a watered-down version of reality; what it has lost in richness, it has gained in strictness. When we talk about a model being *strict*, we mean it in the mathematical sense of "exact, precise," that the concepts, attributes, relations, and behaviors are unambiguous.

People are really complex beings with lots of attributes and lots of relationships. When you decide to focus on name, age, shoe size, and pets, you lose a lot of richness. But you gain precision in what you mean by "a person," a precision that makes it possible to represent this entity in software. Knowing what to sacrifice in richness to gain in precision is hard work, and you need access to people with deep domain knowledge to do this well.

NOTE   The folks who really understand the domain, we call *domain experts.*

Writing software is a collaboration between two kinds of professionals who come from different directions and who need to meet in a productive way: the businesspeople and the developers. Each has different needs that have to be fulfilled to create great software. Businesspeople need to see the terminology they're used to, not some quasi-technical mumbo-jumbo. If they don't recognize their domain, you've failed them.

> ### Some terminology
> - *Domain*—A part of the real world where stuff happens (for example, the domain of baggage handling)
> - *Domain model*—A distilled version of the domain where each concept has a specific meaning
> - *Code*—An encoded version of the domain model written in a programming language

It's not enough to just have some familiar words as labels in the user interface or in the headers of printed reports. The system must also behave in a way that businesspeople think is reasonable, consistent, and understandable. For this to happen, the domain model has to be strict. If the model isn't strict and contains ambiguities, then one part of the system might behave in one way and another part in another way.

For example, a screen at the check-in counter might talk about "number of bags," another at the gate might say "baggage count," and the tablet used by loading staff might say "luggage." To make things worse, some of these terms might count the carry-on as part of the number, while others don't. When the personnel speak to each other, they each have to remember what screen the other person is seeing and whether to add or subtract the carry-on from the number they're seeing. Sometimes there are misunderstandings, and bags are lost. The system fails the business, and not even the domain experts think it makes sense.

> **WARNING** Many "almost synonyms" describing the same concept are often a sign that the model isn't strict.

Another shameful variant is when a model is consistent in the terminology but too lenient in its constraints and relationships. This is often the result of using a standard system and configuring it to the domain, which is the usual way of working with, for example, Enterprise Resource Planning (ERP) products.

One of the first business uses of computers in the 1940s and 1950s was to plan the use of machines and raw materials in manufacturing industry, which provided huge benefits compared to paperwork and manual routines. In the 1980s, *material requirements planning* (MRP) expanded into *manufacturing resources planning* (sometimes called MRP II) to include finance, personnel, marketing, and other so-called resources. But the underlying domain still used resources from a bill-of-material to produce products to sell. Because factories differ, these MRPs were highly configurable.

In the 1990s, these processes evolved into ERP systems, planning the work of entire enterprises and becoming even more configurable to support any enterprise in any kind of business. They were often described and sold as *standard systems*, which could be configured to handle any domain; whereas, under the hood, they were still the same flow-of-materials systems. This line of business has successfully sold such systems to handle customer complaints, police investigations, or other completely different domains. Unfortunately, successfully selling is one thing and successfully delivering value is another. If you want to configure a flow-of-materials system to handle police investigations, you need to do some very nonintuitive abstractions: police can be seen as a machine, and a report about a burglary can be seen as a pile of raw material that is refined by the (police) machine during its investigation.

In order to shoehorn one domain into another, you need to be less and less specific, and less and less precise. The result is often a general *object management system* where everything is an object. Through the user interface, you can update the attributes of the objects, but this watered-down model carries little understanding of what those objects actually represent. Often you can fill in any combination of attributes and relationships.

A system that is so lenient is of course prone to mistakes, and as you saw in the case study of the online bookstore, such lenience can result in security flaws.

> **NOTE** It takes both happy businesspeople and happy developers to make a good system. Both groups need to have their professional needs fulfilled.

Obviously, it's important to pay attention to the businesspeople. They need to recognize the domain they're used to working in, so you should choose terminology that's familiar to them. And it's a big mistake to fail to meet the needs of the domain professionals. It's an equally big mistake to fail to meet the needs of the other professionals: the developers.

As developers, at the end of the day, we write code. And that code is mathematically strict—it tells the computer how to execute based on the data at hand, according to the rules we code. This is why we need strictness. Either we get that strictness from our conversations with the domain experts or we invent that strictness ourselves by filling in the gaps with educated guesses.

It isn't good enough to say that "most people just have one pet." Developers need to know if having a pet is strictly restricted to having just one. This is where it takes some courage to be a developer. You need to ask the questions that make the model strict without ambiguities. If you ask if there can be more than one pet, you might get the answer, "Oh, that's really unusual." This leaves you with two options: either you think, "Then I need to allow for a list of pets," or you think, "Just one pet allowed." In the first case, you end up writing a system with possibly more complexity than necessary, and sooner or later some weird combination occurs. In the second case, you disallow multiple pets, just to get hammered a few months later when it turns out that there are some customers (perhaps customers you get when acquiring another company) who actually have two or more pets. To add insult to injury, this can turn into blame-shifting towards you, with businesspeople saying unfairly, "We told you it could happen," when all you did was make a decent assumption to keep complexity at bay. You need to be able to make decisions to move development forward.

The way out of this dilemma is to actively ask what should be in the model: "Shall we allow for multiple pets, or shall we place a restriction on having just one?" Deciding whether the unusual multipet people should be covered or not isn't a technical decision, it's a business decision. If you don't have system support for multiple pets, then they have to be handled through a separate manual routine. On the other hand, providing scope for lots of diversity doesn't come for free either. It's tempting to allow for more and more general models, but sooner or later everything is in a many-to-many relationship with everything else. That doesn't make anything better in the long run. It can be hard to foresee and get an overview of the ramifications of a general model.

Say there's a function that allows one person to swap pets with another person. If you also allow for multiple pets per person, then you need to figure out what it means to swap pets. Does that mean person A gets all of the pets of person B, and vice versa?

Or do you just swap one pet? If you don't let the model reflect the business domain, you let the businesspeople down. If you don't create a strict model, you let the development people down.

> **NOTE** A good model must not only reflect the business domain, it must be strict. Having a *strict model* means that you eventually can build code using the model as a foundation.

When you design software, you make similar choices; you make simple representations of complex phenomena. Let's have a look at a schoolbook example of object orientation, shown in the following code snippet, where lots of attributes and relationships are ignored and only a narrow view of a person is left:

```
class Person {
    private String name;          The model of the domain concept
                                  "person" captured as code
    private int age;
    private int shoeSize;
    private Animal pet;
    void growOlder() {
        this.age++;
    }
    void swapPetWith(Person other) {
        ...
    }
}
```

In this design, you've removed tons of attributes and behaviors that a person might have, reducing it to four attributes that are essential for the context and purpose at hand. The model has a purpose, a scope of behavior you want to describe. Leaving out details might seem to make the system poorer, but it provides a great benefit—what you gain by leaving out details is the possibility to be precise.

In the domain of people, a *person* is a complex being with complex interactions. But in our model of the domain, a Person is something that has a name, an age, a shoe size, a pet, and the ability to grow older. Period. That's exactly what you mean when you use the word *person*. What you lose in richness, you gain in precision.

3.1.3 *Models capture deep understanding*

The previous example of modeling a person is of course laughingly simplistic. Real-world problems are much more intricate, as is the case of airport baggage handling. The strict understanding that you capture in a domain model is deeper than what most people think. In fact, the knowledge you need to capture is even deeper than the understanding most domain experts exercise in their day-to-day work when they handle situations on a case-by-case basis. The reason for this is that you not only need enough understanding to work in the domain, you need an understanding deep enough to build a machine. Let's compare this with the challenge of riding a bike.

Most of us are experts at riding a bike in the sense that we can do it without actively thinking about what we do.[3] We can prove this by taking a bike and riding it even in pretty challenging conditions, such as on a bumpy road and in windy weather, and, perhaps, even while carrying a large package under one arm. That takes expertise. Compare that with the difficulties faced by a child who's just learning to ride on flat ground on a nice sunny summer day. This expertise is comparable to the proficiency of a domain expert; they know how the domain works. For example, a shipping expert knows how to route cargo containers even when conditions get tough, such as when a container is mistakenly unloaded from a ship and there's no other ship leaving for the same destination for a substantial amount of time. The domain expert is able to handle even tricky cases, taking each case on its own.

Unfortunately, the understanding you need to write a software system goes even deeper. You don't have the luxury of being "at the site" to handle any situation that arises, of being able to assess and improvise to resolve a situation on the spot. You're writing a program that should do this without your being at the site in human form. The challenge you face isn't so much like a youngster riding a bike, but is more like building a bike-riding robot.

If you're to build a bike-riding robot, the understanding of bike riding needed is much deeper than most experts possess, even professional bicycle messengers or BMX pros. For example, how do you turn right while riding a bike? Think about it for a few seconds; you've probably done it a thousand times. Most people spontaneously answer, "I pull on the right handlebar." Unfortunately, doing so would cause you to fall to the left, down onto the asphalt, due to centrifugal force.[4]

What you actually subconsciously do when turning right is to turn the handlebars left, causing you to fall to the right for a very short period of time. After a few milliseconds, you've tilted right just to the appropriate angle, and then you turn the handlebars to the right, taking you into a right turn. Your leaning to the right will be exactly what's needed to compensate for centrifugal force, and you'll turn right, safe and stable (figure 3.5). You do this without thinking and without understanding the subtle kinematics mechanics. If you want to build a bike-riding robot, this is the depth of understanding that you need to have.

This bike-riding robot story provides some bad news and some good news. The bad news is that if you look inside the head of a domain expert, you find no ready-to-go model. There's no *true* model inside. You can't simply ask the domain experts and expect to get all the answers you need. The good news is that working together with domain experts to craft a model is fun and rewarding. Doing so is an iterative process of exploring lots of possible models and choosing one that is appropriate for solving the problems you have at hand.

---

[3] In the Dreyfus model of skill acquisition, these levels of skill are called Expertise and Mastery. Check out *A Five-Stage Model of the Mental Activities Involved in Directed Skill Acquisition* (University of California, Berkeley, 1980) by the brothers Stuart and Hubert Dreyfus.

[4] Yes, centrifugal forces do exist, even if your physics teacher might have told you otherwise. The centrifugal force is a fictitious force that's observed in a rotating frame of reference, such as a bicyclist taking a turn. *Classical Mechanics* (Addison-Wesley, 1951), by Herbert Goldstein, is an excellent book on the subject of kinematics mechanics.

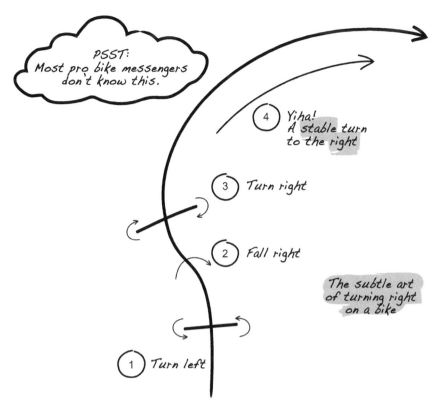

Figure 3.5   To build a bike-riding robot, you need a deep understanding of how to make a right turn.

> **TIP**   The best domain models are evolved in cooperation between developers and domain experts—over time and many iterations.

3.1.4   *Making a model means choosing one*

One of the usual myths of modeling is that there's a true model somewhere, often thought to be embedded inside the head of the domain expert. This isn't the case. Making a model involves an active choice among many possible models, and you need to choose the one that best suits your needs—that which defines the purpose of the model.

> **NOTE**   There is no single *true model*; there are just choices. Make choices that fit the purpose.

DDD practitioners sometimes use the phrase "distilling a model." Let's compare ourselves for a while with a whiskey distiller. Somewhat simplified, the whiskey distiller starts with a large batch of fermented wort, something basically undrinkable, then adds some heat and collects the vapors.[5] The distiller throws away the first part, which

---

[5]   A thorough and accurate description of whiskey distillation is outside the scope of this book... unfortunately.

contains acetone. The middle part consists of most of the alcohol, some of the water, and the natural flavors that are dissolved. This is considered the good part and is kept. The last part consists of some alcohol, a lot of water, and some less attractive flavors. This is also discarded. What is kept is what we call whiskey. Your personal attitude toward whiskey or your tastes might vary, but you get the point. When distilling, we actively keep some parts we want and throw away parts we don't want. In the same way, when you distill a model, you throw away some parts of reality and keep others.

The important point here is that there are many ways for distillers to do their job. They have a choice. Keeping the middle part is a choice because the objective for the distiller is to get a high-alcohol result with some specific flavors. The purpose is to distill something that is pleasurable to drink. The purpose directs how we distill.

NOTE   When distilling a model, you do it for a purpose.

But the distiller could have made other choices, if the purpose had been different. Had the distiller wanted acetone instead, then the distillation would have looked different. The distiller would have kept the first part and thrown away the rest. In the same way, you can distill different models from the same reality depending on what you intend to use the models for.

Our model describing a person with name, age, shoe size, and pet is just one model. Another model could be to describe a person by date of birth, place of birth, mother's name, and father's name. Neither of these two models is more correct than the other (figure 3.6). They're different, and they're good for different purposes. If you're keeping a registry for a dog owners' club, the first model is clearly superior to the second. If you're studying how a family has spread across the world through migration, the first model is worthless, and the second excellent.

When modeling, actively find different models that express your domain. Try to find three different models and compare how good they are at expressing your domain problems. Finding a good model is important because it makes it possible to talk about the domain in an efficient and unambiguous way. A good model forms a language.

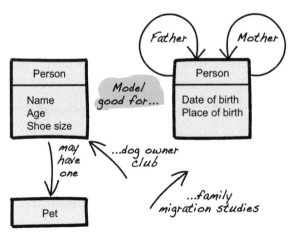

Figure 3.6   Two different models of people—good for different things

3.1.5   *The model forms the ubiquitous language*

An interesting aspect of modeling is that the model creates a language—the language we speak about the system. To start with, realize that when domain experts speak with each other, they use a language of their own. This is the *domain language.* In an English-speaking country, this language might sound like English. But there are subtle differences. There are a lot of words in English that are simply never used in this domain-expert language (for example, chervil will seldom be used in a discussion about accounting). The other way around, the domain-expert language contains domain-specific terms and idioms that aren't used in common English (accrual, for example). What domain experts speak to one another is simply a language that's geared to enabling effective communication.

Take a moment to consider the domain-expert language of system developers. Among ourselves, we easily throw around terminology that makes perfect sense to us but is completely impossible to understand for nondevelopers; for example, we might "pool the connections" or "make that a strategy." And the domain experts of finance, logistics, or healthcare have their own lingo too.

If you're building a logistics system, it seems like a logical approach to take the terminology from logistics and just encode that as a software system. This is a wonderful idea, but unfortunately flawed. The language used by logistics experts isn't logically consistent. This isn't because they're particularly sloppy with terminology. We software developers are equally sloppy with our terminology. Listen in on any two seasoned developers talking, and you'll find that they might use the words *object*, *instance*, and *class* interchangeably, as if they were synonyms. And you know they aren't, because when you explain object orientation to beginners, you're careful to distinguish between classes and objects. But when two experts communicate, they can be sloppy because they understand each other, and the real discussion is elsewhere on a higher level.

> **TIP** Don't turn into the language police, correcting domain experts when they talk to each other. They're allowed to be sloppy, and so are you when talking to your peers.

If you're building a logistics system, wouldn't it be wonderful if you could form a language where you can talk about the system in a precise way without the risk of misunderstanding? This is exactly what a model is. If you jointly (between logistics experts and developers) decide that a *leg* means transport from one place to another using the same vehicle all the way, and you decide that "terminating a leg" means that the cargo is unloaded at the destination, then you can use those terms and make yourselves understood. If you say, "If two transports terminate a leg at the same dock, then they can be cotransported on the next leg," then that phrase can be unambiguously understood, and the functionality can be implemented (figure 3.7).

Figure 3.7   The domain model forms a language in common.

When discussing the functionality of a system, use the words and phrasings that are part of the model. By doing so, you'll quickly realize whether the functionality can be implemented or not. If it's awkward to express the functionality using the terms from the model, this is a sure sign that it'll be awkward to implement. It might be a sign that the model needs to be extended to contain a new term and the system refactored for consistency.

Using the terminology of DDD, you want the model to become the *ubiquitous language* when talking about the system. By ubiquitous, in this case we mean that the terminology should be used everywhere you talk about the system (figure 3.8). The same terms should be used in the user interface, in the manuals, in the requirements or user stories, in the code, and in the database tables. There's simply no point in calling something a quantity in the user interface, referring to it as an amount in the manual, and naming the database column Volume. Insisting on using the same language across disciplines helps in finding ambiguities that could manifest as bugs or security flaws later.

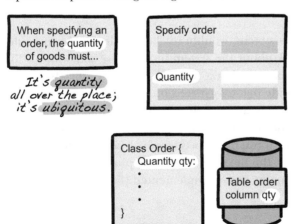

Figure 3.8   The model is ubiquitous; it uses "quantity" consistently all over the place.

It's worth pointing out that, of course, the persistence model might be slightly different from the conceptual model. For example, you might have to split concepts into different tables, and you might need to join tables or synthetic keys that aren't part of the conceptual model. In the same way, the classes in the code might be slightly different from the terms used in the conceptual model for implementation-specific reasons. Nevertheless, the understanding you capture is still the same, and you should use terminology from the ubiquitous language as much as possible when you name your constructs (classes or database tables).

This doesn't mean you're turning into a language police force. The model or the domain model language is the ubiquitous language when talking about the system. The domain experts are still allowed to use their ambiguous domain language among themselves in the same way developers are allowed to be sloppy about objects versus classes in discussions with other developers.

The important point about being precise in the ubiquitous language is that when you talk about the system, you need to be precise. This is especially important when business experts and developers interact and the risk of misunderstanding is the highest. In these situations, you should insist on using the terminology of the ubiquitous language.

> **TIP** Insist on using the words from the domain model in any requirements document. If something is hard to express in the terminology of the domain model, it's probably hard to write as software.

It's also worth pointing out that just because language is ubiquitous doesn't mean that it's universal. It's the ubiquitous language when talking about this specific system, not when talking about other systems (even other logistics systems). Different systems have different needs and different focuses. These will have different models and, thus, different languages. Each domain model language will be the ubiquitous language within its realm but not outside that domain.

The context for the language has an outer bound. In DDD, we refer to this as the *bounded context* for the model. Within the bounded context, each word in the model has a well-defined meaning, but outside the bounded context, words can mean something completely different. We'll cover bounded contexts more deeply later on in this chapter. Understanding more about models and their purpose, you can now move on to some more pragmatic aspects. You need to actually build those models, so some typical building blocks are handy to have.

3.2 *Building blocks for your model*

In order to express your domain model in code, you need a set of building blocks. These building blocks should be well defined, and their purpose is to bring order and structure to complex models. They provide a framework that allows you to keep your domain logic clearly separated from the rest of your code and guides you through the technical difficulties in doing so.

The building blocks from DDD that are of special interest in this book are entities, value objects, and aggregates, as shown in figure 3.9. These are interesting because, used in a certain way, they can also be building blocks for software security.

Understanding the meaning of these building blocks will help you understand the concepts discussed in the rest of this book. In this section, you'll learn the meaning of each of these terms, the details that define them, and how they are used.

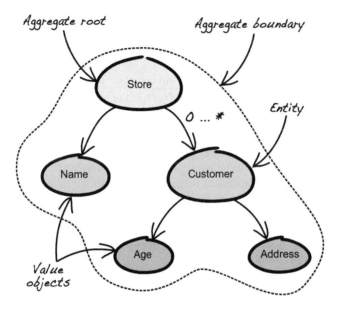

Figure 3.9   Fundamental building blocks of a domain model

3.2.1   Entities

Every part of your domain model has certain characteristics and a certain meaning. Entities are one type of model object that have some distinct properties. What makes an entity special is that

- It has an identity that defines it and makes it distinguishable from others.
- It has an identity that's consistent during its life cycle.
- It can contain other objects, such as other entities or value objects.
- It's responsible for the coordination of operations on the objects it owns.

What this means is that if you need to know if two entities are the same, you look at their identities instead of their attributes. It's the identity of the entity that defines it, regardless of its attributes, and the identity is consistent over time. During the life cycle of an entity, it can transform and take on many different attributes and behaviors, but its identity will always remain the same.

Let's consider a car, for example. Many attributes of a car can change during its lifetime. It can change owners, have parts replaced, or be repainted. But it's still the same car. In this case, the identity of the car can be defined by its vehicle identification number (VIN), which is a unique 17-character identifier given to every car when it's manufactured.

Sometimes an entity's identity is unique within the system, but sometimes its uniqueness is constrained to a certain scope. In certain cases, the identity of an entity can even be unique and relevant outside of the current system. The identity is also what's used to reference an entity from other parts of the model.

Another important trait of an entity is that it's responsible for the coordination of the objects it owns, not only in order to provide cohesion, but also to maintain its internal invariants. The ability to identify information in a precise manner and to coordinate and control behavior is crucial if you want to avoid security bugs sneaking into your code. In upcoming chapters, you'll see that this is what makes entities an important tool for designing secure code.

THE CONTINUITY OF IDENTITY

Sometimes a domain object is defined by its attributes, but sometimes those attributes change over time without implying a change of identity of the domain object. For example, a representation of a customer can be defined by its attributes: name, age, and address. Most of these attributes can change during the time the customer exists in the system, but it's still the same customer with the same trail of history, so its identity shouldn't change (figure 3.10). It would quickly become quite messy if the system were to create a new customer every time an address got updated.

The customer isn't defined by its attributes but rather by its identity and should therefore be modeled as an entity. That way, the customer's identity will stay consistent for as long as the customer exists in the system, regardless of how many state changes it goes through during that existence.

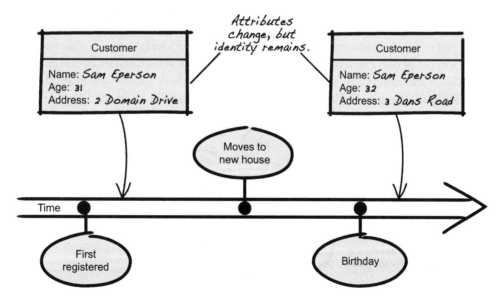

Figure 3.10 The attributes of the customer change, but the identity remains the same.

Choosing the right way to define an entity's identity is essential and should be done carefully. The result of that definition will typically be in the form of an *identifier*. This means that the identity and uniqueness of an entity is determined by its identifier. Sometimes the identifier can be a generated unique ID, and sometimes it can be the result of applying some function to a selected set of attributes of the entity. In the latter case, you need to pay careful attention to not include any attributes that can change over time. This can be tricky because it's hard to know which attributes might change in the future, even though they seem fixed right now. Therefore, it's generally better to use generated unique IDs for identity.

TIP   As a rule of thumb, favor generated IDs over an identity based on attributes.

It's also important to note that what we mean by identity in DDD isn't the same concept of identity, or equality, that's built into many programming languages. In Java, for example, object equality is by default the same as instance equality. Unless you explicitly define your own method for equality, two object instances representing the same customer won't be equal. That's to say, the identity isn't dependent on a specific representation of the entity. Regardless of whether the customer is represented as an object instance, a JSON document, or binary data, it's still the same entity.

LOCAL, GLOBAL, OR EXTERNAL UNIQUENESS

The identity of an entity is important, but the scope in which its identity is unique can vary. Consider, for example, our customer entity. A system could use an identifier that's unique not only to the current system but also outside of the system. This is an *externally unique identifier*. An example of this would be a national identifier like those used by many countries as a means to identify their citizens. In the United States, this would be the Social Security number. Using an externally defined identifier can, however, come with certain drawbacks, one of which is security implications, as you'll see in later chapters.

Perhaps more common than externally unique identifiers are identities made to be unique within the scope of the system or within the boundaries of the current model. Such identifiers can be referred to as being *globally unique*. An example of this is a unique ID generated by the system when a new customer is created (figure 3.11). There

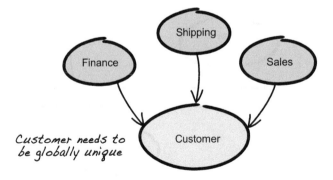

Figure 3.11   Some entities need to be globally unique.

can be some interesting technical challenges involved here that are worth pointing out. If you're dealing with a distributed system and you need the IDs to not only be unique but also sequential, then generating them can be a technical feat in itself.

Some entities will be contained within another entity. Because such encapsulated entities are managed by the entity that holds them, it's usually enough if they have an identity that's only unique inside the owning entity. This identity is said to be *local* to the owning entity (figure 3.12). To go back to our customer entity, say your system is a customer management system for retail stores, and every customer belongs to one, and only one, store. In this case, the identity only needs to be unique within the store the customer belongs to. Modeling an identity to have local uniqueness can simplify the ID generation function. It also makes it clearer that the responsibility for managing those entities lies with the encapsulating entity.

KEEP ENTITIES FOCUSED

One thing to keep in mind when you're modeling entities is to try to only add attributes and behaviors that are essential for the definition of the entity or help to identify it. Other attributes and behaviors should be moved out of the entity itself and put into other model objects that can then be part of the entity. These model objects can be other entities, or they can be value objects, which we'll look at in the next section.

Entities are concerned with the coordination of operations on not only themselves, but also on the objects they own (figure 3.13). This is important because there can be certain invariants that apply to a certain operation, and because the entity is responsible for maintaining its internal state and encapsulating its behavior, it must also own the operations on the internals. Moving the operations outside of the entity would make it anemic.[6]

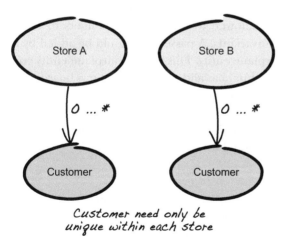

Figure 3.12   Some entities only have local identities.

---

[6]   Fowler, M., "AnemicDomainModel" (2003), http://www.martinfowler.com/bliki/AnemicDomain-Model.html.

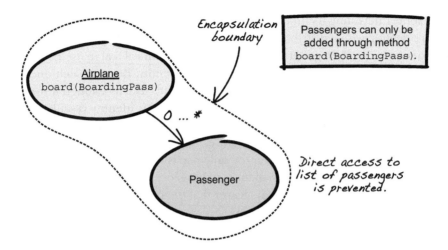

Figure 3.13 Entities coordinate operations.

When boarding an airplane, each passenger must present a boarding pass in order to verify that they're about to enter the correct plane, which makes it easy to keep track of whether anyone is missing when the plane is about to depart. If passengers were allowed to freely walk in and out of the airplane, airline personnel would need to check all the boarding passes after everyone was seated. This would be a lot more time-consuming and possibly cause confusion if passengers had taken seats in the wrong plane. With this in mind, it makes sense to control and coordinate the boarding of passengers. The same goes for the software model to handle this.

   If you model the airplane as an entity with a list of boarded passengers, then other parts of the system shouldn't be allowed to freely add passengers to that list, as it would be too easy to bypass the invariants. A passenger should be added by a method `board(BoardingPass)` on the airplane entity. This way, the airplane entity controls the boarding of passengers and can maintain a valid state. It only allows boarding of passengers with a boarding pass that matches the current flight.

   Entities play a central role in representing concepts in a domain model, but not everything in a model is defined by its identity. Some concepts are instead defined by their values. We use *value objects* to model such concepts.

3.2.2   *Value objects*

As you learned in the previous section, an entity is often made up of other model objects. Attributes and behaviors can be moved out of the entity itself and put into other objects. Some will be other entities, but many will be value objects. The key characteristics of a value object are as follows:

 - It has no identity that defines it, but rather it's defined by its value.
 - It's immutable.

- It should form a conceptual whole.
- It can reference entities.
- It explicitly defines and enforces important constraints.
- It can be used as an attribute of entities and other value objects.
- It can be short-lived.

As you'll see in upcoming chapters, these properties are part of what gives value objects an important role to play when it comes to writing code that's secure by design.

DEFINED BY ITS VALUE

Because a value object is defined by its value rather than its identity, two value objects of the same type are said to be equal if they have the same value. You only care about what they are, not who or which they are.[7] Value objects have no identity. This is the total opposite of how we define entities.

Say you have the concept of money in your domain model. You can choose to model money as a value object because you don't distinguish between different coins or bills. A $5 bill is worth as much as another $5 bill. It's the value of the bill that matters, not which bill it is.

> **NOTE** Whether a concept should be treated as a value object without identity or as an entity with a unique identity is dependent on which context you're currently looking at.

If you were modeling the domain of a central bank, then you probably would choose to model money as an entity, because in the view of a central bank, which is responsible for not only creating banknotes but also keeping track of them and eventually destroying them, each $5 bill is unique. It's created and given a unique serial number that identifies it so it can be distinguished from other $5 bills. It remains in use until one day it's time to destroy it (perhaps to be replaced by a new type of bill with a new identity). In the view of the central bank, money has an identity and a life cycle.

IMMUTABLE

Because a value object is defined by its value, it's important to make sure that the value can't be changed—if the value is changed, it's no longer the same value object. This is why a value object must be immutable. If a value object were mutable, then changing its value could break the invariants of some other object containing the value object. Having immutable value objects also means it's safe to pass them around as arguments and allows for various technical optimizations, such as reusing objects if memory is scarce and ease of use in multithreaded solutions.

CONCEPTUAL WHOLE

A value object can consist of one or more attributes or other value objects. It can also reference, but not contain, entities. The reason for this is that the value of an entity

---

[7] Evans, E., *Domain-Driven Design: Tackling Complexity in the Heart of Software* (Addison-Wesley Professional, 2004), p. 98.

can change. If the value object contained the entity rather than referencing it, then the value object itself would change whenever the entity changed. This would in turn break the immutability of the value object.

When modeling a value object and deciding what it should contain, it's important that it forms a conceptual whole. In other words, it should be a whole value.[8] This means that a value object shouldn't be just a convenient grouping of attributes, objects, and references but should form a well-defined concept in the domain model (figure 3.14). This is true even if it contains only one attribute. When your value object is modeled as a conceptual whole, it carries meaning when passed around, and it can uphold its constraints.

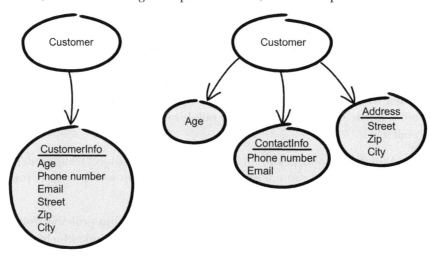

Figure 3.14   A value object should form a well-defined concept.

In figure 3.14, you can see two different ways to model a customer and its related attributes. In the model on the left, all the attributes have been grouped together in a model object called `CustomerInfo`. In the model on the right, the attributes have been modeled so that they are grouped to form well-defined concepts: street, zip, and city have been grouped together in a value object called `Address`. Phone number and email have been put in a value object called `ContactInfo`. Age becomes its own value object.

TIP   Always strive to model your value objects to form a conceptual whole.

It's also important to understand that a value object isn't just a data structure that holds values. It can also encapsulate (sometimes nontrivial) logic associated with the concept it represents. For example, a value object representing a GPS point could have a method that calculates the distance between itself and another GPS point using nontrivial numerical calculations.[9]

---

[8]   Cunningham, W., "The CHECKS Pattern Language of Information Integrity: 1. Whole Value" (1994), http://c2.com/ppr/checks.html#1.

[9]   GPS (Global Positioning System) is a satellite-based navigation system that provides accurate positioning on earth.

DEFINES AND ENFORCES INVARIANTS

Let's say you have a value object Age that has one integer value, as seen in figure 3.15. In Java, for example, an integer can by default take the values from -2^{31} to $2^{31}-1$. You'd probably not consider that range to be typical for a person's age. Therefore, you should model age as a value object with proper constraints or invariants so that its definition becomes clear (figure 3.15).

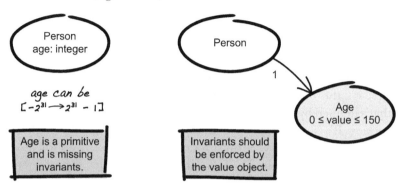

Figure 3.15 Value objects should enforce their own invariants.

You could during your modeling come to the conclusion that the age of a person should be between 0 and 150 years.[10] Or maybe your domain doesn't allow for young children, so the minimum age might be 18. Whatever range you choose, it'll be a lot stricter than allowing the full range of a Java integer.

> **NOTE** These types of invariants should be enforced within the value object itself and not be put into other domain objects or utility methods.

It's also worth noting that the types of invariants we're talking about aren't the types of checks that are commonly referred to as *validation*. Validation checks are typically performed when asserting that a domain object is valid for a certain operation; it's possible to perform a specific action on it. An example of validation would be to check if an order is ready to be sent to the shipping system. The validation could include verifying that the order has been paid for and that it contains the necessary address information. This type of validation often involves multiple domain objects and is generally performed as late as possible.[11]

3.2.3 Aggregates

When dealing with a model object that has a life cycle, such as an entity, it's important to make sure that its state remains valid throughout its entire life cycle. This can require quite a bit of logic to implement and can involve code to handle locking

---

[10] An age of 150 might be a bit of a stretch, but people are living longer and longer, so you might want to future-proof your model.

[11] Cunningham, W., "The CHECKS Pattern Language of Information Integrity: 6. Deferred Validation" (1994), http://c2.com/ppr/checks.html#6.

mechanisms to support concurrent operations and managed updates to persistent storage. Regardless of whether the entity is being persisted or not, the state change can be said to take place within a transaction.[12]

Transaction management is usually feasible when it comes to a single entity. In reality, your domain model is typically not that simple and involves many connections between various entities and value objects. This means the consistency you need to manage spans over multiple domain objects. Once faced with such a situation, the question quickly arises of how to manage transactions that span multiple elements in the model. This is where the aggregate comes in.

An *aggregate* is a conceptual boundary that you use to group parts of the model together. The purpose of this grouping is to let you treat the aggregate as a unit during state changes; it's the boundary within which transactions must be managed. The boundary that's defined by the aggregate isn't randomly chosen or chosen from a technical point of view. It's carefully selected based on deep insights of the model.

When modeling an aggregate, it must follow a strict set of rules for it to work as intended and to fulfill its purpose. The following lists these rules as put forward by Eric Evans:[13]

- Every aggregate has a boundary and a root.
- The root is a single, specific entity contained in the aggregate.
- The root is the only member of the aggregate that objects outside the boundary can hold references to. Thus
  - The root has global identity.
  - The root controls all access to the objects within the boundary.
  - Entities other than the root have local identity. Their identities don't have to be known outside of the aggregate.
  - The root can pass references to internal entities to other objects, but those references can only be used transiently and can never be held onto.
  - The root can pass references of value objects to other objects.
- Invariants between the members of the aggregate are always enforced within each transaction.
- Invariants that span multiple aggregates can't be expected to be consistent all the time, but they can eventually become consistent.
- Objects within the aggregate can hold references to other aggregates.

This is quite a comprehensive set of rules, and you might want to go through them again and think about their meaning and the implications each of them will bring to the design of not only your model but also your code. There are, however, a couple of traits that we'd like to expand on to make things clearer.

---

[12] We're not talking database transactions here but logical state transactions.

[13] Evans, E., *Domain-Driven Design: Tackling Complexity in the Heart of Software* (Addison-Wesley Professional, 2004).

The aggregate is a conceptual boundary, and it contains an entity that's the root of the aggregate. In general, when implementing aggregates, the root entity and the aggregate will be the same object. Reasoning about them might become easier if you think of them as being the same.

The *root* of the aggregate is the only point of reference outside of the boundary. The root also controls all access to everything within the boundary. This makes the root the perfect place for upholding all the invariants that span across the objects within the boundary. And it can't be bypassed, as long as you stick to the rules on how to model aggregates. Another implication of the root being the only point of reference is that the root is the only thing that can be accessed through a *repository* (see sidebar). This again is a way to control how an aggregate is accessed and to make sure an entity within the aggregate can't be manipulated directly by objects outside of the aggregate.

Repositories

We won't delve into detail about repositories, but you can think of them as technology-agnostic storage for aggregate roots. You can put aggregate roots into a repository and then get them back at a later time. You can also use repositories to delete previously stored roots, if your model supports that.

Aggregates, with their boundaries and upholding of consistent state, turn out to be of importance when you start looking at how to use them to drive security in your code. Let's take a look at an example of how you could model a simple aggregate next.

Our example model consists of a company and its employees. We'll make the company an entity because it has a clear identity and, because our system can handle many companies, it also needs to be globally identifiable. The company has a name, but the name is merely a value, so we'll make it a value object. It also has employees who work at the company. An employee definitely has an identity, so it's also modeled as an entity. An employee always belongs to a company, so it becomes a child entity of the company. Each employee will have a specific role, but that's also a value, so it becomes a value object. The resulting model can be seen in figure 3.16.

After discussing the nature of an employee together with the domain experts, you realize that an employee doesn't have to be identifiable outside of the company. The employee object can have local identity. You also realize that when roles are assigned to employees within the company, there are certain roles that can only be held by one person at a time. There can, for example, only be one CTO at any given point. The same goes for many other roles. To uphold these required invariants, the company entity should control the assignment of roles to employees. This leads you to the insight that the company, together with its child objects, should be modeled as an aggregate. You make the company the root of the aggregate. You can see the result in figure 3.17.

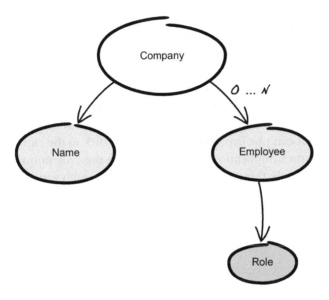

Figure 3.16   The company domain model

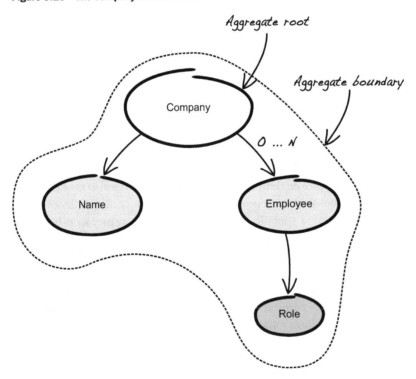

Figure 3.17   The company modeled as an aggregate

This means that the company, which is globally identifiable, can be referenced and looked up by others, but the only way to get to an employee is to go through the aggregate root, the company. The same goes for assigning new roles to employees. The role assignment is handled by a method on the company. Because all operations on the aggregate are controlled by the root, it becomes a straightforward task to uphold the invariants regarding the employees.

In this section, you've learned the basics about the fundamental building blocks used to create domain models in DDD. We've gone through a lot of material so far, and it might take some time to digest all this information properly. But if you stay with us, you'll learn about bounded contexts—the next important concept from DDD that you need to be familiar with before you get into the remaining chapters of this book.

3.3 Bounded contexts

Another interesting concept is the *bounded context pattern*, which defines the applicability of the domain model. As it turns out, it's not only essential in DDD, it's also important from a security perspective. Some complex attacks are easier to understand when using bounded contexts as a basis for the analysis. To see this, you need to fully understand the concept, and therefore we'll start by diving into the semantics of the ubiquitous language.

3.3.1 Semantics of the ubiquitous language

Ubiquitous is defined as "existing or being everywhere at the same time."[14] In DDD, this translates to a language spoken everywhere at all times, by everyone, to promote clarity and common understanding—a ubiquitous language as illustrated in figure 3.18.

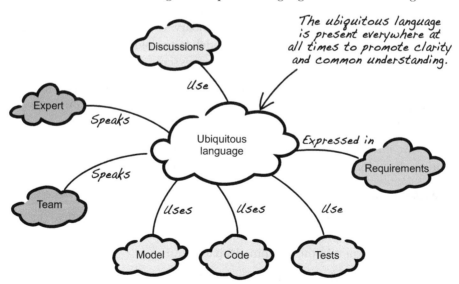

Figure 3.18 Ubiquitous language is present everywhere, at all times, to promote clarity and common understanding.

---

[14] Merriam-Webster, https://www.merriam-webster.com/dictionary/ubiquitous.

It's easy to think that everywhere, at all times, by everyone means there should be a unified language with terms, operations, and concepts that capture the entire business, but that's a huge misunderstanding. Anyone who has tried this knows it's doomed to fail because it's too complex. And the reason is *semantics*.

A term or concept can have the same name in various parts of the business, but each usage can have a different meaning. For example, consider the word *package*. If you ask someone in the shipping department, they'll say that it's a box, but in the IT department, they'll say that it's a logical grouping of files in the codebase—both departments use the term *package*, but with different semantics. Trying to capture this in a unified language is probably not a good idea because it requires a new term that captures both meanings. The obvious conclusion is to allow two coexisting languages instead of a unified language with imprecise semantics. With this in mind, let's see how the ubiquitous language relates to the model and the bounded context.

3.3.2 *The relationship between language, model, and bounded context*

The relationship between language, model, and bounded context becomes clear when you see it from a semantic point of view. A *model* is an abstraction of the domain in which concepts, relationships, and terms of the ubiquitous language are found. This makes the language and model tightly coupled, not only through the terms and relationships but also through semantics—a concept found in the model must have the same meaning in the language and vice versa.

As long as the semantics of terms, operations, and concepts remain the same, the model holds. But as soon as the semantics change, the model breaks, and the boundary of the context is found. Realizing this is important because this is where the meaning of a term could change, only because it crossed the boundary. That means that everything within the context adheres to the semantics of the model, but outside the boundary, the same term can have different semantics. This certainly makes sense, but it feels a bit theoretical.

> **NOTE** Data crossing a semantic boundary is of special interest from a security perspective because this is where the meaning of a term could implicitly change, which could open up security weaknesses.

Let's dive into an example where we define the ubiquitous language, create a model, and use it to identify the semantic boundary of a context.

3.3.3 *Identifying the bounded context*

When identifying a bounded context, a good starting point is to analyze the ubiquitous language. For example, let's consider the following conversation between a developer and a domain expert in the Shipping Department:

> Developer: "What characterizes an order?"
>
> Expert: "Well, an order contains products that are sellable and nonsellable items."
>
> Developer: "Not sure I understand. What do you mean by nonsellable products?"
>
> Expert: "Nonsellable products are items that are bundled with sellable products when shipped as a package to their destination."

Developer: "Oh, I see. Nonsellable items are products without a price?"

Expert: "No no, all products have a value, but bundled products have a price of zero, so they get included for free."

Developer: "Hmm, OK, I guess that makes sense."

Up to this point, lots of confusion exists, but it's possible to identify significant terms and manifest them as a raw version of a domain model, as seen in figure 3.19.

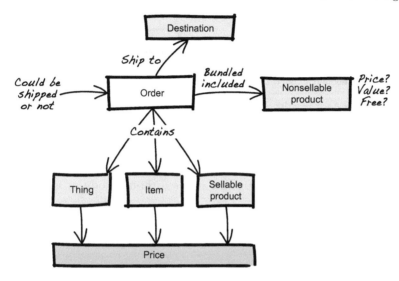

Figure 3.19 Raw domain model

One of the core principles of the ubiquitous language is to avoid ambiguities, because they create a lot of confusion and misunderstanding. We see this in figure 3.19, where the model has lots of ambiguity and duplicated concepts. Let's get back to the conversation and see how the language and model evolve:

Developer: "I'm a bit confused about the terminology. Could we agree on using some of the terms?"

Expert: "Sure, any particular ones in mind?"

Developer: "It seems we only have products—is it OK to stop using words like items, things, nonsellable, and sellable?"

Expert: "OK, that makes sense. From now on, we'll use the term product for all of these."

Developer: "Included and bundled mean the same thing, right?"

Expert: "Yes, so let's only use bundled."

Developer: "What about price and value?"

Expert: "Same thing. Let's use price."

Developer: "Why do we need to care whether a product is free or not?"

Expert: "You're right. We don't. Let's not use free."

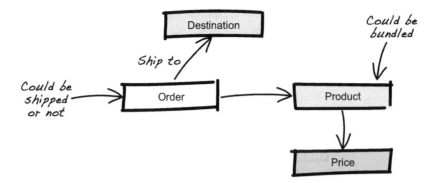

Figure 3.20   A refined domain model with less redundancy

This distillation process results in a much tighter language and a refined domain model, as seen in figure 3.20.

But sometimes, distilling also uncovers missing terms, and this is the case here as well:

> Developer: "An order can have one or more products?"
>
> Expert: "Yes, that's correct. But an order without products isn't much of a package."
>
> Developer: "Package?"
>
> Expert: "Oh, sorry. Yes, a 'package' is what we call the box in which we ship everything."
>
> Developer: "OK, makes sense. But how do we know how many products we need to ship in a package?"
>
> Expert: "Well, the quantity of each product is specified in the order."
>
> Developer: "Ah, I see. Let's introduce 'quantity' and 'package' in our ubiquitous language and add them to the model."

After this last revision (figure 3.21), the developer and expert are quite confident that they share the same view and understanding of an order.

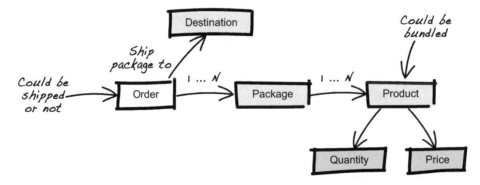

Figure 3.21   Final domain model

But how far does the model reach into the organization? When does the model no longer hold? Determining this is the key to finding the boundary of the context. The developer starts asking around, and everyone in the Shipping Department seems to have a common understanding. But when talking to an expert in the Finance Department, the model suddenly breaks:

> Developer: "Could you please have a look at our model of an order?"
>
> Finance Expert: "Sure. The model makes sense, but you seem to miss a lot of important concepts."
>
> Developer: "Really? Please explain."
>
> Finance Expert: "The payment information and due date are missing. Also, the reserved amount doesn't seem to be represented."
>
> Developer: "Aha. We seem to have a different definition of an order. Thanks for your time."

As soon as the semantics of the model no longer hold, the boundary of the context is found. Finding where the model's semantics didn't hold, the developer quickly realizes that an order in the Finance domain is something different than in the Shipping domain. This tells us where the context boundary is. This can be illustrated as two separate contexts, where an order is present in both but with different meanings, as seen in figure 3.22.

But what happens if you need to communicate and pass an order between the contexts? Are there any other concepts that are similar but with different semantics? This brings us to the next topic: interactions between contexts.

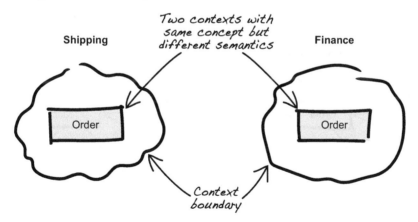

Figure 3.22 Two contexts with the same concept but with different semantics

3.4   *Interactions between contexts*

The context boundary is interesting from a security perspective when you start thinking about interactions between contexts. When data crosses a boundary, it implicitly accepts the semantics of the receiving context's ubiquitous language and model. This implies that every time no action is taken, a potential security vulnerability opens. Although this might be obvious, problems of this kind are surprisingly common.

Ironically, the root cause might be the attempt to satisfy DRY—Don't Repeat Yourself. Andrew Hunt and David Thomas defined the principle as:

> *Every piece of knowledge must have a single, unambiguous, authoritative representation within a system.*
>
> —*Andrew Hunt and David Thomas, The Pragmatic Programmer (Addison-Wesley, 2003)*

Many interpret this as avoiding syntactic duplication (for example, the result of copying and pasting code), but the principle is about semantics. And this brings us back to the ubiquitous language.

The ubiquitous language requires the semantics of the domain model to be unambiguous throughout the context. But if you apply a syntactic interpretation of DRY, the method of how you share data between contexts suddenly becomes a technical matter rather than semantic. And this is a huge problem, because if models are shared to reduce syntactic duplication, but certain concepts mean different things, it opens the door to all sorts of craziness—including security weaknesses. To illustrate this, let's revisit the example with a Shipping and a Finance context, but this time with a shared model to reduce syntactic duplication.

3.4.1   Sharing a model in two contexts

Both Shipping and Finance use concepts such as order, product, and price. Having a shared model is indeed compelling, as it minimizes duplication. But to do this, you need a few more concepts from the Finance domain, as seen in figure 3.23.

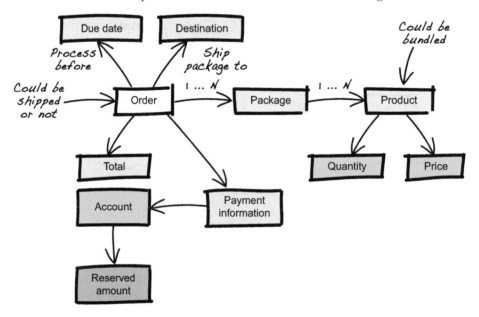

Figure 3.23   A unified order model that's shared between the Shipping context and the Finance context

At first, having a unified model is a great success; the only apparent downside is a rich model with some unused concepts. But let's see what happens when a new business requirement is introduced in the Shipping context:

Expert: "To simplify customs declarations for international shipments, we need to list the actual value of a package."

Developer: "OK. So how should we treat bundled products?"

Expert: "Well, previously we made the product free by faking the price by setting it to zero, but that's no longer OK."

Developer: "Right, so is it OK to just remove the faked price?"

Expert: "Yes, the sum of all prices is the actual value of the package, so that should work."

Developer: "And then we deduct the bundle prices from the total, right?"

Expert: "No, the reserved amount is what's charged by Finance, so we don't need to deduct anything."

Developer: "OK, that makes sense. I'll only remove the faked price then."

Making the changes doesn't require much effort, and initially everything works fine, but after a while, strange behaviors start to emerge in Finance. For some reason, every now and then the invariant *reserved amount ≥ sum of all prices* is false. This seems like a minor problem because it only happens when the products are bundled. But it does, in fact, start a full-blown security investigation. A violation of the invariant is the same as order tampering, and that's a serious security problem!

The investigation doesn't show any security breach, but it's interesting how a simple change could lead to all of this. Analyzing it further shows that the root cause is, in fact, having one model to represent two conceptual views of an order. The invariant *reserved amount ≥ sum of all prices* only makes sense in the Finance context. But as a direct consequence of sharing a model, the Shipping context is forced to respect the invariant, even though it doesn't make sense. Obviously, this isn't a good thing, because it prevents each context from being independent and the master of its own model. But if you don't share a model, how do you know what concepts need special attention when communicating across context boundaries? The solution is to draw a context map.

3.4.2 Drawing a context map

A *context map* is a conceptual view of how different contexts interact. This could be a graphical drawing described in text or simply an understanding communicated between teams. Regardless of how it's manifested, the key point is that it helps identify concepts that cross semantic boundaries.

An incorrect mapping is often the root cause of misunderstandings that can become exploitable. Identifying the context boundary is of great importance therefore, but it can be easier said than done. If you don't know where to start, a good strategy is to use

Conway's Law as a starting point.[15] Mel Conway published the paper "How Do Committees Invent?" in 1968 with the thesis:

> *Any organization that designs a system (defined broadly) will produce a design whose structure is a copy of the organization's communication structure.*
>
> — Mel Conway, "How Do Committees Invent?" (Datamation, 1968)

The implication of the thesis is that the communication structures that exist in the organization are often reflected in the architectural design of the system. This also seems to apply to how bounded contexts are defined. As many teams tend to organize around subsystems, bounded contexts often follow the same rules. Laying out the teams is therefore a good starting point when trying to identify the bounded contexts for your map.

To illustrate what a graphical representation of a context map might look like, we need to revisit the Shipping and Finance contexts one more time. To gain deeper insight, a good starting point is to draw a simple, high-level picture of the system interactions when a new order is processed (figure 3.24).

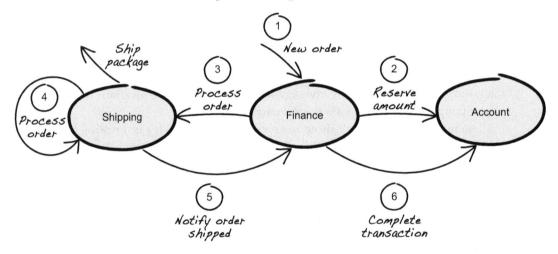

Figure 3.24   Interaction between Finance and Shipping

Here's the interaction between Finance and Shipping:

1. Finance receives a new order.
2. The total value of the order is reserved on the account specified by the payment information.
3. Finance sends the order to Shipping for processing.
4. Shipping processes the order and ships it.
5. Shipping notifies Finance with an updated status.
6. Finance completes the financial transaction.

---

[15] http://www.melconway.com/Home/Conways_Law.html.

The interaction flow diagram is easily converted into a context map where it becomes clear that the Shipping context is downstream of the Finance context (figure 3.25). This might seem obvious, but the mere understanding that a Finance order must be translated to a Shipping order makes a huge difference. The relationship makes it clear that explicit mapping is required and that communication between the teams is needed to ensure success.

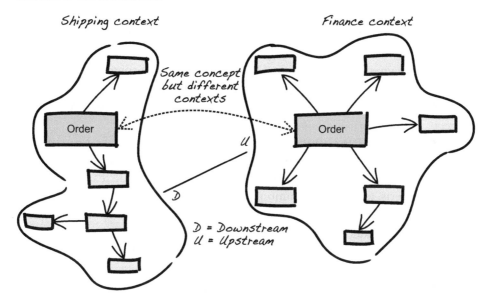

Figure 3.25   The Shipping context is downstream of the Finance context.

You have now gained a conceptual view of why bounded contexts are important and how context maps are created, but we still need to show you how they relate to security. In the upcoming chapters, you'll see how bounded contexts help when analyzing code from a security point of view; for example, in chapter 9, when looking at failure handling, or in chapters 12 and 13, when working with legacy code.

In the next chapter, you'll learn about code constructs that promote security by using ideas from this chapter combined with concepts from other fields. As a result, you'll be able to immediately apply them in your everyday work and learn how to spot exploitable weaknesses in your existing codebase.

Summary

- Building domain models is a good way to promote deep learning about the domain.
- A domain model should be a strict and unambiguous representation of the domain that captures only the most important aspects.
- When creating a domain model, you make a choice among many possible models.

- The domain model forms a language for communicating about the system.
- Entities, value objects, and aggregates are the basic building blocks for your domain model.
- Entities have an identity that's consistent during their life cycle and can contain other entities or value objects.
- The uniqueness of entities always has a scope, and that scope depends on your model.
- A value object doesn't have an identity but rather is defined by its value.
- A value object must always be immutable and should form a conceptual whole.
- An aggregate is a conceptual boundary that groups together other model objects and is responsible for upholding invariants among those objects.
- An aggregate always has an aggregate root and, in code, that root is typically the same as the aggregate.
- The aggregate root has global identity because this is the only part of the aggregate that other parts of the model can hold a reference to.
- The ubiquitous language is spoken by everyone on the team, including domain experts, to ensure a common understanding.
- The domain model is bound by the semantics of the ubiquitous language.
- The bounded context is the context in which the semantics of the model hold. As soon as the semantics change, the model breaks and the boundary of the context is found.
- Using Conway's Law is a good starting point when trying to find the boundary of a context.
- Data crossing a semantic boundary is of special interest from a security perspective because this is where the meaning of a concept could implicitly change.

Code constructs
promoting security

This chapter covers

- How immutability solves security problems
- How fail-fast contracts secure your design
- Types of validation and the order in which to do them

As developers, we're constantly reminded about priorities and deadlines. Cutting corners and dirty hacks are sometimes part of reality that we must accept—or are they? The truth is, at the end of the day, you decide what syntax to use, what algorithms to apply, and how to steer the flow of execution. If you truly understand why certain code constructs are better than others, then using them becomes second nature and no more time-consuming than writing bad code. The same applies to security. Attackers don't care about deadlines or priorities—a weak system is exploitable, regardless of why or under what circumstances it was built.

We all share the responsibility of designing secure software. In this chapter, you'll learn why that doesn't take any longer than building weak, exploitable software. To this end, we've organized this chapter into three sections, each discussing different strategies to solve security problems you might encounter in your daily work (table 4.1).

Table 4.1   Problem areas addressed

Section	Problem area
Immutability	Security problems involving data integrity and availability
Failing fast	Security problems involving illegal input and state
Validation	Security problems involving input validation

This way, we hope to empower you with a new set of tools, mindset, and best practices to use in your daily work. You'll also learn how to spot weaknesses in legacy code and how to address them. As a result, you'll see why security bugs are just bugs and how good design prevents them. We'll start by dealing with change using immutability and provide an example for this.

4.1   *Immutability*

When designing an object, you need to decide whether it should be mutable or immutable. *Mutability* allows state to change; *immutability* prevents it. This might seem of minor importance, but from a security perspective, it makes a big difference. Immutable objects are safe to share between threads and open up high data availability—an important aspect when protecting a system against denial of service attacks. Mutable objects, on the other hand, are designed for change, which can lead to illegal updates and modifications. Often, mutability is introduced because frameworks require it or because it seems easier. But choosing mutability over immutability can be as expensive as it is dangerous. To illustrate, we'll walk through an example where the mutable design of a webshop causes security problems that are easily solved using immutability.

4.1.1   *An ordinary webshop*

Picture an ordinary webshop where customers log in and add items to a shopping cart. Each customer has an associated credit score based on purchase history and membership points. A high credit score allows paying by invoice or credit card, whereas a low credit score allows only credit card payments. The credit score computation is quite expensive and is done continuously to even out the overall system load.

All in all, the system worked fine—until recently. When the last marketing campaign ran, lots of traffic hit the webshop. Then the system didn't handle the load well, and customers complained about orders timing out, long waits, and inconsistent payment alternatives. The latter seemed a minor problem, but when the Finance Department reported that lots of customers with low credit scores had outstanding invoices, a full-blown security investigation started—the system must have been compromised! Obviously, the credit score computation was the primary suspect, but to everyone's surprise, the root cause turned out to be a much bigger problem: the design of the Customer object.

THE DESIGN OF THE CUSTOMER OBJECT

The Customer object in listing 4.1 shows two interesting details. First, all fields are initialized through setter methods, which implies that internal state is allowed to change after object creation. This is problematic because you never know when the object is properly

initialized. The other observation is that each method is marked as synchronized to prevent concurrent field modification, which in turn can lead to *thread contention* (when threads
are forced to wait for another thread to release one or more locks before executing).

Listing 4.1 Mutable `Customer` class

Lower bound that allows paying by invoice

Unique value that identifies the customer

```
public class Customer {
    private static final int MIN_INVOICE_SCORE = 500;
    private Id id;
    private Name name;
    private Order order;
    private CreditScore creditScore;

    public synchronized Id getId() {
        return id;
    }

    public synchronized void setId(final Id id) {
        this.id = id;
    }

    public synchronized Name getName() {
        return name;
    }

    public synchronized void setName(Name name) {
        this.name = name;
    }

    public synchronized Order getOrder() {
        this.order = OrderService.fetchLatestOrder(id);
        return order;
    }

    public synchronized void setOrder(Order order) {
        this.order = order;
    }

    public synchronized CreditScore getCreditScore() {
        return creditScore;
    }

    public synchronized void setCreditScore(CreditScore creditScore){
        this.creditScore = creditScore;
    }

    public synchronized boolean isAcceptedForInvoicePayment() {
        return creditScore.compute() >
                        MIN_INVOICE_SCORE;
    }
    ...
}
```

Holds first and last name of the customer

Service that computes the current credit score

Contains all items displayed in the shopping cart

Initializes the credit score field

Determines if the customer is eligible for invoice payment

How these design choices relate to security isn't obvious, but when categorizing the webshop problems as data integrity or data availability issues, the correlation becomes clear. Let's discuss those issues next.

CATEGORIZING PROBLEMS AS INTEGRITY OR AVAILABILITY ISSUES

Data integrity involves the consistency of data during its entire life cycle; *data availability* ensures data is obtainable at the expected level of performance in a system.[1] Both concepts are essential to understanding the root cause of the webshop problems. For example, failure to retrieve data is an availability problem that often boils down to code that prevents parallel or concurrent access. Similarly, identifying code that allows modification is the place to start when analyzing integrity issues. Table 4.2 shows the webshop problems categorized as availability and integrity issues.

Table 4.2   Categorization of problems experienced in the webshop

Experienced problems	Category	Probable cause
Long waits and poor performance	Availability	The system fails to access customer data in a reliable way and times out.
Orders timing out at checkout	Availability	The system fails to retrieve necessary data to process the order in a timely fashion.
Inconsistent payment alternatives	Integrity	The credit score is changed in an illegal way.

These categories give you an idea of what to look for in the Customer class. Let's start by dealing with how implicit blocking can reduce availability.

IMPLICIT BLOCKING YIELDS REDUCED AVAILABILITY

Choosing to allow or disallow concurrent and parallel access is often a balance between performance and consistency. If state always needs to be consistent and updates interleaved with read operations, then using a locking mechanism makes sense. But if access is mostly reads, then locking can result in unnecessary thread contention. For some reason, contention caused by concurrent access is often easier to reason about in code than contention caused by parallel access. For example, if a method is synchronized, as in listing 4.1, only one thread at a time is allowed to access the method, because the intrinsic lock of the method's object must be acquired.[2] All other threads that try to access the method concurrently must then wait until the lock is released—and this could cause thread contention.

Using synchronized on a method level can also yield thread contention during parallel access of two or more methods. As it turns out, the intrinsic lock acquired for a synchronized method is the same for all synchronized methods in an object. This

---

[1] See "Engineering Principles for Information Technology Security (A Baseline for Achieving Security)" by Gary Stoneburner, Clark Hayden, and Alexis Feringa, at https://csrc.nist.gov/publications/detail/sp/800-27/rev-a/archive/2004-06-21.

[2] For more information, see the Java documentation on intrinsic locks and synchronization at https://docs.oracle.com/javase/tutorial/essential/concurrency/locksync.html.

means that threads accessing `synchronized` methods in parallel implicitly block each other, and this kind of contention can be hard to recognize.

If we go back to the webshop and analyze the ratio between read and write operations, it turns out that reading customer data is far more common than updating it. This is because data is primarily changed by the credit score algorithm, and reads are made by numerous client requests, including Finance's reporting system. This gives you a hint that most of the time parallel and concurrent reads are safe, so why didn't we remove the locking mechanism (`synchronized`) altogether?

Although it's likely that parallel and concurrent reads are safe, you can't ignore writes and remove the locking mechanism to minimize contention. Instead, other solutions must be considered. One is to use advanced locking mechanisms, such as a `ReadWriteLock`, which respects the read dominance.[3] But locking mechanisms add complexity and cognitive load, which is something we'd prefer to avoid.

TIP Immutable values are safe to share between threads without locks: no locking, no blocking.

A simpler and better strategy is to use a design that favors parallel and concurrent access (for example, immutability). In listing 4.2, you see an immutable version of the `Customer` class that doesn't allow state to change. This means it's safe to share `Customer` objects between threads without using locks, and this yields high availability with low contention. In other words, no locking, no blocking.

Listing 4.2 Immutable `Customer` class

Immutable field that uniquely identifies the customer

```
import static org.apache.commons.lang3.Validate.notNull;

public final class Customer {
    private final Id id;
    private final Name name;
    private final CreditScore creditScore;

    public Customer(final Id id, final Name name,
                    final CreditScore creditScore) {
        this.id = notNull(id);
        this.name = notNull(name);
        this.creditScore = notNull(creditScore);
    }

    public Id id() {
        return id;
    }
```

Immutable field that holds the customer's first and last name

Immutable field that holds the credit score value

---

[3] A `ReadWriteLock` is actually two locks: one for reading and one for writing. The read lock can be held by multiple reader threads until there's a writer thread requesting the write lock, hence allowing parallel and concurrent access of data as long as it's not modified. For more information, see https://docs .oracle.com/javase/8/docs/api/java/util/concurrent/locks/ReadWriteLock.html.

```
    public Name name() {
       return name;
    }

    public Order order() {
       return OrderService.fetchLatestOrder(id);
    }

    public boolean isAcceptedForInvoicePayment() {
       return creditScore.isAcceptedForInvoicePayment();
    }
}
```

But you still need to be able to change customer data. How do you do this if `Customer` is immutable? As it turns out, you don't need mutable data structures to support change. What you need is to separate reads from writes and perform updates through channels other than those used when reading. This might seem overly complex, but if your system has an imbalance between reads and writes, it can be worth it. How to achieve this in practice is covered in chapter 7, where we discuss the Entity snapshot pattern in depth.

You've learned how immutability prevents availability issues by design, but what about the integrity issue in the webshop? Does immutability solve that too? Perhaps. Let's see how the mutable design of `Customer` and `CreditScore` opens up the integrity issue.

CHANGING CREDIT SCORE, AN INTEGRITY ISSUE

Before diving into the analysis, let's quickly recap the credit score problem. Each customer has an associated credit score, where a high value allows paying by invoice. During the last campaign, the system failed, and the Finance Department reported that lots of customers with low credit scores had outstanding invoices—a data integrity issue where credit scores changed to favor invoice payment. But how was this possible? Looking at the credit score logic of the mutable `Customer` object in listing 4.3, we see that

- The way `creditScore` is initialized in `Customer` opens up the possibility of changing the credit score at any moment.
- The `creditScore` reference is accidentally escaped in the `getCreditScore` method, which allows modification outside of `Customer`.
- The `setCreditScore` method doesn't make a copy of the argument. This makes it possible to inject a shared `creditScore` reference.

Listing 4.3   Credit score logic in the mutable `Customer` object

```
public class Customer {
  private static final int MIN_INVOICE_SCORE = 500;
  private CreditScore creditScore;                      ◁── A new credit score
  ...                                                        value can be injected
  public synchronized void setCreditScore(                   at any moment.
                    CreditScore creditScore) {       ◁──
    this.creditScore = creditScore;       ◁──── The credit score field can be
  }                                              assigned a shared reference.

  public synchronized CreditScore getCreditScore() {
```

```
      return creditScore;                                    The internal credit score
   }                                                         reference is escaped.

   public synchronized boolean isAcceptedForInvoicePayment() {
      return creditScore.compute() > MIN_INVOICE_SCORE;
   }
   ...
}
```

Let's look at each one of these observations to see how they can cause a data integrity issue.

The first way to cause this sort of data integrity issue involves explicitly changing the credit score through initialization. The `creditScore` field in `Customer` is initialized through the `setCreditScore` method. Although done by design, this way of initializing the field allows changing a customer's credit score at any moment, because the method doesn't guarantee an *invoke at-most-once* behavior. This can seem acceptable because a client is only expected to read data, but the mutable design of `Customer` makes it impossible to prevent anyone from accidentally using the mutable API. This means you can't guarantee the integrity of a `Customer` object.

The second way involves changing the credit score outside of `Customer`. If you look at the `getCreditScore` method in `Customer`, you'll see that the internal `creditScore` field is accidentally escaped. This makes it possible to modify the credit score outside of the `Customer` object without acquiring the lock. This is extremely dangerous because `Customer` is a shared mutable object and updating it without synchronization is a disaster waiting to happen. (We'll talk more about this in chapter 6.) But changing the credit score without a lock is one thing.

Due to the mutable design of `CreditScore`, it's also possible to explicitly change the associated customer ID by invoking the `setCustomerId` method, as shown in listing 4.4. This implies that a `Customer` object can have one ID and the `CreditScore` object another— a dissociation that could yield an incorrect credit score value in the `compute` method!

Listing 4.4 `CreditScore` class

```
public class CreditScore {
   private Id id;
                                                    Sets the ID that uniquely
   public synchronized void setCustomerId(Id id) {  identifies which customer
      this.id = id;                                  the credit score belongs to
   }

   public synchronized int compute() {              Fetches billing history to use
      List<Record> history =                         when computing credit score
         BillingService.fetchBillingHistory(id);
      Membership membership =                        Fetches membership data to use
         MembershipService.fetchMembership(id);       when computing credit score
      return CreditScoreEngine.compute(id, history,
                              membership);            Heavy computation
   }                                                  of credit score
   ...
}
```

To address this, the mutable design of CreditScore needs to be changed. In list-ing 4.5, you see an immutable version of the same object. What's interesting is that the synchronized keyword and the dependency to the customer ID have been removed. This is because there's no longer a need to acquire a lock when checking the credit score value, as it can't change after being assigned in the constructor. This, in turn, means that the dependency to a specific customer is redundant, and the design can be simplified by moving the credit score computation outside of the object. As a result, this allows the credit score to be shared between threads without the risk of illegal updates, blocking, or locking.

Listing 4.5   Immutable `CreditScore` class

```
import static org.apache.commons.lang3.Validate.isTrue;

public class CreditScore {
    private static final int MIN_INVOICE_SCORE = 500;
    private final int score;

    public CreditScore(final int computedCreditScore) {
        isTrue(computedCreditScore > -1, "Credit score must be > -1");
        this.score = computedCreditScore;              ◄─────┐  Score is assigned and
    }                                                         │  never allowed to change.

    public boolean isAcceptedForInvoicePayment() {
        return score > MIN_INVOICE_SCORE;
    }
    ...
}
```

The third way to change creditScore isn't as obvious as the other two—it involves changing a shared credit score reference. If you look at the setCreditScore method in the mutable Customer object, you'll see that the internal field is assigned the exter-nal mutable creditScore reference. This is fine as long as the external reference isn't reused in another Customer object. But if it is, the computed credit score value will be the same for all customers sharing that reference—a major integrity issue that could explain the inconsistent payment alternatives in the webshop.

IDENTIFYING THE ROOT CAUSE

All the scenarios we've explored are plausible explanations of the data integrity prob-lem seen in the webshop, but which one caused it? Well, it doesn't matter. The key point is that the decision to make Customer and CreditScore mutable made the code less secure in various ways. But when choosing a design that favors immutability, the need for locks and protection against accidental change disappears. Such a design yields implicit security benefits.

You've now learned how immutability solves data integrity and availability issues. You might have noticed how on some occasions we aggressively blocked bad data before it had a chance to establish itself in the object. Doing so is also an effective trick to uphold security, so let's move on to how to fail fast using contracts.

4.2　*Failing fast using contracts*

As mentioned in chapter 1, a guiding principle for security is *security in depth.* Even if one security mechanism at the border fails, there are more mechanisms in place that can stop a breach from continuing or spreading. With physical security, the access card a visitor uses to gain entry to a building might also be a badge with a photo that they're required to wear at all times. We've found the software design practices of *preconditions* and *Design by Contract* to be effective in making software more secure in a similar way. In this section, we show the pragmatic coding practices we've come to use, which you'll see plenty of in the examples throughout the book.

Talking about preconditions was part of the theoretical studies of computer science in the late 1960s, especially by Sir C. A. R. Hoare (who also takes the blame for inventing the null-pointer exception).[4] The term *Design by Contract* was coined in the late 1980s by Bertrand Meyer, who used it as a foundation for object orientation.[5] Apart from being theoretically interesting, these ideas have direct practical benefits for security.

Thinking about design in terms of preconditions and contracts helps you clarify which part of a design takes on which responsibility. Many security problems arise because one part of the system assumes another part takes responsibility for something when, in fact, that part assumes the opposite. In this section, we'll walk you through how to use contracts, preconditions, and failing fast to avoid those situations in practice.

How does Design by Contract work, and what do we mean by a contract? Let's start with a nonsoftware example. Imagine you contract a plumber to fix the broken sink in your bathroom. The plumber might require that the door be unlocked and that the water shut-off valve be closed. These are the preconditions for the work. If they aren't fulfilled, things might not go well. On the other hand, the plumber promises that after the work is finished, the bathroom sink will function properly. This is the postcondition of the contract.

Design contracts for objects work the same way. A *contract* specifies the preconditions that are required for the method to work as intended, and it specifies the postconditions for how the object will have changed after the method is completed. In listing 4.6, you see a class that's part of the support system for a cat breeder. This particular class, CatNameList, helps keep track of cat names that can be given to new kittens. When the cat breeders come up with a new idea for a cat name, they queue it up using queueCatName. When they need a good cat name, they look up which is next in turn using nextCatName, and if they decide to use it, they remove the name with dequeueCatName. The method size tells them how many names are in the list.

---

[4]　See his paper, "An Axiomatic Basis for Computer Programming," in the October 1969 issue of *Communications of the ACM.*

[5]　For more information, see his book, *Object-Oriented Software Construction* (Prentice Hall, 1988).

Listing 4.6   `CatNameList` that keeps track of good names for cats

```
public class CatNameList {
    private final List<String> catNames = new ArrayList<String>();

    public void queueCatName(String name) {        ⟵  Should only be called with good cat names
        catNames.add(name);
    }
                                                        Gives the next cat name in the queue,
    public String nextCatName() {          ⟵        but should only be called if a next exists
        return catNames.get(0);
    }
                                                        Drops the next cat name, perhaps
    public void dequeueCatName() {         ⟵        because it's already used
        catNames.remove(0);
    }

    public int size() {      ⟵    Gives the number of cat names waiting to be used
        return catNames.size();
    }
}
```

In the contract for this class, there are some pre- and postconditions, as listed in table 4.3.

Table 4.3   Contract for keeping track of cat names

Method	Precondition requires	Postcondition ensures
nextCatName	Must contain something	`size` is the same after call
		name is guaranteed to contain s (a sound)
dequeueCatName	Must contain something	`size` is one less after call
queueCatName	name isn't null	`size` is one more after call
	name must contain s (a sound)	
	name isn't in list	

The method `queueCatName` has some peculiar preconditions. It makes sense that a cat name can't be null; it must be something, otherwise, this design doesn't work properly. According to Swedish folklore, a good cat name must have an *s* sound in it (that makes the cat listen to it), so that's also a precondition. Finally, cat breeders don't want the same name to appear twice in the list, so this contract requires as a precondition that the new name isn't already in the list.

The contract could have been written in another way. For example, the cat name list could have taken on the burden of avoiding duplicates. In that case, the pre- and postconditions would have been stated differently, as shown in table 4.4.

Table 4.4 Alternative contract that takes responsibility for preventing duplicate names

Method	Precondition requires	Postcondition ensures
nextCatName	Must contain something	size is the same after call
		name is guaranteed to contain s (a sound)
dequeueCatName	Must contain something	size is one less after call
queueCatName	name isn't null	size is one more after call or unchanged if name is already in list
	name must contain s (a sound)	

Note how this contract is about the entire class, not just one method at a time. The contract requires that the name sent to queueCatName contains an *s* and, at the same time, promises that the name returned from nextCatName indeed contains an *s*. This contract is about the responsibility of the class as a whole. The important aspect is that the contract points out the intended design. The task of avoiding duplicates has to fall on either CatNameList or the caller. Stating the contract makes it clear on whom the responsibility falls.

Many security problems arise from situations when one part of the system assumes that another part takes responsibility for something when, in actuality, it doesn't—it assumes the callers would do that. Explicitly thinking in terms of Design by Contract avoids lots of those situations that give rise to vulnerabilities.

What should you do if preconditions aren't fulfilled? Let's look back to the situation of the plumber who comes to fix the broken sink, and who requires a few preconditions (door open, water turned off). If the door is locked, the plumber won't be able to gain access, and if the water is still on, it's not a good idea to start working. If work begins on the pipes with the shutoff valve still open, things might go seriously wrong. The better option is to *fail fast*—to terminate the job as soon as it becomes clear that the preconditions aren't met.[6] This is where the real security benefit comes in.

> **TIP** It's much better to stop bad data or abnormal situations fast than it is to let them slide and wreak security problems later.

To make contracts powerful, the rules have to be enforced in code. The programming language Eiffel, designed by Bertrand Meyer, has support for this built into the language itself. As a programmer, you state the preconditions, postconditions, and invariants, and the runtime platform ensures they are checked. As you probably use other programming languages, you'll need to build these checks into the code yourself. Let's dig into some of those code patterns to help you create more secure software.

4.2.1 Checking preconditions for method arguments

In the contract for CatNameList, there are some restrictions on the names queued up by queueCatName: it's not allowed to send in null, and the name must contain an *s*. If

---

[6] This concept is best explained in Jim Shore's article "Fail Fast" in the September/October 2004 issue of *IEEE Software*, available at https://martinfowler.com/ieeeSoftware/failFast.pdf.

the caller doesn't adhere to the contract, things will probably break sooner or later. If you do nothing in the implementation to uphold the contract, then names without an *s* could be queued, and much later, you'd end up with cats named Fido, Doggy, or Bonnie. To promote security, we advise to fail fast in a controlled manner instead of letting things break later, uncontrolled.

To fail fast, you check the preconditions at the beginning of the method before you do anything else, and fail hard if they aren't met. If the preconditions aren't met, then the program isn't using its classes in a way they were designed to be used. The program has lost control of what's happening, and the safest thing to do is to stop as fast as possible. This is nothing complicated; you can implement it yourself with an `if` statement that throws an exception along the lines of the following listing.

Listing 4.7   Enforcing fail fast of contract preconditions

```
public void queueCatName(String name) {            Must be a cat name, not null
    if (name == null)            ◀
        throw new NullPointerException();          Must be a good cat name
    if (!name.matches(".*s.*"))         ◀
        throw new IllegalArgumentException("Must contain s");
    if (catNames.contains(name))        ◀
        throw new IllegalArgumentException("Already queued");
    catNames.add(name);
}
                                           Must not be in the queue already
```

This code is arguably a little verbose, but it does the trick. It stops if the cat names are missed completely (`null`) or bad cat names and prevents already existing cat names from entering the list. And it does so using an aggressive fast-fail approach.

In Java, if you encounter a `null` when there shouldn't be one, you throw a `Null-PointerException`.[7] In the other cases, you throw an `IllegalArgumentException` to mark that the method call itself was valid but a specific argument couldn't be accepted.

For brevity, we've found it useful to use the `Validate` utility class from Apache's Commons Lang framework.[8] It contains several useful helper methods that do exactly what we want: check a condition and throw an appropriate exception if the condition is false. Using the `Validate.notNull`, `Validate.matchesPattern`, and `Validate.isTrue` methods gives you the code in the following listing.

Listing 4.8   Using `Validate` to enforce preconditions

```
import org.apache.commons.lang3.Validate.*;
...
public void queueCatName(String name) {
```

---

[7]   The documentation states that this type of exception is thrown "when an application attempts to use `null` in a case where an object is required." See http://docs.oracle.com/javase/8/docs/api/java/lang/NullPointerException.html.

[8]   See https://commons.apache.org/proper/commons-lang/javadocs/api-3.1/org/apache/commons/lang3/Validate.html.

```
    notNull(name);                          Must be a cat name, not null
    matchesPattern(name,".*s.*",
                "Cat name must contain s");     Must be a good cat name
    isTrue(!catNames.contains(name),
        "Cat name already queued");      Must not be in the queue already
    catNames.add(name);
}
```

Validate contains a lot of other helpful methods, like `exclusiveBetween` and `inclusiveBetween` to check if a value is within a range of valid values. Look through the documentation to see what's there; it makes it much easier to check preconditions in your code. For brevity, we'll use the framework in the examples in the rest of the book.

> **NOTE** You aren't repeating the bad data in the exception. Such an echo might open up vulnerabilities. We'll cover more about that in chapter 9.

Checking preconditions is pretty easy, but thinking through contracts takes more work. When is it worth the effort? In our experience, formulating contracts and checking preconditions for public methods is definitely worth it. This goes for simple checks like checking for `null`, that numbers are within the expected range, and similar. For package internal methods, it's a judgement call. If the package is large and the class has a lot of usage, it's probably a good idea, but for a helper class with a few uses, we'd skip it. As for private methods, it's not worth the effort. If the class needs internal contracts, it's probably too big, does too many things, and should be split instead.

> **TIP** Check the preconditions for all public methods; at least check that the arguments aren't `null`.

Now that you've looked at checking arguments for methods, let's proceed to the similar subject of arguments for constructors. We'll also talk about one more thing that Meyer mentioned in his theory, apart from preconditions and postconditions: *invariants*, which are things that always should be true for an object. Invariants must initially be upheld by the constructor on object creation.

4.2.2 Upholding invariants in constructors

Arguments to constructors add a bit of complexity compared to arguments for methods. The constructor arguments aren't only primarily to process or to modify the state of the object but to create the object in its initial state. Because an object state can be created in one part of an application and used in a completely different part, an invalid state can produce hard-to-trace bugs that can be a breeding ground for security vulnerabilities. Better to fail fast than let that happen.

Enforcing the contract for a constructor could be as simple as saying one of the fields is mandatory and then checking that the value isn't null. Here, you can interpret the word *mandatory* as meaning the contract of this object contains an invariant that states that this field must always be set to an object, never `null`. By adding a non-`null` check, you're enforcing that invariant. Invariants can be a lot more complicated, but we'll cover that in more depth in chapter 6 when we discuss securing mutable state.

In the next listing, you see the constructor of the class `Cat`. The contract states that as invariants, neither `name` nor `sex` is unspecified, so you must check that both fields are non-null. We also included the now familiar check that cat names must contain an *s*.

Listing 4.9   Enforcing contract for constructor

```
import org.apache.commons.lang3.Validate.*;

enum Sex {MALE, FEMALE;}

public class Cat {

    private String name;
    private final Sex sex;

    public Cat(String name, Sex sex) {            Enforces the invariant
        notNull(name);                            mandatory name
        matchesPattern(name,".*s.*",
                    "Cat name must contain s");    Cat names must
                                                   contain the letter s.
        notNull(sex);
        this.name = name;                 Enforces invariant mandatory sex
        this.sex = sex;
    }
    ...
}
```

Due to a feature in `Validate`, this constructor can be compressed. The method `notNull` not only validates but also returns the validated object. Using this feature, your `Cat` constructor becomes even briefer, as seen in the following listing.

Listing 4.10   Enforcing contract for constructor, condensed version

```
public Cat(String name, Sex sex) {
    this.name = notNull(name);            notNull returns a validated value.
    this.sex = notNull(sex);
    matchesPattern(name,".*s.*",          matchesPattern doesn't
                "Cat name must contain s");   return a validated value.
}
```

Although most `Validate` methods return the validated value, there are a few that don't. The pattern validator `matchesPattern` is one of these and, therefore, can't use the condensed form but needs to stand on a line of its own. You'll still have the desired behavior, where `null` results in a `NullPointerException`, whereas a malformed cat name yields an `IllegalArgumentException`.

You've probably noted that there are now two places in the code that do the same format check for cat names. This is a flagrant violation of the DRY (Don't Repeat Yourself) principle, which states that the same idea should be represented only once.[9] In chapter 5, we'll show our preferred way of solving these kinds of issues by introducing a *domain primitive* that, in this case, takes the form of a class `CatName`.

---

[9]   This principle was formulated by Andy Hunt and Dave Thomas in their book *The Pragmatic Programmer: From Journeyman to Master* (Addison-Wesley, 1999).

Now that you've learned how to ensure that methods get appropriate arguments and that objects are created with constructors that uphold the invariants, it's time to move on to the last kind of contract check we advise: preconditions checking that an object is in an appropriate state.

4.2.3 Failing for bad state

Finally, you want to ensure that preconditions that require an object to be in a certain state for an operation to be valid are met. For example, if the list of cat names is empty, it doesn't make sense to look at the next name in the queue. It's an operation that doesn't fit the state of the `CatNameList`. If you remember from table 4.3, for `nextCatName` and `dequeueCatName`, the contract requires that `CatNameList` must contain something.

The obvious way to check this is to use `Validate` to ensure that the list in `catNames` isn't empty. But the helper method `Validate.isTrue` doesn't do the job well in this case. On failure, that method throws an `IllegalArgumentException`, which would be confusing for someone who had called the no-arg method `nextCatName`. Fortunately, for this situation, there's `Validate.validState`, which you see used in the code for `nextCatName` in the following listing.

Listing 4.11 Enforcing state when looking at next name

```
public String nextCatName() {
    validState(!catNames.isEmpty());          It's only meaningful to look at the
    return catNames.get(0);                    next name if the list isn't empty.
}
```

The next listing shows the `CatNameList` class in its final form, with preconditions that protect the class from bad usage and fast failure if data is received that would, intentionally or by mistake, invalidate the contract.

Listing 4.12 `CatNameList` with contract enforced through fast fails

Can always be called

```
import org.apache.commons.lang3.Validate.*;

public class CatNameList {
    private final List<String> catNames = new ArrayList<String>();

    public void queueCatName(String name) {          Cat names must not be null.
        notNull(name);
        matchesPattern(name,".*s.*",
                    "Cat name must contain s");      Cat names must contain an s.
        isTrue(!catNames.contains(name),
                "Cat name already queued");          No duplicate names in queue
        catNames.add(name);
    }

    public String nextCatName() {
```

```
        validState(!catNames.isEmpty());
        return catNames.get(0);
    }

    public void dequeueCatName() {
        validState(!catNames.isEmpty());
        catNames.remove(0);
    }                                           Can only be called if queue isn't empty

    public int size() {                    Can always be called
        return catNames.size();
    }
}
```

You can see that the class has grown with five lines of code, and it has become much more secure. Invalid argument data is stopped early, and the object can never be in an invalid state. The main effort goes into thinking through the design and phrasing it as a contract, but that's work that needs to be done anyway.

Failing fast is a small code construct that promotes security. It comes in handy in the larger scheme of validating that data is sound and safe to use. In the next section, we'll dig deeper into the different levels of validation.

4.3   *Validation*

To keep a system secure, it's important to validate data. OWASP stresses *input validation* (validating data when it enters the system).[10] This seems like an obvious and sound thing to do, but unfortunately it's not that simple. There's the challenge of structuring the code to ensure input is validated everywhere. There's also the challenge of what constitutes valid data. What is valid or not varies from situation to situation.

Asking whether a particular value is valid or not is meaningless. Is 42 valid input? Is -1 or <script>install(keylogger)</script> valid? That depends on the situation. When ordering books, 42 is probably a valid input as a quantity, but -1 isn't. On the other hand, when reporting temperatures, -1 is certainly sensible. The script string is probably not what you want in most circumstances, but on a site where you report security bugs, it definitely fits.

Validation is also a word that tends to mean lots of different things. One person might claim that AV56734T is a valid order number because it follows the format for order numbers the system uses. Someone else might claim that AV56734T isn't a valid order number because there's no order in the system with that number. Yet someone else might claim that it's not valid even though there's an order with that number because they tried to clear the order for shipping and, at that specific time, it wasn't possible to do so. Obviously, there are many different kinds of validation.

You have probably come across the security advice "validate your input." But with the confusion about validation in mind, this piece of advice is as helpful as "when driving a car, avoid crashing." It's certainly well meant, but it's not helpful.

---

[10] The OWASP Foundation is a worldwide nonprofit organization that works for better software security. There's a lot of excellent resources at their website, www.owasp.org.

To clear up this confusion, we'll walk through a framework that tries to separate the different kinds of validation. The list presented here also suggests a good order in which to do the different kinds of validation. Cheap operations like checking the length of data come early in the list, and more expensive operations that require calling the database come later. In this way, the early controls shield the more expensive and advanced controls.[11] You'll want to perform the following types of validation, preferably in this order:

- *Origin*—Is the data from a legitimate sender?
- *Size*—Is it reasonably big?
- *Lexical content*—Does it contain the right characters and encoding?
- *Syntax*—Is the format right?
- *Semantics*—Does the data make sense?

As mentioned, checking for origin or checking the size can be done cheaply and quickly. Checking the lexical content requires a scan, which takes a bit more time and resources. Checking syntax might require parsing the data, something that consumes CPU resources and occupies a thread for quite some time. And checking if the data makes sense probably involves a heavy round-trip to the database. In this way, the earlier checks can prevent the more expensive later checks from being performed unnecessarily. We'll take a look at these different types of validation one-by-one and see how they fit into a secure design. We'll start with checking where data comes from.

4.3.1   Checking the origin of data

It certainly makes sense to check where data comes from before spending any effort on handling it. The reason for this is that many attacks are asymmetric in favor of the attacker. *Asymmetric* means that the effort required of the attacker to send malicious data is far less than the effort required of your system to handle that data. This is the basic logic of a denial of service (DoS) attack: the system is sent so much trash data that it becomes preoccupied with handling it, so no resources are left for the system to do its proper work.

A popular version is the *distributed DoS* (DDoS) attack, where lots of geographically distributed malicious clients send messages to the system at the same time. The clients of DDoS attacks are often botnets made up of computers that someone has infected with a remote-control function that's silent until it receives a message from its master. Such botnets can be bought or rented on the less respectable street corners of the web.[12]

Unfortunately checking the origin of data doesn't help in all cases, but checking data's origin is a first simple step to change the asymmetry in your favor. If the data comes from a legitimate origin, then continue. If not, discard it. Roughly, there are two mechanisms you can use: checking which IP address the data comes from or requiring an API access key. The simplest thing to do is check the IP address, so we'll start there.

---

[11] To our knowledge, this list was suggested by Dr. John Wilander but hasn't been published.

[12] Media and blogs report that a botnet of 1,000 bots costs about $50 to rent for one hour.

CHECKING THE IP ADDRESS

The most obvious way to check the origin of data is to check the IP address it's sent from. The approach is somewhat losing its applicability as things become more and more connected, but it still has some merits.

If you have a microservice architecture, then some of the services will *sit on the edge*, accepting outside traffic, but others *sit in the inside* and only expect calls from other services. The services in the inside can be restricted to only accept traffic from a specific IP range (of the other services). For the edge services, this is probably not doable, as they possibly need to be accessible from any client.

In practice, this kind of check is nothing you do from inside your application. Instead, access is restricted by network configuration. In a physical hall, this is set up in the physical routers. On a cloud service, such as Amazon Web Services (AWS), you can set up a security group that only allows incoming traffic from a specific range or list of IP addresses. If your system is used inside a company, such as a point-of-sale system, it might also be possible to do origin checks through IP ranges. For example, if servers should only be contacted by the point-of-sale terminals or the office desktops inside the company network, you can lock down access to those IP ranges. Unfortunately, in this more-and-more connected world, such situations are becoming increasingly uncommon.

Also, be aware that IP filters, MAC address filters, and similar provide no guarantee. MAC addresses can be changed from the operating system, IP addresses can be spoofed (or real machines taken over). But at least they provide some sort of first line-of-defense.

USING AN ACCESS KEY

If your system is open for requests from many places, you can't check by IP origin. For example, if your clients could be anywhere on the internet, then all IP addresses are legitimate senders. This is the case for almost all public services facing customers. Sorting out attackers based on IP origin is hard or impossible in these cases. Thankfully, there's one more way to restrict who's allowed to contact your system: requiring an *access key*. Such a key can be given to all legitimate clients. If the client is another system, it can be given to that system on deploy. If the clients are applications, the key can be built into the application. If the clients access an API, the key can be given to them when they sign some kind of end-user agreement. The point is that the holder of an access key proves it's allowed to send data to your system.

Taking AWS as an example, it has a REST API where you can manage your AWS resources, such as the S3 cloud data storage.[13] When sending an HTTP request to this API, you need to provide your access key as part of the HTTP `Authorization` header, as shown in listing 4.13. If there's no such header, the request is denied. It isn't enough to just send the access key, however. A malicious attacker might be able to spoof your access key and could, thereafter, use it to impersonate you. To stop this, the `Authorization` header also contains a signature where the message content has been signed using your *secret key*, which is a secret shared by you and AWS alone. AWS can determine which secret key to use for checking the signature by looking at the access key.

---

[13] See http://docs.aws.amazon.com/AmazonS3/latest/dev/RESTAuthentication.html.

> **Listing 4.13   Calling the REST API of AWS using access key and signature[14]**

```
GET /photos/puppy.jpg HTTP/1.1
Host: johnsmith.s3.amazonaws.com
Date: Mon, 26 Mar 2007 19:37:58 +0000

Authorization: AWS AKIAIOSFODNN7EXAMPLE:frJIUN8DYpKDtOLCwo//yllqDzg=
```

In this case, you need to invest in some computation on the server side, as you need to check that the signature of the message matches. It's not a particularly expensive operation, but you're opening yourself up a little to attacks where someone can send you lots of data and fool you into processing it. The good part is that an attacker needs a real access key, and if they use that maliciously, you can blacklist them for a limited time. The drawback of using access keys is that it's extra work. Fortunately, it's something that typically only needs to be done once and might be provided if you use an API gateway or similar products. If you do the work yourself, remember to do appropriate validation of the access key as well (length, charset, format) so that it doesn't become an attack vector.

> **Access tokens**
>
> Using an access key is a special case of using an access token. There are protocols, such as OAuth, that let an authentication server generate a token that can then be used as a proof of authorization to access other resources. What they share is that there has been an authentication earlier and that the token/key proves that the sender really is the entity it claims to be.
>
> Access control through authentication and authorization is a world of its own. OAuth is a good place to start to learn about this world. Check out www.oauth.com.

Having checked the origin of the data, you can now safely spend some effort processing it. The first step is to check that the data is of a reasonable size.

4.3.2   Checking the size of data

Does it make sense to accept an order number that's 1 GB of data? Probably not. If you've checked that the data comes from a legitimate origin, is the data of a reasonable size? Ideally, this check should be done as early as possible.

What is a reasonable size? That depends fully on the context. For example, an upload to a video site could easily be in the range of 100 MB to a few GB without anything being strange. On the other hand, a business application based on simple JSON or XML messages might not have messages bigger than some KB. What is a reasonable size for your data?

If the data comes over HTTP, you can check the `Content-Length` header and the size of the data.[15] If you run a batch process, you can check the file size.

Apart from checking the size of the data as a whole, it's also useful to check the size of each part when processing it. An attacker might hide a 1 GB order number inside a

---

[14] Example from the documentation at https://docs.aws.amazon.com/AmazonS3/latest/dev/RESTAuthentication.html#RESTAuthenticationExamples.

[15] Web servers and web containers like Tomcat have configuration options that let you set limits on the size of the POST or the size of headers.

request. You might forget to check the size of each particular request, or the total size might be within reasonable limits, but if you also check the size of order numbers, there'll be a defense mechanism every time you create an order number.

Hopefully this seems like sound design to you. If that's the case, then you get a lot of security for free. If you do this trick consistently for order number, phone number, street name, zip code, and so forth, then it's a lot harder for an attacker to find a place to insert big data. You have added protection that no part of the data can have a bizarre size.

For example, if you run an online bookstore, you might get batch files or HTTP requests regarding orders of books. These books are most probably identified using an International Standard Book Number (ISBN), which is a nine-digit number with an additional check digit. Checking that the entire order file or HTTP request is of reasonable size is good, but when you single out a part that should be an ISBN, you also want to check that part specifically. The following listing shows a class that represents an ISBN and validates its length to stop DoS attacks.

Listing 4.14 ISBN class containing a check that the number is short enough

```
import org.apache.commons.lang3.Validate.*;

public class ISBN {
    private final String isbn;

    public ISBN(final String isbn) {          ◄── Checks that the string isn't null and throws
        notNull(isbn);                              an IllegalArgumentException if it is
        inclusiveBetween(10, 10,isbn.length());  ◄──
        this.isbn = isbn;
    }                              Checks that the string is exactly 10 chars and
}                                  throws an IllegalArgumentException otherwise;
                                   long strings will be stopped early.
```

Needs additional checks (follows in refined
versions of this class later in the chapter)

Checking the length of the string might seem redundant in some cases. In later steps, we often check content and structure using a regular expression (often called a *regexp*). Regexps might look like any of the following:

- [a-z]—a single character between a and z
- [A-Z]{4}—four letters, each between A and Z
- [1-9]*—digits between 1 and 9, repeated any number of times

If the next step is a format control matching the regexp [0-9]{20} (any digit between 0 and 9, repeated exactly 20 times), why should you check the length separately? A 25-char string won't match the string anyway, so why check twice? The point here is that the length check protects the regexp engine. What happens if the string isn't 25 chars but 1 billion? Most probably the regexp engine will load and start processing that humongous string, not realizing it's too big. An early length check protects the latter stages.

Once you've checked that the input data is of reasonable size, it's time to look inside the data. The first check is that the data contains the expected type of content, such as the expected characters and encoding, which is called the *lexical content*.

4.3.3 *Checking lexical content of data*

Knowing that the data comes from a trustworthy source and has a reasonable size, you can dare to start looking at the content. Most probably, sooner or later you'll need to parse the data to extract the interesting parts (for example, if you receive the data in JSON or XML format). But parsing is expensive, both in terms of CPU and memory, so before you start parsing, you should do some further checks.

When checking the lexical content of data, we look at the content but not the structure. We scan through the data to see that it contains the expected characters and the expected encoding. If we encounter something suspicious, we discard the data instead of starting a parsing process that could bring our servers to their knees.

For example, if we expect data that only contains digits, we scan the stream to see if there's anything else. If we find anything else, we draw the conclusion that the data is either broken by mistake or has been maliciously crafted to fool our system. In either case, the safe bet is to discard the data. Similarly, if we expect plain text that's HTML-encoded, we scan the data to see that it only contains the expected content. In this case, each < should be encoded as <, so we shouldn't encounter any brackets at all. If we come across a bracket, we get wary. Might it be someone trying to sneak in a JavaScript snippet? To be on the safe side, we discard the data.

Lexical content is how the data is supposed to look when you look at it up close, focusing on the details and not paying attention to larger structures. Simple regexps are a great way of checking lexical content in many simple situations. For example, the ISBN-10 formats for books can only contain digits and the letter *X*.[16] An ISBN can also contain hyphens and spaces for readability, but for simplicity, we'll ignore them. The following listing shows the ISBN class from earlier, now refined to check that an ISBN only contains the expected characters.

> **Listing 4.15** ISBN **class with a regexp to control lexical content**

```
import org.apache.commons.lang3.Validate.*;

public class ISBN {
    private final String isbn;

    public ISBN(final String isbn) {
        notNull(isbn);
        inclusiveBetween(10, 10,isbn.length());      ←  Checks that length is
        isTrue(isbn.matches("[0-9X]*"));             ←  10 chars as expected
        this.isbn = isbn;                               Scans that all characters are
    }                                                   what you expect in an ISBN
}
```

If your input data is more complicated, for example XML, you might want to use a more powerful lexer. A *lexer* (or *tokenizer*) splits a sequence of characters into parts

---

[16] There are actually two ISBN formats in use: ISBN-10 and ISBN-13. In this section, we describe ISBN-10, which consists of nine digits followed by a check digit. ISBN-10 is used for books published before 2007, and ISBN-13 for books published after. We have chosen to discuss ISBN-10 because the format is more interesting from a technical discussion point of view.

called *lexemes* or *tokens*. These can be defined as the smallest part with a meaning or the sequence of characters that forms a syntactic unit. In written English, words are considered to be the tokens. In XML, tokens are the tags and the content within them. The following two listings show an XML document and its tokens.

> **Listing 4.16   XML document with book information**

```
<book>
   <title>Secure by Design</title>
   <authors>
      <author>Dan Bergh Johnsson</author>
      <author>Daniel Deogun</author>
      <author>Daniel Sawano</author>
   </authors>
</book>
```

> **Listing 4.17   Tokens found in book XML document, one token per row**

Tag is a token.

```
<book>              Whitespace such as newlines between tags
<title>             has no meaning in XML and isn't a token.
s
e                   For content, each character is a token.
c
u
r
e
...
```

In some situations, you might not want the full power of XML and might want to restrict it. In chapter 1, we presented an example of how dangerous it can be to allow XML entities in input. The reasonably short XML file you see in the following listing is less than 1,000 characters long. Still, it expands to a billion `lol` strings, something that will most probably break the poor XML parser.

> **Listing 4.18   XML expanding to a billion lols**

```
<?xml version="1.0" encoding="UTF-8" standalone="yes"?>
<!DOCTYPE lolz [
<!ELEMENT lolz (#PCDATA)>
<!ENTITY lol "lol">
<!ENTITY lol1 "&lol;&lol;&lol;&lol;&lol;&lol;&lol;&lol;&lol;&lol;">
<!ENTITY lol2 "&lol1;&lol1;&lol1;&lol1;&lol1;&lol1;&lol1;&lol1;&lol1;&lol1;">
<!ENTITY lol3 "&lol2;&lol2;&lol2;&lol2;&lol2;&lol2;&lol2;&lol2;&lol2;&lol2;">
<!ENTITY lol4 "&lol3;&lol3;&lol3;&lol3;&lol3;&lol3;&lol3;&lol3;&lol3;&lol3;">
<!ENTITY lol5 "&lol4;&lol4;&lol4;&lol4;&lol4;&lol4;&lol4;&lol4;&lol4;&lol4;">
<!ENTITY lol6 "&lol5;&lol5;&lol5;&lol5;&lol5;&lol5;&lol5;&lol5;&lol5;&lol5;">
<!ENTITY lol7 "&lol6;&lol6;&lol6;&lol6;&lol6;&lol6;&lol6;&lol6;&lol6;&lol6;">
<!ENTITY lol8 "&lol7;&lol7;&lol7;&lol7;&lol7;&lol7;&lol7;&lol7;&lol7;&lol7;">
<!ENTITY lol9 "&lol8;&lol8;&lol8;&lol8;&lol8;&lol8;&lol8;&lol8;&lol8;&lol8;">
]>
<lolz>&lol9;</lolz>
```

Needless to say, a billion `lol` strings will make your parser fall off a cliff and die, so you can't allow this to pass. One way of avoiding this is to disallow the use of XML entity definitions by having a lexer that scans the data, not recognizing `<!ENTITY` as a legitimate lexeme. Leaf back to chapter 1, section 1.5, if you want to review the details.

In practice, when working with XML documents, you'll most probably parse them to pick out the interesting parts. You don't want to do two parsings, one for checking content and one for parsing the structure. One way of avoiding this is to interleave the lexical check inside the parsing. The way to do this is to run the lexical check as part of stream processing, which was exactly what we did in chapter 1. Once you know that your data comes from a legitimate sender, is of reasonable size, and contains the right types of tokens, you can invest in digging deeper into the data, parsing it, and seeing if it has the right format and structure.

4.3.4 *Checking the data syntax*

It isn't uncommon for data to arrive as XML or JSON, and to understand it, you need to parse it. In the previous section, we described how we look at the lexical content of data: how it looks up close. When checking the syntax, we zoom out so we can see the larger picture. In XML, is there a closing tag for each opening tag? Are attributes inside the tags well formed?

Sometimes checking syntax is as simple as using a regexp. But to be truthful, regexps aren't always simple; we've seen numerous examples of people creating complex and sometimes incomprehensible things using regexps. We recommend using regexps in a simple way, for simple things. If a regexp makes your head hurt when you look at it, consider writing the logic as code instead.

One example where syntax checking is simple is with ISBNs. As mentioned earlier, an ISBN consists of nine digits and a control digit. The control digit might be 10, which is denoted by the letter *X*. The syntax of an ISBN is something that can be checked with a regexp. To do that, we check if the data matches `[0-9]{9}[0-9X]`. If it does, it has the right format, and not matching this regexp means we discard the data.

More complex data structures, like XML, require a parser. Parsing complex and large data structures is something that requires lots of computational resources. This is why the parser is a desirable target for someone who wants to launch a DoS attack on your system. Many of the preceding steps of checking origin, checking data size, and checking lexical content are there to shield the parser.

We've mentioned that checking syntax consists of checking that data comes in the proper form. We'll look at one more common mechanism, a checksum, to see if the format is correct. An ISBN is a good example of this, as the tenth and last digit in the ISBN is a control digit. Without getting into the details of how the checksum is computed, checking this is also part of checking syntax. The next listing shows the `ISBN` class again, now with a syntax check of the format as well as a control of the check digit.

Listing 4.19   Checking an ISBN's lexical content and syntax

```
import org.apache.commons.lang3.Validate.*;

public class ISBN {
    private final String isbn;

    public ISBN(final String isbn) {
        notNull(isbn);
        inclusiveBetween(10, 10,isbn.length());
        isTrue(isbn.matches("[0-9X]*"));
        isTrue(isbn.matches("[0-9]{9}[0-9X]"));
        isTrue(checksumValid(isbn));
        this.isbn = isbn;
    }

    private boolean checksumValid(String isbn) { /.../ }
}
```

Validates all characters are what you expect in an ISBN

Checks the format

Checks the checksum

When the syntax structure is simple enough, it looks ridiculous to first have a lexical check with one regexp and then a syntax check with a similar regexp. In these cases, the lexical check and syntax check are often collapsed into one step, as in the next listing.

Listing 4.20   Checking an ISBN's lexical content and syntax in one step

```
import org.apache.commons.lang3.Validate.*;

...

    public ISBN(final String isbn) {
        notNull(isbn);
        inclusiveBetween(10, 10,isbn.length());
        isTrue(isbn.matches("[0-9]{9}[0-9X]"));
        isTrue(checksumValid(isbn));
        this.isbn = isbn;
    }
```

Lexical check and syntax check collapse

Checks the checksum

It might look like we're sidestepping the validation order here. What happens in this case is that the lexical analysis and the syntax analysis are so similar that they are done by the same mechanism. You can look at it as if they're interleaved or have collapsed. The essential idea of the validation order is still there. Now that you know that you have well-formatted data that contains the expected content, has a reasonable size, and comes from a legitimate sender, you can see if this data fits in with the data you have—if it makes sense.

4.3.5   *Checking the data semantics*

By checking origin, size, content, and structure, you'll have gathered so much confidence in the input data that you're ready to act on it. Up to this point, you might have performed checks that are CPU-intensive or require lots of memory. For example, you might have processed a large XML message that instructs you to add a lot of items to an order in an order system. But, thus far, you've only worked on the data by itself, not on the data in connection with the rest of the system. Chances are that you've probably not hit the database once during this time.

In the example with a large XML message for extending an order, you might have found a lot of order lines to add, but you haven't checked that the specified product numbers exist, and certainly not their stock status. The specified order might not even exist or is perhaps already shipped and not open for extension. You've only checked the syntax.

Now it's time for the semantic check: is this data sound and consistent with the view of the world that resides in the rest of the system? In the semantic check, you check things like whether this product number exists in your product catalog or if the order described by this order number can be amended with another item. We think the most intuitive place to put these constraints is in the domain model.

A search in your product catalog domain service could be asking does this product number exist? If there's no match, an exception is thrown, and the flow is interrupted. In the same way, if someone tries to add an item to an order that's closed (perhaps paid and shipped), it'll show up as an `IllegalStateException` from the `Order` class. In fact, we think the domain model is such a natural place to put these kinds of checks that we don't think of them as validations—to us, they're part of the domain model.

Yet we agree that semantic validation is rightly part of the list, as the verb *validate* doesn't make sense on its own. You always need to validate with respect to something. You validate that the data adheres to some rules and constraints, and those rules and constraints are what make up the domain model. The domain model states how you've chosen to look at the world. You have modeled order numbers to have a specific format, and you've modeled orders to be closed for amendments when they ship. After passing all these stages, you know that the data is considered sound with respect to the model—it's been validated.

You have now reached the point where you know the data is from a legitimate sender, has a reasonable size, contains the expected content with the expected structure, and makes sense with respect to the rest of the data. You can now safely act on that data by adding a new book to the cart, accepting the payment, or sending the order for shipping.

To secure the design, it's powerful to let the code reflect if data is validated and to what degree. The `ISBN` class you saw earlier is an example of this. It's a small, domain-focused building block that we know contains an ISBN of the valid format. There's no need to validate that number again. In our experience, designing such building blocks does wonders for the security of your system. It's now time to dive into how to craft such blocks, which we call domain primitives.

Summary

- Data integrity is about ensuring the consistency and accuracy of data during its entire life cycle.
- Data availability is about ensuring data is obtainable and accessible at the expected level of performance in a system.
- Immutable values are safe to share between threads without locks: no locking, no blocking.
- Immutability solves data availability issues by allowing scalability and no locking between threads.
- Immutability solves data integrity issues by preventing change.
- Contracts are an effective way to clarify the responsibilities of objects and methods.
- It's better to fail fast in a controlled manner than to risk uncontrolled failures later. Fail fast by checking preconditions early in each method.
- Validation can be broken down into checking origin, data size, lexical content, syntactic format, and semantics.
- Origin checks can be done by checking the origin IP or requiring an access key to counteract DDoS attacks.
- Data size checks can be done both at the system border and at object creation.
- Lexical content checks can be done with a simple regular expression (regexp).
- Syntax format checks might require a parser, which is more expensive in terms of CPU and memory.
- Semantic checks often require looking at the data in the database, such as searching for an entity with a specific ID.
- Earlier steps in the validation order are more economical to perform and protect the later, more expensive steps. If early checks fail, later steps can be skipped.

Domain primitives

This chapter covers

- How domain primitives create secure code
- Mitigating data leaks with read-once objects
- Improving entities with domain primitives
- Ideas from taint analysis

In chapter 4, you learned about powerful design constructs like immutability, failing fast, and validation. Those constructs do indeed address several security issues, such as invalid input, illegal state, and data integrity, but applying them individually isn't an effective way of achieving secure code. Table 5.1 shows the problem areas we'll address in this chapter and those constructs that will help you achieve a greater level of security.

Table 5.1   Problem areas addressed

Section	Problem area
Domain primitives and invariants	Security issues caused by inexact, error-prone, and ambiguous code
Read-once objects	Security problems due to leakage of sensitive data
Standing on the shoulders of domain primitives	Security issues caused by code burdened by too much complexity

The theme of this chapter is how to create a higher-order construct called a *domain primitive,* which combines secure constructs and value objects to define the smallest building block of a domain. This way, you'll learn how to empower your code with a design that facilitates security in depth, as well as bringing overall clarity and understanding. You'll also learn how domain primitives can be used to reduce complexity in entities and how they allow detection of unintentional leakage of sensitive data. With that said, let's dive into domain primitives and invariants.

5.1   *Domain primitives and invariants*

Some of the key properties of value objects in Domain-Driven Design are that they are immutable and form a conceptual whole.[1] We've found that if you take the concept of the value object and slightly tweak it, keeping security in mind, you get something called a *domain primitive.*

When you start using domain primitives as the smallest building blocks in your domain model, you'll be able to create code with a significantly reduced likelihood of security issues, simply by the way you're designing it. You're designing code that's precise and leaves little or no room for ambiguity. This type of code tends to contain fewer bugs and, as a consequence, fewer security vulnerabilities. The code also tends to be easy to work with because domain primitives lower the cognitive load on developers. We'll spend the rest of this section expanding on what domain primitives are, how to define them, and how they can be used to create secure software.

5.1.1   *Domain primitives as the smallest building blocks*

A value object represents an important concept in your domain model. When modeling it, you decide how to represent the value object and what name it should have. If you take this further and also put some effort into determining what it is and what it's not, you'll gain significantly deeper insight into that concept. You can then use that insight to introduce invariants that must be upheld in order for the value object to be considered valid. Continuing, you can say that the value object not only should or can but must uphold these invariants, and that they must be enforced at the time of creation. What you end up with is a value object so strict in its definition that, if it exists,

---

[1] It's important to grok the concept of value objects in Domain-Driven Design before you dive into domain primitives. Revisit chapter 3 if you feel you need a refresher.

it'll also be valid. If it's not valid, then it can't exist. This type of value object is what we refer to as a domain primitive.

> **NOTE** A value object so precise in its definition that it, by its mere existence, manifests its validity is a domain primitive.

Domain primitives are similar to value objects in Domain-Driven Design. Key differences are that you're requiring the existence of invariants, and they must be enforced at the point of creation. You're also prohibiting the use of simple language primitives, or generic types (including `null`), as representations of concepts in the domain model. It's also worth pointing out that even though we call them domain primitives, they can still be complex objects and contain other domain primitives as well as nontrivial logic.

> **NOTE** Nothing in a domain model should be represented by a language primitive or a generic type. Each concept should be modeled as a domain primitive so that it carries meaning when passed around, and so it can uphold its invariants.

Let's say the concept of quantity exists in your domain model. Quantity is the amount a customer wants to buy of a certain item in the webshop you're building. The quantity itself is a number, but instead of representing it as an integer, you create a domain primitive called `Quantity`. When defining `Quantity`, you discuss with the domain experts what's considered to be a valid quantity in the context of the current domain. This discussion reveals that a valid quantity is an integer value between 1 and 200. A zero quantity isn't valid because if the customer wants to buy zero items, then the order shouldn't exist at all. A negative value isn't valid either because you can't un-buy products, and returns are handled separately. Orders for more than 200 items aren't handled by the system at all. Large orders are extremely rare, and if they do occur, they need special handling, so they're dealt with via direct contact with a sales representative instead of through the online store.

You also encapsulate important behavior of the domain primitive, such as the addition and subtraction of quantities. By having the domain primitive own and control domain operations, you reduce the risk of bugs caused by lack of detailed domain knowledge of the concepts involved in the operation. The further away from a concept they are, the less detailed knowledge of the concept can be expected, so it makes sense to keep all domain operations within the domain primitive itself. To give you an example, if you need to add two quantities, and you create a method `add`, then the implementation of that method needs to take into account the domain rules of a quantity—remember, you're not dealing with plain integers anymore. If you were to place the `add` method somewhere else in your codebase, say in a utility class called `Functions`, then it'd be easy for subtle bugs to creep in. If you decide to slightly change the behavior of the `Quantity` domain primitive, will you remember to also update the method in the utility class? Chances are you'll forget, and that's how you introduce hard-to-find bugs that can lead to serious problems. When you're done, the `Quantity` domain primitive should look like the following listing when represented in code.

Listing 5.1   The `Quantity` domain primitive

```
import static org.apache.commons.lang3.Validate.inclusiveBetween;
import static org.apache.commons.lang3.Validate.notNull;

public final class Quantity {

    private final int value;          ◄─── The integer value

    public Quantity(final int value) {
        inclusiveBetween(1, 200, value);   ◄─── Enforces invariants at time of creation
        this.value = value;
    }

    public int value() {
        return value;
    }
                                                Provides domain operations
    public Quantity add(final Quantity addend) {  ◄─── to encapsulate behavior
        notNull(addend);
        return new Quantity(value + addend.value);
    }

    // equals() hashCode() etc...

}
```

This is a precise and strict code representation of the concept of quantity. In the case study of the anti-*Hamlet* in chapter 2, you saw an example of how a small ambiguity in the system could lead to customers giving themselves discount vouchers by sending in negative quantities before completing their orders. A domain primitive like the `Quantity` as created here removes the possibility of some dishonest user sending in a negative value and tricking the system into unintended behavior. Using domain primitives removes a security vulnerability without the use of explicit countermeasures. As this modeling exercise shows, quantity isn't just an integer. It should be modeled and implemented as a domain primitive so that it carries meaning when passed around, and so it can uphold its invariants.

Now you've learned the basics of what a domain primitive is. Let's move on and look at the importance of defining the scope in which a domain primitive is valid.

5.1.2   Context boundaries define meaning

Domain primitives, like value objects, are defined by their value rather than by an identity. This means that two domain primitives of the same type and with the same value are interchangeable with each other. Domain primitives are perfect for representing a wide variety of domain concepts that don't fit into the categories of entities or aggregates.[2] One important aspect to keep in mind when modeling a concept using a domain primitive is that it should be defined to mean exactly what the concept is in the *current domain*.

---

[2]   Go back to chapter 3 if you need to brush up on what entities and aggregates are in Domain-Driven Design.

Say you're building a system that lets users choose and create their own email addresses. A user can choose the local part of the email address (the part to the left of the @), and once created, they can start sending and receiving messages using that address. If a user enters `jane.doe`, then the email address `jane.doe@example.com` would be created (assuming your domain name is `example.com`). When modeling, you realize that an email address is a perfect example of a domain primitive. It's defined by its value, and you can come up with some constraints that you could use to assert that it's valid.

At first, you might be inclined to use the official definition of an email address to figure out what constitutes a valid address.[3] Although this would technically be correct in terms of meeting the requirements of the RFC, it might not be what's considered a valid email address in the context of the current domain (figure 5.1). As an engineer, this might come as a surprise to you. But remember, we're focusing on the meaning of a concept in a specific domain, not what it might mean in some other context, as in the context of a global standard. For example, your domain might define an email address to be case-insensitive, so anything the user enters will be transformed to lowercase. You could go even further and say that the only characters allowed are ASCII alphabetic characters, digits, and dots (`[a-z0-9.]`). This is a deviation from the technical specification, but it's a valid choice in the context of the current domain.[4]

Sometimes you'll encounter situations where the name of the concept you're trying to model is also used outside of the current context, and where its external definition is so prevalent, it would be confusing to redefine it in your domain model. An email address might be such a term, but as you just learned, it can make sense to redefine the term *email* in your current domain.

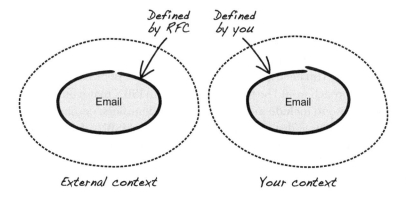

Figure 5.1 The meaning of a term is defined within the boundaries of a given context.

---

[3] Explaining the definition of an email address is beyond the scope of this book, but a good place to start if you'd like to know more is RFC 3696 (https://tools.ietf.org/html/rfc3696).

[4] It might be of interest to know that even RFC 5321 discourages the use of case-sensitive email addresses, although the specification defines email addresses as case-sensitive.

Another example of a well-defined term is an ISBN. The ISBN is defined by the International Organization for Standardization (ISO), and redefining it could cause confusion, misinterpretation, and bugs. These types of subtle differences in meaning are a common cause for security issues, so you want to avoid them, especially when interacting with other systems or other domain contexts (figure 5.2).

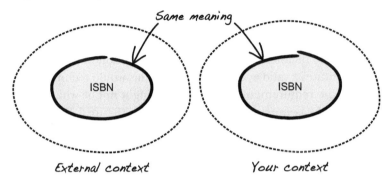

Figure 5.2   Using an externally defined term without changing its meaning

Most times, when you find yourself redefining a well-known term, the need for that is because the term is used to describe more than one thing in your current context. In those cases, try to either split the term into two distinct terms or come up with an entirely new term. The new term is unique to your current context, so you avoid any misinterpretation. It also makes it clear why certain specific invariants are used instead of those associated with the externally defined term. Another benefit of introducing a new term is that the original term can keep its crisp definition and remain a domain primitive. You've maintained full freedom to model important concepts in your domain without losing any of the model's exactness.

 Imagine you're building book-managing software that uses ISBNs to identify books. After a while, you realize you need a way to identify and handle books that haven't received an ISBN yet. One approach would be to redefine the term ISBN to not only represent real ISBN numbers, but also to include internally assigned identifiers, perhaps using a magic prefix or something similar to distinguish them from the real ISBNs. To avoid the possible confusion that comes with redefining an ISO standard, you could instead introduce a new term, BookId, that would contain either an ISBN or an UnpublishedBookNumber (figure 5.3). BookId is what identifies a book, and UnpublishedBookNumber is the internally assigned identifier.

 By introducing two new terms, BookId and UnpublishedBookNumber, you're able to keep the exact and well-known definition of ISBN, while at the same time meeting the needs of your business domain.

5.1.3   *Building your domain primitive library*

Now that you've expanded your toolbox with the versatility of domain primitives, you should strive to use them as much as you can in your code. These are the smallest building

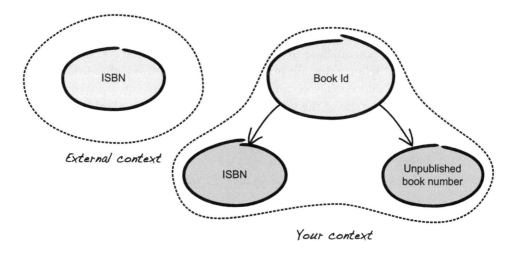

Figure 5.3   Introducing new terms instead of redefining existing ones

blocks and form the basis of your domain model. As such, almost every concept in your model will be based on one or more domain primitives. When you're done modeling, you'll have a collection of domain primitives that you can view as your *domain primitive library*. This library isn't a collection of generic utility classes and methods, but rather a well-defined, ubiquitous set of domain concepts. And because they're domain primitives, it's safe to pass them around as arguments in your code just like regular value objects.

Domain primitives lower the cognitive load on developers because there's no need to understand their inner workings in order to use them. You can safely use them with the confidence that they always represent valid values and well-defined concepts. If they aren't valid, they won't exist. This also removes the need to constantly revalidate data in order to make sure it's safe to use. If it's defined in your domain, you can trust it and use it freely.

5.1.4   *Hardening APIs with your domain primitive library*

You should always strive to use domain primitives in your programmatic APIs. If every argument and return value of a method is valid by definition, you'll have input and output validation in every single method in your codebase without any extra effort. The way you're using domain design enables you to create code that's extremely resilient and robust. A positive side effect of this is that the number of security vulnerabilities caused by invalid input data drastically decreases.

Let's examine this more closely with a code example. Say you're given the task of sending the audit logs of your system to a central audit log repository. Audit logs contain sensitive data, and it's important that they're sent to a designated place to be stored and protected properly. Sending the data to the wrong place can have a significant negative business impact. If you create a method in your API that takes the current audit logs and sends them to a log repository located at a given server address, it could end up looking like this:

```
void sendAuditLogsToServerAt(java.net.InetAddress serverAddress);
```

The issue here is that a method signature like this allows for any IP address to be the destination for the logs. If you fail to properly validate the address before sending the logs, you could potentially send them to an insecure location and reveal sensitive data. If you instead define a domain primitive, `InternalAddress`, that strictly defines what an internal IP address is, you can use that as the type of the input parameter in your method. Applying this to the `sendAuditLogsToServerAt` method leads to the code in the following listing instead.

> **Listing 5.2   Hardening the API with domain primitives**

```
import static org.apache.commons.lang3.Validate.notNull;

void sendAuditLogsToServerAt(InternalAddress serverAddress) {
   notNull(serverAddress);

   // Retrieve logs and send them to server
}
```

The only input validation left to perform is a null check.

Now you've designed your method so that it's impossible to pass invalid input to it. The only form of validation left to do, in terms of verifying that the IP address is internal, is to make sure it's not `null`.

5.1.5   *Avoid exposing your domain publicly*

One thing to remember when hardening your API is that if you have an API that acts as an interface to a different domain, you should avoid exposing your domain model's objects in that API. If you do, you instantly make your domain model part of your public API.[5] As soon as other domains start using your API, it quickly becomes hard to change and evolve your domain independently.

An example of a public API facing a different domain is a REST API exposed on the internet for others to consume via client software. If you expose your internal domain in the REST API, then you can't evolve your domain without forcing the software clients to evolve with you. If your business depends on those clients, then you can't ignore them; you have no other option but to evolve at the same pace as your consumers are able to adapt their clients. To make things even worse, if you have multiple consumers, then you're not only tying yourself to each consumer, but you're tying the consumers together with each other. This is a less than ideal situation, and you can avoid it by not exposing your domain publicly.

What you want to do instead is to use a different representation of each of your domain objects. This can be viewed as a type of data transfer object (DTO) used to communicate with other domains. You can place invariants in those DTOs, but they won't be the same constraints that exist in your domain. Rather, they can, for example, be constraints relevant to the communication protocol defined by the API. The first thing you do in an API method like this is convert the DTO into the corresponding domain primitive(s) in order to ensure its data is valid. By using this layer of translation between

---

[5]   In Domain-Driven Design, this type of shared domain is referred to as a *shared kernel*.

the concepts in your public API and your domain, you're able to uncouple the two. This allows you to evolve the API and your domain independently.

We have covered a lot of important aspects of domain primitives in this section. Before we move on, let's review the key points:

- The invariants of domain primitives are checked at the time of creation.
- Domain primitives can only exist if they are valid.
- Domain primitives should always be used instead of language primitives or generic types.
- Their meaning is defined within the boundaries of the current domain, even if the same term exists outside of the current domain.
- You should use your domain primitive library to create secure code.

So far, you've learned about immutability, failing fast, validation, and domain primitives and how these concepts promote security by design. There's one more code construct we need to go over in this chapter that's also important from a security perspective—the read-once object.

5.2 *Read-once objects*

One common source of security issues in software is leakage of sensitive data. This leaking of information can either be unintentionally caused by the developer or intentionally triggered by an individual. Regardless of the reason behind the leak, you can use a few design techniques to help with this issue. Let's take a look at how you can use a design pattern we call the read-once object to mitigate the possibility of leaking sensitive data. Here's a list of the key aspects of a read-once object:

- Its main purpose is to facilitate detection of unintentional use.
- It represents a sensitive value or concept.
- It's often a domain primitive.
- Its value can be read once, and once only.
- It prevents serialization of sensitive data.
- It prevents subclassing and extension.

A *read-once object* is, as the name implies, an object designed to be read once. This object usually represents a value or concept in your domain that's considered to be *sensitive* (for example, passport numbers, credit card numbers, or passwords). The main purpose of the read-once object is to facilitate detection of unintentional use of the data it encapsulates. Often this object is a domain primitive, but you can apply this pattern to both entities and aggregates as well. The basic idea is that once the object has been created, it's only possible to retrieve the data it encapsulates once. Trying to retrieve it more than once results in an error. The object also makes a reasonable effort to prevent the sensitive data from being extracted through serialization.

An example of a read-once object is shown in listing 5.3. As you can see, the `Sensitive-Value` object has been modeled as a domain primitive with all its invariants enforced at creation. The class is declared as `final` to prevent subclassing, and the value is wrapped in an `AtomicReference`.[6] When the accessor method `value` is called, it sets the sensitive value to `null` and then returns the previous value. If `value` has already been called, then the previous value will be `null` and an exception is thrown.

The object also implements the `java.io.Externalizable` interface and always throws an exception in order to prevent accidental serialization. The `value` field is declared `transient` in case some library uses field access to serialize the object rather than Java serialization (but still honors the `transient` keyword). As a last measure, the `toString` method is implemented so it doesn't output the actual value.

Listing 5.3   Storing sensitive data in a read-once object

```java
import java.io.Externalizable;
import java.io.IOException;
import java.io.ObjectInput;
import java.io.ObjectOutput;
import java.util.concurrent.atomic.AtomicReference;

import static org.apache.commons.lang3.Validate.notNull;

public final class SensitiveValue
        implements Externalizable {

    private transient final
            AtomicReference<String> value;

    public SensitiveValue(final String value) {
        validate(value);
        this.value = new AtomicReference<>(value);
    }

    public String value() {
        return notNull(value.getAndSet(null),
            "Sensitive value has already been consumed");
    }

    @Override
    public String toString() {
        return "SensitiveValue{value=*****}";
    }

    @Override
    public void writeExternal(final ObjectOutput out) {
        deny();
    }

    @Override
    public void readExternal(final ObjectInput in) {
        deny();
    }
```

Makes class final to prevent subclassing

Implements Externalizable

Declares a transient field

Validates domain rules at time of creation

Reminder that the value can only be retrieved once

toString doesn't reveal the sensitive value.

Throws an exception to prevent serialization

---

[6]   See the javadoc for `java.util.concurrent.atomic.AtomicReference` if you're unfamiliar with this.

```
    private static String validate(final String value) {
        // Check domain-specific invariants
        return notBlank(value).trim();
    }

    private static void deny() {
        throw new UnsupportedOperationException(
            "Not allowed on sensitive value");
    }
}
```

To give you a better understanding of the benefits of this design pattern, let's take a look at a scenario where a read-once object can prevent sensitive data from unintentional exposure.

5.2.1 Detecting unintentional use

Imagine you're building simple login functionality, where credentials in the form of a username and password are entered and then used to perform authentication. The authentication is done by calling a second system responsible for verifying the given credentials—the authentication system. Once the password has entered your system, it shouldn't be used for anything other than authentication, as illustrated in figure 5.4. This means that the only point you need to retrieve the password is when you pass it on to the authentication system. Once you've done that, there's no need to keep the password around anymore.

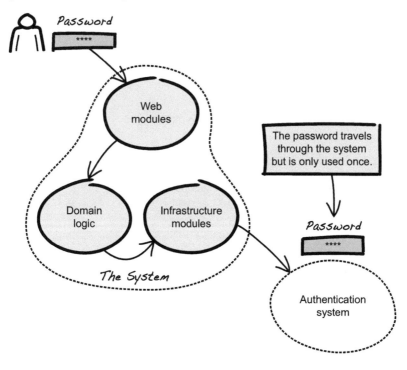

Figure 5.4   The life cycle of a read-once object

Passwords are a typical example of sensitive data. The last thing you want is the user's password to end up as plain text in some log file on disk where anyone can read it, or written out in an error message in the user's browser or in a monitoring dashboard for your operations team to see. If you model your password as a domain primitive and implement it as a read-once object, as shown in the following listing, you're creating a safety net that helps you easily detect if the password starts to leak somehow.

Listing 5.4   Password represented as a read-once domain primitive

```
import static org.apache.commons.lang3.Validate.validState;

public final class Password implements Externalizable {

    private final char[] value;
    private boolean consumed = false;

    public Password(final char[] value) {
        this.value = validate(value).clone();          The input array is cloned.
    }
                                                       Thread-safe accessor
    public synchronized char[] value() {
        validState(!consumed, "Password value has already been consumed");
        final char[] returnValue = value.clone();
        Arrays.fill(value, '0');                       The internal
        consumed = true;                               field is erased.
        return returnValue;          Value is marked
    }                                as consumed.

    @Override
    public String toString() {
        return "Password{value=*****}";
    }

    @Override
    public void writeExternal(final ObjectOutput out) {
        deny();
    }

    @Override
    public void readExternal(final ObjectInput in) {
        deny();
    }

    private static void deny() {
        throw new UnsupportedOperationException(
                "Serialization of passwords is not allowed");
    }

    private static char[] validate(final char[] value) {
        // Validate length, characters and so forth
        return value;
    }
}
```

The internal field is cloned.

With this implementation, unintentionally using the password leads to an error message saying, "Password value has already been consumed" when you try to verify the credentials with the authentication system. This unintentional use could, for example, be in a log message or a result of throwing an exception, where the thrown exception contains the password. Most likely, you'll catch this kind of programming mistake early on, because of a failing test in your continuous delivery pipeline.[7] And if you don't, then the inability to log in will quickly be noticed in production, and the error message should make it fairly easy to understand what's going on.

> **Details of the Password class**
>
> The `Password` object shown in listing 5.4 is similar to the `SensitiveValue` object you saw earlier but with some additional changes worth pointing out. The reasons for these changes are due to how memory is managed by JVMs. We're not going to go into JVM details here, but we'll point these details out for you to use as best practices.
>
> First, the value field has been changed to a `char` array instead of using a `String`. This is because you want to be able to clear it after it's been used. The input array is also cloned for this reason. Making a copy of the array ensures you don't interfere with any cleanup logic performed by the code calling the constructor on `Password` or vice versa. Because you're not using an `AtomicReference` anymore, a boolean flag together with a synchronized accessor method is used to keep track of a consumed value in a thread-safe manner.
>
> When the value is consumed, via the `value` accessor method, a copy of the internal `char` array is returned, then the internal array is cleared. Again, the reason for making a copy of the passed-out array is to have the `Password` class responsibly do its part in handling sensitive data without interfering with the rest of the codebase. Both the calling and the receiving code outside of this class should also properly clean up any references to the password.
>
> The goal of these implementation details is to reduce the exposure of sensitive values in JVM memory. You can take these concepts even further if you want to, but we believe these examples add reasonable value for a relatively low effort and should be considered good practice when coding in Java.

In the case of retrieving the value through the accessor method `value`, the read-once object doesn't prevent the data from leaking but makes it easy to detect the leak once it happens. And if you're making use of good developer practices and have a comprehensive test suite, you have a good chance of preventing the leak from ever reaching your production environment.

5.2.2 *Avoiding leaks caused by evolving code*

Another scenario where it's easy to cause unintentional data leakage is when redesigning or remodeling your code. This is something we've experienced ourselves on

---

[7] Don't worry if you're unfamiliar with continuous delivery and pipelines. You'll learn about them in an upcoming chapter.

occasion, and thanks to the use of read-once objects, we were able to find the leak and prevent it from reaching production. Let's take a look at a scenario similar to what we experienced but slightly tweaked—to protect the innocent.

Imagine you're building a web application where the code often needs to access data about the currently logged-in user. The required information is available in the User domain object. At some point, the developers decide to put the User object in the web session in order to ease access and to act as a cache. This solution works as intended and has the desired benefits. Later, as a result of new business requirements, the User domain object is remodeled and a Social Security number (SSN) is added to it (figure 5.5). The SSN object is implemented as a read-once object because it's only intended to be used once.

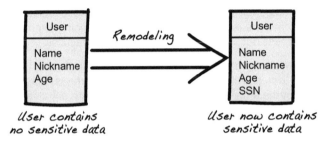

Figure 5.5   Remodeling the User object, causing sensitive data to leak

The new domain model serves the new functionality well, and all tests in your test suite pass. But during acceptance testing in your staging environment, you notice, by chance, that some stack traces are printed every time you shut down the application. The error message is, "Not allowed on sensitive value." You follow the stack trace and see that the exception is caused by an attempt to serialize the SSN. Puzzled that something is trying to serialize your sensitive data, you start to track down the source for this behavior. After some digging, you find that the serialization is triggered by the Tomcat web server you're using. It turns out that, by default, Tomcat persists any active sessions to disk whenever it's shut down or restarted.[8] If you put any sensitive data in the session without turning this feature off, that data might end up on disk, readily available for anyone with disk access to read—a perfect case of exposing sensitive data without proper authorization.

It's common to see these types of data leaks in software systems, and they're almost always unintentional, either because the developers didn't think about the implications or because they weren't aware of them (perhaps because the code they were working on was far away from where the sensitive data had been created). By designing with read-once objects, you allow the developers to be more focused on the task at hand and not have to worry about security.

---

[8]   For more information about this, see https://tomcat.apache.org/tomcat-8.5-doc/config/manager .html#Persistence_Across_Restarts.

Now that you know what domain primitives represent and how to implement them, let's take a look at what they do for the rest of the code—how do they help other parts of the code to become more secure? In particular, let's look at what they do for entities.

5.3   Standing on the shoulders of domain primitives

Without domain primitives, the remaining code needs to take care of validation, formatting, comparing, and lots of other details. *Entities* represent long-lived objects with a distinguished identity, such as articles in a news feed, rooms in a hotel, and shopping carts in online sales. The functionality in a system often centers around changing the state of these objects: hotel rooms are booked, shopping cart contents are paid for, and so on. Sooner or later the flow of control will be guided to some code representing these entities. And if all the data is transmitted as generic types such as `int` or `String`, responsibilities fall on the entity code to validate, compare, and format the data, among other tasks. The entity code will be burdened with a lot of tasks, rather than focusing on the central business flow-of-state changes that it models. Using domain primitives can counteract the tendency for entities to grow overly complex.

As development time goes by, entity classes have their code written, extended, and changed multiple times. It's easy for entities to become magnets of functionality, and their methods to become code clumps spanning several hundred lines and riddled with nested `for` and `if` blocks. Numerous times, we've found security vulnerabilities caused by local changes that didn't take all conditions into account. Imagine you're adding an `else` clause to an `if` statement deep down inside such a method. What are the odds you'll forget to check some condition or another? When the code grows in complexity, important details might be overlooked—in particular, validation has a tendency to be forgotten, with disastrous results for security. A good way to make entities more secure is to offload them by using a library of domain primitives.

Now let's show how standing on the shoulders of domain primitives can relieve entities of the burden of many types of validation. At the same time, validation becomes more consistent, and the code more secure overall.

5.3.1   The risk with overcluttered entity methods

Let's look at an example of an overly cluttered entity and how it can benefit from using domain primitives. Listing 5.5 shows the class `Order` from an online bookstore. The online bookstore is of the same type as in the case study in chapter 2. The state of the application changes when books are added to an order and when the order is paid for later and shipped. The class `Order` is responsible for tracking these changes.

One example of the changes can be seen in the method `addItem`, which tracks when a book is added to the order. It's 10 lines of code, but still it manages to uphold lots of business rules. But there's also a subtle mistake. See if you can spot it. (It's not easy.)

Listing 5.5   `Order` entity that does a lot in its `addItem` method

```
import org.apache.commons.lang3.Validate;

class Order {
    private BookRepository bookCatalog;
    private ArrayList<Object> items;
    private boolean paid = false;
    Inventory inventory;

    public void addItem(String isbn, int qty) {
        if(this.paid == false) {
            notNull(isbn);
            isTrue(isbn.length() == 10);
            isTrue(isbn.matches("[0-9X]*"));
            isTrue(isbn.matches("[0-9]{9}[0-9X]"));
            Book book = bookCatalog.findByISBN(isbn);
            if(inventory.avaliableBooks(isbn) >= qty){
                items.add(new OrderLine(book, qty));
            }
        }
    }
    ...
}

class ShoppingFlow {

    void handleOrderAdd() {
        ...
        String isbnText = ...
        int qty = Integer.parseInt(qtyText);
        ...
        order.addItem(isbn, qty);
        ...
    }

}
```

Checks that the order isn't closed

Validates ISBN format

Uses validated ISBN to search for book

Checks that there are enough books left for sale

Adds the quantity of books to the order

Calls the order entity to update it

Did we validate or not? Should we have?

In 10 lines of code, addItem manages to validate arguments, check the state of the order, check the availability of books, and manage the list of ordered items. Seems solid, doesn't it? In this online bookstore, those snippets of code that validate ISBNs are repeated throughout the code, so often that they are almost an idiom in the codebase.

What about the mistake? There are two. First, the code doesn't verify the checksum of the ISBN. That's a minor flaw and most probably harmless. But second, the code doesn't check for negative quantities—the very flaw that led to the massive loss of money in the chapter 2 case study. If you noticed, good spotting, indeed. If you didn't, don't feel too bad about it. It's hard to spot these kinds of mistakes in a codebase you're shown like this. (In the case study, there was also a restriction that the quantity must be a maximum of 240 books because of restrictions from the storehouse and logistics. That check is also lacking in this code.)

Finding mistakes gets even trickier with a more realistic codebase. A realistic codebase needs to take even more aspects into account. For example, it needs to do error handling, something this example glosses over. A realistic `addItem` would throw `Item-CannotBeAddedException` and `InvalidISBNException` when appropriate. It would also include a `for` loop for finding if the ISBN was already in the order to avoid several `OrderLine`s with the same ISBN. To make even more of a mess, the code would be riddled with outdated functionality, like last year's promotional campaign where you received one cookbook for free if you bought three books on home furnishing. The code that was added then is no longer used and hasn't been removed. The same goes for the code for the Christmas campaign. There would also be the VIP customer cases with a discount on express shipping, and free shipping under certain circumstances would be patched in there somewhere in the mess. The list goes on. In a large and hairy method like that, it wouldn't be strange if you didn't notice a missing range check.

The reason why it's so easy to miss the details even in a simple example is due to some fundamental psychology. We humans are good at recognizing similarities and unconsciously look for supporting evidence. This is why people have to be trained to check ID cards. Without training, you'll look at the person in front of you, look at the card, and think, "Yeah, two eyes, a nose in the middle, a chin at the bottom—seems to match," or some subtly more advanced version of the same idea. Police training includes special classes to avoid doing this. Psychologists call this human trait of looking for matches *confirmation bias*, and the phenomenon has been systematically studied since the 1960s.[9]

How does this apply when looking at code? When you read code, most of the code you see is correct. The lazy brain thinks, "The code I've seen this far looks good," and it subconsciously makes the hypothesis, "The rest is probably OK as well." After that, your tendency for confirmation bias will make you nod every time something looks OK and makes it almost impossible to find the spots where the code is incomplete or wrong.

You've probably experienced this phenomenon the other way around as well. When you find the first bug, the spell is broken, and suddenly you see bugs all over the place. It's a little bit like searching for mushrooms in the forest or bird watching—at first you see none, but when you spot the first, you suddenly see them everywhere. We as humans have a tendency to miss subtle details such as validation when looking at lots of code, and, at the same time, missing validation is something that can cause severe security problems. There's clearly a need to declutter our entities.

5.3.2   *Decluttering entities*

Now that you've seen the security risks of cluttered entities, let's see how to use domain primitives to avoid these problems. Domain primitives naturally contain a lot of relevant validation. When the entity code isn't burdened with those pieces of validation, it

---

[9] Confirmation bias is the human tendency to notice things that confirm our preexisting beliefs and to pay less attention to things that aren't in line with our expectations or prejudices. The term was coined by Peter Wason in his 1960 article in the *Quarterly Journal of Experimental Psychology*, "On the Failure to Eliminate Hypotheses in a Conceptual Task."

can focus on the kind of validation it's best suited to do. Let's quickly revise the different levels of validation we investigated in chapter 4:

- *Origin*—Is the data from a legitimate sender?
- *Size*—Is it reasonably big?
- *Lexical content*—Does it contain the right characters and encoding?
- *Syntax*—Is the format right?
- *Semantics*—Does the data make sense?

The last step, semantic validation, is clearly the kind of validation that entities should do. An entity knows the state and history of data and is well suited to judge whether the incoming data makes sense right here and now. But the earlier steps are checks that should be done before you bring the data to the entity.

Now let's put our domain primitives to use. You have the `Quantity` domain primitive created earlier (listing 5.1), which works well to replace the `int` parameter in `addItem`. Now you need a domain primitive to replace the ISBN `String`. The following listing constructs a domain primitive `ISBN` in the same way.

Listing 5.6   Domain primitive `ISBN` including validation logic

```
import org.apache.commons.lang3.Validate.*;

public class ISBN {
    private final String isbn;

    public ISBN(final String isbn) {
        notNull(isbn);
        isTrue(isbn.length() == 10);
        isTrue(isbn.matches("[0-9X]*"));
        isTrue(isbn.matches("[0-9]{9}[0-9X]"));
        isTrue(checksumValid(isbn));
        this.isbn = isbn;
    }

    private boolean checksumValid(String isbn) {
        // ...
    }
    ...
}
```

The constructor ensures that an ISBN object always contains a valid ISBN.

Here we remembered to verify the checksum— it need only be remembered in one place.

This class is written once, so there's no risk that you'll sometimes remember to verify the checksum and sometimes forget. The class contains all the validations for size, lexical content, and syntax, so when using `ISBN` in an entity, you don't have to clutter your entity code with that.

You can now revise the entity `Order` to peruse the domain primitives `ISBN` and `Quantity`, as seen in in listing 5.7. In the new version of the `Order` class, you'll see the improvement. To begin with, there's less code, but that's mostly due to some of the code having been moved elsewhere. More important is that the code is more to the point. It's about how to handle what needs to be done when adding a new item to the order.

Listing 5.7 Order using Quantity

```
class Order {

    public void addItem(ISBN isbn, Quantity qty) {          ◄────── The ISBN and quantity are
        Validate.notNull(isbn);                                    already validated in a neat
        Validate.notNull(qty);                                     package.

        if(this.paid == false) {          ◄────── Checks that the order isn't closed—
            Book book =                            this is still awkward, we'll work on it
                bookcatalogue.findByISBN(isbn);    in chapter 7.
            if (inventory.avaliableBooks(isbn)
                .greaterOrEqualTo(qty)) {          ◄────── The code actually says, "If
                addToItems(new OrderLine(book, qty));        inventory of available books
            }                                                of said ISBN is greater than or
        }                                                    equal to the quantity...."
    }

    private void addToItems(OrderLine bookQuantity) {
        ...
        items.add(new OrderLine(book, qty));      ◄────── Adds a new order line or
        ...                                                updates an existing one if
    }                                                      book is already in order
}


class ShoppingFlow {

    void handleOrderAdd() {
        ...
        String isbn = ...
        int qty = ...
        ...                                  Anything calling the entity
        order.addItem(new ISBN(isbn),        needs to package each data
                    new Quantity(qty));      ◄────── item in a validated wrapper.

        ...
    }
}
```

The format of ISBN is already done. (annotation pointing to `bookcatalogue.findByISBN(isbn)`)

The method addItem doesn't have to carry the burden of earlier stages of validation, only the final part—the step we called *semantics*—which asks, "Does the data make sense right now?" You can see that here there's less code in the method, so there's less risk for mistakes should you need to update it. Also, the validation is handled consistently by domain primitives, so there's no risk of forgetting to verify the checksum of the ISBN or that the quantity isn't a negative number.

The client code in ShoppingFlow from listing 5.5 can no longer send in a naked String for the ISBN and an int for the quantity. Any attempt at doing so generates a compiler error. To be able to call Order.addItem, the client code needs to create an ISBN object and a Quantity object, and because the constructors of ISBN and Quantity contain validation, there's no longer any risk of sending the entity unvalidated data. The validation is pushed to the caller.

There could be validation problems when the calling client tries to construct ISBN or Quantity. If that happens, the client code needs to get back to the calling GUI to have those problems resolved; for example, by asking the user to correct the data. Note the separation of concerns: the client code ensures that the validation is done, but how it's done is the responsibility of the domain primitives ISBN and Quantity.

Up to this point, we've discussed method arguments. The same discussion applies to arguments of constructors. We've also found it valuable to apply the same ideas for the return values and data fields that the entity holds.

> **TIP**   Use domain primitives for method arguments, constructor arguments, return values, and data fields in entities.

The main benefits of using domain primitives in entity code include the following:

- *Input is always validated.* The type system ensures you use domain primitives.
- *Validation is consistent.* It's always done by the domain primitive constructor.
- *Entity code is less cluttered and more to the point.* It doesn't need to do boundary checks, format controls, and so on.
- *Entity code is more readable.* It speaks the language of the domain.

Using domain primitives isn't the only way to reap these benefits. We've found that using domain primitives as the arguments for methods in particular is just the best way for ensuring that entities use well-validated input.

5.3.3   *When to use domain primitives in entities*

Offloading the burden of validation to entities by using domain primitives is a powerful technique. In fact, it's so powerful we have a hard time finding examples of when *not* to use it. It needs to be a situation where there's no (or almost no) need to validate input, a situation where all data would be allowed. Perhaps a time series of temperatures would be simple enough? But even then, you don't want to accept a temperature below absolute zero ($0°$K, which equates to $-273°$C or $-460°$F).[10] Finding a situation where something is just an int or a completely unrestricted String is hard.

We sometimes hear the argument that the extra wrapper object (such as the ISBN around the String) adds a performance penalty at runtime. In principle, that's true, but it's seldom a practical concern. Remember that you want to run the ISBN validation anyway, and you either do it inside the ISBN constructor or in some other way so that it doesn't add to the performance penalty. It's the allocation and management of an extra object that's extra.

Using modern garbage collection, there'll be almost no penalty for this kind of short-lived object: the allocation of memory only takes about 10 machine instructions, and the deallocation of memory is most often zero-cost.[11] And all of these concerns are dwarfed as soon as you touch a database or make a call over the network.

---

[10] Absolute zero is the lowest possible temperature, where nothing could be colder and no heat energy remains in a substance. See https://www.sciencedaily.com/terms/absolute_zero.htm.

[11] For more on this, see Brian Goetz's September 27, 2005, article "Urban Performance Legends, Revisited" at http://www.ibm.com/developerworks/library/j-jtp09275/.

The performance constraints mentioned are in the range of nano- to microseconds, whereas a database round-trip is measured in milliseconds. It takes an extreme situation to care about object allocation, perhaps big data analysis, but if you have a situation where you are crunching enormous amounts of numbers in memory or programming for a restricted device, you might not use entities at all.

It's worth noting that the pattern of using domain primitives inside entities doesn't only apply to greenfield development, where you're creating a new entity. When you touch an entity for maintenance or further development, you take the chance of improving it by changing the signature to use domain primitives. If there's no suitable domain primitive, you've probably found a suitable time to introduce a new one. (We've had codebases that we've slowly turned around by using this trick and doing one small step each time we worked on the code.) After a while, your domain primitive library grows richer, and your entities become more focused. In chapter 12, we talk about what to do with legacy code, and we'll dive deeper into this aspect.

Now you've seen how domain primitives provide a solid building ground, due largely to the fact that they relieve the rest of the code of the burden of validation. Let's end this chapter by taking a look at some computer science research that has been done that's relevant to this area. In computer science, tracing potentially dangerous input and ensuring that it's validated (to some degree) before it's used is known as *taint analysis*.

5.4 Taint analysis

In the field of security research, taint analysis investigates how to stop malicious attack data from being used by marking input as tainted. Attack data can be web content with embedded JavaScript that installs a keylogger, or it might contain embedded SQL commands that attempt to destroy the database or reveal its content. Every input is considered suspicious until it has been cleared of suspicion, which is done when the data is checked through some mechanism. Should uncleaned (still tainted) data be used in a sensitive way (for example, if it's shown to a user or written to the database), then you've found a security risk, and the taint analysis will raise an alert.

The interesting part is that taint analysis can be done at runtime and can track every input on its way through the system by setting a *taint bit*. If data that's still tainted is sent to the database or otherwise used in a sensitive way, the taint analysis system intercepts it and stops this from happening (figure 5.6).

Each taint analysis tool has specific rules for what to check, when to intercept, and how to clean data. But most follow the same framework for terminology.[12] The framework consists of four parts:

- *Taint sources*—The places where dirty input might come into the system, which can be user interfaces, import jobs, or integrations with external systems
- *Untainting*—The way data is cleaned of suspicion through some type of check

---

[12] The framework is described in "Dytan: A Generic Dynamic Taint Analysis Framework" (2007) by James Clause, Wanchun Li, and Alessandro Orso of the Georgia Institute of Technology (https://www.cc .gatech.edu/~orso/papers/clause.li.orso.ISSTA07.pdf).

- *Propagation policy*—What determines whether the result is marked tainted or not when data is processed or combined
- *Taint sinks*—The places where data is used in a sensitive way: rendered to the user, written to the database, or similar

The taint analysis tool that implements the framework needs to interact with the runtime platform. For example, an implementation for systems written in Java would interact with the JVM as it runs the bytecode.[13] It extends the memory representation on the heap of each object with a taint bit and places itself between the bytecode and the JVM so that it can do taint analysis at all times.

In Java, the *taint sources* can be defined by pointing out specific methods in the standard libraries. For example, it would probably be interesting to trace anything that enters the system through `InputStream.read` but not `Random.nextBytes`. The tool can also distinguish between different input streams; for example, by tainting `InputStream.read` if the `InputStream` is a result of a `Socket.getInputStream` but not if it was created through `new FileInputStream(...)`.

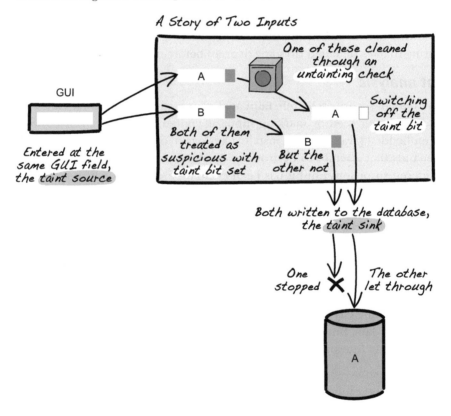

Figure 5.6   Tainted data stopped; cleaned data let through

---

[13] See, for example, "Dynamic Taint Propagation for Java," by Vivek Haldar, Deepak Chandra, and Michael Franz (https://www.acsac.org/2005/papers/45.pdf).

Untainting happens when data is considered to be checked. The analysis tool, however, doesn't know when the data is checked because it neither knows the domain rules of the application nor has any insight into the programmer's brain. Instead, it has to rely on heuristics. For example, if a `String` is matched to a regexp through `String.matches`, the tool can assume that the programmer has done some sensible check, but strictly it cannot know. Usual approaches for tools to do untainting include looking for regexp checks for strings, comparisons (`<`, `=`, `>`) for numbers, and so on. If the code doesn't react, then the taint analysis considers that the programmer has accepted the data as clean, and the taint bit is switched to false. Another case is when the data is passed as an argument to a constructor. If the constructor doesn't react, then the platform takes it as a sign that the programmer thought that the string was OK, and it's no longer considered tainted.

The taint *propagation policy* needs to determine when the taint bit should change. For example, if two strings are concatenated, then the resulting string is tainted if either of the concatenated strings is tainted; it's clean only if both strings are clean. If a string is substringed, then the result is clean if the original string is clean; otherwise, it's tainted, and so on.

Finally, *taint sinks* are those methods that are deemed sensitive. The method `java.sql.Statement.execute` is certainly deemed sensitive. Writing to a local file through `FileWriter.write` might be deemed uncontroversial, or it could require a taint check. If the taint check fails, the taint analysis intercepts the execution and throws a `SecurityException`.

> **NOTE** Running an application with taint analysis instrumentation is currently undergoing research, not something we advise you to do in production—the performance penalty is way too high.

What's interesting is to compare the role that taint analysis puts on the constructor. Clearly the constructor is considered a central place for validation—if a string has passed the constructor, it should be validated. Obviously, if you were to write a constructor that didn't validate string parameters, you'd render the taint analysis worthless.

Many contemporary systems would probably not run for many seconds with concurrent taint analysis before the taint check at a taint sink threw an exception. In many systems, we've seen numerous ways for a string to end up in a database without being checked by a regexp or in a constructor, and when that happens, the taint system will protest. On the other hand, a system with a design that's built on domain primitives would probably run smoothly.

Taint analysis has no formal connection to our idea about domain primitives, but it's refreshing to see that the two ideas are so well aligned. Although concurrent taint analysis during runtime sounds like an interesting idea, it's unfortunately not practical for production yet. In the meantime, you can design your systems with domain primitives and get a lot of the security benefits anyway.

This chapter has focused on how to form a stable foundation for the domain representation. Domain primitives form sound and secure building blocks on which larger structures can be built. You have seen what domain primitives can do directly for entities. The next chapter will dive into other challenges that entities face, how they might become insecure, and what you can do about it.

Summary

- Domain primitives are the smallest building blocks and form the basis of your domain model.
- You should never represent a concept in your domain model as a language primitive or a generic type.
- If a term in your domain already exists outside of your domain but with a slightly different meaning, you should introduce a new term instead of redefining the existing one.
- A domain primitive is immutable and can only exist if it's valid in the current domain.
- When domain primitives are used, the rest of the code is greatly simplified and becomes more secure.
- You should harden APIs by using your domain primitive library.
- A read-once object is a useful way to represent sensitive data in your code.
- The value of a read-once object can only be retrieved once.
- The read-once object design pattern can mitigate leakage of sensitive data.
- Domain primitives provide the same type of security that concurrent taint analysis would.

Ensuring integrity of state

This chapter covers

- Managing mutable states using entities
- Ensuring an entity is consistent on creation
- Ensuring an entity keeps its integrity

Mutable state is an important aspect of systems. To some degree, changing state is the point of many systems, like the online bookstore of chapter 2. The system keeps track of a variety of state changes: books are put in a shopping cart, the order is paid for, and the books are shipped to the customer. If there aren't state changes, not much interesting happens.[1] Mutable state can be represented technically in many different ways. We'll take a look at some alternatives and explore our preferred way—explicitly modeling mutable state in the style of Domain-Driven Design (DDD) as entities, as described in chapter 3.

Because entities contain the state that represents your business, it's important that a newly created entity follow the business rules. Entities that can be created in an inconsistent state can cause both bugs and security flaws that are hard to find or

---

[1] Some conceptually interesting programming languages, such as Haskell, attempt to achieve this when programming with strictly immutable constructs. But most languages (Java, C, C#, Ruby, and Python, to name a few) do it using mutable constructs such as stateful objects.

detect. But fulfilling all the constraints at the moment of creation can be difficult. How difficult depends on how strict or complicated the constraints are. We'll walk through a couple of techniques that are suitable for handling most mutable states, starting with simple techniques for simple constraints and ending up with the builder pattern, which can handle even pretty complicated situations.

Once entities are created consistently, they need to stay consistent. We'll guide you through some common traps that can risk the integrity of your entities, as well as providing advice on how to design so that your entities stay secure. Let's get started with different ways of managing state so you can see why using entities is our preferred way.

6.1   *Managing state using entities*

A central theme for most systems is to track how the state of things changes. As a bag is loaded onto a plane, both the state of the bag and the state of the plane change, and suddenly new rules apply. The bag can't be opened any longer, which it could be before it was loaded. On the other hand, it can now be unloaded—something that wasn't possible before. For the plane, the load it carries increases. This is what computer scientists call *mutable state*. In the systems you write, you need to keep track of these state changes and ensure that all the changes follow the rules.

If the systems you write don't handle change properly, you'll have security issues sooner or later, whether mild or severe. A luggage handling system at an airport needs to keep track of bags. If a bag hasn't been screened, it's not allowed to be loaded onto a plane, and the system must stop that from happening. The system must also keep track of what bags belong to which passenger and whether that passenger boards the flight. If the passenger doesn't show, the bags must be unloaded. Not doing so is a severe security risk and could be dangerous.

All designs in this chapter revolve around modeling change as *entities* (to use the terminology of DDD). As we described in chapter 3, DDD describes entities as things with a durable identity, whose state can change over its lifetime. The baggage in the airport is a good example. It can be checked in, screened, loaded onto, and unloaded from flights, but we still perceive it as the same bag with a changed state. Entities are our preferred way to implement mutable state, but let's briefly look at the alternatives (figure 6.1).

When implementing a system, there are many ways to track and handle how state changes:

- You can keep state in a cookie.
- You can make changes in the database directly using SQL or stored procedures.
- You can use an application that loads the state from the server, updates the state, and sends it back.

All of these approaches are possible and have various merits. Unfortunately, a lot of systems are made up of an inconsistent mix of these approaches. This is a risk. If the responsibility for holding state and controlling its changes is too spread out, there's a danger that the different parts won't fit together perfectly. Those small logical cracks are what open up the possibility of security breaches. Therefore, what we prefer is a

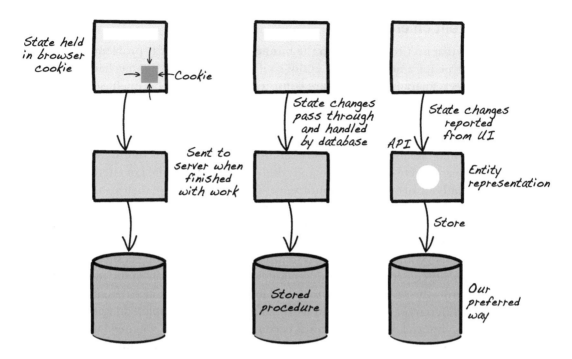

Figure 6.1 Some different ways to implement state

kind of design where it's easy to see what states are allowed and what changes are permitted according to the state.

In our experience, the most effective way to ensure a mutable state is handled in a safe and secure way is to model states as entities in the style of DDD. During modeling, you decide what concepts are most important to model. Is it bag, flight, and passenger that makes it easiest to understand the rules, or should you think about the situation in terms of check-in, loading, and boarded travelers? In the first case, the business rule can be expressed as "a bag is only allowed to be on the same flight as the passenger that checked in the bag." In the second case, the same rule would be rephrased as "the loading of the plane may only contain checked-in bags that belong to the boarded travelers." In this example, you might agree that the first phrase reads more easily, so that would be your model. But it's effort well spent to explore different models, as we described in chapter 3, and to seek deeper understanding, as the case study in chapter 2 showed.

Entities have the benefit of collecting all the understanding of state and how it changes in the same place. We also prefer to implement mutable state using a class that keeps the data with the associated behavior as methods in the same class. You'll see numerous examples of this in this chapter and the following chapter, which focuses on how to reduce the complexity of state.

Entities can be designed in an infinite number of ways, so we're going to share some of our favorite tricks and patterns to keep your design and code clear and secure. The rest of this chapter is about how to create and keep entities in a consistent state that upholds business integrity. Let's get started with how to create entities in a secure way.

6.2   *Consistent on creation*

An entity that isn't consistent with the business rules is a security problem. This is particularly true for a newly created entity, so it's important that the mechanism for creating objects guarantees entities are consistent on creation. This might seem obvious, but still it's sometimes treated as a technicality—and the consequences just might be disastrous.

A colleague of ours was once working with a large Asian bank. He found several security vulnerabilities, but they were all dismissed as minor technical flaws. It wasn't until he managed to create an account without an owner that he got attention. A bank account without an owner is an abhorrence, and the existence of such an account could cause a bank to lose its banking license. Suddenly the issue was escalated to top management, who gave it the highest priority.

An entity that isn't consistent with the rules is a security problem, and the best way we've found to counteract this risk is to insist that every entity object should be consistent *immediately* on creation. In this section, we'll show the perils of the most common anti-pattern—the no-arg constructor—and look at some alternative designs. We'll walk through different ways to create an entity, starting with the simplest and progressing to the more advanced. When constraints become more complex, you need more complicated constructions. Simple constructions suffice for simple constraints. We'll start with the simplest construction of all, the no-arg constructor, which is so simple, it's useful for almost nothing at all. We'll end with the builder pattern for handling the most complex situations.

Because entities often represent data that's stored and changed over a long period of time, entities are often saved in a database. If you have a relational database together with an object-relational mapper (ORM) such as JPA or Hibernate, there's often confusion that leads to bad and insecure design. We'll comment on different ways of using such frameworks in a way that doesn't violate security.

Although our introductory example in this chapter was from the financial domain, the problem isn't restricted to that domain. We find inconsistent newly created entities in code in all kinds of domains. One thing that many have in common is that they often stem from constructing objects using a no-arg constructor.

6.2.1   *The perils of no-arg constructors*

The simplest way to create an entity is definitely using the constructor. And what could be simpler than calling a constructor without any arguments (aka, a *no-arg constructor*)? The problem is that no-arg constructors seldom live up to the promise of creating a fully consistent, ready-to-use object.

If you think about it, a no-arg constructor is a strange thing to find in code. It promises not only to create a Car object, for instance, but a car for which you don't need to specify any attributes at all. It doesn't have a color, a number of doors, or even a brand. Or, if it has any of those attributes, it's a default value that should apply to all cars on creation. In practice, no-arg constructors don't stand up to the contract for constructors to create consistent objects that are ready to use.

Often, we encounter entities that seem to have a convention for creation: first you call a no-arg constructor, then you call a number of setter methods to initialize the object before it's ready to be used. But there's nothing in the code that enforces this convention. And, sadly, the convention is often forgotten or broken in a way that leads to inconsistent entities.

> **WARNING** Where there's a no-arg constructor for an entity, there's probably setter-based initialization, which is most probably trouble. Setter-based initializations risk becoming incomplete; incomplete initializations result in inconsistent objects.

Let's look at the kind of code we often encounter. In listing 6.1, you see an `Account` class with some attributes: an account must have an account number, an owner, and an interest rate. It might also have an optional credit limit, which allows the account to go into debt to a certain degree, or a fallback account (often a savings account), from which money will be drawn if needed to prevent the account from becoming empty or going into debt. The method `AccountService.openAccount` shows how this no-arg constructor is intended to be used. First the constructor is called, and then the `Account` object is filled with data by calling one setter method after another.

Listing 6.1 Account class with no-arg construction and setter initialization

```java
public class Account {
    private AccountNumber number;
    private LegalPerson owner;            ── Mandatory
    private Percentage interest;
    private Money creditLimit;
    private AccountNumber fallbackAccount;  ── Optional

    public Account() {}      ◄──── In Java, if you leave out the constructor,
                                   you'll get a public no-arg constructor.

    public AccountNumber getNumber() {
        return number;                      Clients must remember to
    }                                       call these methods before
                                            the object is ready to use.
    public void setNumber(AccountNumber number) {  ◄──
        this.number = number;
    }

    public LegalPerson getOwner() {
        return owner;
    }

    public void setOwner(LegalPerson owner) {  ◄──
        this.owner = owner;
    }
    ...
}
```

```
class AccountService {

    void openAccount() {
        Account account= new Account();
        account.setNumber(number);
        account.setOwner(accountowner);
        account.setInterest(interest);
        account.setCreditLimit(limit);
        ...
    }
}
```

An inconsistent, newly created object needs setter-based initialization.

Client code required to set all mandatory fields, forgetting none

Setting one optional field

What this approach lets you do is create a completely blank object and then fill in the fields you want. But there's no guarantee your Account object will fulfill even the most fundamental and important business constraints. Furthermore, the design is brittle because it relies on every creation to remember all the steps. If the conditions change, there's an update nightmare. For example, as part of international attempts to curb corruption, many countries have passed financial regulations on people classified as politically exposed. People in government, for instance, might be more exposed to temptations of corruption or bribery due to the influence of their office. Each account has to trace whether the owner is a politically exposed person or not.

Imagine you're working with Account and are given the requirement that it needs a new mandatory field, boolean politicallyExposedPerson. Also, it's required to set the field explicitly each time an entity is created. Now you need to find every single place the constructor new Account() is called and ensure that setPolitically-ExposedPerson is also called.

The compiler doesn't point out mistakes as it would if you added a parameter to a constructor argument list. A well-honed suite of unit tests would catch the errors, but the codebases with no-arg constructors we see have seldom had those kinds of test suites. Unfortunately, some places will be overlooked each time an attribute is added; not necessarily the same place every time, but rather different places each time. Over time, that kind of process tends to result in an inconsistent codebase, where sooner or later there are security loopholes.

> **TIP** Where there's a no-arg constructor for an entity, there's probably setter-based initialization, which is most probably trouble.

6.2.2   *ORM frameworks and no-arg constructors*

If you use an object-relational mapper framework such as JPA (Java Persistence API) or Hibernate, it might seem like you're forced into having a no-arg constructor for your entities. Tutorials for these frameworks inevitably start with creating an entity with a no-arg constructor, and it looks like that's the way code should or must be written. But that's not completely true. If you use such frameworks, you have two options for avoiding security loopholes in this regard: either separating the domain model from the persistence model or ensuring that the persistence framework is secured from exposing inconsistent objects.

The first alternative is to conceptually separate from the persistence model. If you do this, your persistence model resides in a separate package, together with other infrastructure code. When you load data from the database, the persistence framework loads it into objects in the persistence package. Thereafter, you construct domain objects using those objects before letting the domain objects handle business-logic calls. In this way, you're completely in charge of any creation of domain objects, and any JPA annotations stay in the persistence package.

> **TIP** Separate the domain model and persistence model to emphasize that they are different contexts and to make the mapping explicit.

If you don't make this distinction and directly map your domain objects using the persistence framework, you'll need to do due diligence on how you use the framework instead. We know this style is pretty common, and it's possible to do it in a secure way, so we'd like to share some tricks for doing so.

When it comes to no-arg constructors, it's true that persistence frameworks like Hibernate and JPA do need a no-arg constructor. The reason for this is that the framework needs to create objects when it loads data from the database. The way it does so is by internally creating an empty object and then filling it with data from the database through reflection. It therefore needs to have a no-arg constructor to start with. But neither JPA nor Hibernate needs a public constructor—they can do well with a private no-arg constructor. Furthermore, the frameworks don't need setter methods to inject the data; it can be done through reflection directly into private fields if you set the persistence style to field annotations.

> **TIP** If you use your domain model as a persistence model, then create *private* no-arg constructors and use field annotations to avoid opening up your domain objects to the risks of inconsistent creation or usage.

Now, let's move on to what you can do about this situation. Because you don't want a no-arg constructor, you can instead use a constructor that sets all mandatory fields.

6.2.3 *All mandatory fields as constructor arguments*

Let's take a look at the simplest way of solving the security problem of inconsistent entities: instead of using a no-arg constructor that doesn't convey enough information for consistent creation, use a constructor where you pass in all the required information (figure 6.2).

Figure 6.2   We don't want half-finished cars to be visible to the outside.

Extend the constructor parameter list until all mandatory information is sent. There's no need for parameters for optional information at this stage. Ensure that the entity is created in a fully consistent state. Optional information can be supplied after the entity is constructed by calling one method at a time.

Listing 6.2 shows the result of applying this approach to the previous Account example. The constructor requires an account number, owner, and interest rate—all the mandatory attributes. The optional attributes for credit limit and fallback account aren't in the constructor list but are set afterwards via separate method calls.

Listing 6.2   Constructor takes the mandatory attributes, methods the optional

```
import org.apache.commons.lang3.Validate.*;

public class Account {
    private AccountNumber number;
    private LegalPerson owner;
    private Percentage interest;
    private Money creditLimit;
    private AccountNumber fallbackAccount;

    public Account(AccountNumber number,        Takes all arguments needed
                   LegalPerson owner,           to create a fully valid object
                   Percentage interest) {
```

```
        this.number = notNull(number);
        this.owner = notNull(owner);
        this.interest = notNull(interest);
    }

    protected Account() {}

    public AccountNumber number() { ... }

    public LegalPerson owner() { ... }

    public void changeInterest(
                Percentage interest) {
        notNull(interest);
        this.interest = interest;
    }

    public Money creditlimit() { ... }

    public void changeCreditLimit(
                Money creditLimit) {
        notNull(creditLimit);
        this.creditLimit = creditLimit;
    }

    public AccountNumber fallbackAccount() {
        return fallbackAccount;
    }

    public void changeFallbackAccount(AccountNumber fallbackAccount) {
        notNull(fallbackAccount);
        this.fallbackAccount = Validate.notNull(fallbackAccount);
    }

    public void clearFallbackAccount() {
        this.fallbackAccount = null;
    }
}

class AccountService {
    void openAccount() {
        AccountNumber number = ...
        LegalPerson accountowner = ...
        Percentage interest = ...
        Money limit = ...
        Account account =
            new Account(number,
                        accountowner,
                        interest);
        account.changeCreditLimit(limit);
        accountRepostitory.registerNew(account);
    }
}
```

Checks that nothing tries to sneak in null arguments

Nonpublic constructor might be needed for persistence framework

Accessor method with a more domain-friendly name than one prefixed with get

It's possible to change the interest rate even after the account is created.

The interest rate is mandatory even if it's changed and can't be null.

Domain-friendly name of method that changes the credit limit

Number, owner, interest, and limit are fetched from other services.

No risk of forgetting any mandatory data

Optional field (not in constructor) as separate method call

Because the constructor list contains mandatory fields, don't expect any of them to have a `null` argument at any time. You can include such checks in the constructor.

TIP   Check your constructor arguments for `null` values.

The history of the JavaBeans set/get naming conventions

In listing 6.2, we renamed setter and getter methods to names that better describe their role in the domain. As mentioned in the previous section, there's a misconception that persistence frameworks need set/get methods to work properly. The same functionality can be obtained without set/get methods by using field annotations. Frameworks such as Hibernate and Spring Data JPA do their work using reflection and can find private attributes that way. There's no need for public methods with some specific naming convention for that reason.

We'd also like to put the set/get naming convention into perspective. The convention was created in 1996 as part of the JavaBeans specification.[*] The basic idea of JavaBeans was to create a framework that enabled suppliers to provide off-the-shelf components (called *beans*) that could be bought separately and then assembled to work together using graphical tools. This vision was never successful, and the specification never got beyond version 1.01. But for some reason the strange naming convention of using set and get as prefixes stuck. The framework also contained a more interesting part on how to make components communicate through events, which sadly didn't catch on in the same way.

Apart from the residual naming convention of set and get, the JavaBeans specification is basically dead. We see little value in following a naming convention with a purpose no longer found to be desirable. We prefer to name methods in the code according to the original idea of object orientation—that methods correspond to actions in the domain, as in an object has a method to handle a message it receives.

----

[*]   See http://download.oracle.com/otndocs/jcp/7224-javabeans-1.01-fr-spec-oth-JSpec/.

We are slowly moving from the most basic objects with only mandatory attributes toward more complex conditions, sometimes with more attributes. Taking all those attributes as parameters to the constructor soon becomes awkward. We guess you've felt the awkwardness of 20-parameter constructors at some point.[2] Also, with more complex conditions that span between attributes, it's hard for a constructor to uphold them.

The most complex types of entities will need the builder pattern to be created in a feasible way. But, on our way to the builder pattern, we'll first look at an interesting way to create objects with mandatory and optional fields in a way that makes the code on the client side read fluently. We turn our attention next to fluent interfaces.

----

[2]   If you have 20 parameters, then some of them might feasibly be "baked together" to something that is conceptually whole. For example, a monetary amount and a currency might be put together into a Money object. See the discussion on conceptual whole in chapter 3.

6.2.4 Construction with a fluent interface

For construction of more advanced entities with more constraints, you need a more potent tool. Eventually we'll get to the builder pattern, but we aren't there yet. On our way to this, we'll start with a design style that makes the builder pattern easier to understand and use, as well as making the client code simpler to read and ensuring it does the right thing. We're talking about the fluent interface.

This style of interface design was given its name by Eric Evans and Martin Fowler in 2005, even though the design style it describes has roots in the Smalltalk community that dates back to the 1970s. The ambition of a *fluent interface* is to make the code read more like a fluent text in a natural language, and this is often accomplished through the form of method chaining.

Let's describe this style by applying it so you can see how it affects the code needed to set up an entity. Listing 6.3 shows the code for `Account`, adapted to provide a fluent interface. The constructor doesn't change, but note the methods for the optional credit limit and fallback account. These methods also return a reference to the modified instance, the object itself. You can see in `AccountService.openAccount` how this enables the client code to chain or cascade these method calls so that the code almost reads as text.

> **Listing 6.3 `Account` class with a fluent interface**

```
public class Account {
    private final AccountNumber number;
    private final LegalPerson owner;
    private Percentage interest;
    private Money creditLimit;
    private AccountNumber fallbackAccount;

    public Account(AccountNumber number,
        LegalPerson owner,
        Percentage interest) {
        ...          ◄──────────────────┤ Same, same, no difference
    }

    public Account withCreditLimit(Money creditLimit) {
        this.creditLimit = creditLimit;
        return this;
    }

    public Account withFallbackAccount(AccountNumber fallbackAccount) {
        this.fallbackAccount = fallbackAccount;
        return this;
    }
}

class AccountService {
```

The with... methods return a reference to the object itself to allow chaining.

```
void openAccount() {
    Account account = new Account(number,
                                  accountowner,
                                  interest)
                       .withCreditLimit(limit)
                       .withFallbackAccount(fallbackAccount);

    ...

}
}
```

> A new account with a credit
> limit and fallback account set

There's no doubt that fluent interfaces yield code that reads differently from conventional code; it reads more fluently. But there are trade-offs. Most importantly, this design style clashes with one flavor of the command-query separation (CQS) principle, which states that a method should either be a command or a query.[3] A usual interpretation is that a command should change state but return nothing, and a query should return the answer but change nothing. In this example of a fluent interface, the with... methods do change state but don't have void as a return type—perhaps a small violation, but certainly something to take into account.

Nonfluent fluent interface

If you start at lots of setters and take a half-step toward fluent interfaces, you end up with setters that return this.

```
class Person {
  private String firstname;
  ...
  public Person setFirstName(String firstname) {
    this.firstname = firstname;
    return this;
  }
  ...
}
```

This makes it possible to chain the setters in the same way as in a fluent interface. In this way, you might get code like the following:

```
Person p = new Person()
          .setFirstName("Deve").setLastName("Loper")
          .setProfession("Developer");
```

From a technical perspective, it's very similar to fluent interfaces. In a way, the object acts as its own builder (more on the builder pattern in the next section). But it completely misses the fluent part—it doesn't read well, which is an important ambition for fluent interfaces.

Fluent interfaces work well when you want to enrich your object under creation, one step at a time (first credit limit, then fallback account). But the object needs to be consistent after each step. By themselves, fluent interfaces aren't enough to enforce

---

[3] This concept was introduced by Bertrand Meyer in his book *Object-Oriented Software Construction* (Prentice Hall, 1988).

advanced constraints. Alone, this approach doesn't handle restrictions that span multiple properties; for example, if an account is required to have either a credit limit or a fallback account but isn't allowed to have both. To handle these more advanced constraints, we'll combine fluent interfaces with the builder pattern—but first, you'll see what advanced constraints might look like.

6.2.5 *Catching advanced constraints in code*

Advanced constraints on an entity might be restrictions among attributes. If one attribute has a certain value, then other attributes are restricted in some way. If the attribute has another value, then the other attributes are restricted in other ways. These kinds of advanced constraints often take the form of *invariants*, or properties that need to be true during the entire lifetime of an object. Invariants must hold from creation and through all state changes that the object experiences.[4]

In our example of the bank account, we have two optional attributes: credit limit and fallback account. An advanced constraint might span both of these attributes. For the sake of the example, let's look at the situation where an account must have either but isn't allowed to have both (figure 6.3).

As a diligent programmer, you need to ensure that you never leave the object with any invariant broken. We've found it fruitful to capture such invariants in a specific method, which can be called when there's a need to ensure that the object is in a consistent state. In particular, it's called at the end of each public method before handing control back to the caller. In listing 6.4, you can see how the method `checkInvariants` contains these checks. In this listing, the method checks that there's either a credit limit or a fallback account, but not both. If this isn't the case, then `Validate.validState` throws an `IllegalStateException`.

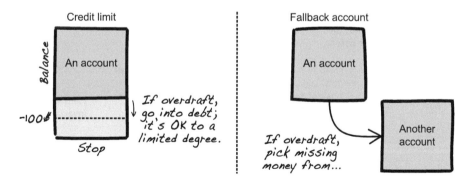

Account must have either overdraft safeguard mechanism but can't have both.

Figure 6.3 Safeguarding a bank account by either a credit limit or a fallback account

---

[4] Invariants were first described in *Object-Oriented Software Construction* by Bertrand Meyer (Prentice Hall, 1988).

Listing 6.4   Checking advanced constraints in separate method

```
import static org.apache.commons.lang3.Validate.validState;

    private void checkInvariants()
        throws IllegalStateException {
        validState(fallbackAccount != null
                ^ creditLimit != null);
    }
```

It isn't necessary to declare the exception, but it's done for clarity.

Fallback account or credit limit but not both (^ is the Java syntax for XOR operator.)

You don't need to call this method from outside the Account class—an Account object should always be consistent as seen from the outside. But why have a method that checks something that should always be true? The subtle point of the previous statement is that the invariants should always be true as seen from outside the object.

After a method has returned control to the caller outside the object, all the invariants must be fulfilled. But during the run of a method, there might be places where the invariants aren't fulfilled. For example, if switching from credit limit to fallback account, there might be a short period of time when the credit limit has been removed, but the fallback account isn't set yet. You can see this moment in listing 6.5: after creditLimit has been unset but before fallbackAccount is set, the Account object doesn't fulfill the invariants. This isn't a violation of the invariants, as the processing isn't finished yet. The method has its chance to clear up the mess before returning control to the caller.

Listing 6.5   Changing from a credit limit to a fallback account

After removing the credit limit, the account is temporarily inconsistent.

```
    public void changeToFallbackAccount(AccountNumber fallbackAccount) {
        this.creditLimit = null;
        this.fallbackAccount = fallbackAccount;
        checkInvariants();
    }
```

Fallback account set and invariants hold again

Checking invariants before returning control to the outside

TIP If you have advanced constraints, end every public method with a call to your home-brewed checkInvariants method.

The design pattern of having a validation method together with the fluent interface design lets you tackle a lot of complexity. But there'll always be situations where that doesn't suffice. The ultimate tool is the builder pattern, which is the topic of the next section.

6.2.6 *The builder pattern for upholding advanced constraints*

You have seen how to ensure an object is created consistently by adding all mandatory fields to the constructor and using setters for optional attributes. But if there are constraints between optional attributes, this doesn't suffice.

Let's continue the example where a bank account must have either a credit limit or a fallback account set but not both. We'd like to do the construction in steps but still ensure that the object is fully created with all constraints fulfilled before the rest of the code gets access to it. This is what the *builder pattern* does.[5]

The basic idea of the builder pattern is to hide the complexity of constructing an entity within another object, the builder. Figure 6.4 shows how a car builder hides the car so that you never need to see the half-built car; it's revealed when the assembly is finished and the car is complete.

Now let's see what this looks like in code using the account example. In listing 6.6, you see the client code. We start by creating an `AccountBuilder`, fiddle around with it (ordering it to build an account inside itself), and when we're satisfied, we tell the `AccountBuilder` to reveal the finished account.

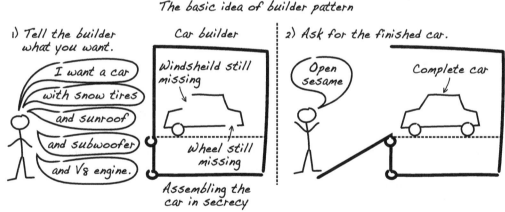

The basic idea of builder pattern

1) *Tell the builder what you want.*
I want a car
with snow tires
and sunroof
and subwoofer
and V8 engine.

Car builder
Windsheild still missing
Wheel still missing
Assembling the car in secrecy

2) *Ask for the finished car.*
Open sesame
Complete car

You don't need to see the car in its incomplete and inconsistent intermediary stages.

Figure 6.4   Hiding a half-finished car until it's finished

---

[5]   This pattern was initially described by Erich Gamma, Richard Helm, Ralph Johnson, and John Vlissides, aka the "Gang of Four" (GoF), in their book *Design Patterns: Elements of Reusable Object-Oriented Software* (Addison-Wesley, 1994).

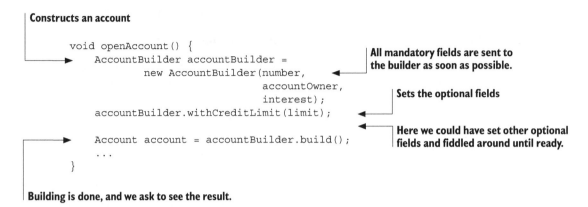

Listing 6.6   Account with a credit limit constructed using `AccountBuilder`

Constructs an account

```
void openAccount() {
    AccountBuilder accountBuilder =
            new AccountBuilder(number,
                                    accountOwner,
                                    interest);
    accountBuilder.withCreditLimit(limit);

    Account account = accountBuilder.build();
    ...
}
```

All mandatory fields are sent to the builder as soon as possible.

Sets the optional fields

Here we could have set other optional fields and fiddled around until ready.

Building is done, and we ask to see the result.

In this example, if you had wanted an account with a fallback account, you would have called `withFallbackAccount` before finishing the build. This pattern extends well to more complex situations too. In those cases, you fiddle around with the builder for a little bit longer, calling more methods to configure the product before calling `build` to obtain the final product. There's no need for a multitude of constructors or overloaded methods. And if `AccountBuilder` has a fluent interface where the method `withCredit-Limit` returns a reference to the builder itself, the code can be even more elegant:

```
void openAccount_fluent() {
    Account account =
            new AccountBuilder(number,
                                    accountOwner,
                                    interest)
                .withCreditLimit(limit)
                .build();
    ...
}
```

AccountBuilder with mandatory fields

Configured with credit limit

Calls build to yield the Account

The tricky part of the builder pattern is how to implement the builder. The account builder needs to be able to manipulate an `Account` object even when it's not consistent (something you want to avoid to start with). Remember that you can't let the builder leave the product in an inconsistent state, because the account builder can't work on the account from the outside.

The classic way of putting the builder on the inside is to put both classes (`Account` and its builder) in a module, then provide one interface that the account can show the rest of the world and another interface that the builder can work with. This works, but sooner or later you'll get a headache from doing that.

Listing 6.7 shows how we can get around this dilemma using inner classes in Java. The inner class `Builder` inside `Account` has access to the inner mechanics of `Account` without any special methods. Because `Builder` is a static class, it can create a not-yet-complete `Account` using the private constructor and work on it until the client on the outside calls the method `build` to reveal the finished `Account` object.

Listing 6.7 Builder of accounts implemented as an inner class

```
import static org.apache.commons.lang3.Validate.notNull;
import static org.apache.commons.lang3.Validate.validState;

public class Account {
    private final AccountNumber number;
    private final LegalPerson owner;
    private Percentage interest;
    private Money creditLimit;
    private AccountNumber fallbackAccount;

    private Account(AccountNumber number,
                    LegalPerson owner,
                    Percentage interest) {          The constructor is private because it's not
        this.number = notNull(number);             intended to be used from the outside.
        this.owner = notNull(owner);
        this.interest = notNull(interest);
    }

    ...

    private void checkInvariants() throws IllegalStateException {
        validState(fallbackAccount != null
                ^ creditLimit != null);            Fallback account or credit
    }                                              limit but not both

    public static class Builder {          Builder class to build an account
        private Account product;

        public Builder(AccountNumber number,        Constructor with mandatory
                       LegalPerson owner,           attributes to get building started
                       Percentage interest) {
            product = new Account(number, owner, interest);
        }
                                                            Methods to add optional
        public Builder withCreditLimit(Money creditLimit) {  arguments to the account
            validState(product != null);
            product.creditLimit = creditLimit;
            return this;
        }

        public Builder withFallbackAccount(AccountNumber fallbackAccount) {
            validState(product != null);
            product.fallbackAccount = fallbackAccount;
            return this;
        }
                                                Ensures the produced account
        public Account build() {                is consistent before releasing it
            validState(product != null);
            product.checkInvariants();          The builder object self-destructs
            Account result = product;           so it can't be used twice.
            product = null;
```

Support for fluent interface

```
        return result;      ◄─────┐  Releases a reference to the newly
    }                              │  constructed and consistent account
  }
}
```

By making the Account constructor private, you ensure that the only way to construct an account is with the Builder class and build method. The account under construction can be inconsistent as long as it can only be accessed by the builder object that's building it. But when it's time to release the account from the builder, it's required to fulfill all invariants.

When the Account is delivered to the caller using build(), you also make the builder object release the reference to the product (Account). This is to ensure that another call to build won't hand out another reference to the same Account. Once the builder produces an Account, it self-destructs. From an object-orientation theoretical point of view, the concept of an inner class is a bit strange, but from an implementation point of view, it's practical in this specific situation.

> **TIP** Think of a builder as a multistep constructor. When the constructed object is released, it must be consistent.

Used this way, the builder process replaces calling the constructor. Phrased slightly differently, you can say that when creating an object is a complex process, use the builder process in multiple steps; when it's a simple process, use a constructor in a single step. Note the similarity between the words *constructor* and *builder*—they mean the same thing.

Constructors galore

In theory, we can ensure some complicated constraints using constructors. You could have a constructor that has every single attribute as a parameter, whether mandatory or optional, and then check all constraints inside the constructor. But that would require you to allow null or Optional.empty() as constructor arguments—something that's confusing and not recommended. Another alternative would be to have one constructor for every valid combination of arguments. A class Foo with mandatory fields A, B, and C and an optional field D would need two constructors: Foo(A,B,C) and Foo(A,B,C,D). If there were instead two optional fields, D and E, it'd need four constructors: Foo(A,B,C), Foo(A,B,C,D), Foo(A,B,C,E), and Foo(A,B,C,D,E).

Under the hood, all these constructors would call the same underlying code, so there'd be no code duplication between them. Still, the number of outward-facing constructors can quickly grow unmanageable. With 3 parameters, there would need to be 8 constructors; with 7 parameters, there would need to be over 100; and with 10 parameters, you'd need more than 1,000 different constructors! You can't design code in such an unmanageable fashion. The builder pattern provides the same flexibility in a much more condensed way.

6.2.7   *ORM frameworks and advanced constraints*

When you have entities with the kind of complexity we're handling here, with constraints that span attributes, you need to think about how you relate to the database. This is true if you use an ORM framework such as JPA or Hibernate to directly map your domain objects to the database.

If your domain is small and you have full control of the only application that touches the database, you might consider it to be inside your security region, your trusted area of control. In that case, you might assume that the data in the database is consistent with your business rules and that you can safely load it into your application without validation. Things stay simple, but you should be sure you have strict control over your data.

If your domain is a little richer, or if you can't guarantee that you're the only one touching the database, we recommend that you look at the database as a separate system and validate data when loading it. If you're using your domain entities to directly map to the database using the ORM, things get more delicate. It's still possible, but we advise that you read up on persistence frameworks.

For advanced constraints, you'll need to ensure that the invariants hold after you've loaded the data from the database, which is exactly what the checkInvariants method does. All you need to do is ensure that it's run on load. This is what the annotation @PostLoad, demonstrated in the following listing, does in both JPA and Hibernate.

Listing 6.8   Integrating invariants check with an ORM framework

```
                    Runs after data has been
                    loaded from the database
@PostLoad   ◄───┘
private void checkInvariants() throws IllegalStateException {
    Validate.isTrue(fallbackAccount != null
            ^ creditLimit != null);   ◄───── Either fallback account or credit limit but not
}                                            both (^ is the Java syntax for XOR operator.)
```

6.2.8   *Which construction to use when*

In this section, we showed three patterns for ensuring that entities are created in a consistent state: constructor with mandatory attributes, fluent interface, and the builder pattern. All three have the common goal of ensuring that an object is consistent on creation by moving away from the perils of a no-arg constructor.

Even if the builder pattern makes it possible to build the construction over the run of lots of calls to the builder, we recommend that the builder be a short-lived object—the main limitation of all these approaches. Exactly what short-lived means depends on the situation, but for a web-based system, we recommend finishing the construction in the same request or client-server round-trip. If the construction is so complex that it needs several steps of interaction with the client, we'd rather recommend that you make initialization a state of its own in the entity.

Now that your entity is constructed in a nice and consistent state, you certainly want it to stay that way. You don't want the integrity of your entity to be compromised so that its security is in the hands of the calling code.

6.3   *Integrity of entities*

Entities that are created following all the business rules are a good thing. It's even better if they continue to follow the rules, and one of the points of designing entities as objects is that you can encapsulate all the relevant business logic close to the data. What you want to avoid at this stage is designs that leak that data into the hands of your clients in a way that enables them to change the data in violation of the business rules. This is what information security professionals refer to as protecting the *integrity* of the information.

If there are ways to change entity data without the entity being in control, you can be almost sure that sooner or later there'll either be a mistake or a malicious attack that changes the data in violation of the rules. In either case, bad integrity of entities is a security problem. The basic trick of ensuring the integrity of entities is to never leave anything mutable accessible to the outside.

> **NOTE** If you give the client access to something mutable, it can modify the entity without the entity being in charge of the change—exactly what you want to avoid.

In this section, we want to share some common pitfalls of designs that don't protect the integrity of entities, as well as ways of designing so that integrity is protected. We'll look at some different cases: fields with getter and setter methods, mutable objects, and collections.

6.3.1   *Getter and setter methods*

Most developers agree that leaving a data field open as a mutable public field is a bad idea—and to many, it's close to taboo to even discuss it. But to our surprise, there are many developers who are happy to leave fields equally open by providing a pair of unrestricted setter and getter methods. It might be aesthetically more pleasing according to some tastes, but from a security point of view, it's equally bad. Let's look at the ramifications of setters and getters.

In the following listing, the attribute `paid` of an order is protected as a private field. But it can still be manipulated by the outside in the same way as if it was unprotected because it has an unrestricted setter and getter method pair.

> **Listing 6.9   Data field not really protected when there is a setter method**

```
class Order {
    private CustomerID custid;
    private List<OrderLine> orderitems;
```

```
    private Addr billingaddr;
    private Addr shippingaddr;          The field is protected by
    private boolean paid;          ◀──── the private access modifier.
    private boolean shipped;

    public void setPaid(boolean paid) {    Data is open to arbitrary change
        this.paid = paid;          ◀────── through the setter method.
    }
    public boolean getPaid() { return paid; }
}
                                    Not possible, compiler would complain
Order order = ...
order.paid = true;         ◀───┘
order.setPaid(true);    ◀───┐ No problem, unrestricted change
                            │ to the same effect as public field
```

Let's work with this for a while. You want to protect the field `paid` from being changed arbitrarily. Making it private, like the data field `boolean paid` in the `Order` class, is a good start. But protecting data fields doesn't help much when the data is open to arbitrary modification through setter methods. In some cases, there's intelligent functionality in the setter and getter methods, and they do some good for security by encapsulating behavior. But often setters and getters open up the data field to arbitrary access and modification.

> **WARNING**   Protecting data fields with `private` and providing a setter method is like buying a high-class security door and leaving the key in the lock.

What kind of behavior might be interesting to encapsulate? Let's return to the `paid` field. Is it sensible that its value can be changed without restrictions? Probably not. In this case, it only makes sense to go from not paid to paid, which happens when you receive a payment for the order. There's no business case for going in the opposite direction.

You can secure this design by restricting how the data can change. The obvious way is to replace the arbitrary `setPaid` with a method for the specific situation of marking an order as paid:

```
class Order {
    private boolean paid = false;    ◀───┘ Orders aren't paid to start with.
    private boolean shipped;

    public void markPaid() { this.paid = true; }    ◀──┐ The attribute paid can only move
    public boolean isPaid() { return paid; }           │ in one direction, from false to true.
}
```

Now you've ensured that the attribute `paid` can only change according to business rules. It's important to note that encapsulation is about enclosing the interpretations and rules about the data together with the data. It's not about just technically protecting a data field from direct access.

6.3.2   *Avoid sharing mutable objects*

An entity needs to share its data with its surroundings. The Order entity in listing 6.9 will certainly need to share the shipping address sooner or later. The safest way for an entity to do this is by sharing domain primitives, which are immutable and therefore safe to share (as explained in chapter 5).

Sharing an object that's possible to mutate comes with the risk that the reference will be used to change the object you're using for your state representation. In listing 6.10, the attribute Person.name is represented by an immutable String, but the attribute Person.title is represented by a mutable StringBuffer. Even if the code for accessing them looks alike, the difference is fundamental. When the immutable name is used, the object Person keeps its integrity. But when the mutable title is used, it accidentally changes the representation that Person uses for keeping its state. The integrity of the Person object is violated.

> **Listing 6.10   Person class that shares one immutable object and one mutable one**

```
class Person {
    private String name;
    private StringBuffer title;

    String name() {
        return name;          ◄── Returns copied reference to
    }                             the same immutable object

    StringBuffer title() {    ◄── Returns copied reference to
        return title;             the same mutable object
    }
}

String personalizedLetter(Person p) {
    String greeting =
        p.name()
          .concat(", we'd like to make you an offer");  ◄── Uses the immutable name
    String salute =                                         to construct new objects
        p.title()
          .append(", we'd like to make you an offer")
          .toString();        ◄── Uses the mutable title by changing it
    ...
}
```

The risk of changing mutable objects in data fields is why we advise using immutable domain primitives instead, both for representation of data fields and for method arguments and return types.

> **WARNING**   Sometimes Java is explained as pass-by-reference for objects. It isn't. Java is always pass-by-value, but the value is either a primitive type (boolean, int, and so forth) or a reference to an object. When a method is called, the method gets a copy of the reference to the same object. The difference is important! You

can't change the outside reference within a method, because you only have a copy of it. But you can use the reference to change the object that's referred to.

A bad date

Designing things as mutable when they shouldn't be might seem like a beginner's mistake, but even the smartest API designers have made such mistakes. The first version of the Java standard libraries contained a `Date` class with a severe design flaw.[*] It represented a specific date, such as the 28th of January 1972 at 08:24 UTC. Unfortunately, it was also mutable: if you had a reference to the object, you could change it through mutator methods like `setHour`, `setYear`, and so forth. This put a huge challenge on any entity that used a date as an attribute. Many mistakes occurred where a date object was returned from an entity and thereafter changed from the outside. Several of these mistakes ended up as security issues.

Obviously, this is a design flaw of the `java.util.Date` class. A date should be a value object, and value objects shouldn't be mutable. A value object that can change its value doesn't make sense at all. You don't say, "This is today's date but changed to tomorrow instead." No, today is one day, and tomorrow is another day.[†] Unfortunately, the `java.util.Date` class was designed as mutable, and even though many of the methods are now deprecated, the `setTime` mutator method remains undeprecated.

Our advice for `java.util.Date` is short: don't use it. We recommend using a modern library such as the `java.time` package instead.[‡]

---

[*] See http://web.mit.edu/java_v1.0.2/www/javadoc/java.util.Date.html.
[†] Niklas Strömstedt, "I Morgon Är En Annan Dag" (1992).
[‡] See https://docs.oracle.com/javase/tutorial/datetime/index.html.

If for some reason you find yourself in a situation writing code where your only option is to work with a mutable object, there's a trick. When your methods return a reference to an encapsulated object, first clone the object. In this way, you avoid having your mutable object changed by someone else. If they use the reference you give them to mutate the object, they'll only change their copy, not your original. In the following listing, you see this trick applied to `java.util.Date`.

Listing 6.11   Person class that returns a clone of `birthdate`

```
class Person {

    private Date birthdate;

    Date birthdate() {
        return birthdate.clone();          ⟵——— Ensures that a copy is returned
    }
}
```

Most often, it's not too hard to avoid sharing mutable objects because many modern libraries have good immutable classes. But there's one case that often surfaces as a problem—collections.

6.3.3   Securing the integrity of collections

Even if a class is well designed so as not to leak mutable objects, there's one tricky area: collections such as lists or sets. For example, an `Order` object of an online bookstore might have a list of order lines, where each line describes a book being bought together with the quantity. On the inside, this is stored as a data field, `List<OrderLine> orderItems`. For such collections, we've seen a few pitfalls that we'd like to share.

To start with, you obviously must not expose the list to the outside. Making the field `orderItems` public would allow anyone to replace the list arbitrarily. Neither should you use a setter method like `void setOrderItems(List<OrderLine> orderItems)` that does the same thing. Instead of exporting the collection to the outside and letting the client work on the list, you want to encapsulate what is done *inside* the entity.

For example, to add items to the list, you should have a `void addOrderItem(OrderLine orderItem)` method. If you want to know the total quantity of items in the order, you don't give the client the list to do the sum; instead, you capture the calculation inside an `int nrItems()` method. Think of the entity as a gravity well for functionality and let computations move into the entity. The result over time is a much greater consistency of business rules, as well as greater integrity of data. You might even come to the point where there's no need to expose the list at all because everything that works on that list is now inside the entity abstraction.

If there's still a legitimate need for the rest of the code to work on the list of order items, then you need to share it in some form; for example, by providing a method `List<OrderItem> orderItems()`. But now you're back to the same problem as before. The list is a mutable object, and there's nothing that stops a client from obtaining a reference to the order item list and then modifying it by adding new order items or removing existing items. In the following listing, you can see how `void addFreeShipping(Order)` works directly on the order item list.

> **Listing 6.12   Violating integrity by working on the list from outside**

```
void addFreeShipping(Order order) {
    if(order.value().greaterThan(FREE_SHIPPING_LIMIT) {
        List<OrderLine> orderlines = order.orderItems();
        orderlines.add(                              ◄──── Adds directly to the list, without
            new OrderLine(SHIPPING_VOUCHER, 1));           the consent of the Order object
    }
}
```

In this example, the method orderItems gives out a reference to the list where order items are stored. The client directly changes this list, and the Order object doesn't get a chance to control the change. This is definitely a security loophole, and something we see quite often.

The way to secure this design is to ensure that when an entity returns its data, it should be a nonmodifiable copy. For data fields of primitive types, this isn't a problem. In the previous example of boolean isPaid(), the value returned is a copy of the boolean value in the data field. The receiver can do whatever it likes without affecting the Order. To secure the design for List<OrderItem> orderItems(), you must ensure the copy that's returned can't be used to make changes to your internal list. You can clone the list in the same way as you did with Date, but for collections, there's also a special trick using a read-only proxy.

Starting with cloning, the usual way to copy collections isn't by using clone but instead by using the so-called copy constructors. Every class in the collections library in Java has a constructor that takes another collection as an argument and creates a new collection with the same content. You can see in the following listing how this is used for orderItems, which returns a copy of the list of order items.

> **Listing 6.13 Copy constructor to return a copy of the list of order items**

```
class Order {
    private List<OrderLine> orderitems;      ◄────── Collection that carries the internal state
    public List<OrderLine> getOrderItems() {
        return new ArrayList(orderitems);    ◄────── The caller is handed a copy of the list.
    }
}
```

The caller of orderItems gets a copy of the collection, and any changes are made to that copy, not to the list inside Order. The drawback of this approach is that the caller can still do operations on the list, thinking they should result in state changes. This can lead to hard-to-find bugs. But, as we mentioned, for collections there's another neat trick available. In the handy Collections utility class, there are many useful static methods. One of them is

```
static <T> List<T> unmodifiableList(List<? extends T> list)
```

You can see this used in listing 6.14. The method returns a read-only proxy to the original list. Any attempt to call a modifying method on the returned list results in an UnsupportedOperationException.[6]

---

[6] This is really a horrible design—to implement an interface but not really provide implementations for all methods. It's a make-believe fulfillment that pretends to have compile-time type checking but replaces it with runtime checks instead.

Listing 6.14   Exporting unmodifiable collections to protect internals

```
class Order {
    private CustomerID custId;
    private List<OrderLine> orderitems;
    public List<OrderLine> orderItems() {
        return new Collections.unmodifiableList(orderitems);
    }
}

List<OrderItem> items = order.orderItems();
items.add(new OrderItem(SHIPPING_VOUCHER, 1));
```

> The caller gets an unmodifiable proxy to the underlying list.

> Trying to modify the list causes an exception.

A word of caution: even if the list is unmodifiable from the outside, that's not the same as immutable. It's still possible to change the underlying list `orderitems` from inside the `Order` object; for example, by adding a new item. It's a way of locking out changes made by clients, not a way to make the list immutable. Either way, by copying the list or returning an unmodifiable proxy, you've now secured the integrity of the order item list. It can't be modified from the outside, either by mistake or by malicious manipulations, which was the original intent of making the data field private.

What you've now secured is the content of the list, which consists of references to objects. You've also ensured that those references can't be removed and no new references can be added to the list. The next step is to ensure that the objects in the list can't be changed themselves. The best way to do this is to make the items in the list immutable, as described earlier in this chapter.

The trouble of modifiable items in a list

A metal hardware online store had the price of each item the shop sold stored in a list. It wasn't possible to modify the list itself from the outside—the list was unmodifiable. But the items in the list weren't protected. It was possible to first add 100 kg of wire to your basket in the normal way at the price of $9.00/kg. After that, you could change the price of copper wire in your basket to $0.01/kg. Having integrity of the list of items doesn't help if you don't have integrity of the items themselves.

TIP If a data field in an entity is a collection (list, set, or similar), make the entries in the list immutable and expose the collection to the outside in an unmodifiable form.

This chapter has been devoted to entities as a secure way of representing mutable states. In particular, we've dived into the important aspects of ensuring that entities are created in a state that's consistent with business constraints, and that entities uphold their integrity and stay consistent. In this chapter, you've learned about the patterns listed in table 6.1.

Table 6.1   What pattern serves which purpose and addresses which problem?

Pattern	Purpose	Security concern
Creation through a constructor with all mandatory attributes; optional attributes set via method calls	Entities fulfill simple business rules from the start.	Integrity
Creation through fluent interface	Simplified client code for creating entities with simple business rules	Integrity
Creation through builder pattern	Consistent creation for advanced constraints	Integrity
Public fields only for final attributes that can't change	Encapsulate behavior, not data as such	Integrity
Restrictions on getter/setter methods	Without restrictions, there's no encapsulation.	Integrity
Securing collections through immutability	Avoid opening collection data for access or modification by mistake.	Integrity, confidentiality

In the next chapter, we're going to consider another aspect of entities: what to do when the number or complexity of states grows unmanageable. We'll look at what designs you have at your disposal to keep the entities secure even in these conditions.

Summary

- Entities are the preferred way to handle mutable states.
- Entities must be consistent on creation.
- No-arg constructors are dangerous.
- The builder pattern can be used to construct entities with complex constraints.
- You need to protect the integrity of attributes when they're accessed.
- A private data field with unrestricted getter and setter methods isn't more secure than a public data field.
- You should avoid sharing mutable objects and use immutable domain primitives instead.
- You shouldn't expose a collection, but rather expose a useful property of the collection.
- Collections can be protected by exposing an unmodifiable version.
- You must take care so that the data in a collection can't be changed from the outside.

Reducing complexity of state

This chapter covers
- Making entities partially immutable
- Using entity state objects
- Looking at entities through entity snapshots
- Modeling changes as a relay of entities

If mutable state isn't handled properly, bad things happen. For example, a flight taking off with a bag in the hold belonging to a passenger who never showed up for boarding might be a security risk. But keeping the state of entities controlled becomes hard when entities become complex, especially when there are lots of states with complex transitions between them. We need patterns to deal with this complexity, to reduce it in a manageable way.

On top of the problems with complex mutable states, entities are also hard to code. This is because they represent data with a long lifespan, during which they are changed. The problem occurs if two different agents try to change the same entity at the same time. Technically, this boils down to two threads trying to change the same object simultaneously. The patterns you use to control complexity need to handle this situation as well. We'll look more closely at this to distinguish between single-threaded environments, such as the inside of an EJB container, and multi-threaded environments.

In this chapter, we'll cover four patterns that can reduce complexity. We'll start with two patterns that are useful in single-threaded environments: partially immutable entities and state objects. Later, we'll look at the entity snapshot pattern that's well-suited to multithreaded environments. Finally, we'll explore the large-scale design pattern of entity relay as a way to reduce overall conceptual complexity in both single-threaded and multithreaded environments.

> **NOTE** One tricky thing about entities is the environment in which they are found. Whether you're working in a single-threaded or multithreaded environment makes a huge difference in how you implement them.

When first learning about object orientation, students are taught to implement entities using an object with mutable data fields. In the following listing, for example, you can see how the account `balance` is updated and how the update is protected by a check to see that there are sufficient funds in the account.

Listing 7.1 Naive implementation of `withdraw` in class `Account`

```
void withdraw(Money amount) {
    if(this.balance.moreThan(amount)) {            Checks balance
        Money newBalance = this.balance.subtract(amount);    Calculates new balance
        this.balance = newBalance;
    } else {                                       Updates balance
        throw new InsufficientFundsException();
    }
}
```

But this code isn't safe in a multithreaded environment. Imagine the account balance is $100, and there are two different withdrawals that accidentally happen at the same time: one ATM withdrawal of $75 and an automatic transfer of $50. The second withdrawal might reach the balance check before the first withdrawal has reached the stage of reducing the balance. Consider this sequence of events:

1 ATM withdrawal checks balance ($100 > $75): OK, proceed.
2 Automatic transfer checks balance ($100 > $50): OK, proceed.
3 ATM withdrawal calculates new balance: $100 - $75 = $25.
4 ATM withdrawal updates balance: $25.
5 Automatic transfer calculates new balance: $25 - $50 = -$25.
6 Automatic transfer updates balance: -$25.

Because the two threads weren't executed consecutively (one after the other) but concurrently, the balance check was circumvented. The balance check for the second transaction was performed before the first transaction was completed, so it made no difference—it didn't protect from overdraft.

This is an example of a so-called *race condition*. Things can be even worse: if the events happen in the order 1, 2, 3, 5, 4, 6, then the ending balance would be wrong. In that scenario, the final balance would be $50. Even though $125 has been transferred from an account holding $100, a credit remains in the account. (Walk through the scenario if you like.)

To handle this situation, you need to either build a shielding environment to ensure each entity is only accessed by one thread at a time or design your entities so that they handle multiple concurrent threads well. There are many approaches to creating a single-threaded shielding environment. One of the simplest is having each client request run in a separate thread, then loading an entity object separately in each thread. This way, you're guaranteed to have only one thread accessing each entity instance. But if two threads are working on the same entity (the same data), then two entity instances change simultaneously, one in each thread. In that situation, it'll be the database transaction engine that resolves what happens.

Another approach is to use a framework, such as Enterprise JavaBeans (EJB), that handles the load/store cycle of the entity. In this case, it'll be the framework that ensures only one thread at a time accesses the entity, while minimizing the traffic to the database. Whether an entity instance is shared or not is up to the configuration. Perhaps the most up-to-date way of creating a single-threaded environment is to use an actor framework like Akka. In Akka, an entity might reside inside an actor that guarantees that only one transaction thread at a time touches the entity.

Multithreaded environments are typical when you want to avoid communication with the database and, instead, keep entity instances in a shared cache, such as Memcached. When a thread wants to work with an entity, it first looks up the entity in the cache. In this scenario, your entities need to be designed to work correctly even with multiple concurrent threads. The traditional—ancient and error-prone—way of doing this is to add semaphores in the code to synchronize the threads with each other. In Java, the most low-level way of doing this is through the keyword `synchronized`.

You can use many other options and frameworks, but common to all of them is that guaranteeing correct behavior is a challenging task. Let's start with reducing the complexity of mutable states in single-threaded environments by looking at situations where you can make an entity partially immutable.

7.1   *Partially immutable entities*

When something is mutable, there's a risk of some other part of the code changing it. And when something changes in code, there's a risk of it changing in an unwanted way. Unwanted changes can happen because some other piece of the code is broken or because someone has identified a weakness and used it to launch an attack. If *moving parts* are dangerous, it makes sense to reduce the number of moving parts. And, even if entities are bearers of change, we've found it fruitful to look at parts of entities and ask, "Does this particular part need to change?"

Let's return to the `Order` class, and this time let's take a look at the attribute for customer identity, `custid`. Customer IDs don't need to change: why should a shopping cart of books for one customer suddenly be transferred to another customer? That doesn't make sense, and keeping that possibility open can result in a security issue. Say an order has been paid for but not yet shipped. If an attacker at that moment manages to change the customer ID associated with the order, they'll have, in effect, kidnapped the order. You don't need to leave that possibility open.

An effective way to avoid these issues through design is to make entities partially immutable. To do that, ensure that you set the customer ID once and that it isn't possible to change it thereafter. Listing 7.2 shows an example of this, where the `custid` attribute of the `Order` class is set to `private final`. This enforces that `custid` must be set in the constructor and isn't allowed to change after that. The method `getCustid` returns the same reference every time it's called—a reference to the same `CustomerID` object. In this listing, `CustomerID` is a domain primitive and is designed to be immutable.

Listing 7.2   `Order` class with an immutable customer identity

```
class Order {
    private final CustomerID custid;
    Order(CustomerID custid) {
        Validate.notNull(custid);
        this.custid = custid;
    }
    public CustomerID getCustid() {
        return custid;
    }
}
class SomeOtherPartOfFlow {
    void processPayment(Order order) {
        registerDebt(order.getCustid(), order.value());
        ...
    }
}
```

Ensures that this field can't be changed after the Order object is created

The compiler enforces that a final field is set by the constructor.

Guarantees the getter always returns the same customer ID

Thinking further about this code, it becomes evident that the method `getCustid` doesn't encapsulate anything interesting and can be replaced with direct access to the field. Listing 7.3 shows how `custid` can be exposed directly, but in a secure way. The reference in the data field can't be changed, and the `CustomerID` object the reference points to is immutable and can't be changed either. Even if `processPayment` gets direct access to the field `order.custid`, it can't do anything insecure with it.

Listing 7.3   Protecting the `Order` attribute `custid` at compile time

```
Order order = ...
order.custid = new CustomerID(...);
```

Doesn't compile; custid is final.

An interesting feature of this code is that we've enlisted the compiler's help to ensure the integrity of the `custid` data field. Any attempt to change the attribute will never get to runtime but is caught at compile time.

> **TIP**   When there are attributes that shouldn't change, make entities partially immutable to avoid integrity-breaking mistakes.

You've seen how data fields can be protected either by encapsulation, as discussed in section 6.3, or by making them partially immutable. Now let's turn to a trickier aspect of entities: the fact that behavior, or allowed behavior, can change depending on what state entities are in.

7.2 Entity state objects

One thing that makes working with entities difficult is that not all actions are allowed in all states. Figure 7.1 shows two marital states: unmarried and married. Most of us would agree that for someone who's unmarried, it's acceptable to date. But after marrying, you're in the married state, and dating isn't appropriate behavior (except with your spouse, of course). Someone who's married can divorce and reenter the unmarried state; at which point, they're free to date and to marry again. But while you're married, it isn't possible to marry again. Similarly, when you're unmarried, it isn't possible to divorce.

Obviously, this is a coarse model. It doesn't take into account polygamy or that you might be unmarried but still not free to date (for example, when you're engaged or in a committed relationship). Still, it serves the purpose as an example of when actions aren't allowed at all times for entities.

7.2.1 Upholding entity state rules

Moving over to software, the design must ensure that these rules on entity states are upheld. Failing to do so can lead to security problems; for example, a bookstore providing goods without payment. And this isn't an uncommon problem. Missing, incomplete, or broken management of entity state is something we encounter often in almost every codebase of significant size.

The cause of this security problem is that the state rules are often not designed at all or are implicit and vague. It's often obvious that there's no conscious effort at design; rather, the rules have gradually appeared in the codebase, most probably on a case-by-case basis.

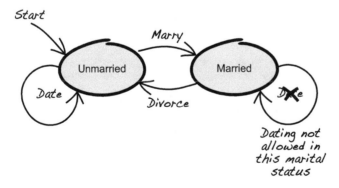

Figure 7.1   Entities should behave in a way that's appropriate to their state.

WARNING   Hearing something like, "It's just an `if` statement," is a sign that you're on a dangerous slope, heading downhill toward broken entity states. Listen carefully during story-planning or solution-design meetings.

The manifestation in code is often one of two variants: rules embedded in service methods or `if` statements in entity methods. In listing 7.4, you see the first variant. There's a rule that states if the person `boss` is married, then it's not appropriate for them to turn an after work chat into a date. That rule is upheld by the `afterwork` method in the class `Work`, not by the class `Person`.

Listing 7.4   Entity state rule upheld by a service method

```
public class Person {
    private final boolean married;
    public Person(boolean married) {
        this.married = married;
    }
    public boolean isMarried() {
        return married;
    }
    public void date(Person datee) {}       ◀──┐ Not called when married
}

public class Work {
    private Person boss;
    private Person employee;

    void afterwork() {
        // boss attempts to date
        if (!boss.isMarried()) {             ◀──┤ Method upholds rule for entity state
            boss.date(employee);             ──┐ This part is often forgotten.
        } else {                          ◀──┘
            logger.warn("bad egg");
        }
    }
}
```

Looking at the code once again, you realize something odd. The rule about not dating when married is a general rule. But in the codebase, it appears as a rule that specifically applies to the `afterwork` scenario. This would better fit as a rule about when a person is allowed to date. In that case, it would better reside inside the `date` method of `Person`.

In real-life codebases, we regularly see entities that are just *structs* (classes with private data fields, setters, and getters). The rules for how entities can behave must then be upheld by service methods. Practically, this might be possible to start with when the system is small. But as code evolves over time, upholding rules becomes inconsistent. Some parts of the system uphold some rules, whereas others don't. Also, it's hard to get an overview of what rules apply. To do so, you must mine all the code where the entity is used and search for guarding `if` statements. In short, there's no practical way to audit what rules apply to the entity.

Closely related to how hard it is to audit is how hard it is to test. Imagine that you want to write a unit test that checks that the boss isn't allowed to date when married. To do so, you need to test the conditional inside the `afterwork` method, which means you have to mock any dependencies it might have, such as a connection to the database. You also need to craft test data: both the `boss` itself and the dating object, `employee`, must be provided. Finally, you need to ensure that the `afterwork` method does the right thing to report an inappropriate dating attempt, so you'll need to mock the logging framework and scan the log for bad egg. And, should there be a `coffeeBreak` method somewhere else in the codebase, you'll need to do the same thing there to ensure no attempts to initiate dating are made during coffee breaks. This isn't an easy way to test the rule "a married boss isn't allowed to date."

A somewhat better version is when entity methods uphold the state rules. But even this approach might lead to exploitable inconsistencies. Listing 7.5 shows another version of the dating code. Here it's the responsibility of the `Person` class to check that the person `boss` isn't married before proceeding with dating. (Note the `if` statement in the method `date`.)

Listing 7.5 Entity state rule upheld by entity method

```
public class Person {
    private boolean married;

    public Person(boolean married) {
        this.married = married;
    }

    public boolean isMarried() {
        return married;
    }                                          │ Entity method upholds rule for entity state

    public void date(Person datee) {    ◄──────┘
        if (!isMarried()) {          ◄────────── The check might be embedded
            dinnerAndDrinks();                  │ some way down in the code.
        } else {          ◄─────────────────────┘
            logger.warn("bad egg");
        }                            │ This part is often forgotten.
    }

    private void dinnerAndDrinks() {}
}

public class Work {
    Person boss = new Person(true);
    Person employee = new Person(false);

    void afterwork() {
        // boss attempts to date
        boss.date(employee);
    }
}
```

This approach is definitely a step in the right direction. Business rules are at least inside the `Person` class. If dating can be initiated both after work and during coffee breaks, then at least it's the same code that does the checking, which means there's less risk of inconsistencies that can lead to security flaws.

Unfortunately, the state handling is still implicit, or at least convoluted. We've often seen these `if` statements sprinkled around deep inside the entity methods. When digging through the history of the code, it often becomes clear that they have been added one by one to handle some special cases. Sometimes the big picture of all the rules isn't even a logically consistent model.

> **TIP** When you encounter an entity with lots of `if` guards inside it, try to draw a state graph and give a name to each state.

Obviously, having a state implemented as `if` statements in service methods or entity methods isn't good design, but is it a security problem? Well, yes. If an entity leaves an opening for using a method that shouldn't be open in that state, then that opening can potentially be used as the starting point of an attack that exploits the mistake. For example, a mistake that makes it possible to add items to an order after it has been paid might be exploited by an attacker to get goods without paying.

Let's return to the online bookstore. In the webshop, it's important that you ensure that an order has been paid for before you ship it. The following listing shows what that would look like if the logic were upheld in the service method `processOrderShipment` outside the `Order` class.

> **Listing 7.6 Business rule upheld by a service method**

```
class Order {
    final public CustomerID custid;
    Order(CustomerID custid) {
        Validate.notNull(custid);
        this.custid = custid;
    }
    ...
}

class SomeOtherPartOfFlow {
    void processOrderShipment(Order order) {        Shipping is protected by an if
        if(order.getPaid()) {            ◀──────    statement in the shipping flow.

            warehouse.prepareShipment(order.custid, order.getOrderitems());
        } else {
            ...                    ◀──────┐
        }                                 │ Some kind of error alert should go here.
        ...
    }
}
```

There's one small `if` statement in `processOrderShipment` that protects goods that haven't been paid for from being shipped—and that small `if` statement resides in some other class. It's easy to imagine such checks being missed or gradually undermined as more and more code is added over time. If you omit to check that an order is paid for before it's shipped, you get a loophole for customers not paying for their goods. If that loophole becomes known, you might start losing big money as unpaid-for goods suddenly start streaming out of your warehouse. Missing entity state handling is indeed a security issue.

Online gambling sites and free money

Online gambling sites often have campaigns where they give away free credit or free spins. Lots of people try hard to convert these to real money they can withdraw. In doing so, they add some credit, gamble a little, lose a little, win a little, and add some more credit in the hopes of sooner or later confusing the system about what is real money and what isn't. Many gambling sites have lost real money through such attacks.

The sites that have succeeded the best at blocking these attacks are those that have put effort into modeling this scenario as an interesting set of entities that capture the intended rules in a logically coherent way. Is the credit in the account playable? Is it possible to withdraw it and, if so, how much of it? The credit isn't just a dollar amount; it's a complicated entity with many states.

7.2.2   *Implementing entity state as a separate object*

We suggest that entity state be explicitly designed and implemented as a class of its own. With this approach, the state object is used as a delegated helper object for the entity. Every call to the entity is first checked with the state object.

Returning to the example of marital status, you can see in listing 7.7 what a Marital-Status helper object looks like. It encapsulates the rules around marital status, but nothing else. For example, you see in the method date how a call to the Validate framework helps to uphold the rule about not dating when married.

Listing 7.7   `MaritalStatus` helper object encapsulating the rules of marital status

```
import static org.apache.commons.lang3.Validate.validState;

public class MaritalStatus {

    private boolean married = false;        ◀── We all start out as singles.

    public void date() {        ◀── No need to know the datee, it's all about the person.
        validState(!married,
                "Not appropriate to date when married");
    }

    public void marry() {        ◀── To date or marry, you must be unmarried.
        validState(!married);
        married = true;
    }
```

```
        public void divorce() {
            validState(married);                    You can only divorce if you're married.
            married = false;
        }
    }
```

The code of the helper object is concise. The married versus the unmarried examples are almost the simplest state graph possible. The state graph would be slightly more complicated if you introduce support for the state dead by adding a private boolean variable `alive`, which initially would be set to `true`. When the person dies, the flag would be switched to `false`, and at that point, the value of the flag `married` would be meaningless.

Having logic for dead or alive in the entity would probably result in a couple of `if` statements that would decrease both readability and testability and, over time, lead to less secure code. Alternatively, you could add the same logic in the helper class `Marital-Status`, and the code would still be manageable. A direct effect of the conciseness of the helper object's code is that the code is also testable. In the following listing, you see a few possible tests that check that the rules are upheld by `MaritalStatus`.

> **Listing 7.8   Some test cases for `MaritalStatus`**

```
public class MaritalStatusTest {
    @Test
    public void should_allow_dating_when_unmarried() {
        MaritalStatus maritalStatus = new MaritalStatus();
        maritalStatus.date();
    }

    @Test(expected = IllegalStateException.class)
    public void should_not_allow_dating_when_married() {
        MaritalStatus maritalStatus = new MaritalStatus();
        maritalStatus.marry();
        maritalStatus.date();
    }

    @Test
    public void should_allow_dating_after_divorces() {
        MaritalStatus maritalStatus = new MaritalStatus();
        maritalStatus.marry();
        maritalStatus.divorce();
        maritalStatus.date();
    }
}
```

Note how well the code reads. The code of the test `should_allow_dating_after_divorces` clearly states that if you marry and then divorce, then you're free to date. Naming your classes after concepts that exist in the domain, such as marital status, helps.

TIP   Find a good name for your state helper class. `MaritalStatus` is a much better name than `PersonStateHelper`. Good naming aids good thinking.

It's time now to look at how to weave this state representation into the entity. In the following listing, we let the entity `Person` consult its helper object `MaritalStatus` at the beginning of every public method to detect whether the call is legal.

Listing 7.9   The class `Person` aided by the class `MaritalStatus`

```
public class Person {

    private MaritalStatus maritalStatus =
            new MaritalStatus();

    public void date(Person datee) {          Checks that it's OK to date,
        maritalStatus.date();          ◄──────  throws an exception otherwise
        buydrinks();
        offerCompliments();
    }
                                               Checks that a person is married and
    public void divorce() {                    changes status to unmarried
        maritalStatus.divorce();       ◄──────
        ...
    }
    ...
}
```

Extracting your state management into a separate object makes your entity code much more robust and much less prone to subtle business integrity problems like customers avoiding to pay for their orders before they're shipped. We recommend using a separate state object when there are at least two states with different rules and when the transitions between them aren't completely trivial. We would probably not use a separate state object to represent the state of a light bulb (on/off, and where switch is always allowed and always switches to the other state). But for anything more complicated than that, we recommend you consider using a separate state object.

This kind of entity representation as a mutable object works well in single-threaded environments as mentioned. But in multithreaded environments, you'd need to have lots of `synchronized` keywords in your code to stop threads from thrashing the state. Unfortunately, that leads to other problems, such as limited capacity and potential deadlocks. Next, we look at a different design that works well in multithreaded environments.

7.3   *Entity snapshots*

Let's turn now to multithreaded environments, where the same entity instance can be accessed by multiple threads. In a high-performance solution where response times are critical, you want to avoid hitting the database. This is usual in financial trading, streaming, and multiuser gaming applications, as well as highly responsive websites. The round-trip time to fetch data from the database would kill the quick responses you're after in these situations. Instead, you might hold your entities in memory as much as possible; for example, using a shared cache (such as Memcached). All threads that need to work with an entity fetch the data from the cache, and the entity representation becomes shared between threads. This results in fast response times and high capacity, but it puts an additional burden on the design of entities: they must live well in an environment with multiple threads.

One way of handling this situation would be to add a lot of synchronized keywords to the code, but that would result in lots of threads waiting for each other and would reduce capacity drastically. Even worse, it might cause a *deadlock*, where two threads wait for each other indefinitely. Instead, let's take a look at another design pattern for handling this situation—representing entities as *entity snapshots*.

7.3.1 *Entities represented with immutable objects*

When designing with entity snapshots, you have an entity, but that entity isn't represented in code through a mutable entity class. Instead, there are snapshots of the entity that are used to look at that entity and take action. This is most easily described through a metaphor.

Imagine an old friend who you haven't seen in a while. You live in separate cities, but you keep in contact by following each other on a photo-sharing site. On a regular basis, you see photos of your friend, and you can follow how they change over time. Perhaps they try out a new hairstyle or move to a new house, and they certainly slowly grow older, as we all do. No doubt your friend is someone with an identity that transcends all these attribute changes. You see the changes and you stay in touch, although you never meet up in person (see figure 7.2).

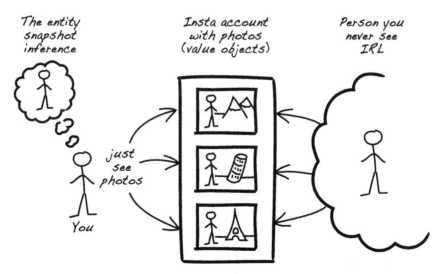

Figure 7.2   A series of photos gives an impression of a real person, even if you never meet up in real life.

What about the photos? Are those your friend? Of course not. Those are snapshots of your friend. Each photo is a representation of your friend at a particular point in time. The photo can be copied and disposed of, the copy replacing the original, without you caring. Your friend will still be there, in the far-away city, living their life.

The *entity snapshot pattern* follows the same idea. In an online webshop, orders are created when customers purchase products. Each order has a significant lifespan and evolves as the customer adds items, selects a payment method, and so on. Technically, the state might be kept in the database. But when it's time for the code to look at the state, you take a snapshot of it and represent it in a class `OrderSnapshot`, which is an immutable representation of the underlying entity as shown in the following listing. It provides a snapshot of what the order looks like at the moment you ask for it.

Listing 7.10   Class `OrderSnapshot`

```
import static org.apache.commons.lang3.Validate.*;

public class OrderSnapshot {                        ◄─── Not the order entity per
    public final OrderID orderid;                        se, but a snapshot of it
    public final CustomerID custid;
    private final List<OrderItem> orderItemList;

    public OrderSnapshot(OrderID orderid;
                         CustomerID custid,
                         List<OrderItem> orderItemList) {
        this.orderid = notNull(orderid);
        this.custid = notNull(custid);
        this.orderItemList =
            Collections
                                                    ItemList is directly
                .unmodifiableList(                  stored as immutable.
                    notNull(orderItemList));   ◄───
        checkBusinessRuleInvariants();
    }

    public List<OrderItem> orderItems() {
        return orderItemList;       ◄──────────────┐
    }                                              The entity snapshot contains intelligent
                                                   business logic for observing the state.
    public int nrItems() {      ◄──────────────────┘
        ...
    }

    private void checkBusinessRuleInvariants() {
        validState(nrItems() <= 38, "Too large for ordinary shipping");
    }
}            ◄─── No mutating methods at all

public class OrderService {
    public OrderSnapshot findOrder(OrderID orderid) ...
    public List<OrderSnapshot> findOrdersByCustomer(CustomerID custid) ...
}
```

Even if the order entity still exists conceptually, it doesn't manifest itself as a mutable entity class in the code. Instead, the `OrderSnapshot` class does the job of bringing you the information you need about the entity, probably to visualize it in the webshop GUI. The idea behind the snapshot metaphor is that the domain service goes down to the database, bringing a camera with it, and brings back a snapshot photo of what the order looked like. `OrderSnapshot` isn't just a dumb reporting object, it contains interesting domain logic like a classical entity. For example, it's able to compute the total number of items in the order and ensure that the number stays within the prescribed range for shipping.

But what about the underlying entity? Does it exist when there isn't a mutable entity class? Well, the entity order does still exist, conceptually, in the same way as your faraway friend. Like your friend, you never see the order entity directly but only see snapshots of its state. The only place where the order is represented as a mutable state is in the database: the row in the `Orders` table and the corresponding rows in the `OrderLines` table.

7.3.2 *Changing the state of the underlying entity*

We've shown how a mutable entity can be represented through immutable snapshots. But if this is a true entity, it needs to be able to change its state. How do you achieve this if the representation is immutable?

There needs to be a mechanism to mutate the entity (by which we mean the underlying entity data). To this end, you can provide a domain service to which you send updates. In the following listing, you can see that the domain service `OrderService` has been given another method, `addOrderItem`, to provide such updates.

Listing 7.11 `OrderService` with methods for updating the order in the database

```
class OrderService {

    public void addOrderItem(OrderID orderid,
                    ProductID pid, Quantity qty) {          Validates that the specified
        //...                                                quantity can be added
        //...
    }              Updates the underlying database
}                  with the new information
```

The method `addOrderItem` validates the conditions to ensure the change is allowed and then performs an update of the underlying data, either through SQL commands sent directly to the database or via the persistence framework you use. With this approach, you get high availability because you avoid locks when reading, which is assumed to be much more common than writing (in the form of changing data). Writing, which might require locks, is separated from the reads, and you avoid the security problem of not having data available.

A drawback of this approach is that it violates some of the ideas of object orientation—especially the guideline to keep data and its accompanying behavior close together, preferably in the same class. Here, you've ripped the entity apart, putting the read side in a value object in one class and the write side in a domain service in another class. Architecture often involves trade-offs. In cases like this, you might value availability so highly that you're willing to sacrifice other things, like certain principles of object-oriented code.

The idea isn't as strange as it might sound. Similar approaches have been suggested elsewhere, sometimes in slightly different settings. The pattern of Command Query Responsibility Segregation (CQRS), suggested by Greg Young, and the Single Writer Principle, proposed by Martin Thompson, both bear similar signs.

Apart from availability, the entity snapshot pattern also supports integrity. Because the snapshot is immutable, there's no risk at all of the representation mutating to a foul state. An ordinary entity with methods that change its state is vulnerable to bugs of that kind, but the snapshot isn't. There's code that changes the state of the underlying data, and that code can contain bugs, but at least the snapshot that's used to show the state of the entity can't change.

How databases make entities lock

In some situations, read performance (in terms of both response time and capacity) is important. In the online bookstore, for example, there might be peak times when lots of clients are looking up books they intend to buy (say, just before Christmas). Each of these clients wants a fast response with a description of the book, the price, and how many there are left in stock. If each lookup puts a read/write lock on that book's row in the database, the product catalogue would soon come to a grinding halt. It wouldn't be feasible to tell customers, "I'm sorry, I can't give you the description of *Hamlet* at the moment because someone else is looking at it. Please wait until that customer is finished, and we'll get back to you."

When working with an entity that's stored in a database, it's pretty normal to put some kind of lock on the database row. Exactly what type of lock and how it's managed depends on the persistence framework, the database management product, and the table's configuration, but it's not unusual that fetching a mutable entity sets a read/write lock on that entity's row. In this way, the database guarantees that no other client modifies the same entity at the same time.

If entities lead to this kind of restriction, they're clearly not a good modeling choice when there are many clients that want to look at an entity at the same time. We'll soon get back to this situation, but let's first look at what happens when there's high traffic load, but each client is only interested in one specific entity.

If we return to our online bookstore, it seems like a good idea to model orders as entities. The entire point of orders is to capture the changes in state when books are added to an order and the order is paid for, packed, and delivered. Each order is stored in the database in a few tables: the `Orders` table, the `OrderLines` table, and perhaps a few others. This should be fine even under high load, right? No one else apart from the customer to whom the order belongs will look at its row or rows in those tables. Hence, there'll never be two clients locking each other out.

In principle, this sounds fine, but in practice, things are slightly more complicated. The problem is that many database management systems don't lock individual rows separately. Instead, they put locks on blocks of rows for efficiency, as shown in the figure.

Rather than a single row, an entire memory page (and all the rows in it) is locked and loaded into memory!

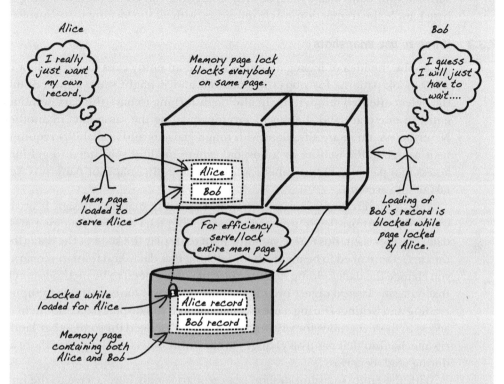

Locking one row also locks other rows because of page locking.

The reason for page-level locking is read/write efficiency, which is crucial for a database management system. During a transaction, the system reads an entire page from disk and loads it into memory. The transaction makes some changes to the data contained in this page. On commit, the entire page is written back to disk. It's an efficient way of handling I/O. But what happens if some other client wants to work on data that resides on the same page? How does the system ensure that clients don't overwrite each other's changes?

The simplest and most naive way is to lock the entire page while someone is working on it. If some other clients want to access data from the same page while it's locked, they're put on hold until the first client commits. Then and only then is the next client in turn given the opportunity to load the page and perform its operations. This is a simplification—database management systems are much more sophisticated than we can get into here, but you get the gist. The unfortunate effect is that one customer accessing their order locks not only their row in the database but also neighboring rows. If other customers arrive at the same time, they'll have to wait until the lock is released. This puts you in a situation where clients are forced to wait for each other, which results in worse response times as well as lower capacity—not good. The availability of your system is at risk, which is a security concern.

Implementing entities using the entity snapshot pattern makes it possible for them to live well in a multithreaded environment without causing the drawbacks you get if you sprinkle your code with `synchronized`. You also avoid contention by letting the database handle the transaction synchronization, with all the locking issues involved.

7.3.3   *When to use snapshots*

No doubt, the idea of having an entity without an entity class doesn't follow ordinary schoolbook patterns for object orientation, and it might seem counterintuitive. To the object-oriented mind, it might also be disturbing to have the data definition of an entity in one place and the mechanics for updating the same data in another place. Nevertheless, there are situations with tough capacity and availability requirements— be it a high-traffic website or a hospital, where medical staff need to get immediate access to a patient's notes—where we think the entity snapshot pattern is well worth taking into account.

Another interesting security benefit of the entity snapshot design is in situations where different privileges are needed for reading data and for changing and writing data. For user scenarios where you only want to display the state of the data (looking at the cart), there need to be methods for fetching that data. And for user scenarios where you change the data (adding items to the cart), there need to be methods for changing that data. In classical object orientation, the entity will have methods to support both reading and writing. During a user scenario where you display data, the client code has access to those methods for writing as well. There's a need for some other kind of security mechanism that controls changes to the entity object, making sure there are none during read scenarios.

With the entity snapshot design, read scenarios only have access to the immutable snapshot, and it's impossible for them to call a mutating method. Only the clients that are allowed to make changes will have access to the domain service used for updating the underlying entity. In this way, the entity snapshot pattern also supports integrity for some common scenarios. In an environment where multiple threads access the same entity, perhaps at the same time, using entity snapshots is therefore an effective design to ensure high availability together with integrity.

Now you've studied two designs: one that works well in single-threaded environments and one that works well in multithreaded environments. But there's another way complexity might arise: when an entity has a lot of different states. Handling more than 10 states in an entity can get awkward, but often it's possible to apply an alternative design—splitting the complex states into an entity chain.

7.4 *Entity relay*

Many entities have a reasonably low number of separate states, and they are fairly easy to grasp. For example, the civil status of an individual in the marital status example has few states and transitions among them, as figure 7.3 shows.

A state graph of this size is easy to understand. It'd also be easy to implement using the state object pattern from section 7.2 for example.

Sometimes an entity state graph grows and becomes quite large and less easy to grasp. It might well be designed that way from the beginning, but more often, such a design is the result of a long history of many changes. Most of the changes were probably perceived as a small fix at the time they were made, but the accumulative result as time passes is a lot of states. You can imagine that an online bookstore might start out having two states for its orders, received and shipped. After a while, the state graph might look like that shown in figure 7.4.

It can be hard to understand all the possible states and transitions for such an entity, even when you're looking at the graph. To implement these states in code and to ensure that all the different rules are enforced in all the different states would be a nightmare. When this entity is implemented as one single class, that class becomes so complex that it risks containing hard-to-spot inconsistencies. Something has to be done if you have a state graph like that for the online order in figure 7.4. You need to break it up. Having five states is manageable. Having 10 states is endurable. Having to juggle 15 states is simply too risky. And this is where we suggest entity chaining.

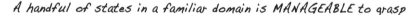

A handful of states in a familiar domain is MANAGEABLE to grasp

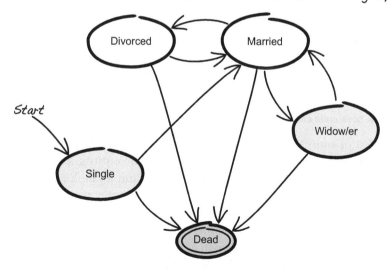

Figure 7.3   Civil status: single, married, divorced, widow/er, dead

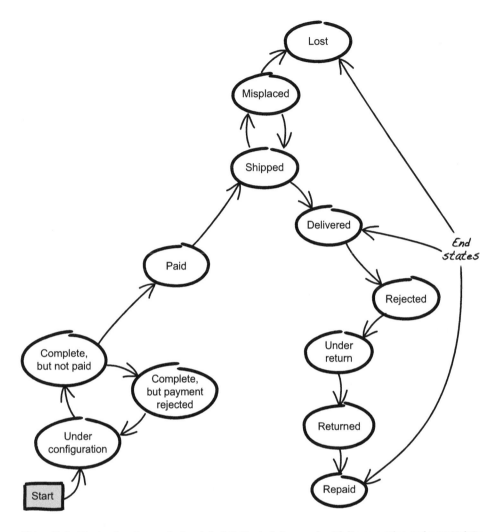

Figure 7.4   The book order can be in a lot of distinct states, each with its own rules and constraints.

The basic idea of *entity relay* is to split the entity's lifespan into phases, and let each entity represent its own phase. When a phase is over, the entity goes away, and another kind of entity takes over—like a relay race. As an example, look at figure 7.5, which views the life of a person in two ways: first as one single entity that goes through many states of life, then as a chain of entities.

On the left side of figure 7.5, you see the life of a person viewed as one single entity: a person is born and spends a few years in childhood, then some time in adolescence before shouldering the responsibilities of adulthood, followed by aging, until death. You can view the person as the same entity, which passes through the states of birth, childhood, adolescence, adulthood, aging, and death.

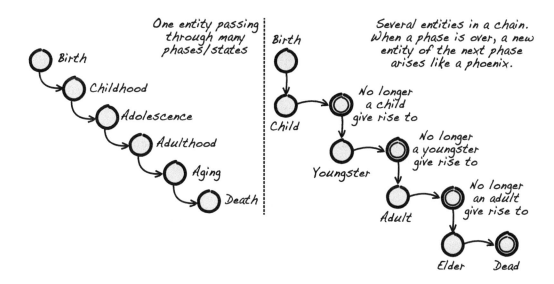

Figure 7.5 The life of a person viewed in two ways: as a single entity and as a chain of entities.

On the right side of the figure, you see the same life viewed as a chain of entities. A child is born and grows. One day, the child is gone, and there's a youngster standing in its place, taking over the relay baton. A few years later, the youngster is gone and is replaced by an adult. The adult eventually yields to an elder, who finally dies. In this case, you can view this life as a succession of different characters.

We've presented two ways of looking at the same thing. Neither representation is more true or better than the other; they focus on different aspects and are good at different things. Shifting focus from one to the other might help you sometimes—when you have an entity with a lot of states is one such occasion. We've found that this design shift can be a powerful way to handle entities that have far too many states. You split the too large state graph into phases, model each phase with an entity of its own, and let these entities form a relay chain. Each entity in the relay has a few states to manage, and you've overcome risky complexity.

The power of entity relay comes from the ability to split the overall lifespan of the entity into phases and instead model the phases as one entity following another. For this to work well, there should be no looping back to a previous phase. If there are loopbacks, then you can still apply the same idea, but the simplicity of the relay metaphor is lost, as well as much of the gain. Next, we'll return to the scary state graph of the book order and show how you can turn it into a more manageable relay chain.

7.4.1 Splitting the state graph into phases

Let's take another look at the overcomplex entity in figure 7.4 and see how you can remodel it as a relay race of entities. Look for places where one group of states leads to another group of states. Preferably, there should be no way back to the first group once you've left it. Figure 7.6 shows one way to partition the states.

Now you see that the complex graph of the online order can be viewed as two phases: up until payment and after payment. Call the first phase a preliminary order and the second phase a definitive order. These are the phases that you want to redesign to be separate entities instead. The runners that make up the relay race include the first entity (or preliminary order), which starts the race, and the second entity (or definitive order), which takes over when the first entity completes. When a preliminary order is paid for, a definitive order is born as a result.

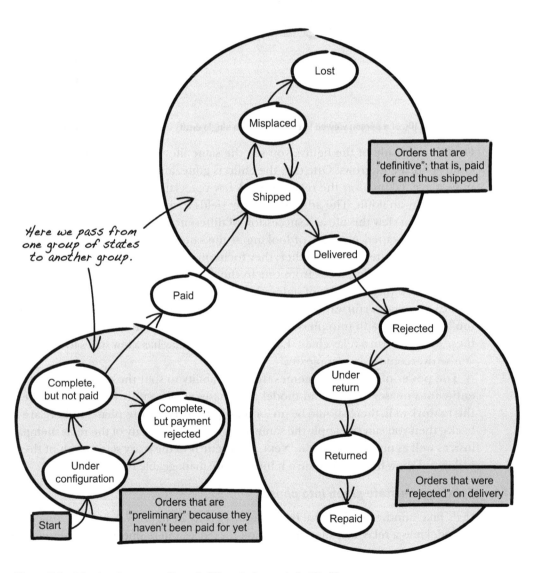

Figure 7.6   A book order passes through different phases during its lifespan.

TIP   When applying this strategy, look for places where you can't go back, so
that an earlier entity in the chain never needs to be reborn. It's also preferable
if there's only one end state for each entity in the relay that gives rise to a new
entity—the next runner in the race.

If you take another look at the state graph in figure 7.6, you'll see that there's one
more place that meets these requirements—when the delivered package is rejected by
the receiver. The difference here is that not all delivered orders give rise to a rejected
order, just some. It's still a good place to split the state graph. You need to remember
that the birth of a rejected order isn't automatic, it's conditioned on the recipient not
accepting the delivery.

After these transformations, you now have a simpler setup. As you can see in figure 7.7, you no longer have one entity with an overwhelming amount of states. Instead,
you have three entities, each of which is reasonably simple.

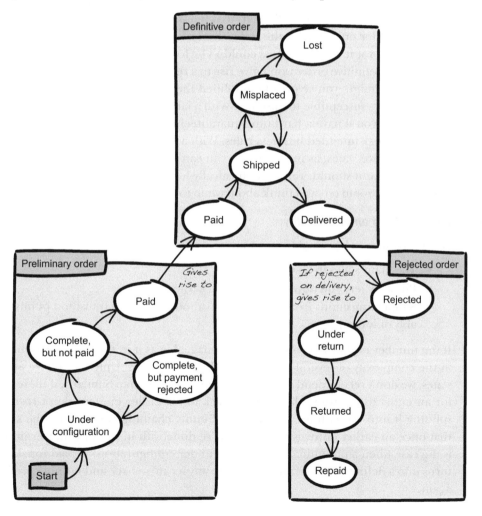

Figure 7.7   A book order as a chain of three entities

The three entities (preliminary order, definitive order, and rejected order) have four or five possible states each, so implementing them on their own is pretty straightforward. Using the previous design of state objects, you'll be able to implement all three entities in a secure way.

Let's briefly look at the transitions, the baton handovers between the entities in the relay. When a preliminary order is finally configured completely and paid for, it moves into the state paid, which is its end state. At that time, a definitive order is born in its start state, paid. The baton is handed from the preliminary order, which has reached its goal, to the definitive order, which starts its run. This is the same situation as when a youngster entity moves into the state no longer youngster and, at the same time, an adult entity arises. In the same way, as an adult can't move back and become a youngster again, a preliminary order can't move back before its start state, paid.

The transition between definitive order (paid for and shipped to the customer) and rejected order works almost the same way, but with a small twist. When a definitive order reaches its end state, delivered, that doesn't always cause a next entity to arise. A rejected order only arises if the definitive order is rejected on delivery (no one was willing to sign for it, or the address couldn't be found, for example). In most cases, the delivery of a definitive order won't give rise to a rejected order.

With this design, you've greatly simplified the task of writing code and made your code much less susceptible to mistakes. With a large and complex state graph, like that in figure 7.4, you'll have a hard time guaranteeing that there are no strange, esoteric paths that break intended business rules. With a simpler design of three entities, each with four or five states, as in figure 7.7, you can more easily validate and test that the code does what it should. You have drastically lowered the risk of security vulnerabilities. Let's now zoom out and think about when to apply this pattern or not.

7.4.2   *When to form an entity relay*

For this pattern to be valuable, you want to see three factors in place:

- Too many states in an entity
- Phases where you never go back to an earlier phase
- Simple transitions from one phase to another and few transition points (preferably only one)

If the number of states in your entity is manageable as it is, there's no reason to bring in the complexity of several entities with different names. Unless you have at least 10 states, we don't recommend splitting your entity into a relay. Similarly, if there are ways for an entity to go from a later phase back to an earlier one, we don't recommend splitting it into two entities. The power of entity chaining comes from the simplicity that once an earlier entity is finished, you're done with it. In our order example, this is the case when a preliminary order (still under configuration) is paid for. Then that turns into a definitive order, and there's no way it can go back and become preliminary again.

If it's possible to reopen an earlier entity, that would be comparable to having one runner hand the baton over to an earlier runner. Now, you no longer have the simple succession of one runner handing the baton on to the next until the relay race is over. Instead, you get some kind of directed graph where entities of different phases can be revived. The simplicity of a relay race is lost.

If there are many ways that an earlier entity can give rise to a later entity, you should consider whether the benefits of entity relay outweigh the costs. There's a simplicity in having only one place where the next entity is born. If there are several, consider remodeling. Perhaps you can add an end state for the phase? If not, perhaps the two phases should be seen as one.

Finally, sometimes you get a huge state graph with a lot of states and where the transitions look like a tangled ball of yarn. Don't even try to resolve that by creating relays. No amount of effort to design it nicely will help. A mess like that continues to be a mess, even if you pull a few threads. Instead, we recommend that you take the model back to the drawing table. Sit down with the domain experts and talk it over:

- What are the real drivers for the model being this complex?
- Is all that complexity really needed?
- Is there a valid business driver for each part of the complexity?
- Is that business driver so valuable that it justifies the cost of such complexity and, perhaps, an insecure system?

We've covered a few ways of reducing complexity in this chapter. Table 7.1 provides a concise summary of the central aim of each pattern and the security concerns it addresses.

Table 7.1 Patterns of this chapter: purposes and security concerns

Pattern	Purpose	Security concern
Partially immutable entity	Locks down parts of entities that shouldn't change anyway	Integrity
Entity state object	Makes it easier to grasp what states the entity can have	Integrity
Entity snapshot	Supports high capacity and fast response times by avoiding locking	Availability, integrity
Entity relay	Makes it easier to handle large and complex state graphs	Integrity

The first pattern we looked at was minimizing the number of moving parts by making the entity partially immutable where possible. The next pattern, the entity state object, focused on capturing state transitions of one entity and worked well in single-threaded environments. In multithreaded environments, it becomes more feasible to represent the entity through entity snapshots to avoid threading issues. Finally, for a complex entity with lots of states, an alternative design is to model it as an entity relay, reducing the number of states you need to keep in mind at the same time.

Summary

- Entities can be designed to be partially immutable.
- State handling is easier to test and develop when extracted to a separate object.
- Multithreaded environments for high capacity require a careful design.
- Database locking can put a limit on availability of entities.
- Entity snapshots are a way to regain high availability in multithreaded environments.
- Entity relay (when fulfillment of one entity gives rise to another) is an alternative way to model an entity that has lots of different states.

Leveraging your delivery pipeline for security

This chapter covers

- Security-style unit tests
- A security perspective on feature toggles
- Writing automated security tests
- Why availability tests are important
- How misconfiguration causes security issues

Most developers agree that testing should be an integral part of the development process. This way, the perils of having a separate bug-fixing phase after development is avoided. Methodologies such as test-driven development (TDD) and behavior-driven development (BDD) have made it the de facto standard to execute thousands of tests each time a change is integrated. But for some reason, perhaps because security is an afterthought for many people, this only seems to apply to nonsecurity tests. In our opinion, this doesn't make sense. Security tests are no different than regular tests and should be executed as frequently. This doesn't mean you need a penetration test at every commit.[1] Instead, you need a different mindset,

---

[1] A test performed on a system to uncover possible security weaknesses; see https://www.owasp.org/index.php/Web_Application_Penetration_Testing.

where security concerns are seamlessly integrated into the delivery pipeline and exercised every time a change is made—and that's what this chapter is about.

Each section in this chapter is more or less independent, but a common theme is to teach you how to integrate different security tests into your delivery pipeline. This may require thinking explicitly about security for a change, but doing this in your daily work instantly gives you feedback on and an understanding of how secure your software is. Before we dive into the details, let's have a quick refresher on what a delivery pipeline is.

8.1   *Using a delivery pipeline*

A *delivery pipeline* is an automated manifestation of the process for delivering software to production (or to some other environment).[2] Although this sounds advanced and overly complex, it's just the opposite. Suppose you have the following delivery process:

1 Make sure all files have been checked into Git.
2 Build the application from the master branch.
3 Execute all unit tests and make sure they pass.
4 Execute all application tests and make sure they pass.
5 Execute all integration tests and make sure they pass.
6 Execute all system tests and make sure they pass.
7 Execute all availability tests and make sure they pass.
8 Deploy to production (if all previous steps pass).

The first couple of steps ensure that all files have been included in the build and that the code compiles. Steps 3 to 7 exercise different quality aspects, and the last step allows deployment to production if all previous steps pass. Regardless of whether you choose to run the process manually or automatically, the main objective is to prevent bugs from slipping through to production. If you choose to use a build server, you end up with an automated manifestation of the process—a delivery pipeline as illustrated in figure 8.1.

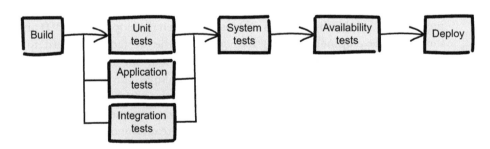

Figure 8.1   Example of a delivery pipeline

---

[2] See Jez Humble and David Farley's *Continuous Delivery: Reliable Software Releases Through Build, Test, and Deployment Automation* (Addison-Wesley, 2010).

As illustrated, unit tests, application tests, and integration tests run in parallel, whereas the other steps run sequentially. Although not required, a benefit of automating the process is the ease of moving around the process steps. Although it's interesting to analyze how to do this best, what's far more important is the choice of making this an automated process.

Using a delivery pipeline guarantees that the process is executed consistently—no one can choose to skip a step or cheat when delivering to production or some other environment. You can take advantage of this to ensure that security checks are done continuously during development. By including security tests in the pipeline, you gain immediate feedback and an understanding of how secure your software is. This makes a huge difference to quality, so let's see how you can secure your design using unit tests.

8.2 Securing your design using unit tests

When securing a design using unit tests, you need to think a bit differently from what you may be used to. Using TDD helps you focus on what the code *should* do rather than what it *shouldn't* do. This is a good strategy, but unfortunately, it only takes you halfway. Only focusing on what the code should do makes it easy to forget that security weaknesses often are unintended behavior.

For example, if you represent a phone number as a string, you probably expect phone numbers as input and nothing else. But the definition of a string is much broader than the definition of a phone number, and this makes you automatically accept any input that could be represented by a string—a weakness that opens up the possibility of injection attacks. This justifies the need for a different test strategy that includes both what the code should do and what it shouldn't do.

When testing your objects, we suggest using four different test types, as described in table 8.1. That way, you'll gain confidence that the code truly does what it claims to do and that unintended behavior is avoided.

Table 8.1   Test types and their objectives

Test type	Objective
Normal input testing	Verifies that the design accepts input that clearly passes the domain rules, ensuring that the code handles *vanilla* input in a correct way.
Boundary input testing	Verifies that only structurally correct input is accepted. Examples of boundary checks are length, size, and quantity, but they could also include complex invariants and domain rules.
Invalid input testing	Verifies that the design doesn't break when invalid input is handled. Empty data structures, `null`, and *strange* characters are often considered invalid input.
Extreme input testing	Verifies that the design doesn't break when extreme input is handled. For example, such input might include a string of 40 million characters.

To give you a feel for and understanding of how to use these tests, we'll walk you through an example where sensitive patient information in a hospital is sent by email. Although designing and testing an email domain primitive might seem trivial, the methods and reasoning used are universal and can be applied to any object you create.

Picture a hospital with an advanced computerized medical system. The system includes everything from medical charts to drug prescriptions to x-ray results—a vital system with thousands of transactions per day. As part of the daily routine, doctors and nurses use the system when discussing sensitive patient information. This communication is email-based, and for patient integrity reasons, it's critical that information is never sent to email addresses outside the hospital domain.

Configuring the email servers to only accept addresses in the hospital domain is the natural strategy of choice. But what if the configuration changes or is lost during an upgrade? Then you'd silently start to accept emails to invalid addresses—a security breach that could lead to catastrophic consequences. A better strategy is to combine email server configuration with the rejection of invalid addresses in the system. This way, security in depth is achieved, which makes the system harder to attack because it's not enough to circumvent one protection mechanism.[3] But to do this, you need to understand the rules for an email address in the hospital domain.

8.2.1   *Understanding the domain rules*

In chapter 1, you learned that talking to domain experts helps you gain a deeper understanding about the domain. This is also the case for the hospital domain. As it turns out, the rules for an email address in this context are quite different from what you might expect.

The email address specification, RFC 5322, is quite generous when it comes to what characters an accepted address can have.[4] Unfortunately, you can't use the same definition in the hospital domain because several legacy systems have character restrictions that need to be considered. Because of this, the domain experts have decided to allow only alphabetic characters, digits, and periods in a valid email address. The total length is restricted to 77 characters, and the domain must be hospital.com. Several other requirements include:

- The format of an email address must be local-part@domain.
- The local part can't be longer than 64 characters.
- Subdomains aren't accepted.
- The minimum length of an email address is 15 characters.
- The maximum length of an email address is 77 characters.
- The local part can only contain alphabetic characters (a-z), digits (0-9), and one period.
- The local part can't start with nor end with a period.

---

[3] For a discussion of security or defense in depth, see https://www.us-cert.gov/bsi/articles/knowledge/ principles/defense-in-depth.

[4] Request for Comments, Internet Message Format, available at https://www.ietf.org/rfc/rfc5322.txt.

At first, it can be tempting to represent an email address as a `String` because of the generous definition in RFC 5322. But the requirements defined by the domain rules suggests that a better choice would be to represent it as a domain primitive, `Email-Address`. One way to ensure it complies with the domain rules is to drive the design using unit tests, so let's start by testing normal behavior.

8.2.2 *Testing normal behavior*

When testing normal behavior, you want to focus on input that clearly meets the domain rules. For `EmailAddress` that means input that fits within the length constraints (15 to 77 characters); has hospital.com as the domain; and has a local part containing only alphabetic characters (a-z), digits, and at most one period. This way, confidence is gained that the implementation works as expected when *vanilla* input is provided.

In listing 8.1, you see an example of how to capture the normal behavior of `Email-Address`. The test is executed with JUnit 5, and the construction is quite clever in the sense that it uses a stream of input values (valid email addresses), which are mapped to a lazily executed test case—a dynamic test.[5] Compared to an ordinary test case, a dynamic test case is different in that it's not defined at compile time but rather at runtime. That way, it's possible to dynamically create test cases based on parameter input, as is done in the listing. In addition, using a parameterized test construction is often preferable when confirming a theory because it lets you easily add or remove input values without affecting test logic.

> **TIP** When designing tests that need to confirm a theory (for example, the normal behavior), use a parameterized test construction that lets you inject different values in the same test.

Listing 8.1 Test capturing the normal behavior of `EmailAddress`

```
import static org.junit.jupiter.api.Assertions.assertDoesNotThrow;
import static org.junit.jupiter.api.DynamicTest.dynamicTest;

class EmailAddressTest {                    Creates a stream of input values
  @TestFactory
  Stream<DynamicTest> should_be_a_valid_address() {        Input values that clearly
    return Stream.of(   ◄                                  satisfy the domain rules
          "jane@hospital.com",
          "jane01@hospital.com",
          "jane.doe@hospital.com")
        .map(input ->                                   Creates a dynamic test
          dynamicTest("Accepted: " + input,   ◄         case at runtime
            () -> assertDoesNotThrow(   ◄
              () -> new EmailAddress(input))));     Asserts that the input doesn't
  }                                                 throw an exception when an
}                                                   EmailAddress object is created
```

---

[5] The JUnit 5 documentation is available at http://junit.org/junit5/docs/current/user-guide/.

Having this test in place allows you to start designing the `EmailAddress` object. According to the domain rules, only alphabetic characters, digits, and one period are allowed in the local part. This adds some complexity, but the next listing shows a solution that addresses this using a regular expression (regexp). The domain is also restricted to hospital.com, which prevents any other domains from being accepted.

Listing 8.2   `EmailAddress` **meeting the normal behavior criteria**

```
import static org.apache.commons.lang3.Validate.matchesPattern;

public final class EmailAddress {

    public final String value;

    public EmailAddress(final String value) {
        matchesPattern(value.toLowerCase(),
            "^[a-z0-9]+\\.?[a-z0-9]+@\\bhospital.com$",
            "Illegal email address");

        this.value = value.toLowerCase();
    }
    ...
}
```

Normalizes the input into lowercase and passes it to the regexp engine

Regexp that ensures the local part contains alphabetic characters, digits, and at most one period, explicitly requiring the domain to be hospital.com

Assigns the input to the value field if it matches the regexp

---

But testing normal behavior is only one step toward making `EmailAddress` secure. You also need to ensure that addresses close to the semantic boundary behave as expected. For example, how do you know if an email address longer than 77 characters is rejected or that an address can't start with a period? This justifies adding a new set of tests where the boundary behavior is verified.

8.2.3   *Testing boundary behavior*

In chapter 3, we discussed the importance of understanding the semantic boundary of a context and how data could implicitly change meaning when crossing a boundary. For a domain object, it's often a combination of simple structural rules (for example, length, size, or quantity) and complex domain rules that defines the semantic boundary. For example, consider a shopping cart on a web page that's modeled as an entity. It's fine to add items up to a certain limit and modify the cart as long as you haven't gone through checkout. After that, the order is immutable, and updates are illegal. This state transition makes the order cross a semantic boundary because the meaning of an open order isn't the same as that of a submitted order. This is important to test because many security problems tend to lie around these boundaries.

Returning to `EmailAddress` and the hospital domain, you need to ensure the design truly satisfies the boundary conditions defined by the domain rules. Fortunately, you can simplify the testing a little because the rules don't impose any complex state transitions like those in the shopping cart example. Instead, you only have structural requirements, such as length restrictions and which symbols to allow, and they are quite easy to test. Table 8.2 summarizes the boundary conditions that need to be verified.

Table 8.2   Boundary conditions to verify

Accept	Reject
Address that's exactly 15 characters long	Address that's 14 characters long
Address with a local part that's 64 characters long	Address with a local part that's 65 characters long
Address that's exactly 77 characters long	Address with a local part containing an invalid character
	Address with multiple @ symbols
	Address with a domain other than hospital.com
	Address with a subdomain
	Address with a local part that starts with a period
	Address with a local part that ends with a period
	Address with more than one period in the local part

Having this list in place allows you to start designing unit tests that verify boundary behavior for each particular case. In listing 8.3, you see an example of how to implement this with JUnit 5. The first test, should_be_accepted, verifies that an address is accepted if it's part of the hospital.com domain and between 15 and 77 characters long. The second test, should_be_rejected, is a bit longer and focuses on rejecting input that's outside the boundaries; for example, input that's too short, too long, has invalid characters, or has an invalid domain.

Listing 8.3   Tests verifying that addresses meet boundary conditions

Should accept a 15-character address

```
import static org.apache.commons.lang3.StringUtils.repeat;
import static org.junit.Assert.assertEquals;
import static org.junit.jupiter.api.Assertions.assertDoesNotThrow;
import static org.junit.jupiter.api.Assertions.assertThrows;
import static org.junit.jupiter.api.DynamicTest.dynamicTest;

class EmailAddressTest {
    @TestFactory
    Stream<DynamicTest> should_be_accepted() {          // Should accept a
        return Stream.of(                                // 77-character address
            "aa@hospital.com",
            repeat("X", 64) + "@hospital.com")
            .map(input -> dynamicTest("Accepted: " + input,
                () -> assertDoesNotThrow(() -> new EmailAddress(input))));
    }
                                                         // Should reject a
                                                         // 14-character address
    @TestFactory
    Stream<DynamicTest> should_be_rejected() {           // Should reject a
        return Stream.of(                                // 78-character
            "a@hospital.com",                            // address
            repeat("X", 64) + "@something.com",
            repeat("X", 65) + "@hospital.com",           // Should reject a
                                                         // 65-character local part
```

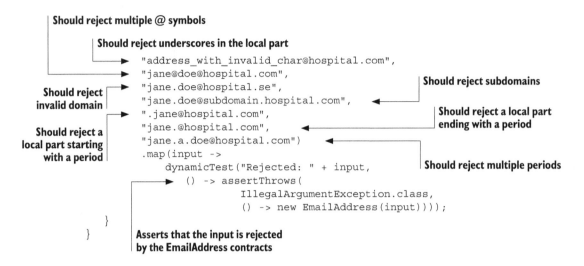

Should reject multiple @ symbols

Should reject underscores in the local part

Should reject invalid domain

Should reject a local part starting with a period

```
                "address_with_invalid_char@hospital.com",
                "jane@doe@hospital.com",
                "jane.doe@hospital.se",
                "jane.doe@subdomain.hospital.com",
                ".jane@hospital.com",
                "jane.@hospital.com",
                "jane.a.doe@hospital.com")
            .map(input ->
                dynamicTest("Rejected: " + input,
                    () -> assertThrows(
                        IllegalArgumentException.class,
                        () -> new EmailAddress(input))));
    }
}
```

Should reject subdomains

Should reject a local part ending with a period

Should reject multiple periods

Asserts that the input is rejected by the EmailAddress contracts

Executing this test shows that the implementation of `EmailAddress` is too weak. The regular expression `^[a-z0-9]\+\.?[a-z0-9]\+@\bhospital.com$` is a bit naive because it doesn't limit the length of the local part or the total length of an address.

Listing 8.4 shows an updated version of `EmailAddress` where length is explicitly checked before applying the regexp. In chapter 4, you learned that a lexical scan should always be applied before processing the input. This can be achieved using a positive lookahead in the regular expression, but we've deliberately skipped it because the length check ensures the input is safe to parse regardless of which characters it contains.[6] However, in more complex situations, you should protect the parser by doing a lexical scan first.

> **Listing 8.4   `EmailAddress` with explicit length check**

```
import static org.apache.commons.lang3.Validate.inclusiveBetween;
import static org.apache.commons.lang3.Validate.isTrue;
import static org.apache.commons.lang3.Validate.matchesPattern;

public final class EmailAddress {

    public final String value;

    public EmailAddress(final String value) {
        inclusiveBetween(15, 77, value.length(),
            "address length must be between 15 and 77 chars");

        isTrue(value.indexOf("@") < 65,
            "local part must be at most 64 chars");

        matchesPattern(value.toLowerCase(),
```

Ensures that the input is 15 to 77 chars long

Ensures that the local part is at most 64 chars long

---

[6] For more information about positive lookaheads, see http://www.regular-expressions.info/lookaround.html.

```
                "^[a-z0-9]+\\.?[a-z0-9]+@\\bhospital.com$",
                "Illegal email address");

        this.value = value.toLowerCase();
    }
    ...
}
```

Adding the explicit length check does indeed make the design appear solid. Unfortunately, this is where most developers stop their testing efforts, because the implementation appears to be good enough. But from a security perspective, you need to go further.

It's also important to verify that harmful input can't break the validation mechanism. For example, the design of `EmailAddress` relies heavily on how regular expressions are interpreted. This is fine, but what if there's a weakness in the regexp engine that could make it crash when parsing a certain input, or if there's input that takes an extremely long time to evaluate? Flushing out these types of problems is the objective of the last two test types: invalid input testing and extreme input testing. Let's see how to apply invalid input testing on the `EmailAddress` object.

8.2.4 *Testing with invalid input*

Before you design tests with invalid input, you need to understand what invalid input is. As a general rule of thumb, any input that doesn't satisfy the domain rules is considered *invalid*. But from a security perspective, we're also interested in testing with invalid input that causes immediate or eventual harm, and for some reason, `null`, empty strings, and strange characters tend to have this effect on many systems.

Listing 8.5 illustrates how `EmailAddress` is tested with invalid input. The input is a mix of addresses containing strange characters, `null` values, and input resembling valid data. With this type of testing, you increase the probability that the design truly holds for simple injection attacks that could exploit weaknesses in the validation logic.

> **Listing 8.5   Testing with invalid input**

```
import static org.junit.Assert.assertEquals;
import static org.junit.jupiter.api.Assertions.assertThrows;
import static org.junit.jupiter.api.DynamicTest.dynamicTest;

class EmailAddressTest {
    @TestFactory
    Stream<DynamicTest> should_reject_invalid_input() {
        return Stream.of(
                null,
                "null",            Invalid input that tries to break
                "nil",             the validation logic in the
                "0",               constructor of EmailAddress
                "",
                " ",
                "\t",
                "\n",
```

```
"john.doe\n@hospital.com",
"   @hospital.com",
"%20@hospital.com",
"john.d%20e@hospital.com",
"john..doe@hospital.com",
"--",
"e x a m p l e @ hospital . c o m",
"=0@$*^%;<!->.:\\()&#\"",
"©@£$∞§|[]≈±´•Ωé®†μüιœπ'~ß∂ √ç<>''‚…")
.map(input ->
    dynamicTest("Rejected: " + input,
        () -> assertThrows(
            RuntimeException.class,
            () -> new EmailAddress(input))));
   }
}
```

Invalid input that tries to break the validation logic in the constructor of EmailAddress

Asserts that the input is rejected by the contracts in the EmailAddress constructor

After running the boundary tests, it appears that the design of `EmailAddress` was good enough. But testing with invalid input revealed that `null` causes the implementation to crash when invoking `value.length()`. The next listing is an updated version of `EmailAddress` where `null` is explicitly rejected by a `notNull` contract.

Listing 8.6   Updated version of `EmailAddress` that rejects `null` input

```
import static org.apache.commons.lang3.Validate.inclusiveBetween;
import static org.apache.commons.lang3.Validate.isTrue;
import static org.apache.commons.lang3.Validate.matchesPattern;
import static org.apache.commons.lang3.Validate.notNull;

public final class EmailAddress {

    public final String value;

    public EmailAddress(final String value) {          Guards against null input
        notNull(value, "Input cannot be null");

        inclusiveBetween(15, 77, value.length(),
            "address length must be between 15 and 77 chars");

        isTrue(value.indexOf("@") < 65,
            "local part must be at most 64 chars");

        matchesPattern(value.toLowerCase(),
            "^[a-z0-9]+\\.?[a-z0-9]+@\\bhospital.com$",
            "Illegal email address");

        this.value = value.toLowerCase();
    }
    ...
}
```

Testing with input that causes eventual harm

Testing with input that causes eventual harm is interesting from a security standpoint because it's the underlying foundation of second-order injection attacks.[*]

In chapter 3, we talked about context mapping and how data changes meaning when crossing a semantic boundary. A similar reasoning applies when trying to understand where and when input might cause eventual harm in a system. This is because the input isn't trying to exploit a weakness in the receiving context, but rather in a context where it's used at a later stage. For example, when analyzing how the `EmailAddress` is used in the hospital domain, you might find that it's used in SQL queries and displayed on a web page. Although this isn't the primary concern of the `EmailAddress` object, knowing this should inspire you to test against SQL injection and cross-site scripting (XSS) attacks.

In the following code example, the `EmailAddress` object is tested with 10 SQL injection statements to ensure that it rejects the input. There are of course a lot more SQL injection statements to test for, but this gives you an idea of how to gain confidence that the `EmailAddress` object isn't susceptible to SQL injection attacks. (A better solution might be to dynamically load thousands of injection strings from an SQL dictionary instead of listing them explicitly.[†])

Testing that SQL injection statements are rejected

```
import static org.junit.Assert.assertEquals;
import static org.junit.jupiter.api.Assertions.assertThrows;
import static org.junit.jupiter.api.DynamicTest.dynamicTest;

class EmailAddressTest {
  @TestFactory
  Stream<DynamicTest> should_reject_SQL() {
    return Stream.of(
        "'or%20select *",
        "admin'--",
        "<>\"'%;)(&+",
        "'%20or%20''='",
        "'%20or%20'x'='x",
        "\"%20or%20\"x\"=\"x",
        "')%20or%20('x'='x",
        "0 or 1=1",
        "' or 0=0 --",
        "\" or 0=0 --")
        .map(input ->
          dynamicTest("Rejected: " + input,
            () -> assertThrows(
                RuntimeException.class,
                () -> new EmailAddress(input))));
  }
}
```

Example of SQL injection statements that normally would be imported from a dictionary

Asserts that the input is rejected by the contracts in the EmailAddress constructor

---

[*] For details on this type of attack, see the NCC Group white paper, "Second-Order Code Injection Attacks," available at https://www.nccgroup.trust/uk/our-research/second-order-code-injection-attacks/.

[†] For an example of a tool that can help, see the open source project Wfuzz, the Web fuzzer, at https://github.com/xmendez/wfuzz.

NOTE   Testing for XSS injections can be done in a similar fashion by using dictionaries with different ways of expressing <script>, along with the less than (<) character.[7]

Running the invalid input tests shows that the validation logic is sound. But to ensure it's really secure, we also need to test the extreme.

8.2.5 Testing the extreme

Testing the extreme is about identifying weaknesses in the design that make the application break or behave strangely when handling extreme values. For example, injecting large inputs can yield poor performance, memory leaks, or other unwanted behaviors. Listing 8.7 shows how EmailAddress is tested using a Supplier lambda with inputs ranging from 10,000 to 40 million characters. This clearly doesn't meet the domain rules, but the point isn't to test them; it's rather to see how the validation logic behaves when parsing the input. Ideally, it should reject it, but if a poor evaluation algorithm is used, then all sort of craziness might happen.

Listing 8.7 Testing EmailAddress with extreme values

```
import static org.apache.commons.lang3.StringUtils.repeat;
import static org.junit.Assert.assertEquals;
import static org.junit.jupiter.api.Assertions.assertThrows;
import static org.junit.jupiter.api.DynamicTest.dynamicTest;

class EmailAddressTest {
    @TestFactory
    Stream<DynamicTest> should_reject_extreme_input() {      // Generates a string with 100,000 characters
        return Stream.<Supplier<String>>of(
            () -> repeat("X", 10000),                        // Generates a string with 10,000 characters
            () -> repeat("X", 100000),                       // Generates a string with 1,000,000 characters
            () -> repeat("X", 1000000),
            () -> repeat("X", 10000000),                     // Generates a string with 10,000,000 characters
            () -> repeat("X", 20000000),                     // Generates a string with 20,000,000 characters
            () -> repeat("X", 40000000))                     // Generates a string with 40,000,000 characters
            .map(input ->
                dynamicTest("Rejecting extreme input",
                    () -> assertThrows(                      // Asserts that input is rejected by the contracts in the EmailAddress constructor
                        RuntimeException.class,
                        () -> new EmailAddress(input.get())))));
    }
}
```

As it turns out, running the extreme input test shows that the design of EmailAddress truly holds. The input is rejected in an efficient way, but this might not have been the case. In chapter 4, we talked about validation order and the importance of validating input length before parsing contents. Listing 8.7 is an example where it really matters.

[7] See https://www.owasp.org/index.php/XSS_Filter_Evasion_Cheat_Sheet for the possibilities.

The length check can seem redundant, but without it, the extreme input yields such terrible performance that the application more or less halts. This is because when the regexp engine fails to match an expression, it backtracks to the character next to the potential match and starts over again. For large input, this could lead to a catastrophic performance drop due to the vast number of backtracking operations.[8]

> **WARNING** Input length should always be checked before passing data to a regexp engine. Otherwise, you might open up security weaknesses caused by inefficient backtracking.

This concludes the `EmailAddress` example and how to use a security mindset when designing unit tests. But this is only one step toward making software secure by design. Another way is to ensure you only have the features you want in production, and this brings us to the next topic: verifying feature toggles.

8.3 Verifying feature toggles

With continuous delivery and continuous deployment increasingly becoming best practices in software development, the use of feature toggles when developing systems has also found greater acceptance. *Feature toggling* is a practice that allows developers to rapidly develop and deploy features in a controlled and safe manner. Feature toggling is a useful tool, but if used excessively, it can quickly become complex and nontrivial. Depending on what functionality you're toggling, a mistake made in the toggling mechanism can lead to not only incorrect business behavior, but also severe security complications (as you'll soon see).

When using feature toggles, it's important to understand that a toggle alters the behavior of your application. And like any other behavior, you should verify it using automated tests. This means you shouldn't verify only the feature code in your application, but also the toggles themselves. Before we start looking at how to verify toggles, let's take a look at an example of why it's important you verify them.

8.3.1 The perils of slippery toggles

Here's a story about a team of experienced developers and an unfortunate mishap with feature toggles—a mishap that led to exposure of sensitive data in a public API.[9] This mishap could have been avoided if the developers had used automated tests to verify the toggles. If you're not familiar with feature toggling, don't worry, you'll get a primer before we move on with the rest of the section.

The members of the team had been working together for some time, and it had become a tight group that was delivering working software at a high pace. The team applied many software development practices from continuous delivery, and they also used test-driven development when writing code. In addition to that, they'd built an extensive delivery pipeline that ensured only properly working features made it all the way to production.

---

[8] For details, see http://www.regular-expressions.info/catastrophic.html.

[9] The story is based on true events, but obfuscated for the purpose of this book.

The team was working on a set of new functionality. One of the first things they did, as they'd done many times before, was to add a feature toggle that allowed them to turn the new functionality on and off. This toggle was used when executing local tests on a developer's computer and the CI server, or when running tests against a deployed instance in the test environment. The new functionality was to be exposed through a public API, and when finished, it would have proper authentication and authorization so that only certain users could call the new API endpoints. The authorization would be based on some new permission rules that hadn't been developed yet and would be developed by a different team. But the new permission rules weren't needed to verify the rest of the business behavior. This allowed the team to continue to work while the other team was finishing up on its side. The toggle for the unfinished functionality was configured to be off during production in order to prevent it from being exposed in the public API. It was to remain off until the new functionality was completely finished and had passed all acceptance tests.

At one point during development, the toggle accidentally got enabled in the production configuration. This happened because of a mistake made by a developer when merging some code changes in the configuration files. The number of toggles used in the application had built up over time, and the configuration for the toggles had become rather complex. Spotting a subtle mistake in the configuration wasn't easy, and it was a mistake any one of the developers could have made. This mishap resulted in the new functionality being exposed in the public API—but without any form of authorization controls in place, because they hadn't been implemented yet. This made it possible for almost anyone to access the new endpoints. Fortunately, the mistake was soon discovered by the team, and the error in the configuration was corrected before the exposed functionality was ever executed in production.

Had an ill-minded person discovered those publicly exposed endpoints, they could have caused significant damage to the company. Even though this particular story ended well, there's still an interesting observation to make: none of the toggle configurations were verified to work as expected. If the team had employed automatic verification of the behavior of each toggle, it would have prevented the mishap from ever happening.

We wanted to share this story with you to show you a real example of how feature toggles can lead to quite serious problems if not implemented correctly. You're now ready to start looking at how to verify feature toggles from a security perspective.

8.3.2   *Feature toggling as a development tool*

A full exploration of the topic of feature toggling is beyond the scope of this book. But in order to understand why and how you should test your feature toggles, we feel it's fitting to begin with a brief introduction to the subject. If you're already familiar with feature toggling, you can view this section as a quick refresher.

In essence, a feature toggle works much like an electric switch. It lets you turn on and off a certain feature in your software, like an electric switch turns a light bulb on and off (figure 8.2). Apart from turning features on and off, toggles can also be used to switch between two different features, letting you alternate between different behaviors.

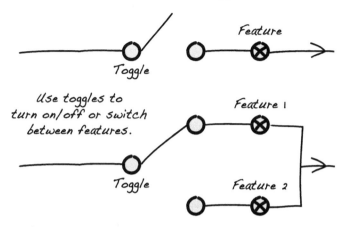

Figure 8.2   Feature toggles let you switch between features or turn them on and off.

When working on new functionality, you can use a toggle to turn on, or enable, that functionality when you need to run tests or deploy the application to a test environment. This gives you full access to the new functionality while you're working on it. At the same time, the toggle lets you turn off, or disable, the functionality when the application is deployed to your staging or production environment. This ability to turn specific functionality on and off gives you full control over when the functionality is made available to end users.

Another aspect of using feature toggles is that it lets you perform development on the main branch of the version control system instead of a long-lived feature branch. This is something many consider to be a necessity in order to follow best practices from continuous integration and, as a consequence, continuous delivery. (This is yet another reason for why feature toggles are becoming more common among developers.)

There are various types of feature toggles. Some are used to toggle features still in development, others to enable or disable functionality in production, depending on runtime parameters like time or date or certain aspects of the current user. You can also implement toggles in different ways. The most basic implementation is by changing a piece of code to either include or exclude certain parts of the codebase, as seen in listing 8.8.

As you can see, the code toggles between an old and a new functionality. The old functionality is invoked via the `callOldFunctionality` method. When the old functionality is enabled, you disable the new functionality by commenting out the `callNewFunctionality` method. When you want to use the new functionality instead, you do the opposite: you comment out the `callOldFunctionality` method and invoke `callNewFunctionality`, as is done in the listing with `usingNewImplementation`.

Listing 8.8   Feature toggling by code in its most rudimentary form

```
void usingOldImplementation() {

    doSomething();
    callOldFunctionality();        ◄─────┐ Enables current (old) implementation
    //callNewFunctionality();       ◄───┐ Disables new implementation
    doSomethingElse();

}

void usingNewImplementation() {

    doSomething();
    //callOldFunctionality();       ◄─────┐ Disables old implementation
    callNewFunctionality();        ◄───┐ Enables new implementation
    doSomethingElse();

}
```

A more elaborate toggle can, for example, be controlled via configuration provided at application startup. An example of this is shown in listing 8.9, where the functionality executed depends on the value of a system property called `feature.enabled`. If you want more dynamic toggles, you can make them controllable during runtime via some administrative mechanism.[10]

Listing 8.9   Feature toggling by configuration—a simple example

```
void branchByConfigurationProperty() {

    final String isEnabled = System.getProperty("feature.enabled", "false");
    if (Boolean.valueOf(isEnabled)) {    ◄───────┐
        doSomething();                            If the system property feature.enabled is
    }                                             set to true, then doSomething executes.
    else {
        doSomethingElse();
    }

}
```

Regardless of what type of toggles you use, or what mechanism you use to toggle them, it's important to understand that a feature toggle alters the behavior of your application. When you're flipping the toggle's switch, you're changing the behavior of your system. When you make use of feature toggles, you're designing your system to allow for alternating behavior, and, like any other behavior in your application, you should

---

[10] If you're interested in runtime toggles, there are several popular open source alternatives available that are worth taking a look at.

verify it with as many automated tests as you can. Because feature toggles can lead to security implications, it's important you get them right. Now that we've reviewed the basics of feature toggles, we can start looking at how you can verify them using automated tests.

8.3.3   *Taming the toggles*

Whenever you use feature toggles, you introduce complexity. The more toggles you add, the more complexity you end up with, especially if the toggles depend on each other. If you can, minimize the number of toggles you use at any given point. If that's not possible, then you'll have to learn how to deal with the complexity they add.

Complexity increases the likelihood of making mistakes, and when talking security, even a simple mistake can lead to severe problems. For example, exposing unfinished functionality in a public API can lead to a variety of security problems, ranging from direct economic loss to sensitive data being exposed.

> **TIP**   For every toggle you create, also create a test verifying the toggle works as intended.

If you create automatic tests that verify every toggle works as intended and you add those tests to your delivery pipeline, you get a safety net that ensures the toggles behave as expected. Because the tests are executed automatically, and for every build, they also work as regression tests for future changes, preventing you from accidentally messing things up. The scenario from the story at the beginning of this section, where a bad code merge led to API endpoints being exposed to the public, could've been prevented if there had been automatic tests in place that made sure the new functionality was never enabled in production.

Always strive to test feature toggles automatically rather than manually. Automated tests are the most reliable and deterministic way to verify not only feature toggles but any behavior of your code. There are exceptions to the rule, and sometimes you'll find it too costly to automate the verification. In those cases, it makes sense to resort to manual verification. When you need to perform manual testing, make sure you add that as a manual step in your delivery pipeline. By doing so, you avoid the risk of forgetting to perform the testing before a deliverable is marked as ready for production, because you can't accidentally skip a step that's in the pipeline.

Table 8.3 shows a few examples of how you can verify different types of feature toggles. These are basic suggestions, and often the verification will be more elaborate, but they'll suffice to give you an idea of how to verify a toggle using an automated test.

Table 8.3 Examples of methods for verifying feature toggles

Type of toggle	Typical methods of verification
Remove functionality in public API	If removed successfully, the API should: ■ Return 404 in an HTTP API call ■ Discard/ignore sent messages ■ Refuse connections on a socket
Replace existing functionality	Try to perform a new action. New behavior shouldn't be observed until finished (can be checked via resulting data or nonexisting UI elements, and so forth).
New authentication/authorization	Should be unable to log in/access system with new functionality/users/permissions. Only the old way should work.
Alternating behavior	When enabling feature A, then feature B shouldn't be executed/accessible, and vice versa when enabling feature B.

Listing 8.10 shows an example of a slightly more realistic OrderService that provides the ability to place an order. The OrderService has been extended with a new feature that sends data about the placed order to a business intelligence (BI) system. The new feature is toggled with the help of a ToggleService, which is a fictional library for managing feature toggles. Whenever the placeOrder method is executed, the OrderService checks to see whether the new or old order mode is enabled and acts accordingly.

Listing 8.10 `OrderService` with a new feature placed in a toggle

```java
import static org.apache.commons.lang3.Validate.notNull;

public class OrderService {

    // ...

    public void placeOrder(final Order order) {
        notNull(order);

        if (OrderMode.OLD.equals(toggleService.orderMode())) {
            orderBackend.process(order);      ◄──────  With the old order mode
        }                                               enabled, only the order is
        else if (OrderMode.NEW.equals(toggleService.orderMode())) {   processed; no additional
            orderBackend.process(order);                               processing is done.
            biBackend.record(order);       ◄─┐ Order data is sent to the BI system
        }                                    └ if the new order mode is enabled.
        else {
            throw new IllegalStateException("No supported order mode");
        }
    }

}
```

```
public class ToggleService {          ┌─ Used by OrderService to keep track of
                                      │  what order mode is currently enabled
    public enum OrderMode {
        OLD("old"),
        NEW("new");

        private final String key;

        OrderMode(final String key) {
            this.key = key;
        }

        public String key() {
            return key;
        }
    }

    private OrderMode orderMode = OLD;

    public OrderMode orderMode() {
        return orderMode;
    }

    public void setOrderMode(final OrderMode orderMode) {
        this.orderMode = notNull(orderMode);
    }
}
```

An example of how to write tests for this toggle is shown in listing 8.11. The tests aren't focusing on the behavior of the underlying functionality of placing an order and sending data to a BI system. They're only concerned with verifying if correct behavior is triggered based on the setting of the toggle. If the order mode of the toggle is set to OLD, then the order should be sent for processing, but nothing should be sent to the BI system. If the order mode is set to NEW, then data about the order should be sent to the BI system in addition to the order being processed. The tests are using mocks to verify interaction with the supporting services (the BI backend and the order backend). Don't worry if you're not familiar with using mocks in tests. In this example, it's a way to verify if any calls have been made to the supporting services.

Listing 8.11 Testing the toggle in `OrderService`

```
import org.junit.Test;

import static org.mockito.Matchers.any;
import static org.mockito.Mockito.*;

public class OrderServiceToggleTests {

    @Test
    public void should_process_order_if_old_order_mode_is_enabled() {
        givenOrderModeIs(OLD);

        whenPlacingAnOrder();
```

```
      thenOrderShouldBeProcessed();          ◄────  Verifies that the order has
   }                                                been sent for processing

   @Test
   public void should_not_send_to_BI_if_old_order_mode_is_enabled() {
      givenOrderModeIs(OLD);

      whenPlacingAnOrder();

      thenOrderShouldNotBeSentToBI();    ◄──────  The order shouldn't be sent to the BI system.
   }

   @Test
   public void should_process_order_if_new_order_mode_is_enabled() {
      givenOrderModeIs(NEW);

      whenPlacingAnOrder();
                                               Verifies that the order has
      thenOrderShouldBeProcessed();    ◄────  been sent for processing
   }

   @Test
   public void should_send_to_BI_if_new_order_mode_is_enabled() {
      givenOrderModeIs(NEW);

      whenPlacingAnOrder();

      thenOrderShouldBeSentToBI();    ◄──────  The order should be sent to the BI system.
   }

   private ToggleService toggleService;
   private OrderBackend orderBackend;
   private BIBackend biBackend;

   private void givenOrderModeIs(final OrderMode orderMode) {
      toggleService = new ToggleService();
      toggleService.setOrderMode(orderMode);
   }

   private void whenPlacingAnOrder() {
      createOrderService().placeOrder(new Order());
   }

   private OrderService createOrderService() {
      orderBackend = mock(OrderBackend.class);
      biBackend = mock(BIBackend.class);       │─  Mocks the supporting services
      return new OrderService(orderBackend,    │   injected to the OrderService
                              biBackend,
                              toggleService);
   }
                                                        │   Verifies that the process(Order)
   private void thenOrderShouldBeProcessed() {          │   method is called
      verify(orderBackend).process(any(Order.class));  ◄─┘
   }
                                                 │  Verifies that no calls have
   private void thenOrderShouldNotBeSentToBI() { │  been made to the BIBackend
      verifyZeroInteractions(biBackend);    ◄────┘
```

```
    }

    private void thenOrderShouldBeSentToBI() {
        verify(biBackend).record(any(Order.class));
    }

}
```

◄─── **Verifies that the record method is called**

So far, you've learned why it's important to test your toggles, and you've seen a few examples of how to test them. There are a few more things to discuss before we close the section on feature toggles: dealing with a large number of toggles and the fact that the process of toggling can be subject to auditing.

8.3.4 *Dealing with combinatory complexity*

If you're using multiple toggles, you should strive to verify all combinations of them, especially if there are toggles that affect each other. Even if they aren't directly related, you should test all the combinations, because there might be indirect coupling between them. Indirect coupling can occur at any time during development. As you might guess, it can quickly become a combinatory nightmare if you have a large number of feature toggles to verify. But the more toggles you have, the more likely it is you'll get something wrong—and the more important it is you test them. This is one of the reasons why you should always try to keep the number of feature toggles as low as possible.

One could argue that it isn't necessary to test all combinations if you first perform a risk analysis—evaluating how much more confidence or less risk you get by testing all combinations versus testing a few of them—and then only choose a selected set of combinations to test. This approach might appear reasonable, but it's based on the assumption that you can assess security flaws you're unaware of. If you're aware of them, you most likely have already addressed them.[11] Our recommendation is to verify all combinations of your toggles and mitigate the testing complexity by reducing the number of toggles in your codebase.

8.3.5 *Toggles are subject to auditing*

One thing to keep in mind when using runtime toggles is the importance of exposing the toggle mechanism in a safe manner. Because these types of toggles are changing the behavior of the application in production, the mechanism you use to change the state of the toggles should be protected so that only authorized access is possible. You should also consider if any modifications to the state of a toggle should be logged for auditing purposes. It should always be possible to identify when and by whom a toggle was changed in production.

> **NOTE** When and by whom a toggle is changed in production is a fundamental question you should be able to answer.

---

[11] This is similar to the reasoning about the shortcomings of the traditional approach to software security we discussed in chapter 1, where we identified the problems with trying to explicitly protect yourself against threats you aren't aware of.

The use of feature toggling is becoming more and more popular, and we predict many developers will come to see such toggles as a natural part of how software is developed. An effect of this is that it'll be increasingly important to verify your toggles in an automatic way and to make that verification part of your delivery pipeline. We're advocates of using feature toggles because they bring many benefits to software development. As long as you're aware of the potential pitfalls and how to mitigate them, we believe the benefits far outweigh the drawbacks. In the next section, we'll take a look at how to get started writing automated tests that explicitly verify security features and vulnerabilities.

8.4 Automated security tests

Most developers will agree that security testing is important and should be performed regularly. The reality, though, is that most software projects will never be subjected to a security audit or a penetration test, perhaps because the software has been deemed low risk or because security has been overlooked by the developers. Another common reason for why these tests are skipped, in our experience, is because penetration tests are often considered too time-consuming and costly.

Security testing tends to be time-consuming because a lot of the testing involved can be hard to automate. It's hard to automate because it's the experience and knowledge of the security expert that's needed to expose possible flaws and weaknesses in an application.

In a way, the work (and value) of a penetration tester is not that different from that of a normal tester performing exploratory testing. Humans can perform tasks and logical reasoning in ways computers are still incapable of. Trying to replace a human tester with automated tests is not a realistic option, nor do we suggest it should be your goal. But some of the testing performed during a penetration test can be automated. In this section, you'll learn how to write tests that can be used to perform a mini pen test as part of your delivery pipeline.

8.4.1 Security tests are only tests

One thing you should realize is that security tests are no different from any other tests (figure 8.3). The only difference is that as developers, for whatever reason, we choose to label the tests with the word *security*. If you know how to write regular automated tests to verify behavior and find bugs, you can apply the exact same principles to security testing.

- Do you handle failed login attempts correctly? Write a test for it.
- Does your online discussion forum have adequate protection against XSS? Write a test that tries to enter malicious data.

Once you understand that there's nothing magical about security testing, you can start using automated tests to verify security features and to find security bugs.[12]

Let's take a closer look at what types of checks a security tester performs. Some are more or less mandatory in the sense that they will always be performed regardless of what the goal of the testing is. A lot of these checks can be considered hygiene-level,

---

[12] OWASP publishes a number of cheat sheets that you can use as a guide when writing your own security tests. See https://www.owasp.org/index.php/OWASP_Cheat_Sheet_Series.

Figure 8.3 Security tests are no different from other tests.

and an application should always pass them. As it turns out, many of them aren't that hard to perform through automated tests. The checks that are easy to automate are usually also the ones where having a human performing them adds little value. Converting these into automated tests not only allows you to run them at will, but it also allows the testers to focus on more elaborate testing. Supplying malicious data to check for flaws in input validation, such as flaws that enable SQL injection or buffer overflow attacks, isn't only a mundane task but also a good example of testing that can be automated.

8.4.2 *Working with security tests*

To help you understand what features to test and how to structure the work with test automation, we can categorize security tests into two main categories: application and infrastructure (as seen in table 8.4). Apart from these two types of tests that explicitly focus on security, there are also tests with a domain focus. We covered domain testing in the first part of this chapter and, as you learned, those tests will also help secure your system. We'll now take a look at the other two categories of tests.

Table 8.4 Types of security tests

Category	Types of checks
Application focused	These tests verify the application in parts other than the domain. Examples include checking HTTP headers in a web application or testing input validation.
Infrastructure focused	These tests verify correct behavior from the infrastructure running the application. Examples include checking for open ports and looking at the privileges of the running process.

For tests focusing on the application and infrastructure, there are a number of tools available that might be worth exploring. Port scanning tools can, for example, be set up to run against the server you deploy your application on. Likewise, a web testing tool can scan your web application or run predefined use cases, while at the same time checking for vulnerabilities.[13] You can also use tools to scan your code for vulnerable third-party dependencies.[14] Any unexpected results from a test run should fail and cause the delivery pipeline to be stopped.

These types of tests can sometimes take a while to execute, so you might choose to run them less often than other tests in your pipeline. If you have other long-running tests such as performance tests executed nightly, a good approach can be to run the scanning tools before or after them.

8.4.3   *Leveraging infrastructure as code*

With the adoption of cloud computing, the idea of infrastructure as code (IaC) is becoming more common. The basic concept of IaC is that it allows you to declaratively define infrastructure. This can be anything from servers and network topologies to firewalls, routing, and more. This has multiple advantages, one of which is making the setup of your infrastructure deterministic, giving you the ability to recreate your entire infrastructure as many times as you want. It also becomes a breeze to use version control to track the history of every change to your infrastructure, no matter how small or big.

From a security perspective, this is exciting. Not only do you minimize the risk of human error, but you can also use this approach to automatically verify your infrastructure. Because you're putting all changes in a version control system, you get traceability of any changes made, and the automated nature of IaC means you can verify the changes before pushing them into production.

For example, say you're updating a firewall. Before applying the changes in production, you first apply them in a preproduction environment. The ideal way to do this is to completely recreate the entire infrastructure in a mirrored setup. Once you've created the preproduction environment, you can run automated security tests against it, verifying that no previous functionality has been unintentionally altered and that the changes made have the expected effects. You can then safely deploy the changes in production. If you are using IaC or are about to move in that direction, you should definitely look into the opportunities it provides in terms of securing your infrastructure.

8.4.4   *Putting it into practice*

By writing tests with an explicit security focus and adding them to your pipeline, you can pick a lot of low-hanging fruit. If you couple that with the execution of existing tools in an automated fashion, you get a mini pen test you can execute at will and as often as you want. This field is still developing, but we'll be watching it with interest in

---

[13] OWASP has a great list of tools at https://www.owasp.org/index.php/Category:Vulnerability _Scanning_Tools.

[14] OWASP Dependency Check is an example of a tool you can use to scan for vulnerable dependencies; see https://www.owasp.org/index.php/OWASP_Dependency_Check.

the upcoming years because we're hoping the tools will become more mature and accessible to both developers and QA.

You have now learned the basics of how to automate explicit security testing. In the next section, we'll take a look at why availability is important and how it relates to secure software.

8.5 Testing for availability

It's easy to think that the classical security concerns of confidentiality, integrity, and availability (CIA) only apply to information security, but they're also important when designing secure software.[15] For example, *confidentiality* is about protecting data from being read by unauthorized users, and *integrity* ensures data is changed in an authorized way. But what about *availability*? Many developers find it easy to understand but difficult to test because it concerns having data available when authorized users need it.

For example, suppose a fire breaks out and you call 911 (or 112 in Europe), but your call doesn't get through, not because you dialed the wrong number but because the switchboard is flooded with prank calls. Not good! Another less serious example is when you're trying to buy tickets to a popular concert online, and the website crashes or can't be accessed. Often, this isn't the result of malevolent behavior, but rather that everyone tries to buy tickets at the same time; people's intentions are good, but the consequences are equally as bad as those of an evil attack.

Testing availability is therefore something every application needs to do, but how do you do this in practice? One way is to simulate a denial of service (DoS) attack, which lets you understand what the behavior is before and after data becomes unavailable.[16] To do this, you need to start by estimating the headroom.

8.5.1 Estimating the headroom

Estimating the headroom is about trying to understand how much load an application can handle before it fails to serve its clients in a satisfactory way. Typical things to look for are memory consumption, CPU utilization, response times, and so on. But it can also be a way to understand how the application behaves before it fails and where the weak spots are in the design.

Figure 8.4 shows an example of a distributed denial of service (DDoS) attack, where a massive number of parallel requests are made from different servers against an application. Regardless of how many requests are made or how much load they generate, the main objective is to limit the availability of the application's services. When talking about DDoS attacks, it's not uncommon to use the more generic term DoS attack. The main difference between the two is that DoS attacks are made from a single server instead of multiple ones. The objective is, however, the same, and from now on, we'll use the terms DDoS and DoS interchangeably.

---

[15] See NIST Special Publication 800-27, "Engineering Principles for Information Technology Security (A Baseline for Achieving Security)," available at https://csrc.nist.gov/publications/detail/sp/800-27/rev-a/archive/2004-06-21.

[16] To simulate this type of attack, see US-CERT Security Tip ST04-015, "Understanding Denial-of-Service Attacks" at https://www.us-cert.gov/ncas/tips/ST04-015.

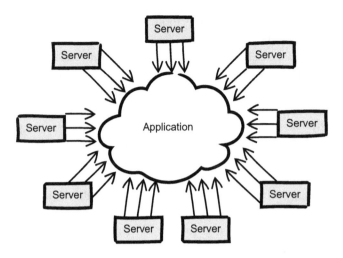

Figure 8.4   Denial of service attack (DDoS, but more commonly referred to as DoS attack)

By simulating a DoS attack, you can easily get a feel for how well your application scales and how it behaves before it fails to meet its availability requirements. It's important to note that regardless of how well a system is designed, an attack large enough will eventually break it. This makes it practically impossible to design a system that's 100% resilient, but estimating the headroom is a good strategy to use when trying to understand where the weak spots are in your design.

Several commercial products and open source alternatives let you load test your application. One example is "Bees with Machine Guns,"[17] which is a utility for creating EC2 server instances on the Amazon Web Services platform that attack an application with thousands of parallel requests.[18] In listing 8.12, you see an example of how to configure eight EC2 instances that issue 100,000 requests, 500 at a time, against a website.

> **WARNING**   Attacking a website is illegal unless you have explicit permission to do so, and consuming resources this way can lead to a painful experience on your credit card.

Listing 8.12   Simple example of configuring a test running a DDoS attack

Spins up eight EC2 server
instances to attack the website

```
bees up -s 8 -g public -k your_ssh_key
bees attack -n 100000 -c 500 -u website_url
bees down
```

Sends 100,000 requests, 500
at a time, to the specified url

Spins down the EC2 server instances

---

[17] See https://github.com/newsapps/beeswithmachineguns.

[18] See https://aws.amazon.com for more information on the Amazon Elastic Compute Cloud.

Regardless of which product you choose, having tests in your delivery pipeline that place your system under a heavy load is an efficient way of flushing out weaknesses that could be exploitable by an attacker in production. But a DoS attack doesn't require thousands of parallel requests to be successful. Availability could be affected in a more sophisticated way; for example, by exploiting domain rules that execute under the radar.

8.5.2 *Exploiting domain rules*

When exploiting domain rules, you're actually creating a domain DoS attack in which rules are executed in a way that's accepted by the business, but with malicious intent.[19] To illustrate, let's consider the example of a hotel that has a generous cancellation policy.

> **WARNING** Domain DoS attacks are extremely difficult to detect because there's no difference between benevolent and malevolent use of domain rules—it's only the intent that differs.

To provide great customer service, the hotel manager has decided to fully refund any reservation that's canceled before 4 p.m. on the day of arrival. This allows for great flexibility, but what if someone makes a reservation without the intent of staying at the hotel? Won't that prevent someone else from making a reservation, causing the hotel to lose business? It certainly will, and that's how a domain DoS attack works. By exploiting the domain rules for cancellation, it's possible to reserve all the rooms at the hotel and cancel them at the latest possible moment without being charged. This way, an attacker might be able to block out a certain room type or direct customers to a competitor's hotel.

This type of attack might seem fictitious and unlikely, but there are several real-world examples where this has happened. One was in San Francisco, where the ride-sharing company, Lyft, accused rival Uber of booking and then canceling over 5,000 rides in an attempt to affect its business.[20] Another was in India, where Uber sued its competitor Ola for booking over 400,000 false rides.[21]

Simulating this in tests might seem pointless, but the fact is that by exercising domain rules in a malicious way, you gain deeper understanding of weaknesses in the domain model—knowledge that could be invaluable when designing alarms to trigger on thresholds and user behavior, for example, or when using machine learning to detect malicious activity. But testing availability is only one thing to consider when adding security to your delivery pipeline. Another is to understand how an application's behavior changes with its configuration, especially the security aspects. And this brings us to the next topic: validating configuration.

---

[19] See Johan Arnör's master's thesis "Domain-Driven Security's Take on Denial-of-Service (DoS) Attacks," available at http://www.diva-portal.org/smash/record.jsf?pid=diva2%3A945831.

[20] See the August 12, 2014, *TIME* article, "Lyft Accuses Uber of Booking Then Canceling More Than 5,000 Rides," available at http://time.com/3102548/lyft-uber-cancelling-rides/.

[21] See the March 23, 2016, *Bloomberg* article, "Uber Sues Ola Claiming Fake Bookings as India Fight Escalates," available at https://www.bloomberg.com/news/articles/2016-03-23/uber-sues-ola-claiming-fake-bookings-as-india-fight-escalates.

8.6   *Validating configuration*

In contemporary software development, common features are often realized through configuration; you bring in an existing library or framework that allows you to enable, disable, and tweak functionality without having to implement it yourself. In this section, we'll take a look at why it's important to verify your configuration and how automation can be used to protect against security flaws caused by misconfiguration.

If you're building a web application, you probably don't want to spend time writing your own HTTPS implementation to serve web requests or implementing a home-grown ORM framework for database persistence—both of which can be hard to get right. Instead of implementing these generic features yourself, you can use an existing implementation in the form of a library or a framework. For most developers, this makes a lot of sense, because bringing in generic functionality via an external tool lets you focus on what's unique about your business domain.

Even if you do decide to roll your own in-house implementation of generic functionality, you're most likely going to distribute it as a library for development teams to reuse in their applications. Regardless of which approach you take, the result is that important features of an application are provided by code external to the current team, and those features are controlled through configuration. The features provided can be generic but can, nonetheless, play a central role in the security of your application. As a consequence, errors in the configuration can directly lead to security problems. Automated tests can effectively be used to mitigate these problems.

8.6.1   *Causes for configuration-related security flaws*

Security flaws resulting from faulty configuration can generally be said to stem from either unintentional changes, intentional changes, or misunderstood configuration (figure 8.5).

Let's take a look at each one of these underlying causes to give you an understanding of how they can arise, and why it's so important that you use automated tests to prevent these types of flaws from occurring.

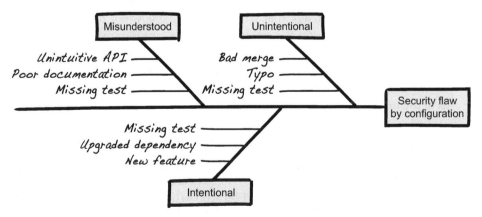

Figure 8.5   Underlying causes for security flaws induced by configuration

UNINTENTIONAL CHANGES

Being able to control functionality through configuration makes the lives of developers a lot easier. Not only does it speed up development, but it can also make your application more secure. Using well-known, community-reviewed, battle-tested, open source implementations is most likely going to be more secure than writing your own libraries. Getting security features right in software is hard, even for the most seasoned security experts.

When features are controlled via configuration, it's easy to alter the behavior of your application. Even substantial changes can be made by altering one line in a configuration. But although it's easy to change the behavior to something you want, it's equally easy to unintentionally change it to something you don't want. Say you mistakenly alter a line in your configuration or you misspell a string parameter, and suddenly the behavior of your application is silently changed; there's no exception or other error when you run the application. If you're unlucky, the changed behavior makes your application vulnerable in one way or another, and if you're really unlucky, you're not going to notice until after it's been deployed to production.

What you need is a safety net that can catch many of the problems caused by unintentional configuration changes. Creating automated tests that check features and behavior enabled via configuration is a relatively economical and easy way to implement such a safety net.

INTENTIONAL CHANGES

It's not only unintentional changes that can make your application insecure through unwanted side effects. Sometimes an intentional change can have unwanted side effects too.

Say you're implementing a new feature and, as part of that, you need to make a change in your application's configuration. You verify the new behavior—ideally by adding a new automated test as you just learned—and then continue implementing the rest of the new feature. But what you didn't notice when verifying the new behavior was that by making the change, you also altered the behavior in a different part of the application. Maybe the configuration you changed had been carefully placed there by another developer as the result of a previously conducted security audit or penetration test, or in order to prevent the exposure of a certain weakness. When altering the configuration, you also disabled those security features, leaving your application exposed.

Unknowingly changing the behavior in one part of a system while making changes in another part isn't an uncommon scenario. The scenario is similar to the one with the unintentional changes, but it's worth pointing this one out because, as a developer, you're not doing anything wrong here.

Unintentional changes are caused by someone making a mistake, so you might think you can protect yourself by being more careful or introducing more rigorous processes. But, in this case, you're making the correct code changes with a deliberate intent. You might even add automated tests for the changes you're currently making. The tests you add might protect you from *unintentional* changes of the feature you just implemented, but unless you have tests for the already existing features, your *intentional* change can break existing behavior. This is something to look out for when working in existing codebases where, historically, not many tests have been written.

MISUNDERSTOOD CONFIGURATION

The third main cause of misconfiguration is not understanding the configuration mechanism used. In essence, this occurs when you think you're configuring a certain behavior, whereas in reality, you're configuring something else. This can easily happen when the configuration API for the library you're using hasn't been designed to be unambiguous.

Integer values, magic strings, and negating statements are typical giveaways of an ambiguous configuration API. When you use such configuration, chances are you're not getting what you think you are. Every time you configure a feature, make it a habit to add a test that verifies your configuration is doing what you intend.

8.6.2   *Automated tests as your safety net*

How can you protect yourself from accidentally introducing security vulnerabilities in other parts of the software than the one you're currently working on? How can you ensure the intention and tribal knowledge behind important configuration don't get lost as a codebase evolves? As we've already hinted, an efficient way is to write automated tests to verify the expected behavior and use those tests as a regression suite in your delivery pipeline.

If you're new to this view on testing configuration from a security perspective, it helps to think in terms of configuration hot spots. A *configuration hot spot* is an area in your configuration where the type of behavior you're controlling has a direct or indirect impact on how secure your system will be. To give you an idea of some typical configuration hot spots, table 8.5 lists examples of functionality it's important to have automated tests for.

Table 8.5   Examples of configuration hot spots to test

Type of configuration	Examples of behavior controlled
Web containers	▪ HTTP headers
	▪ CSRF tokens
	▪ Output encoding
Network communication	▪ Transport Layer Security (HTTPS and so on)
Data parsing	▪ Behavior of data parsers (such as XML and JSON parsers)
Authentication mechanisms	▪ Authentication on/off
	▪ Integration settings (for example, for CAS and LDAP)

Our experience is that the functionality that is controlled via configuration and is interesting from a security perspective is often fairly straightforward to write automated tests for. In a web application, for example, it isn't hard to write a test that checks for proper HTTP headers or that a form uses CSRF tokens.[22] These types of tests are best created as you're developing an application, but because they tend to be straightforward to write, it's fairly easy to add them to an existing codebase.

When discussing test automation for functionality controlled by configuration, sometimes arguments are made against this practice. One common argument is that testing your configuration is similar to testing a setter method that sets a simple value and therefore adds little value. Although this can be true for some types of configuration, it isn't true for the one we're discussing here.

The type of configuration you should test is configuration that alters the behavior of your application. In the same way you write tests to verify the behavior you implement, it's equally important to write tests for the behavior you configure. Once you realize that you aren't testing the configuration itself but rather the resulting behavior, it becomes clearer why this is so important.

8.6.3 *Knowing your defaults and verifying them*

In addition to the behaviors you explicitly configure, it's also important to verify the implicit behaviors you get when using a library or framework. An *implicit behavior* is one you get without adding any configuration. This is sometimes also referred to as a *default* behavior. Because there's no configuration, the tricky part here is even knowing you have an important feature to verify. In order to gain that knowledge, you need to know the defaults of the tool you use.

As an example, most modern web frameworks make it easy to write HTTP APIs or RESTful web services. Numerous frameworks and libraries allow the developer to declaratively write code to define the HTTP endpoints. These types of frameworks can boost your productivity because they let you focus on your business logic instead of generic plumbing and boilerplate code. What enables the code you write to be clean and concise is usually the application of sensible default behavior by the framework. As long as you stick to the defaults, there's little code to write. This is all good when writing code tutorials or small proof-of-concept applications, but for real business-critical projects, you must make sure you understand exactly what the defaults are. In many cases, the defaults will help make your application more secure, but in some cases, they might sacrifice some level of security for an increased ease of use. If you aren't aware of those trade-offs, you might expose security vulnerabilities without knowing it.

Say you're writing an HTTP service. It could be in the form of a RESTful API or some other API approach based on HTTP. In order to reduce the number of attack vectors, it's a good security practice to only enable the HTTP methods required by the API. If an API endpoint is meant to serve data to clients accessing it using an HTTP GET, you should make sure it doesn't return a normal response when accessed with any other HTTP method. Instead, it can respond with a status code 405 Method Not Allowed or 501 Not Implemented to let the client know the requested HTTP method is not

---

[22] A good place to start to learn more about HTTP headers to consider is the OWASP Secure Headers Project at https://www.owasp.org/index.php/OWASP_Secure_Headers_Project.

supported. The more HTTP methods the endpoint responds to, the more security vulnerabilities it opens up. For example, TRACE is an HTTP method known to be used to perform cross-site tracing (XST) attacks, so you don't want to enable TRACE unless you have to.[23]

Listing 8.13 shows an example of how to write a test that verifies only specific HTTP methods are enabled for an endpoint. Note that the example is simplified and that a real implementation depends on how the API under test is designed and what the definition of an enabled endpoint is. Other aspects to consider are, for example, if custom HTTP methods are allowed and if authentication is enabled.

Listing 8.13   Testing enabled HTTP methods

```java
import org.junit.Test;
import java.net.URI;

import static java.util.Arrays.asList;
import static java.util.stream.Collectors.toList;
import static java.util.stream.Collectors.toSet;
import static org.apache.commons.lang3.Validate.notNull;
import static org.junit.Assert.assertEquals;

public class OnlyExpectedMethodsAreEnabledTest {

    enum HTTPMethod {
        GET, HEAD, POST, PUT, DELETE, CONNECT, OPTIONS, TRACE
    }

    URI uri;
    List<Result> results;

    @Test
    public void verify_only_expected_HTTP_methods_are_enabled() {    ⟵ The endpoint under test
        givenEndpoint("http://example.com/endpoint");

        whenTestingMethods(HTTPMethod.values());    ⟵ Tests all HTTP methods

        thenTheOnlyMethodsEnabledAre(GET, PUT, HEAD);    ⟵ Only GET, PUT, and HEAD are enabled
    }

    void givenEndpoint(final String uri) {
        this.uri = URI.create(uri);
    }

    void whenTestingMethods(final HTTPMethod... methods) {
        results = Arrays.stream(methods)
                        .distinct()
                        .map(method -> getStatus(method, uri))
                        .collect(toList());
    }
```

---

[23] See https://www.owasp.org/index.php/Cross_Site_Tracing for details.

```
void thenTheOnlyMethodsEnabledAre(final HTTPMethod... methods) {
    final Set<HTTPMethod> enabled = enabledHttpMethods();
    assertEquals(new HashSet<>(asList(methods)), enabled);
}

Set<HTTPMethod> enabledHttpMethods() {
    return results.stream()
                  .filter(r -> isEnabled(r.status))
                  .map(r -> r.method)
                  .collect(toSet());
}

static class Result {

    final int status;
    final HTTPMethod method;

    Result(final int status, final HTTPMethod method) {
        this.status = status;
        this.method = notNull(method);
    }

}

boolean isEnabled(final int statusCode) {
    // Check if the status code is considered
    // as "enabled"
}

Result getStatus(final HTTPMethod method, final URI uri) {
    // Call the URI with the given HTTP method
    // and return the status
}

// ...

}
```

Implementation details left out for brevity

Remember that the mindset you should have here isn't to explicitly forbid HTTP methods, but to only enable those that are needed for the functionality you're implementing. Also, even if the default settings are what you need, you should add tests that verify the behavior. Even if the defaults are what you need right now, a later release of the framework might change the defaults; if you have tests for those behaviors, you'll immediately catch those changes.

In this chapter, you saw several ways to use your delivery pipeline to automatically verify security concerns. Some approaches we've discussed have involved a more explicit focus on security than other concepts in this book. If you're already familiar with some of these approaches, we hope you've learned how to view them from a slightly different perspective. In the next chapter, you'll learn how to securely handle exceptions and how you can use different design ideas to avoid many of the issues with traditional error handling.

Summary

- By dividing tests into normal testing, boundary testing, invalid input testing, and extreme input testing, you can include security in your unit test suites.
- Regular expressions can be sensitive to inefficient backtracking, and, therefore, you should check the length of input before sending it to the regular expression engine.
- Feature toggles can cause security vulnerabilities, but you can mitigate those vulnerabilities by verifying the toggle mechanisms using automated tests.
- A good rule of thumb is to create a test for every toggle you add, and you should test all possible combinations of them.
- You should watch out for the combinatory complexity that large numbers of toggles can lead to. The best way to avoid this is by keeping the number of toggles as small as possible.
- The toggle mechanism itself can be subject to auditing and record keeping.
- Incorporating automated security tests into your build pipeline can give you the ability to run a mini penetration test as often as you like.
- Availability is an important security aspect that needs to be considered in every system.
- Simulating DoS attacks helps in understanding weaknesses in the overall design.
- A domain DoS attack is extremely difficult to protect against because it's only the intent that distinguishes it from regular usage.
- Many security problems are caused by misconfiguration, and the cause for faulty configuration can be either unintentional changes, intentional changes, or misunderstood configuration.
- Configuration hot spots are good indicators for finding areas in your configuration where testing is most critical.
- It's important to know the default behavior of the tools you use and assert that behavior with tests.

Handling failures securely

What is it that makes failures so interesting from a security perspective? Could it be that many systems reveal their internal secrets when they fail? Or is it how handling failure defines a system's level of security? Regardless, recognizing that failures and security go hand-in-hand is incredibly important when designing secure software. This, in turn, requires understanding what the security implications are when making certain design choices. For example, if you choose to use exceptions to signal errors, you need to make sure you don't leak sensitive data. Or when integrating systems, if you don't recognize the danger of cascading failures, you could end up with a system as fragile as a house of cards.

Regardless of which design choices you make, or why, you need to consider *failure*. The focus of this chapter isn't to tell you which design is better, but rather to give you insight into the security implications when making certain design choices. Also, the scope of failures is huge. To give you an idea of how complex the topic is, we'll show you examples ranging from low-level code constructs to high-level system design. All in all, this is a good starting point for learning how to handle failures securely. With that said, let's start with one of the most common design choices—exceptions.

9.1   *Using exceptions to deal with failure*

Exceptions are often used to represent failures because they allow you to disrupt the normal flow of an application program.[1] Because of this, it's common that exceptions carry information about why and where the execution flow was disrupted—the *why* is described in the message and the *where* by the stack trace. In listing 9.1, you see a stack trace resulting from a closed database connection. At first glance, it seems harmless, but if you look carefully, you'll see that it reveals information that you might want to keep secret. For example, the first line shows that the exception is a `java.sql.SQL-Exception`. This tells you that data is stored in a relational database, and the system can be susceptible to SQL injection attacks. The same line also shows that the code is written in Java, which hints that the overall system might be vulnerable to exploits present in the language and the Java Virtual Machine (JVM).

> **Listing 9.1   Stack trace of a SQL exception when the database connection was closed**

java.sql.SQLException shows Java is used.

SQLException indicates that data is stored in a relational database.

```
java.sql.SQLException: Closed Connection
    at oracle.jdbc.driver.DatabaseError...
    at oracle.jdbc.driver.DatabaseError.throwSqlException(...
    at oracle.jdbc.driver.PhysicalConnection.rollback(...
    at org.apache.tomcat.dbcp.dbcp.DelegatingConnection...
    at org.apache.tomcat.dbcp.dbcp.PoolingDataSource$
                     PoolGuardConnectionWrapper.rollback(...
    at net.sf.hibernate.transaction.JDBCTransaction...
...
```

org.apache.tomcat.dbcp shows that Apache Tomcat's database connection pool component is used.[2]

net.sf.hibernate shows that Hibernate is used as an object relational mapper.[3]

Obviously, the level of detail in a stack trace is meant for troubleshooting rather than sharing. But why is it that stack traces get revealed to the end user every now and then? The answer lies in a combination of sloppy design and not understanding why

[1] See the Oracle documentation on exceptions at https://docs.oracle.com/javase/tutorial/essential/exceptions/definition.html.

[2] See the Apache Commons DBCP documentation at https://commons.apache.org/proper/commons-dbcp/index.html.

[3] See "Hibernate ORM: What Is Object/Relational Mapping?" at http://hibernate.org/orm/what-is-an-orm/.

exceptions are thrown. To illustrate this, we'll walk you through an example where sensitive business information is leaked from the domain because of intermixing business and technical exceptions of the same type. The example also helps to demonstrate why it's important to never include business data in technical exceptions, regardless of whether it's sensitive or not.

9.1.1 Throwing exceptions

As illustrated in figure 9.1, there are three main reasons why exceptions are thrown in an application: business rule violations, technical errors, and failures in the underlying framework. All exceptions share the same objective of preventing illegal actions, but the purpose of each one differs. For example, *business exceptions* prevent actions that are considered illegal from a domain perspective, such as withdrawing money from a bank account with insufficient funds or adding items to a paid order. *Technical exceptions* are exceptions that aren't concerned about domain rules. Instead, they prevent actions that are illegal from a technical point of view, such as adding items to an order without enough memory allocated.

We believe separating business exceptions and technical exceptions is a good design strategy because technical details don't belong in the domain.[4] But not everyone agrees. Some choose to favor designs that intermix business exceptions and technical exceptions because the main objective is to prevent illegal actions, regardless of whether the illegality is technical or not. This might seem to be a minor detail, but intermixing exceptions is a door opener to a lot of complexity and potential security problems.

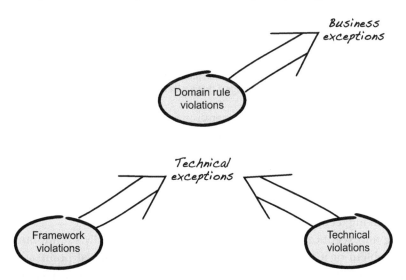

Figure 9.1   Three reasons for throwing exceptions in an application: domain rule violations, technical violations, and framework violations

---

[4]   See Dan B. Johnsson's essay "Distinguish Business Exceptions from Technical" in *97 Things Every Programmer Should Know: Collective Wisdom from the Experts*, edited by Kevlin Henney (O'Reilly, 2010).

In listing 9.2, business and technical exceptions are intermixed using the same exception type. The main flow is fairly straightforward: a customer's accounts are fetched from a database, and the account matching the provided account number is returned. As part of this, an exception is thrown if no account is found or if an error occurs in the database.

Listing 9.2   Intermixing business and technical exceptions using the same type

```java
import static java.lang.String.format;
import static org.apache.commons.lang3.Validate.notNull;

public Account fetchAccountFor(final Customer customer,
                               final AccountNumber accountNumber) {
    notNull(customer);
    notNull(accountNumber);

    try {
        return accountDatabase                               // Fetches the customer's
                .selectAccountsFor(customer)                 // accounts from the database
                .stream()
                .filter(account ->                           // Selects only the accounts
                        account.number().equals(accountNumber))  // that match the provided
                .findFirst()                                 // account number
                .orElseThrow(
                    () -> new IllegalStateException(         // Throws an IllegalStateException
                        format("No account matching %s for %s",  // if there's no matching account
                            accountNumber.value(), customer)));  // for the provided account number
    } catch (SQLException e) {
        throw new IllegalStateException(
                format("Unable to retrieve account %s for %s",
                        accountNumber.value(), customer), e);
    }
}
```

Selects the first matching account because there can only be one matching account per account number

Translates a SQLException into an IllegalStateException with a specific message if there's an error in the database

The documentation of `IllegalStateException` specifies that it should be used to signal that a method has been invoked at an illegal or inappropriate time. It could be argued that not matching an account is neither illegal nor inappropriate and using an `IllegalStateException` is incorrect—a better choice might be `IllegalArgument-Exception`. But using `IllegalStateException` as a generic way of signaling failure is quite common, and we've decided to follow this pattern to better illustrate the problem of intermixing technical and business exceptions.

Throwing an exception when no account is found is logically sound, but is this a technical problem or a business rule violation? From a technical point of view, not matching an account is perfectly fine, but from a business perspective, you might want to communicate this to the user—for example, "Incorrect account number, please try again." This motivates having business rules around it, which makes the exception a business exception.

The second exception (thrown in the catch clause) is caused by a failing database connection or a malformed SQL query in the database. This also needs to be communicated, but not by the domain. Instead, you could rely on the surrounding framework to give an appropriate message—for example, "We're experiencing some technical problems at the moment, please try again later." This means the domain doesn't need rules for this exception, which makes it a technical exception. But how can you tell if you're dealing with a business or technical exception when both are of type `IllegalState-Exception`? Well, this is why you shouldn't intermix business and technical exceptions using the same type. But sometimes things are just the way they are, so let's find out how to handle this and learn what the security implications are.

Be careful using findFirst

The Java Stream API offers a rich set of functionality, where `findFirst` is a method that lets you short-circuit stream processing by selecting the first occurrence of an object. In listing 9.2, it's assumed that a one-to-one mapping exists between account and account number. Applying `findFirst` might then seem to be the natural choice, but this is where you need to be careful.

If you choose to use `findFirst`, it implies you don't care which element you choose as long as it exists. But that's not the case when fetching accounts: associating an account number with the correct account is imperative, and anything else is a disaster. The only reason that `findFirst` works in `fetchAccountFor` is because of the underlying relationship between account and account number. If this suddenly changes (either intentionally or because of a bug), the behavior of fetching accounts becomes random, and that's a hard bug to find!

A better solution is to use the Stream API's `reduce` method instead of `findFirst` to state the uniqueness assumption explicitly and to fail if multiple elements are found. The `reduce` operation is sometimes perceived as complex and hard to understand, but the essence is that it reduces the number of elements in a stream by applying an associative accumulation function to derive a new element. For example, summation can be expressed as `reduce((a, b) → a + b)`. This implies that `reduce` executes only if there are two or more elements present in a stream, and this is something you can use as a guarantee or contract. If `reduce` executes, you know the uniqueness requirement has been violated, but instead of reducing two elements into one, you throw an exception; for example, `reduce((accountA, accountB) → throw new IllegalStateException(...))`. This way, assumptions are stated explicitly, along with avoiding ambiguities and random behavior by design.

9.1.2 Handling exceptions

Handling exceptions seems easy at first; you surround a statement with a `try-catch` block and you're done. But when different failures use the same exception type, things get a bit more complicated. In listing 9.3, you see the calling code of the `fetchAccountFor` method in listing 9.2. Because you want to deal with only business exceptions in the domain, you need to figure out how to distinguish between business exceptions and technical exceptions, even though both are of type `IllegalStateException`.

Unfortunately, you don't have much to go on, because both exceptions carry the same data. The only tangible difference is the internal message: the business exception message contains "No account matching," and the technical exception contains "Unable to retrieve account." This allows you to use the message as a discriminator and pass technical exceptions to a global exception handler that catches all exceptions, logs the payload, and rolls back the transaction due to technical problems.

Listing 9.3   Separating technical and business exceptions by message contents

```
import static org.apache.commons.lang3.Validate.notNull;

private final AccountRepository repository;

public Balance accountBalance(final Customer customer,
                              final AccountNumber accountNumber) {
   notNull(customer);
   notNull(accountNumber);

   try {
      return repository.fetchAccountFor(customer, accountNumber)
                       .balance();
   } catch (IllegalStateException e) {
      if (e.getMessage().contains("No account matching")) {
         return Balance.unknown(accountNumber);
      }
      throw e;
   }
}
```

Checks the internal message to determine if it's a business exception or not

Returns an unknown balance for the requested account number if the message matches

Propagates the exception further up the call stack if the message doesn't match

---

But what happens if you change the message or add another business exception with a different message? Won't that cause the exception to propagate out of the domain? It certainly will, and this is how sensitive data often ends up in logs or accidentally being displayed to the end user.

In listing 9.1, you saw how stack traces reveal information that doesn't make sense to show to a normal user. Instead, displaying a default error page with an informative message would be far better; for example, the message "Oops, something has gone terribly wrong. Sorry for the inconvenience. Please try again later." A global exception handler is often used for this purpose because it prevents exceptions from propagating to the end user by catching all exceptions. Different frameworks use different solutions for this, but the idea is the same. All transactions execute via a global exception handler, and if an exception is caught, the exception payload is logged and the transaction is rolled back. This way, it's possible to prevent exceptions from propagating further, which makes it a lot harder for an attacker to retrieve internal information when a transaction fails.

Let's turn back to the `accountBalance` method in listing 9.3. It's obvious you can't discriminate based on the exception message, because it makes the design too fragile.

Instead, you should separate business and technical exceptions by explicitly defining exceptions that are important for the business.

In listing 9.4, you can see an explicit domain exception (AccountNotFound) that signifies the event of not matching an account. The exception extends the generic type AccountException, which acts only as a marker type—a design decision that helps to prevent accidental business exceptions from leaking from the handling logic.

Listing 9.4 An explicit domain exception signifying that no account has been found

```
import static org.apache.commons.lang3.Validate.notNull;

public abstract class AccountException extends          ◄───── Generic domain type that all
                          RuntimeException {}                   account exceptions extend

public class AccountNotFound extends         ◄───────────       Explicit domain exception
                          AccountException {                    that signifies that no
   private final AccountNumber accountNumber;                   account has been found
   private final Customer customer;

   public AccountNotFound(final AccountNumber accountNumber,
                          final Customer customer) {
      this.accountNumber = notNull(accountNumber);
      this.customer = notNull(customer);
   }
   ...
}
```

In listing 9.5, the fetchAccountFor method is revised to use the AccountNotFound exception instead of a generic IllegalStateException. This way, the code is clarified in the sense that you don't need to provide a message or worry about intermixing its purpose with other exceptions.

Listing 9.5 Explicitly defining a domain exception to signal that no account is found

```
import static java.lang.String.format;
import static org.apache.commons.lang3.Validate.notNull;

private final AccountDatabase accountDatabase;

public Account fetchAccountFor(final Customer customer,
                               final AccountNumber accountNumber) {
   notNull(customer);
   notNull(accountNumber);

   try {
      return accountDatabase
            .selectAccountsFor(customer).stream()
            .filter(account -> account.number().equals(accountNumber))
            .findFirst()
            .orElseThrow(() ->
                new AccountNotFound(accountNumber,customer));
```

Replaces the generic IllegalStateException with an explicit domain exception

```
    } catch (SQLException e) {
      throw new IllegalStateException(
           format("Unable to retrieve account %s for %s",
                  accountNumber.value(), customer), e);
    }
}
```

In listing 9.6, the handling logic is revised to catch the exceptions AccountNotFound and AccountException. From a security perspective, this is much better because it allows less complex mappings between business rules and exceptions, compared with using only generic exceptions such as IllegalStateException. Catching AccountException seems redundant, but this safety net is quite important. Because all business exceptions extend AccountException, it's possible to guarantee that all business exceptions are handled and that only technical exceptions propagate to the global exception handler.

Listing 9.6   Revised handling logic with explicit domain exception

```
import static java.lang.String.format;
import static org.apache.commons.lang3.Validate.notNull;

private final AccountRepository repository;

public Balance accountBalance(final Customer customer,
                              final AccountNumber accountNumber) {
    notNull(customer);
    notNull(accountNumber);

    try {
       return repository.fetchAccountFor(customer, accountNumber)
                    .balance();
    }
    catch (AccountNotFound e) {        ◀── Handles AccountNotFound exception explicitly without parsing the internal message
       return Balance.unknown(accountNumber);
    }
    catch (AccountException e) {       ◀── Catches all unhandled business exceptions
       throw new IllegalStateException(    ◀── Signals that an unhandled domain exception has been detected and that the transaction should be aborted
           format("Unhandled domain exception: %s",
                  e.getClass().getSimpleName()));
    }
}
```

Separating business exceptions and technical exceptions clearly makes the code less complex and helps prevent accidental leakage of business information. But sensitive data isn't leaked only through unhandled business exceptions. It's often the case that business data is included in technical exceptions for debugging and failure analysis as well; for example, in listing 9.5, the SQLException is mapped to an IllegalStateException that includes the account number and customer data, which are needed only during failure analysis. To some extent, this counteracts the work of separating business and technical exceptions, because sensitive data leaks regardless. To address this issue, you need a design that enforces security in depth—so let's have a look at how to deal with exception payload.

9.1.3 Dealing with exception payload

There are two parts of an exception that are of special interest when analyzing failures: the type and the payload. By combining type information and payload data, you get an understanding of what failed and why it failed. As a consequence, many developers tend to include lots of business information in exceptions, regardless of how sensitive it is. For example, in the next listing, you see a snippet from the fetchAccountFor example where an IllegalStateException is populated with the account number and customer data, even though it's a technical exception.

Listing 9.7 Including sensitive data in a technical exception

```
import static java.lang.String.format;

catch (SQLException e) {
    throw new IllegalStateException(
        format("Unable to retrieve account %s for %s",
            accountNumber.value(), customer), e);    ◄────
}
```

Leaks account number and customer data from the business domain when logged by the global exception handler

Having the account number and customer data during failure analysis certainly helps, but from a security perspective, you have a major problem. All technical exceptions propagate to the global exception handler that logs all exception data before rolling back the transaction. This means that the account number and customer data, like Social Security number, address, and customer ID, get logged when a database error occurs—a major security problem that requires logs to be placed under strict access and authorization control. And this isn't what you want when developers need access to production logs.

Obviously, you don't want sensitive data to escape the business domain, but sometimes it's hard to recognize what's sensitive. Exceptions can travel across context boundaries, and insensitive data in one context could become sensitive when entering another context. For example, a car's license plate number tends to be seen as public information, but if someone runs your car's plate against the Department of Motor Vehicles database to identify you, it suddenly becomes information you don't want to share. This puts you in a difficult position. On one hand, you need enough information to facilitate failure analysis; on the other hand, you want to prevent data leakage. How does this affect the design?

To start with, you need to recognize that almost any business data is potentially sensitive in another context. This means it's good design practice to never include business data in technical exceptions, regardless of whether it's sensitive or not. Also, you need to make sure to provide only information that makes sense from a technical perspective; for example, "Unable to connect to database with ID XYZ," instead of the account number and customer data that caused the failure. This way, you know that it's safe to propagate technical exceptions from the domain and that the payload never contains sensitive business data.

But following this practice gets you only halfway. You also need to identify sensitive data in your domain and model it as such. In chapter 5, you learned about the *read-once* pattern, which prevents data from being read multiple times and accidentally serialized; for example, when sent over the network or written to log files. If the account number and customer data had been modeled as sensitive and the read-once pattern used, illegal logging in the global exception handler would have been detected.

The choice of using exceptions to represent technical errors and valid results primarily opens the door to data leakage problems. By separating business and technical exceptions along with using the read-once pattern, it's possible to solve this—but is it the best solution, or is there another way? Perhaps, so let's evaluate how to handle failures without exceptions and see what security benefits there are.

9.2   *Handling failures without exceptions*

Using exceptions to represent failures in domain logic is a common practice, but another equally common approach is to not use exceptions at all. This approach starts with the design mindset that failures are a natural and expected outcome of anything we do. Because exceptions represent something exceptional (the name kind of gives it away) and failures are expected outcomes, it doesn't make sense to model them as exceptions. Instead, a failure should be modeled as a possible result of a performed operation in the same way a success is. By designing failures as unexceptional outcomes, you can avoid several of the problems that come from using exceptions—including ambiguity between domain and technical exceptions, and inadvertently leaking sensitive information.

If you look at the logic you implement in an application, it quickly becomes obvious that it's not only about happy cases. When you execute a method, you have an intention of performing a specific action. Performing that action can almost always have multiple outcomes. At the very least, it can succeed or it can fail. In this section, you'll learn how to gain more security by designing failures without using exceptions.

To explain this design approach, let's illustrate the difference between designing failures as exceptions versus designing them as expected outcomes. We'll do this by solving the same task using the two different approaches. The task is to implement a system to transfer money between bank accounts. In the current domain of banking, a money transfer can have two possible outcomes: either the transaction is performed or it fails due to insufficient funds (figure 9.2).

9.2.1   *Failures aren't exceptional*

If you choose to design using exceptions, your implementation will look something like listing 9.8. The method to transfer money from one bank account to another is called `transfer` and takes two arguments: the amount to transfer and the destination account. The first thing that needs to be done in the `transfer` method is to check that there are enough funds in the source account to cover the transfer. If the source account is lacking funds, an `InsufficientFundsException` is thrown; in which case, the exception needs

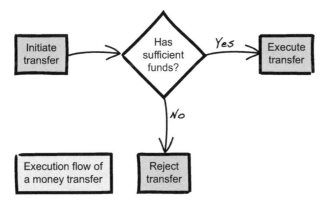

Figure 9.2 The possible outcomes of a money transfer between bank accounts

to be handled appropriately—perhaps by asking the user to adjust the amount or abort the transaction. If sufficient funds are available, you can execute the transfer by calling another backend system through the executeTransfer(amount, toAccount) method. This method can also throw exceptions in case of a failure. If the executeTransfer method is successful, nothing more happens and the code calling transfer continues to execute as normal.

Listing 9.8 Using exceptions for business logic

```
import static org.apache.commons.lang3.Validate.notNull;

public final class Account {

  public void transfer(final Amount amount,
                       final Account toAccount)
      throws InsufficientFundsException {
    notNull(amount);
    notNull(toAccount);

    if (balance().isLessThan(amount)) {          ◄─── Checks whether there are sufficient funds
      throw new InsufficientFundsException();     ◄─── Throws an exception if there
    }                                                  aren't enough funds

    executeTransfer(amount, toAccount);          ◄─── Calls underlying systems to execute the
  }                                                   transfer; may also throw exceptions

  public Amount balance() {
    return calculateBalance();
  }

  // ...
}
```

```
import static org.apache.commons.lang3.Validate.isTrue;
import static org.apache.commons.lang3.Validate.notNull;

public final class Amount implements Comparable<Amount> {
   private final long value;

   public Amount(final long value) {
      isTrue(value >= 0, "A price cannot be negative");
      this.value = value;
   }

   @Override
   public int compareTo(final Amount that) {
      notNull(that);
      return Long.compare(value, that.value);
   }

   public boolean isLessThan(final Amount that) {
      return compareTo(that) < 0;
   }

   // ...

}
```

With this approach, you're handling the flow of your business logic using two mechanisms in the programming language. One is the result from calling a method (in this case, the result is void), and the other is the exception mechanism. You're using the exception mechanism of the programming language as part of your control flow.

Let's stop for a second and think about the semantics of using exceptions as a control flow in the transfer method. By doing so, you're saying that not having sufficient funds in the source account is an exceptional occurrence. You're treating the negative result as something exceptional. This is a common way of designing code, but there's an alternative way to view failures. This alternative way stems from the perspective that failures aren't exceptional but rather an expected outcome of any task you try to perform.

9.2.2   *Designing for failures*

In banking, it's not uncommon for users to try to initiate a transfer of an amount that's larger than the current account balance. This can, for example, happen if the amount is entered incorrectly, or if the user thinks they have more money in the account than they actually have. For whatever reason, it's relatively common for a money transfer to fail due to insufficient funds. Not having sufficient funds is therefore an expected outcome of the operation "trying to transfer money." Because it's an expected outcome, it shouldn't be modeled as an exceptional one. Rather, it should be modeled as a possible result of the action.

If you redesign the transfer method from listing 9.8 so that insufficient funds are an expected outcome, you'll have something like that in listing 9.9. This new method won't throw any exceptions as part of the logical flow. Instead, it returns the result of the transfer operation. The result can either be a success or a failure, and in the case of a failure, it's possible for the calling code to find out what type of failure it was by inspecting the result. If there aren't enough funds, an INSUFFICIENT_FUNDS failure is returned. Otherwise, the method continues and will try to execute the transfer via the executeTransfer(amount, toAccount) method. The executeTransfer method also returns a result that can either be a success or a failure due to difficulties in executing the transfer. When the executeTransfer method finishes, the money transfer either succeeds or fails, with a failure message indicating the reason for failure.

Listing 9.9 Expected results not modeled as exceptional

```
import static Result.Failure.INSUFFICIENT_FUNDS;
import static Result.success;
import static org.apache.commons.lang3.Validate.notNull;

public final class Account {

  public Result transfer(final Amount amount,
                         final Account toAccount) {
    notNull(amount);
    notNull(toAccount);

    if (balance().isLessThan(amount)) {        ◄─────┤ Checks whether there are sufficient funds
      return INSUFFICIENT_FUNDS.failure();     ◄───── Returns the failure as a result
    }                                                 instead of throwing an exception

    return executeTransfer(amount, toAccount); ◄───── Returns the result of calling
  }                                                   the underlying systems to
                                                      execute the transfer
  public Amount balance() {
    return calculateBalance();
  }

  // ...
}

-------------------------------------------------

import java.util.Optional;

public final class Result {

  public enum Failure {
    INSUFFICIENT_FUNDS,       ◄─────┤ Different types of possible failures
    SERVICE_NOT_AVAILABLE;

    public Result failure() {
      return new Result(this);
    }
  }

  public static Result success() {
    return new Result(null);
  }
```

```
    private final Failure failure;

    private Result(final Failure failure) {
        this.failure = failure;
    }

    public boolean isFailure() {
        return failure != null;
    }

    public boolean isSuccess() {
        return !isFailure();
    }

    public Optional<Failure> failure() {
        return Optional.ofNullable(failure);
    }
}
```

It's worth pointing out that the `Result` shown in listing 9.9 is a basic implementation. Once you start using result objects, you'll probably find that you want to design them in certain ways to make them easy to work with and error-free. As an example, if you're using a functional style of programming, you might want to add the ability to perform operations such as map, flatmap, and reduce to simplify dealing with results. Exactly how you choose to design them is up to you or your team.

By designing failures as expected and unexceptional outcomes, you completely eliminate the use of exceptions as part of the domain logic. By doing so, you're able to either avoid or reduce the risk of many of the security issues you faced when designing your code with exceptions. Some of the security benefits of this approach are listed in table 9.1.

Table 9.1 Security benefits of designing failures as expected outcomes

Security issue	Solved through
Ambiguity between domain exceptions and technical exceptions	Domain exceptions are completely removed.
Exception payload leaking into logs	Failures aren't handled by generic error-handling code, and, therefore, the data the payload carries doesn't accidentally slip into error logs.
Inadvertently leaking sensitive information	Failures are handled in a context that has knowledge about what's sensitive and what's not and knows how to handle sensitive data properly.

In our experience, another benefit of treating failures as unexceptional is that once you start designing both successes and failures as results, the only exceptions that can still occur are those caused by either bugs or a violation of an invariant.

So far, you've seen how to handle failures in a secure way on a code level by either using exceptions or designing your failures as unexceptional. In the next section, we'll discuss more high-level designs to show you how you can use design principles commonly used for resilience to gain security benefits.

9.3 Designing for availability

The availability of data and systems is an important security goal and is part of the CIA acronym (confidentiality, integrity, and availability).[5] The National Institute of Standards and Technology (NIST) publication "Engineering Principles for Information Technology Security" talks about five different goals for IT security: confidentiality, availability, integrity, accountability, and assurance.[6] It defines *availability* as the "goal that generates the requirement for protection against intentional or accidental attempts to (1) perform unauthorized deletion of data or (2) otherwise cause a denial of service or data." In this section, you'll learn about design concepts that improve the availability of a system—concepts you can use to create more secure systems.

We've gathered some well-known and commonly used concepts that promote availability, and it's our belief that they're also some of the most important and foundational principles on the subject. We could easily write an entire book on how to build systems that are robust and that will stay available even when experiencing failures. Going into great depth on each concept is beyond the scope of this book, but it's our intention to provide you with enough knowledge to understand each one and how they promote the security of a system. Once you see the connection to security for the concepts described, they will become even more valuable as guiding design principles.

9.3.1 Resilience

It's becoming increasingly common to design and build systems to be *resilient*. A system that's resilient is designed to stay functional even during high stress. Stress for a system can be caused by both internal failures (such as errors in code or failing network communication) and external factors (such as high traffic load). Stress can cause a resilient system to slow down or run with reduced functionality, and parts of the system can crash, but the system as a whole will stay available, and it'll recover once the stress it's been put under disappears.

Another way to describe a system that's resilient is to say it's stable. You can design stable systems in several ways (some of which you'll learn about in this chapter), but the main goal of a resilient system is to survive failures and continue to provide its service. Put differently, a resilient system is a system that stays available in the presence of failures.

Because availability is an explicit security goal, and a resilient system stays available during failures, a system that is resilient must also by definition be a more secure system. This, in turn, leads to the conclusion that all contemporary and well-established design practices that promote the resilience and stability of a system are also beneficial to use when designing secure systems.

---

[5] Go back to chapter 1 for more details on CIA.

[6] NIST Special Publication 800-27 Rev A, "Engineering Principles for Information Technology Security (A Baseline for Achieving Security)," by Gary Stoneburner, Clark Hayden, and Alexis Feringa. Available at https://csrc.nist.gov/publications/detail/sp/800-27/rev-a/archive/2004-06-21.

9.3.2 *Responsiveness*

Say you've built a system that's resilient and stays available during high stress. It doesn't crash, but when the load on the system becomes high enough, the response times increase dramatically. When the system is available but responds slowly, another system calling the slow system eventually gets a response, but it can take an unacceptably long time. From the caller's point of view, the system under load can be considered to be unusable, even though it's technically still available. This is where responsiveness comes in as an important trait when discussing availability.

For a system to be *responsive*, it not only needs to survive stress but also has to respond quickly to anyone trying to use it during times of stress. Even if you've optimized the processing logic as much as possible to make the system run faster, the system will still have a threshold for how much stress it can handle before the response times go through the roof. When this happens, you might wonder how you can possibly make the system respond any faster. In this situation, it's important to realize that to stay responsive, it's far better to answer quickly with an error saying that the system is unable to accept any more requests than to have the caller sit around waiting for an answer that might never come. Any answer is better than no answer, even if that answer is rejecting the request.

To make the system more responsive without rejecting requests, you could, for example, place all the processing work in a queue. Separating the requests for processing and the actual processing makes the system more asynchronous. This way, even if the work queue is growing because of a high load and the requested work takes a long time to finish, the system will be able to accept new requests. The caller gets a fast response saying that the request has been accepted, but it'll have to wait before the result of the work is available. The work queue might eventually get full; in which case, you'll have to decide how to handle that situation—possibly by denying more work to be queued and asking the caller to try again later.

Staying responsive is important for security, because for a system to be truly available, it's not enough that it be resilient and survive stress, it's also necessary for it to continue to respond quickly. How quickly it needs to respond depends on the system you're building and the maximum acceptable response time before the system is considered to be unavailable.

9.3.3 *Circuit breakers and timeouts*

A useful design pattern when building resilient systems is the *circuit breaker pattern*.[7] This pattern is handy for dealing with failures in a way that promotes system resilience, responsiveness, and overall availability—and therefore, also security.

The general idea of the circuit breaker pattern is to write code that protects a system from failures in the same way that an electrical fuse protects a house in the case of failure in the electrical system. A fuse is designed to break the electrical circuit if an

---

[7] See Michael T. Nygard's *Release It! Design and Deploy Production-Ready Software* (The Pragmatic Bookshelf, 2007).

excessive load is placed on the system (for example, by a faulty appliance or a short-circuit somewhere). If the circuit doesn't break, a high electrical current can generate so much heat that a fire can start. By breaking the circuit, and thereby isolating or stopping the failure, it's possible to prevent the entire house from burning down.

In the same way that a fuse protects a house, a circuit breaker in software can isolate failures and prevent an entire system from crashing. Just as an electrical current passes through a fuse during normal operation, you use a circuit breaker to protect your system by having your method calls or requests to other systems pass through it. Figure 9.3 shows an example of a rudimentary circuit breaker.

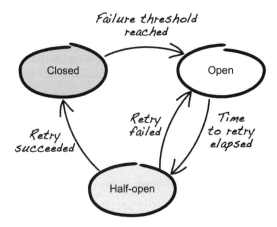

Figure 9.3 The three states of a circuit breaker

Depending on which state the circuit breaker is in, the request is handled differently. If it's in the closed state, any request performed passes through it. If the request completes successfully, nothing more happens. If the request fails, it'll increment a failure counter. If multiple subsequent calls fail, then the failure count eventually reaches a threshold that triggers the circuit breaker to open. Once it's in its open state, any new requests won't pass through but will fail immediately by the circuit breaker.

When a circuit breaker is open, it's effectively applying the fail-fast pattern instead of letting the requests pass through. If a circuit breaker is open, after a while it'll transition into a half-open state. In the half-open state, it can let one or more requests pass through to see if they'll succeed. In the event of success, the circuit breaker can return to its closed state and let all requests pass through. In the event of failure, the circuit breaker goes back to its open state until it's ready to let another trial request through.

When you make a call to another service, it's important to specify a timeout for that request. If an integration point is unresponsive, you don't want your application to hang forever, waiting for a response, because that eventually makes your system unstable. Because both timeouts and circuit breakers deal with protecting a system when making requests to other systems, they typically go hand-in-hand. It's common for implementations of circuit breakers to track timeouts separately and sometimes to even provide built-in functionality for managing timeouts for requests.

> ## Always specify a timeout
>
> In Java, for example, the default timeout for a network call is infinite—meaning that if a timeout isn't explicitly set, a network call waits forever for a response. As a result, the number of systems that have turned into unresponsive memory hogs due to unresponsive integration points is almost infinite too. Whatever environment you're in, whatever programming language or framework you use, always make sure you explicitly set a timeout for all your network requests.

Circuit breakers are typically used when making inter-process requests from one service to another, but they can also be used within the same service if it makes sense to do so. What makes the circuit breaker pattern so effective is that it works well for preventing failures from spreading from one part of a system to another. Isolating the failures and offloading the part of the system currently experiencing stress increases the stability of the system. Through the use of the fail-fast approach, it also improves the responsiveness of the system. Because circuit breakers promote both the resilience and the responsiveness of a system, this is an effective design pattern for improving the security of a system by increasing its availability.

A NOTE ON CIRCUIT BREAKERS AND DOMAIN MODELING

When using circuit breakers, it's common to use a default answer when a call fails. This is sometimes called a *fallback answer*. This pattern is quite effective and allows systems to continue to function despite failures, albeit with reduced or limited functionality.

One thing that's important to remember is that the way the system should behave if a request fails is usually a decision that affects your domain logic, and, therefore, it's a decision that needs to be made together with the domain experts. For example, if you're unable to check the inventory for an item when a customer places an order, do you refuse to take the order and lose a sale, or do you continue processing the order and deal with the unlikelihood of the item being out of stock? The answer is that it depends on how the business wants to handle this scenario. Another example is if you need to get a list of all books written by a particular author. Is it OK to return an empty list if the remote service you need to call is down? Sometimes that might be acceptable, but at other times, it's necessary to convey the failure so the client can distinguish a failure from the fact that no books exist for a given author.

> TIP   When you use default or fallback answers with circuit breakers, make sure to involve the domain experts. Then model and design your failure-handling code as you would any other business logic.

The approach of designing for failures that you read about earlier in this chapter is a great way of handling these scenarios. It forces you to handle failures within your domain logic rather than as part of your infrastructure logic.

Finally, circuit breakers are typically a design tool brought into a codebase by developers, and it's easy to think they are only relevant from a technical perspective. More often than not, the opposite is true. We encourage you to involve your domain experts and stakeholders in the use of circuit breakers so you can design systems that not only technically stay available, but also continue to work as intended from a business perspective.

9.3.4 Bulkheads

The bulkhead design pattern is another tool you can use to efficiently prevent failures in one part of a system from spreading and taking down the entire system. Bulkheads can be applied as both a high-level design pattern when architecting infrastructure (such as servers, networks, routing of traffic, and so on) and a low-level design pattern for designing resilient code. Because bulkheads are so commonly used and do such a good job of isolating failures, it's a pattern that you should become familiar with to create systems with a high degree of availability.

In ship building, the term *bulkhead* refers to a wall or panel used to compartmentalize the hull into sections that are sealed against both water and fire (figure 9.4). Constructing a ship with these types of compartments means that if a water leak or fire were to occur in one part of the ship, the bulkheads would prevent the ship from taking on too much water and sinking or the fire from spreading.

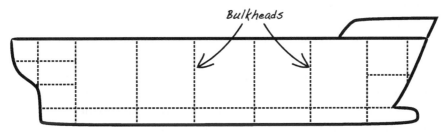

Figure 9.4   A ship hull constructed with bulkheads

In software, the same design techniques can be used to build resilient systems. One thing that's interesting with the bulkhead pattern is that it can be applied on different levels in your architecture. Let's take a look at each of these levels so you can get an idea of various ways to apply this pattern.

LOCATION LEVEL

At a high level, a system's availability can be improved by running the system on servers distributed over multiple geographical locations. If one location becomes inoperable—perhaps because of a power outage, a network fiber dug up during construction work, or an earthquake—then the other location or locations will still be available to provide the service. When deploying systems this way, you typically design each location to be completely self-sustained so that no interdependencies exist. How you choose the geographic locations depends on the business requirements, but they can be anything from different parts of a town to different parts of the world.

INFRASTRUCTURE LEVEL

Zooming in a bit, you can also apply the bulkhead pattern when designing your system infrastructure. For example, if you have a backend for a webshop, you can have one set of servers handling the load of customers browsing products and adding them to the shopping cart and another set of servers handling the checkout and payment flow, as seen in figure 9.5.

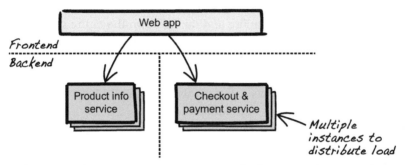

Figure 9.5   Protecting business functionality by partitioning workload

By partitioning the workload on your backend servers, you separate different areas of business functionality so they don't affect each other. (You could also choose to partition your frontend servers, but we'll disregard that in this example.) For example, a release of a popular product that you sell could potentially generate so much traffic that the servers handling product information start to slow down due to the high load. But because the checkout process is handled by a different set of servers, the ongoing sales aren't affected by the high demand on product information. The use of bulkheads ensures that the reduction or loss of availability in one part of the system doesn't affect the availability of another part. Service-oriented architectures are typically a good fit for applying bulkheads in this manner.

One thing to watch out for when partitioning services and servers is hidden dependencies. If you have multiple services using the same database, for example, then one service can cause slow responses or deadlocks in the database, which in turn can reduce the availability of another service. In this scenario, you've failed to properly apply the bulkhead by not separating the persistence solution. Other common hidden dependencies are message queues; network storage, like storage area networks (SANs) and network-attached storage (NAS); and shared network infrastructure, like routers and firewalls. It's also common to see bulkheading applied via use of virtualization technologies, such as containers and virtual machines. These technologies are great, but if you run everything on the same physical hardware, you've managed to create not only a lot of complexity, but also a hidden dependency. If the hardware crashes, it doesn't matter how many containers you partitioned your system on—they'll all go down together.

CODE LEVEL

You can also use bulkheads when designing your code. A common example of the bulkhead pattern applied on a code level is thread pools. The reason this is common is that if you let your code create an unlimited number of threads, your application inevitably grinds to a halt and possibly crashes. An easy and effective way to limit the number of threads is to use a thread pool. A thread pool lets you set a limit on how many threads the code can create. You can then use the threads in the pool to process work. Regardless of how much work needs to be processed, there'll never be more threads than are allowed in the pool. You also have the benefit of reusing threads in the pool instead of constantly creating new ones. Request pools in web servers and connection pools for databases are typical real-world uses of thread pools that you might have encountered before.

Queues are another code construct you can use in order to isolate failures in your code base. Queues are often used together with thread pools. If all the threads in the pool are busy, additional work can be put in a queue. As soon as a thread becomes available in the pool, the queue can be queried for work to be processed. If work is added to the queue at a higher rate than the thread pool can process, the queue grows in size. If this continues, the queue eventually becomes full and, at that point, the application can refuse to accept any new work.

Going back to the example of the webshop backend that provides product information and processes orders, you can write your code to use different thread pools and queues for different types of work. If one thread pool becomes so busy it needs to put work in a queue for later processing, the other thread pool can continue unaffected. Moreover, if the queue for fetching product information becomes full and the system starts to refuse more requests for product information, the queue for order processing can still accept new work and continue processing.

By using thread pools and queues as bulkheads, you're preventing the consumption of resources in one part of your code from affecting another part. If one part of your code becomes unavailable, other parts will remain available even if they're within the same service instance. This effectively increases the availability of your system.

The Reactive Manifesto

The Reactive Manifesto defines four important traits that need to be present for what it calls a reactive system: the system must be responsive, resilient, elastic, and message driven (http://reactivemanifesto.org). A *reactive system*, according to the manifesto, is a system that's "more robust, more resilient, more flexible, and better positioned" to meet the demands put on modern systems. But, as it turns out, the Reactive Manifesto is also interesting from a security perspective. Let's take a look at why.

The goal of the manifesto is to promote good design practices by creating a common, ubiquitous vocabulary to use when discussing modern system design. The manifesto talks about the four traits and what defines each of them, and it also discusses how to achieve them.

(continued)

The main focus of the manifesto is how to build systems that can live up to the demands put on them. Modern systems need to live up to far higher demands than their predecessors. They need to serve more data to more users and with shorter response times. Downtime should be minimal, and it's necessary for modern systems to be able to adapt to fluctuations in load. Reactive systems meet these demands and are also typically more modular in their design, which tends to make them easier to develop and to evolve.

A reactive system stays resilient and responsive during periods of high stress. It's designed to have a high degree of availability. This makes the Reactive Manifesto interesting from a security perspective, because availability is an important trait for secure systems. If you're designing your systems to be reactive, you not only are getting the benefits of scalability and high capacity, but you're also improving the security of the systems.

You've now learned that availability is an important security goal, and you've learned how you can improve the availability of a system by making it more resilient. You've also seen some common techniques for designing resilient and responsive systems. If you weren't familiar with them before, you now have a good starting point for learning more about building resilient systems. In any case, you've hopefully grokked the connection between resilient systems and security, and learned yet another reason for building systems that survive failures. Now it's time to take a look at how to avoid security flaws when dealing with bad data.

9.4   *Handling bad data*

When dealing with data, whether it's from a database, user input, or an external source, there's always a chance it'll be partially broken by having trailing spaces, missing characters, or other flaws that make it invalid. Regardless of the cause, how your code handles bad data is essential for security. In chapter 4, you learned about using contracts to protect against bad state and input that doesn't meet the defined preconditions. This certainly tightens the design and makes assumptions explicit, but applying contracts often leads to discussions about repairing data before validation to avoid unnecessary rejection. Unfortunately, choosing this approach is extremely dangerous because it can expose vulnerabilities and result in a false sense of security.

But modifying data to avoid false positives isn't the only security problem to consider. Another interesting issue is the urge to echo input verbatim in exceptions and write it to log files when a contract fails. This can be justifiable for debugging purposes, but from a security perspective, it's a ticking bomb waiting to explode. To see why, we'll guide you through a simple example of a webshop where it has been decided to expand the membership database with data from another system. Unfortunately, the data quality is poor, which makes the business decide to apply a repair filter before validation. This turns out to be a great mistake because, combined with echoing validation failures, it opens up security vulnerabilities such as cross-site scripting and second-order injection attacks. Let's see how this happens by starting with why you shouldn't blindly repair data before validation.

> ## Cross-site scripting and second-order attacks
>
> In a cross-site scripting (XSS) attack, the attacker sends malicious strings to a site, hoping that the site will repeat the same strings in the output on the page. For example, if a news site lets you search for words in articles, it might return "Cannot find an article containing Jane Doe" if you search for Jane Doe. But if a visitor searches for `<script>alert(0) </script>`, they'll get a result page saying "Cannot find an article containing" and at the same time cause the server to run some JavaScript that pops up an alert box. This doesn't sound so alarming, but an XSS attack might do something much nastier, like installing a keylogger, sending cookies to a remote server, or worse.
>
> Unfortunately, even logs can be used as the starting point of an attack, and a browser-based admin tool used for viewing logs might have a vulnerability for specific formats. In that case, an attacker can cause an attack string to be logged and then wait for the admin to look at that log entry using the vulnerable tool. This is called a *second-order attack* because the attacker isn't attacking the system they face, but rather a second system behind it.

9.4.1 Don't repair data before validation

Picture a webshop where users sign up for a membership to get better deals. The registration form asks them to enter their name, address, and other information that's needed to create a membership. The domain model is well defined, and each term in the membership context has a precise meaning and definition. For example, in listing 9.10, you see that a name has a tight definition and is restricted to alphabetic characters (a-z and A-Z) and spaces, and a length between 2 and 100 characters. This seems a bit strict, but names containing special characters, such as Jane T. O'Doe or William Smith 3rd, are considered rare enough that the business has decided to require users to drop special characters instead of loosening the contracts; for example, Jane T. O'Doe needs to be registered as Jane T ODoe.

Listing 9.10 The name domain primitive

```
import static org.apache.commons.lang3.Validate.inclusiveBetween;
import static org.apache.commons.lang3.Validate.matchesPattern;
import static org.apache.commons.lang3.Validate.notBlank;

public final class Name {
   private final String value;

   public Name(final String value) {
      notBlank(value);                                  ← A name can't be empty or null.
      inclusiveBetween(2, 100, value.length(),          ← A valid name contains
          "Invalid length. Got: " + value.length());      between 2 and 100 characters.
      matchesPattern(value,"^[a-zA-Z ]+[a-zA-Z]+$",     ← A name can only contain
                  "Invalid name. Got: " + value);         alphabetic characters (a-z
      this.value = value;                                 and A-Z) and spaces.
   }
   ...
}
```

But restricting names this way only worked well until it was decided to expand the membership database with data from another system, then the `Name` contracts blew up like fireworks on New Year's Eve. A failure investigation revealed that the quality of the new data was poor: some names were empty, others had special characters, and some contained < and > characters originating from an XML import that went bad a few years ago.

The preferred solution is to address this at the source, but modifying data to fit the membership context isn't as simple as it seems. This is because data is consumed by several systems, and making adjustments for one system (for example, removing special characters in a name) might not be acceptable for another. Consequently, the business decides to leave the data as it is in the database and apply a repair filter before it's validated in the membership context. This strategy turns out to be a great success, as it significantly reduces the frequency of unnecessary rejections in the membership context. In fact, the result is so good that it's decided to apply the filter for all types of input sources, as illustrated in figure 9.6.

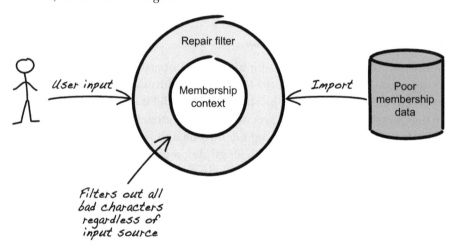

Figure 9.6   Bad characters filtered out for all data sources

Unfortunately, this is also when things start to get bad from a security perspective. To see how, you need to understand the relationship between the repair logic, validation, and failures, as shown in figure 9.7.

As illustrated, input is mutated every time it passes through the filter, and validation failures are echoed in the browser and log files. Although the data mutation is intentional, it also means the repair filter creates a derivative from the original input that could become dangerous. For example, consider the problem of cleaning up names with sporadic < and > characters. Applying a filter to remove them seems like the right thing to do; it creates a win-win situation by minimizing unnecessary rejection and avoiding XSS attacks by dismantling the `<script>` tag. Or at least, that's what many tend to believe. The

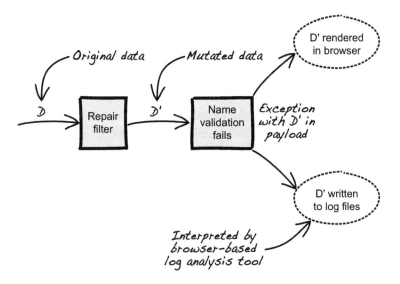

Figure 9.7   Relationship between repairing data and validation

truth is, dropping < and > only adds a false sense of security—it's still possible to launch an XSS attack. Consider injecting

```
%3<Cscript%3>Ealert("XSS")%3<C/script%3>E
```

to the repair filter.[8] Dropping the < and > characters yields

```
%3Cscript%3Ealert("XSS")%3C/script%3E
```

which is the same JavaScript code as `<script>alert("XSS")</script>`. The only difference is that < and > are expressed in hexadecimal. But passing JavaScript code to the membership context isn't dangerous per se unless it gets executed!

9.4.2   *Never echo input verbatim*

In listing 9.11, you see the validation logic applied in the `Name` constructor. When `%3Cscript%3Ealert("XSS")%3C/script%3E` is validated, the regular expression of `matchesPattern` fails and an error message is created. As developers, we often want to know why a contract failed—was it because of a programming error or invalid input? Consequently, many choose to echo input verbatim in error messages because it facilitates the failure analysis, but it could also expose vulnerabilities such as XSS and second-order attacks.

> **Listing 9.11   Validation applied in the `Name` constructor**

```
Validate.notBlank(value);
Validate.inclusiveBetween(2, 100, value.length(),
            "Invalid length. Got: " + value.length());
```

---

[8]   `<script>alert("XSS")</script>` is the classic way of testing if a system interprets input as data or code (JavaScript).

```
Validate.matchesPattern(value, "^[a-zA-Z ]+[a-zA-Z]+$",
                    "Invalid name. Got: " + value);
```

> Input is echoed verbatim in the validation failure message.

By echoing the input verbatim in the validation failure message, the webshop practically allows attackers to control the output of the application, especially if exception payload is logged or displayed to the end user. It can seem harmless to log

```
%3Cscript%3Ealert("XSS")%3C/script%3E
```

but if log data is analyzed in a browser-based tool without proper escaping, `%3Cscript%3Ealert("XSS")%3C/script%3E` could be interpreted as code and executed. This simple example only results in an alert box popping up, but the mere fact that JavaScript is allowed to execute is extremely dangerous—an attacker could take advantage of this to install a keylogger, steal credentials, or hijack a session.

Although it sounds far-fetched, this kind of attack isn't unlikely. In chapter 3, you learned about the importance of context mapping and semantic boundaries. Injecting data with the intention of targeting vulnerabilities in a second system (a second-order attack) builds on the behavior of a broken context map, where data is misinterpreted only because it enters a different context. For instance, in our example, the JavaScript string only becomes harmful when interpreted as code in the log analyzer tool. Because of this, it can be difficult to determine whether it's OK to echo input or not—if you're unsure, play it safe and avoid doing so completely.

XSS Polyglots

Cross-site scripting (XSS) is an interesting type of attack because an attack vector can be crafted in an almost infinite number of ways. This makes it difficult to identify and to remove XSS flaws from a web application. The general recommendation is to do a security audit to find places where user input could end up in the HTML output, but the complexity of XSS makes it hard to guarantee that all places are found.[*] A complement could therefore be to test an application using an XSS polyglot, which is an attack vector that's executable in multiple contexts (places in the HTML where input is rendered as output). To illustrate, let's consider the following injection contexts:

- `<div class="{{input}}"></div>`
- `<noscript>{{input}}</noscript>`
- `<!--{{input}}-->`

An XSS polyglot is an attack vector that successfully executes a JavaScript (for example, `alert('XSS')`) in all three contexts, so let's see how to do this.

The first context is a `class` attribute in a `div` element. To allow script execution, you need to break out of the `class` attribute and close the `div` using a double quote and a greater than character (`">`). This is possible with a string that starts with `">` followed by a script. For example, injecting

```
"><svg onload=alert('XSS')>
```

results in an HTML string that looks like

```
<div class=""><svg onload=alert('XSS')>"></div>
```

This in turn creates an alert box with the message XSS when rendered in a browser. But to be an XSS polyglot, the attack vector must also apply to all other contexts as well.

The second context is a `<noscript>` block into which the attack vector is inserted. To allow for script execution, you need to break out of the context using a `</noscript>` tag. This results in

```
"></noscript><svg onload=alert('XSS')>
```

which is a slightly more complex attack vector that successfully executes the JavaScript.

The third context is within a comment block. To allow for script execution, the attack vector must contain `-->` before the script. Adding this to the existing vector results in

```
"></noscript>--><svg onload=alert('XSS')>
```

which is an XSS polyglot that allows for script execution in all three contexts.

You've now learned how to create an XSS polyglot for three contexts presented by the XSS Polyglot Challenge (a contest that challenges you to create an XSS polyglot for up to 20 contexts using as few characters as possible).[†] But XSS polyglots are actually part of a bigger class of attacks called polyglot injections.[‡]

Polyglot attacks exploit the fact that many applications are implemented using several languages (for example Java, SQL, and JavaScript), which potentially makes them susceptible to attack vectors that combine these languages. For example, the attack vector

```
/*!SLEEP(1)/*/alert(1)/*/*/
```

combines SQL and JavaScript, which could exploit weaknesses in systems using these languages.[§]

[*] See "OWASP Cross-Site Scripting (XSS)" at https://www.owasp.org/index.php/Cross-site_Scripting_(XSS).
[†] See "XSS Polyglot Challenge" at https://polyglot.innerht.ml.
[‡] See "Polyglots: Crossing Origins by Crossing Formats" at https://research.chalmers.se/publication/189673.
[§] See "Polyglot Payloads in Practice," by Mathias Karlsson, at https://www.slideshare.net/MathiasKarlsson2/polyglot-payloads-in-practice-by-avlidienbrunn-at-hackpra.

By now, you've learned why failures need to be considered and how failure handling affects security. In the next chapter, we'll shift focus and explore several design concepts used in the cloud that use security; for example, immutable deployments, externalized configuration, and the three R's of enterprise security.

Summary

- Separating business exceptions and technical exceptions is a good design strategy because technical details don't belong in the domain.
- You shouldn't intermix technical and business exceptions using the same type.
- It's a good design practice to never include business data in technical exceptions, regardless of whether it's sensitive or not.

- You can create more secure code by designing for failures and treating failures as normal, unexceptional results.
- Availability is an important security goal for software systems.
- Resilience and responsiveness are traits that add security by improving the availability of a system.
- You can use design patterns like circuit breakers, bulkheads, and timeouts to design for availability.
- Repairing data before validation is dangerous and should be avoided at all costs.
- You should never echo input verbatim.

Benefits of cloud thinking

This chapter covers

- How externalizing configuration improves security
- Structure as separate, stateless processes
- How centralized logging improves security
- Structuring admin functionality
- The three R's of enterprise security

To successfully run applications in a cloud environment, you need to design them in a way that enables you to fully take advantage of the possibilities the cloud can give you. This means your applications are required to adhere to certain principles and display certain properties, such as being stateless or environment-agnostic. Cloud environments bring a new set of standards for building applications. An interesting observation is that this new way of building applications and systems has proven to be beneficial regardless of whether you're running them in the cloud or not. Even more interesting is that we've found there are also benefits from a security perspective.

This chapter starts by introducing the twelve-factor app and cloud-native concepts. We'll then go on to show you cloud design concepts for handling things such as logging, configuration, and service discovery. Moreover, you'll learn why and how they improve security. What you're not going to learn about in this chapter is how to manage security on cloud platforms, how to harden cloud platforms, or whether a public cloud environment is more secure than an on-premise setup (or vice versa). Those are all interesting topics, but they are topics for another book. The focus here is design concepts with security benefits.

Once you've learned about the fundamental cloud concepts with security benefits, you'll see how they all come together and work as enablers for something called the three R's of enterprise security. The *three R's*—rotate, repave, repair—is an approach for creating secure systems that is radically different from traditional approaches but will allow you to (equally) radically improve your security to a level where only the cloud—sorry, the sky—is the limit.

10.1   *The twelve-factor app and cloud-native concepts*

If you're new to building and designing software for the cloud, there are two concepts we recommend looking at: the twelve-factor app methodology and cloud-native development. Together, these provide a condensed, easy-to-consume compilation of several design concepts that have turned out to be important and useful in the cloud era. In this chapter, we'll use the twelve-factor app methodology and the cloud-native concepts as a base for discussing the security benefits you can gain by applying cloud design concepts to your software, regardless of whether you're running it in the cloud or on-premise. We're not going to give you a full explanation of these concepts, because that would be beyond the scope of this book, but in order to understand where the topics in this chapter come from, you'll get a brief introduction here.

The *twelve-factor app* is "a methodology for building software-as-a-service" applications.[1] It was first published somewhere around 2011, and its main purpose was to provide guidance to avoid common problems in modern application development, as well as providing a shared terminology.[2] The twelve factors include[3]

1   *Codebase*—One codebase tracked in revision control, many deploys
2   *Dependencies*—Explicitly declare and isolate dependencies
3   *Config*—Store configuration in the environment
4   *Backing services*—Treat backing services as attached resources
5   *Build, release, run*—Strictly separate build and run stages
6   *Processes*—Execute the app as one or more stateless processes
7   *Port binding*—Export services via port binding
8   *Concurrency*—Scale out via the process model
9   *Disposability*—Maximize robustness with fast startup and graceful shutdown

---

[1]   For more, see https://12factor.net.
[2]   This methodology was published by employees at the cloud company Heroku.
[3]   As of Git commit edc6406, March 21, 2016. The public repository can be found at https://github. com/heroku/12factor/blob/master/content/en/toc.md.

10 *Dev/prod parity*—Keep development, staging, and production as similar as possible

11 *Logs*—Treat logs as event streams

12 *Admin processes*—Run admin/management tasks as one-off processes

These twelve factors are all interesting design concepts in and of themselves, and if you aren't familiar with them, we recommend taking the time to read up on them to fully understand them. But there are some that we've found are of special interest from a security perspective because they promote the security of a system when applied correctly (even if that's not why they were chosen to be one of the twelve factors). You'll learn exactly how they relate to security later in this chapter.

The twelve-factor app methodology provides easy-to-follow guidelines for building applications that behave well in the cloud. The twelve factors are good design practices, but they aren't all-encompassing. Because of this, there was a need for a more general term to describe applications that are designed to behave well in the cloud, and that term is *cloud-native*. You'd be hard-pressed to find one single definition of this term, because it can mean slightly different things to different people. We think the definition put forward by Kevin Hoffman in his book *Beyond the Twelve-Factor App* (O'Reilly, 2016, p. 52) is a reasonable one:

> *A cloud-native application is an application that has been designed and implemented to run on a Platform-as-a-Service installation and to embrace horizontal elastic scaling.*

From the perspective of this chapter, the interesting part of this definition is that a cloud-native application is designed to be run on a Platform-as-a-Service (PaaS).[4] The implication of this is that, as a developer, you're focusing on functional requirements and leaving the nonfunctional ones to the platform. As you'll see in this chapter, a good PaaS provides you with tools you can use to create a higher level of security when designing your systems. Once you understand the concepts behind these tools, you can apply those concepts to your design regardless of whether you're using a PaaS or running on barebone hardware.

Now that you understand the background of the topics in this chapter, let's start by looking at how the design practice of moving application configuration to the environment can help promote better security.

10.2 *Storing configuration in the environment*

Most applications depend on some sort of configuration to run properly, such as a DNS name or a port number. Although configuration management is important, it's often seen as trivial compared to writing code. But if you consider it from a security perspective, it suddenly becomes a challenge. This is because configuration isn't always

---

[4] A cloud-based platform that allows you to focus on building and running applications rather than spending time managing infrastructure.

about nonsensitive data. Sometimes you need to include secrets as well—for example, credentials, decryption keys, or certificates—and that's a lot more complicated.

In the cloud, it's recommended to externalize configuration because an application often needs to be deployed in different environments, like development, user acceptance testing, or production. Unfortunately, externalizing configuration increases the overall complexity of a system because it needs to dynamically load configuration at runtime. Consequently, not many use this pattern for applications running on-premise, because the environments seldom change. But seen from a security perspective, code and configuration should always be separated, regardless of whether you're running on-premise or not. This makes it possible to automatically rotate keys and apply the concept of ephemeral secrets. To visualize this, it's important to understand why configuration that varies between deployments belongs to the environment and not in code. Let's look at an example where the anti-pattern of storing environment configuration in code is used.

10.2.1 *Don't put environment configuration in code*

Picture an application connected to a database. (It's not important what the application does—it could be anything from a full-blown webshop to a microservice. What's important is that it uses the anti-pattern of storing environment configuration in code, which becomes a security issue if you store sensitive data.) The application is a prototype, but the code is in pretty good shape, and management decides to proceed with a full-scale project. There's no time to redo all the work, and the team is instructed to polish things up to ensure it's ready for production. Because the application is a prototype and only deployed in the development environment, configuration data has been implemented as hardcoded constants all over the codebase.

The strategy of placing environment configuration in code sounds naive, but in our experience, many developers choose this approach, especially when prototyping, because it's easy to start with. The problem is that when things get more complicated (for example when adding secrets), the strategy tends to remain. In listing 10.1, you see an example of how credentials have been added as constants in code. This should raise a warning flag, because it allows anyone with access to the codebase to read the secrets. But it follows the same pattern as other configuration values, so why bother to do anything different?

Listing 10.1   Content management system connector class with secret values

```
public class CMSConnector {
    private static int PORT_NUMBER = 34633;
    private static long CONNECTION_TIMEOUT = 5000;
    private static String USERNAME = "service-A";
    private static String PASSWORD = "yC6@SX5O";
    ...
}
```

Username hardcoded as a configuration value

Secret password hardcoded as a configuration value

From a development perspective, it makes sense to add credentials the same way as other configuration values, because a username or password isn't much different from a port number; it's just a configuration value. But from a security perspective, it's a disaster, because placing credentials in code makes them more or less public. Unfortunately, the security aspect isn't what tends to trigger the need for a redesign. Instead, it's the need to deploy to multiple environments, because each environment has a different configuration. Consequently, many choose to group configuration values by environment and move them into resource files—a strategy that works but makes things worse from a security perspective because now secrets also end up on disk.

10.2.2 *Never store secrets in resource files*

By placing configuration in resource files, you allow code and configuration to be separated. This turns out to be a key component in allowing deployment to multiple environments without changing any code, because an application can then load environment-specific configuration data like an IP address or port number at runtime. But although this sounds great, it's unfortunately an anti-pattern from a security perspective because it yields the same problems as storing secrets in code. The only difference is that sensitive data now also ends up on disk, which means that anyone with server access could potentially access the information—not good! But nevertheless, this pattern is a common choice in many applications, so let's have a deeper look at it.

In listing 10.2, you see a resource file (written in YAML) with two environments, dev and prod, where each has a unique set of configuration values for the content management system (CMS).[5] This file is bundled with the application, and the appropriate set of configuration values is loaded at runtime. This way, the same codebase can be deployed in dev and prod without the need to rebuild the application.

Listing 10.2   Resource file with configuration for all environments

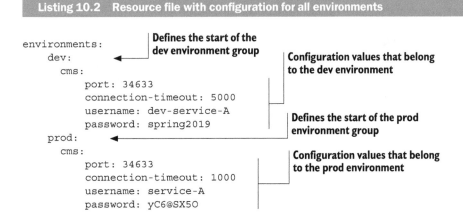

---

[5] YAML Ain't Markup Language is a human-readable data serialization language. For more information, see http://yaml.org.

At first glance, this makes perfect sense because it separates the environments, but it makes the security situation worse. To start with, as with storing secrets in code, anyone with access to the codebase is able to read the sensitive data without creating an audit trail. This sounds like a small problem, but accessing sensitive data without creating an audit trail makes it impossible to know how data has been shared—and that's certainly a big problem! Unfortunately, this can't be addressed adequately when storing secrets in code or in resource files, and the problem is therefore often ignored.

> **WARNING** Never store sensitive data in resource files unless it's encrypted. Otherwise, it can be accessible even after the application has terminated.

Another security problem with storing sensitive data in resource files is that data is stored on disk while the application is running. Secrets such as passwords and decryption keys can then become accessible outside of the application, regardless of whether the application is running or not, which requires you to encrypt all resource data. This seems acceptable at first, but it does add significant complexity; for example, where do you store the decryption key, and how do you provide it to the application? It almost sounds like the chicken-and-egg problem, doesn't it?

A third issue, which is less obvious, is that secrets are shared with everyone in the development team, regardless of whether they're stored in code or in resource files. Ideally, you shouldn't need to care about credentials, certificates, or other sensitive information when designing an application. Secrets should be provided at runtime, and the responsibility for managing them should rest with a limited set of people, not everyone with access to the codebase. Unfortunately, not many developers realize the problems with this approach until the day they need to share code with an external party or choose to go open source, then it suddenly becomes extremely important that secrets aren't leaked. But addressing this at a late stage could be a costly operation. Let's see how you can solve this and the other problems up front by using a better design.

10.2.3 *Placing configuration in the environment*

The security problems discussed so far have in common that code and configuration values haven't been fully separated, which becomes a problem when dealing with secrets—so what's the best way to separate code and configuration? Well, the idea is simple. Any configuration value that changes between deployments should be provided by the environment instead of placed in source code or in resource files. This makes your application environment-agnostic and facilitates deployments in different environments without changing any code.

There are several ways to do this, but a common practice used in the cloud and suggested by the twelve-factor app methodology is to store configuration data in environment variables; for example, in env variables if you're using UNIX. That way, an application only needs to depend on a well-defined set of environment variables that exists in all environments to retrieve the necessary configuration values at runtime (figure 10.1).

The concept is indeed elegant, but how does it affect the security issues identified earlier: audit trail, sharing secrets, and the need for encryption?

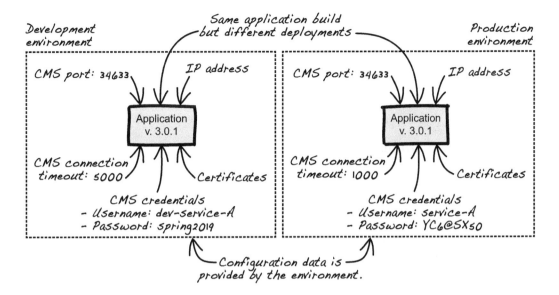

Figure 10.1 Configuration data provided by the environment

AUDIT TRAIL

Moving sensitive data into the environment doesn't solve the problem of change management per se. But from a development perspective, using this pattern makes life a whole lot easier because it reduces implementation complexity. This is because the responsibility of creating audit trails shifts from the application code to the infrastructure layer, which means it becomes an identity and access management (IAM) problem. For example, only authorized accounts are allowed to access the environment, and doing so should create an audit trail that contains every operation performed.

SHARING SECRETS

The strategy of storing secrets in environment variables is an interesting alternative to placing them in code or in resource files. This is because development and configuration management can be separated by design, which in turn allows secrets to be shared only among those responsible for an environment. Application developers can then focus on using secrets rather than managing them, which definitely is a step forward. But unfortunately, this doesn't solve the security problem completely. In most operating systems, a process's environment variables can be flushed out, which becomes a security problem if secrets are stored in clear text. For example, in most Linux systems, it's possible to inspect environment variables using `cat /proc/$PID/environ` (where $PID is your process ID). The question is, therefore, how to address this—perhaps using encryption is a way forward?

ENCRYPTION

Storing encrypted secrets in environment variables certainly minimizes the risk of leaking sensitive data, but the general problems with decryption remain. For example, how do you provide the decryption key to the application? Where do you store it? And how do you update it? These are questions that must be considered when choosing this design. Another strategy, which we prefer, is to use ephemeral secrets that change frequently in an automatic fashion, but this requires a different mindset—we'll get back to this at the end of the chapter, where we talk about the three R's of enterprise security.

You've now learned why code and configuration should be separated and why secrets shouldn't be stored in environment variables. But what about building and running an application—are there any security benefits you can learn from the cloud? There certainly are, so let's see why you should run your application as separate stateless processes in your execution environment.

10.3   Separate processes

One of the main pieces of advice on how to run your application in a cloud environment is to run it as a separate stateless process. To our delight, this design guideline has security benefits as well.

The main direct security advantage is improving the availability of the service; for example, by easily spinning up new service instances when needed to meet a rise in client traffic. You also get some improvement in integrity because you can easily decommission a service instance with a problem, be it memory leakage or a suspect infection. Later in this chapter, you'll see how this ability also lays the foundation for other designs that improve confidentiality, integrity, and availability. The three R's of enterprise security use this ability to its pinnacle, as you'll see in the closing section of this chapter.

Let's elaborate a little about the practice of separate processes. A cloud application should be run as a specific process (or processes), separated from the activity of building it or deploying it to the execution environment. These processes shouldn't keep the client state between requests and should only communicate via backing services, like a database or a distributed cache, that are plugged in. Let's dive a little deeper into what that means.

10.3.1   Deploying and running are separate things

First, let's consider the separation of deploying the service and running the service. Deploying the service is most often done by an operating system user with high privileges, enough to install dependent packages or reconfigure directories. Root access (or similar) can even be needed for deploying new versions of the software. Most of these privileges aren't needed to run the application. A web application might only need privileges for opening a socket for incoming HTTP requests, opening a socket to connect to the database, and writing to some temporary directory it uses while processing requests. The system user running the web application doesn't need to have the broad privileges required for deployment and installation.

> ### Principle of least privilege
>
> The principle of *least privilege* says that it's unnecessary for a process or component to have more privileges than it needs and uses during normal operation:*
>
> *Every program and every privileged user of the system should operate using the least amount of privilege necessary to complete the job.*
>
> *—Jerome Saltzer*

To take it a step further, it's not only unnecessary, it's even harmful to have higher privileges than necessary. If the process or component is hacked, then the hacker can do things there's no need to allow. The principle also leads to practices such as sandboxing or bulkheading, where the reach of what a component can do is limited by some security mechanism.

---

* Jerome H. Saltzer, "Protection and the Control of Information Sharing in Multics," Commun. ACM 17, 7 (July, 1974), pages 388-402.

10.3.2 *Processing instances don't hold state*

Second, an application process shouldn't depend on state from one request being available to another. Sometimes applications assume that two requests from the same client end up at the same server process. For example, in an online bookstore application, the customer might first add a copy of *Hamlet* to the shopping cart and later add a copy of *Secure by Design*. The requests are handled by a set of active instances. In figure 10.2, you can see some ways they are handled and end up in the database.

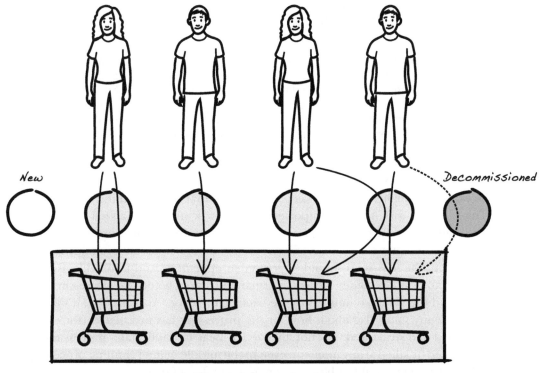

New *Decommissioned*

Backing database of orders

Figure 10.2   Processes serving stateless requests, only communicating via backing services

As you see in the figure, a well-designed cloud application shouldn't assume a specific instance is linked to a specific client. Each and every call from each client should end up at any of the instances that are on duty at the moment.

Let's think about those two consecutive requests from the same customer: one for *Hamlet* and the other for *Secure by Design*. These two requests might be served by the same instance, but a well-designed cloud application shouldn't rely on that. The second request might be served by another instance, and it should work equally well. The second instance might not have even existed when the first request was processed; it might be a new instance that has been spun up to meet a surge in load. Similarly, the instance that served the request for *Hamlet* might not still be around when the request for *Secure by Design* comes in. That first instance might have been killed in the meantime because of some administrative routine. Whatever happens to the instances, it shouldn't matter which route the request takes—the result should be the same. For this reason, the processes shouldn't save any client conversation state between calls. Any result of processing a client request must either be sent back to the client or stored in a stateful backing service, usually a database.

Backing services

A *backing service* is an external resource your application uses, typically by accessing it over the network. This can be a database for persistent storage, a message queue, a logging service, or a shared cache.

An important aspect of backing services is that they should be managed by the environment—not by the application. An application shouldn't connect to a database specified in code. Instead, which database to use should be part of the deployment, as mentioned in the previous section on storing configuration in the environment. When the connection to the database is managed by the environment, it's possible to detach the database and attach another to replace it during runtime.

If the process is doing some heavy or long-running processing, we advise you to split the work into smaller steps and keep a status flag that says something to the effect of "This piece of work has been imported but not structured or analyzed yet." Also, the flag should be updated by each process that advances the computation a step.

A process might well use a local filesystem to temporarily save a result during its processing, but the filesystem should be treated as ephemeral and unreliable as primary memory. You can't consider the work permanently saved before the processing is completed and the result committed to the backing database. At that point, it's advisable to update any status flag about how far the processing has proceeded (for example, "Imported and structured, but not analyzed"). Bear in mind that a process might be interrupted or killed at any moment, even in the middle of long-running processing.

The filesystem shouldn't be relied on as a safe, longtime storage in the way you're used to from computing on a machine with a local filesystem. Some cloud environments even forbid using local files, and any attempt to use APIs to reach them throws an exception.

10.3.3 *Security benefits*

Separating installation and deployment from running the application works well with the principle of least privilege. We've too often seen applications running client requests in a process where the system user has root privileges. If an intruder is able to compromise such a process, it can cause severe damage. But if the process can do only what the application is intended to do—contact the database or write to a log file, for example—the effects will be contained. The attacker can't compromise the integrity of the system itself.

When processes are stateless and share nothing (except backing services), it's easy to scale capacity up or down according to need. Obviously, this is good for availability: fire up a few more servers, and they immediately share the load. You can even do zero-downtime releases by starting servers with a new version of the software at the same time you kill the old servers.

The ability to kill any server at any time is also good for protecting the integrity of the system. If there's any suspicion that a specific server has been infected, it can immediately be killed and replaced. Any work in progress on the server will be lost, but the data will still be in a consistent state, and the new server will be able to redo the work. In the section on the three R's of enterprise security, you'll see how to elevate this ability to effect a drastic increase in security.

Now that you've seen the security benefits of running an application as separate processes and having resources as attached backing services, let's have a closer look at one of those resources—logging.

10.4 *Avoid logging to file*

Logging is a fundamental part of most applications because it helps in understanding why something has happened. Logs can contain anything from user interactions to debug information to audit data, information that most people would consider boring and irrelevant but that, from a security perspective, is like El Dorado.[6] This is because log data tends to include invaluable information, like sensitive data and technical details that could be useful when exploiting a system.

From a security perspective, logs should be locked away and never looked at; but in practice, logs are consumed in a completely different way. For example, when unexpected behavior or bugs are analyzed, logs are used as the primary source of information. This means logs must be accessible at all times, but the data they contain must also be locked away because of its sensitive nature—a contradiction in terms, it seems.

But great security and high accessibility aren't mutually exclusive features. In fact, there's a design pattern used by cloud-native applications that addresses this dichotomy; it's called *logging as a service*. Not many see it as a universal pattern though, and people often choose to log to a file on disk, favoring the needs of development and

---

[6] El Dorado is a mythical city of gold with immense wealth that legend says exists somewhere in South America. See https://www.nationalgeographic.com/archaeology-and-history/archaeology/el-dorado/.

failure investigation only. Before learning more about why logging as a service is preferable, you need to understand what security issues logging to a file on disk brings, so let's analyze it from a CIA perspective.[7]

10.4.1 *Confidentiality*

Many choose to log to a file on disk for several reasons. One is reduced code complexity: logging can be implemented using standard output stream (stdout) or your favorite logging framework. Another is the ease of access during development or failure investigation, because logs can be accessed via remote login to a server. The first reason, in fact, yields better security, because reduced complexity is always good, but the latter is where the security problems start. Allowing logs to be easily fetched is the key to high accessibility, but it also introduces the problem of confidentiality.

Many choose to log massive amounts of data when the trace or debug logging level is enabled. This certainly helps during failure investigations, but the logged information could be sensitive and be used to identify someone; for example, it might reveal a person's political standpoint, geographical location, or financial situation.[8] This certainly isn't acceptable, and implementing an audit trail and restricting access to log data is a must, but applying this process to a file on disk is difficult, if not impossible.

Another issue along the same lines is the need to prevent illegal access. Storing log data on disk and accessing it using remote login makes log access an IAM problem. At first this sounds like a good strategy, because it lets you apply authorization roles and limit overall access, but the strategy only holds as long as no one is able to download any files. If logs can be downloaded, it becomes extremely difficult to uphold access rights, which more or less defeats the purpose of IAM.

10.4.2 *Integrity*

Maintaining the integrity of log files is extremely important, but this requirement is often forgotten when discussing logging strategies. One reason could be that logs are typically only used to help out during development or failure investigations. Preventing modification of log data isn't then a top priority, because why would you modify log data in the first place? A system behaves the same way no matter what you write in the logs.

This certainly makes sense, but if you consider logs as evidence or proof, then integrity suddenly becomes important. For example, if logs are used in a court case claiming that a transaction has been made, then you want to be sure the logs haven't been tampered with. This becomes important when logging to a file. If you allow remote access, you need to

---

[7] Review the section "Designing for availability" in chapter 9 to freshen up on the CIA concept and why availability is important.

[8] This is one of the concerns of the General Data Protection Regulation (GDPR) in the European Union, but that topic is too big for this book to cover. For more information about the GDPR, see https://ec.europa.eu/info/law/law-topic/data-protection_en.

ensure that no one other than the application is able to write to the log files. Otherwise, you could end up in a difficult situation the day you need to prove log integrity.

10.4.3 *Availability*

It seems that guaranteeing the availability of log data should be an easy task when logging to a file on disk, but there are, in fact, several implicit problems that emerge. Storing data on disk is convenient, but it introduces the problem of state. For example, when a server needs to be decommissioned and replaced by a new instance, you need a process to ensure logs are preserved and moved to the new server. Otherwise, critical log data can be lost, and you'll have a gap in the transaction timeline—and that's not good if your logs contain audit data.

Another subtle issue relates to limited disk size. When logging to a file on disk, you need to ensure that the log file doesn't become too large, or you might run out of disk space. A classic dilemma is when the logging process of your application crashes due to lack of available disk space and fails to report it in the logs because there's no space. A common way to mitigate this is to have an admin process that automatically rotates logs. This adds some complexity that we'll get back to in section 10.5, but let's take a quick look at how log rotation works.

Suppose you have a log file called syslog. When that file reaches a certain size or age, the rotation process renames it (say, syslog.1) and creates a new log file called syslog. This way, syslog.1 can be moved, stored, and analyzed without affecting the current log file. This sounds easy, but a common pitfall is that the rotated logs aren't moved and fill up the disk anyway.

You do, indeed, need to consider several security issues when logging to a file on disk. Some are harder and some are easier to resolve than others, but one can't help thinking that there must be a better way to do this—and there is. The solution is found in the cloud, and it involves logging as a service rather than logging to a file on disk.

10.4.4 *Logging as a service*

When running an application in the cloud, you can't depend on external infrastructure, such as a local server disk. This is because a server instance can be replaced at any time, which makes logging to a file on disk problematic. Figure 10.3 illustrates a logging strategy that takes this into account by centralizing all logging to a backing service.

From a code perspective, logging to a service rather than a file doesn't make much difference; you're still able to use your favorite logging framework, but instead of writing to a local disk, data is sent over the network. Conceptually this makes sense, but it's not clear why using a centralized logging service is preferable from a security standpoint—so let's put our CIA glasses on again.

```
public void cancel(final ReservationId reservation) {
    notNull(reservation);

    reservationRepository.cancel(reservation);
    loggingService.log(new ReservationCancelled(reservation, Type.AUDIT));
}
```

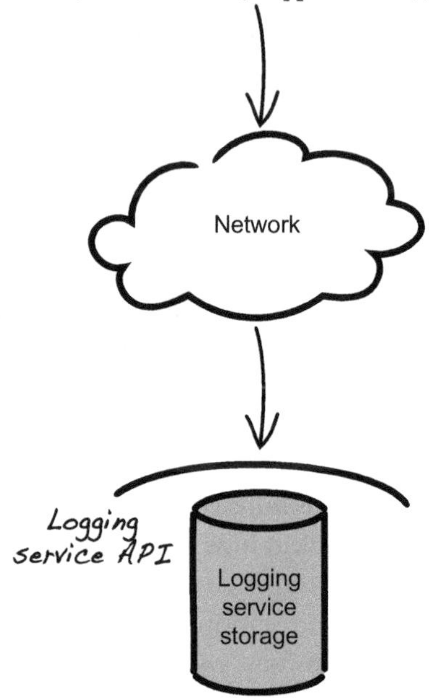

Figure 10.3   Every log call is sent over the network to the logging service.

CONFIDENTIALITY

From a confidentiality perspective, you want to ensure that only authorized consumers get access to log data. This is a challenge when logging to a file on disk, mostly because it's difficult to restrict access to specific data, but also because it's hard to create an audit trail of what data was accessed when and by whom. Using a centralized logging service lets you address this, but only if you choose the proper design. For example, restricting access to the logging system isn't enough on its own to solve the sensitive data access problem, but if you choose to separate log data into different categories, such as Audit, System, and Error, then the logging system could easily restrict users to seeing only log data of a certain category. And, as a developer, this makes perfect sense, because you're probably interested in technical data only (for example, debug or performance data) and not sensitive audit information. How to do this in practice is a topic of its own though, so we'll get back to this in chapter 13.

Another interesting challenge is how to establish a proper audit trail. In comparison to file-based logging, establishing an audit trail is a whole lot easier when using service-based logging. Each time you access log data, the system registers your actions and fires an alarm if you're trying to do anything illegal. This in turn improves the overall credibility of how log data is handled and consumed, even after an application has terminated or been decommissioned.

As a final note, there's one more significant distinction between file-based and service-based logging to remember. When logging to disk, you might consider the disk to be within the same trust boundary as your application. If so, you don't need to worry about protecting data while in transit (from your application to the disk). But if you use a logging service, data is sent over a network, which opens up the possibility of eavesdropping on log traffic. This means that using service-based logging requires data protection while in transit, which is often done using TLS (Transport Layer Security) or end-to-end encryption.

INTEGRITY

Preventing unauthorized access to data is indeed important, but so is ensuring its integrity, especially if you view logs as evidence or proof. Many logging strategies struggle with this, but if you choose service-based logging, the task becomes more or less trivial. This is because the logging system can easily be designed to separate read and write operations, where writes are only performed by trusted sources. For example, if you set up your application to be the only one authorized to write data and give all other consumers read access, then your logs can only contain data written by your application. If you also choose an append-only strategy, then you ensure that log data is never updated, deleted, or overwritten, but only appended to the logs. This way, you can easily ensure a high level of integrity at a low cost.

The need for log aggregation is also an aspect to consider when running a system with multiple instances. When logging to a file on each server instance, logs become separated, and you need to aggregate them manually or run them through a processing tool to get a complete picture of a transaction. This opens up the risk of integrity problems if the aggregation process allows modification—how do you know that data hasn't changed in the aggregated view compared to its individual parts? The solution lies in using a centralized logging service that appends and aggregates data by design. (We'll get back to this when covering logging in a microservice architecture in chapter 13.)

AVAILABILITY

Availability is perhaps the most interesting security aspect to analyze. When you introduce the idea of using a logging service, you're most likely going to be asked, "What if the logging service is down or can't be accessed over the network?" This is a fair question that sounds complex, but the answer is surprisingly easy.

The way to address access failures of the logging service is the same as how you'd deal with disk failures. For example, if transaction rollback is your preferred strategy to handle disk failures, then you'd do the same when failing to access the logging service—it's as simple as that. But if the network is less reliable than disk access and the service can't be accessed, then log data might need to be buffered in local memory to minimize rollbacks if the risk of losing data is acceptable.

Another interesting aspect is the ability to scale. When logging to a file on disk, you're bounded by disk size, and logging can't scale beyond the disk storage capacity. For example, if you need to log a massive amount of data over a long period of time, chances are you'll run out of disk space at some point. But if you choose to use a logging service, then you can adapt the storage capacity based on need and improve overall availability. This is particularly easy if the service is running in the cloud.

A final important comment is that when using a central logging service, you implicitly know where all your log data is; it isn't spread out over hundreds of servers, where some have been decommissioned and some are up and running. This might sound irrelevant, but in a situation where you need to retrieve or remove all the data that you've stored about a person or when you need to run advanced analysis algorithms, it becomes invaluable to know where all your log data is.

10.5 *Admin processes*

A system is not complete without administrative tasks, such as running batch imports or triggering a resend of all messages from a specific time interval. Unfortunately, these admin tasks are often treated as second-class citizens compared to what is seen as the real functionality that customers directly interface with. Sometimes the admin functionality isn't even given the basic standards of version control or controlled deploys, but exists as a collection of SQL and shell command snippets in a file somewhere that's copied over to the server when needed and executed in an ad hoc manner.

Admin functionality should be treated as a first-class citizen; it should be developed together with the system, version controlled on par with the rest of the functionality, and deployed to the live system as a separate interface (API or GUI). You get several security benefits from this (we'll elaborate on how these benefits manifest themselves later in this section):

- You get better confidentiality, because the system can be locked down.
- Integrity is improved, because the admin tools are ensured to be well synchronized with the rest of the system.
- Availability of admin tasks is improved even under system stress.

Administration tasks can be understood as the functionality that isn't the primary purpose of the system but is needed to fulfill that purpose over time. You might have a system whose primary purpose is to sell items to customers over the web. But in doing so, the system interacts with the product catalogue, warehouse, pricing, and so forth. Admin tasks that need to be done might include:

- Auditing the number of warehouse updates that have been executed
- Rerunning failed imports of pricing updates
- Triggering a resend of all messages to the warehouse

Unfortunately, such functionality is often forgotten or overlooked during system development. This might be because these tasks aren't often perceived as value-adding user stories, at least not if you restrict *user* to mean only customer end users, and they aren't given priority.

10.5.1 *The security risk of overlooked admin tasks*

Overlooking admin tasks often opens up security vulnerabilities. All these tasks need to be done anyway, and if there aren't built-in tools for this, the system administrator is forced to use other tools (perhaps overgeneral ones) to get the job done.

To perform admin tasks, the sysadmin might use ssh to log on to the server or to connect directly to the database using a GUI. The tasks might be performed directly in bash using UNIX/Linux commands or SQL commands sent to the database. Some of these scripts and commands will be used more often, and after a while, there will emerge some file of usable scripts, command lines, and SQL that's maintained as part of the sysadmin lore—but those handy scripts won't be maintained together with the rest of the codebase. The security risk is twofold.

First, having such a means of general access as ssh opens up the attack surface more than is necessary. If ssh access is allowed, there's a risk of it being used by the wrong people for the wrong reasons. An attacker that happens to get their hands on root-level ssh access can do almost unlimited harm. The risk might be reduced by closing down access to the machines and only allowing it via bastion hosts or jump hosts that are set up with more strict auditing and so forth. But the risk is further reduced if you have no ssh access at all. Problems might also happen by mistake; for example, during a system emergency, a sysadmin might attempt to clear up space on a partition that becomes full but accidentally erase important data.

The second risk is that if (or rather when) the system and the admin scripts get out of sync, bad things can happen. For example, if the development team refactors the database structure, and the sysadmin SQL commands aren't updated accordingly, applying the old SQL commands on the new table structure can cause havoc and potentially destroy data.

Actually, there's a third risk. Having system code maintained separately from system admin scripts by different groups of people tends to contribute to a strained diplomatic relationship between the two groups of people—something that's not beneficial in the long run.

We'd rather keep the use of such general-purpose and highly potent system administration tools as a last resort. Root-level ssh access or SQL GUIs can definitely get the job done, but they can be used to do almost anything. Explicitly providing the administration functionality that's needed ensures that the attack surface is kept minimal and that the functionality is available when needed.

10.5.2 *Admin tasks as first-class citizens*

The functionality needed for administrative tasks should be developed and deployed as part of the rest of the system. It will reside on the nodes, ready to be called via its API, as seen in figure 10.4.

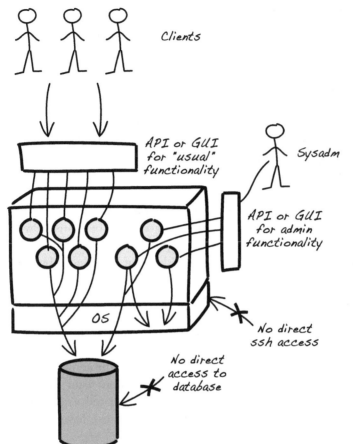

Figure 10.4 Administrative tasks deployed to the server, ready to run via a separate API

In the figure, note how the admin functionality exists on the nodes already; you have to trigger it from the outside. Even if an attacker gains access to the admin API, they'll only be able to trigger the predefined functionality, not any general OS or SQL command—the attack surface is kept low.

Another consideration is that even if admin functionality is part of the deployed system, you'll still want it as a separate process. In particular, you'll probably want to have the admin parts available when things are getting slow and unresponsive. If the admin functionality is embedded in the same process as the usual functionality, there's a risk that it'll become unavailable at the wrong time. For example, if your web server is clogged down by lots of queued-up and waiting requests, you don't want to put your admin requests into the same queue. The solution to this, as indicated in figure 10.4, is to have admin functionality run as a separate process, called via a separate API. One way of doing this is to put it in a separate runtime container.

If you're developing in Java, the admin functionality could be put in a separate JVM of its own, or your admin might be written in Python and deployed separately. If you want to increase availability further, you can put the sysadmin API on a separate network, making it completely independent from what happens with the usual clients.

> ### Admin of log files
>
> A classic admin task is rotating logs. More than one server in the history of computing has stopped working because the disk partition where logs were written suddenly became full (the famous "no space left on device" error). In this situation, it usually becomes the task of operations to log in via `ssh` and remove some old log files.
>
> If you follow some or all of the advice given here, your log file admin will be much easier. If logs are sent to a connected backing service, and you avoid logging to file (see section 10.4), there will be no logs at all on the instances. But if there are, there's no need to delete old logs to get the instance up and running again. All you have to do is decommission that instance and spin up a new one (as they are separate processes, as described in section 10.3). Should you want to keep some logs before deleting the instance, you can do that by having an admin task for retrieving the logs from a specific instance.

If you structure your admin functionality according to the guidelines in this section, you get all three kinds of security benefits:

- Confidentiality increases because the system is locked down to only provide specific admin tasks and not, for example, a general SQL prompt.
- Integrity is better because you know that the administration tools are in sync with the application, so there's no risk of those tools working on old assumptions and causing havoc.
- Availability is higher because it's possible to launch administration tasks even under high load.

The ability to dynamically launch new instances is a key feature both for admin tasks and the usual functionality. To make this work, clients need to be able to access those new instances. Also, you need to ensure that instances that have been decommissioned don't get client calls. For this, you need some kind of service discovery and load balancing, so let's continue on with how to do that.

10.6   *Service discovery and load balancing*

Service discovery and load balancing are two central concepts in cloud environments and PaaS solutions. They also share a common trait in that they both enable continuous change in an environment. It might not be obvious at first, but service discovery can improve security, because it can be used to increase the availability of a system. As you learned in chapters 1 and 9, availability is part of the CIA triad and is an important security property for a system.

Service discovery also increases security by allowing a system to stay less static, which is a topic we'll talk about in more detail in the next section. Let's start by looking at some common patterns for implementing load balancing with and without service discovery.

10.6.1   *Centralized load balancing*

Although load balancing in itself is an old concept, it's performed on a different scale in cloud environments. The basic purpose of load balancing is to distribute workloads across multiple instances of an application. Traditionally, this was commonly done by using dedicated load-balancing hardware, configured to spread requests across a set number of IP addresses (see figure 10.5). Configuring such load balancers is more often than not a manual and brittle process that also involves the risk of downtime if something goes wrong. This approach of spreading load doesn't always work well in a cloud environment.

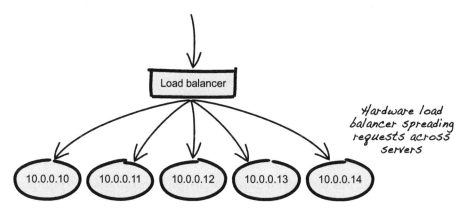

Figure 10.5   Centralized load balancing

Cloud-native applications are stateless and elastic by definition, which means individual instances come and go, and they should be able to do so without the consumer of a service being affected. The number of instances and the IP addresses and ports used by each instance are constantly changing. Because of this, the management of load balancing is transferred to the PaaS you deploy your applications on. The platform is then responsible for constantly keeping track of what instances it should use to spread the workload. This turns load balancing management into a fully automated and more robust task.

When you're using centralized load balancing, the consumer, or the caller, is unaware of how many instances of an application are sharing the load and which instance will receive a specific request. The distribution of the load is managed centrally.

10.6.2 *Client-side load balancing*

An alternative approach to centralized load balancing is client-side load balancing (figure 10.6). As the name implies, this puts the decision of which instance to call on the caller.

You might want to use client-side load balancing instead of centralized load balancing for several reasons, one being that it can simplify your architecture and deployment processes. Another reason is that it allows the caller to make informed decisions on how to distribute the load. In order to do client-side load balancing, you need something called *service discovery*. Service discovery allows one application (the client) to discover, or look up, where the instances of another application are located. Once the client knows about the instances, it can use that information to perform load balancing. Because the discovery is performed at runtime, service discovery works well in ever-changing cloud environments.

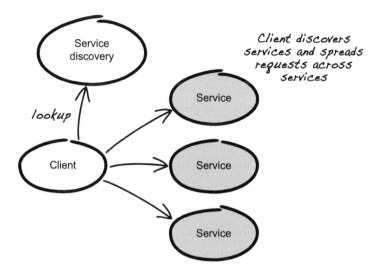

Figure 10.6   Client-side load balancing using service discovery

10.6.3 *Embracing change*

If you can deploy your application in an environment that supports dynamic load balancing and service discovery, be it a PaaS or a homegrown infrastructure, you'll have the basic tools to support an environment that's constantly changing and where individual instances come and go. Change can happen because of elasticity (increasing or decreasing the number of instances), application updates, infrastructure changes, or changes in operating systems.

What's interesting is that from a security perspective, change is good for several reasons. From a pure load balancing point of view, spreading load across multiple instances can increase the availability of a system, and, therefore, it'll also increase the security of the system. Another aspect is that a system, application, or environment that's constantly changing is far more difficult to exploit than one that stays static. Taking advantage of continuous change to improve security is what the three R's of enterprise security are all about.

10.7 *The three R's of enterprise security*

If you design your applications and systems based on the twelve-factor app and cloud-native ideas, you'll not only be able to run them in a cloud environment, but they'll also behave well. Once you're able to run your systems on a cloud platform, you can use the tools provided by the platform to take the security of those systems to the next level. The way to do this is by using the three R's of enterprise security.

The tools and possibilities available to you in a cloud environment are often radically different from those in traditional infrastructure and applications. It shouldn't seem too far-fetched that the approach used to create secure systems in the cloud is equally different from the more traditional approaches of enterprise security. Justin Smith took some of the most important concepts of enterprise security in cloud environments and summarized them in what he called *the three R's:*[9]

1 Rotate secrets every few minutes or hours
2 Repave servers and applications every few hours
3 Repair vulnerable software as soon as possible (within a few hours) after a patch is available

In this section, you'll learn what these concepts mean and how they improve security. You'll also see how the concepts discussed previously in this chapter work as enablers for the three R's.

10.7.1 *Increase change to reduce risk*

Applying the three R's to create secure systems is in many aspects fundamentally different from the traditional approaches used to mitigate security risk in IT systems. One common traditional rationale is that change increases risk. Therefore, in order to reduce risk, rules are made to prevent change in systems or in software in various ways. For example, limitations are put on how often new versions of applications are allowed to be released. Protocols and processes are introduced that turn the cycle time for getting new updates and patches on the OS level out to production into months. Secrets such as passwords, encryption keys, and certificates are rarely or never changed, because the risk of something breaking when doing so is considered to be too high. Reinstalling an entire server is almost unheard of, because not only would it take weeks to get all the necessary configuration in place, it'd also take a significant amount of testing to verify that everything was done correctly. Suffice it to say that this traditional approach to IT security is largely based on *preventing* change.

The purpose of the three R's is the total opposite—reduce risk by increasing change. The observation that Justin Smith makes is that many attacks on IT systems have a greater chance of succeeding on systems that rarely change. A system that stays largely static is also the perfect target for advanced persistent threat (APT) attacks, which usually result in significant damage and data loss. If your system is constantly changing, you effectively reduce the time an attacker will have to inflict any significant damage.

Advanced persistent threats

In an APT attack, the adversary is usually highly skilled and targets a specific system. The results of these attacks are often costly and can hurt a company to the point of bankruptcy. Some characteristics of an APT are that it's performed over a long period of time and involves advanced techniques to allow the attacker to gradually work further into the system, searching for the targeted data. The techniques used often involve finding several vulnerabilities or flaws in software that, in combination, can be used to gain access to new parts of the system.

---

[9] Smith, J., "The Three Rs of Enterprise Security: Rotate, Repave, and Repair" (2016), https://builtto-adapt.io/the-three-r-s-of-enterprise-security-rotate-repave-and-repair-f64f6d6ba29d.

Now that you're familiar with the general concept, let's take a closer look at each of the three R's.

10.7.2 Rotate

Rotate secrets every few minutes or hours. If your application is using passwords to access various systems, make sure they're changed every few minutes and that every application has its own user to access the system with. This might sound like something that's complicated to set up, but if you've designed your application in line with the twelve-factor app methodology and placed your configuration in the environment, your application can remain unaware of the rotation. All it needs to know is how to read the password from the environment.

The PaaS running the application will take care of rotating the passwords on a regular basis and injecting the new values into the environment for the application to consume (figure 10.7). Most solutions for cloud environments, both public and private, have the ability to perform these tasks, and, if not, it's usually not that hard to set up.

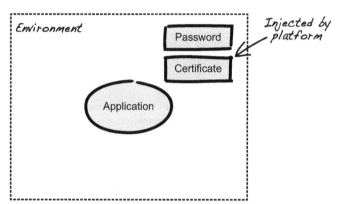

Figure 10.7 The platform injecting ephemeral secrets into the environment

Another benefit of this practice is that passwords can be treated as ephemeral by the platform. They're generated on demand and then injected directly into the environment of a running container or host. They will only ever live in nonpersistent RAM. This helps reduce possible attack vectors, because they're not placed in some file or central configuration management tool that can be more easily compromised. You also don't have to deal with the hassle of encrypting the passwords placed in the configuration file.

Once you understand this concept of ephemeral credentials and how the cloud platform enables you to use unique passwords that don't live for more than a couple of minutes, there's no reason why you shouldn't do the same with other types of secrets. Certificates, for example, can be rotated in a similar fashion. Because you can rotate them instead of renewing them, you're reducing the time frame for which a certificate is valid. If someone were to steal it, they wouldn't have much time to use it. In addition, you'll never again have a problem with a certificate expiring because you forgot to renew it. (Expired certificates are an all too common reason for security issues caused by system unavailability.) The same goes for API tokens used to access various services and any other type of secret used.

TIP   Keep secrets short-lived and replace them when they expire.

Sometimes the application needs to be aware of how the credentials are being rotated, perhaps because it involves details better encapsulated in the application rather than making the platform aware of application-specific details. In these cases, the application itself will receive the ephemeral secrets by directly interacting with a service providing these features (figure 10.8).

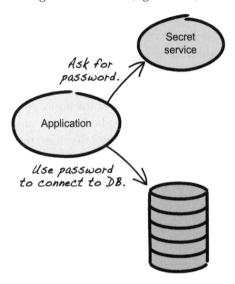

Figure 10.8   The client retrieves secrets from a dedicated service.

With this approach, the application is now responsible for retrieving updated secrets before they expire. In terms of responsibility, this approach is similar to client-side load balancing in that it puts more responsibility on the application.

Rotating secrets doesn't improve the security of the secrets themselves, but it's an effective way of reducing the time during which a leaked secret can be misused—and, as you've learned, time is a prerequisite for APTs to succeed. Reduce the time a leaked secret can be used, and you've made it a lot harder for such an attack to be successful.

10.7.3 *Repave*

Repave servers and applications every few hours. Recreating all servers and containers and the applications running on them from a known good state every few hours is an effective way of making it hard for malicious software to spread through the system. A PaaS can perform rolling deployments of all application instances, and if the applications are cloud-native, you can do this without any downtime.

Instead of only redeploying when you're releasing a new version of your application, you can do this every other hour, redeploying the same version. Rebuild your virtual machine (VM) or container from a base image and deploy a fresh instance of your application on it. Once this new instance is up and running, terminate one of the older ones (see figure 10.9). By *terminate*, we mean burn it down to the ground and don't

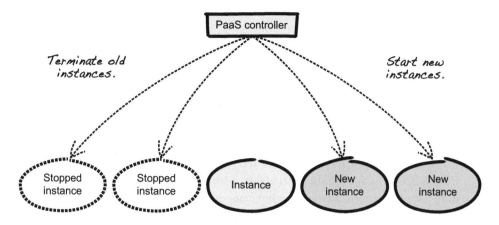

Figure 10.9 Repaving instances by rolling deployment

reuse anything. This includes erasing anything put on a file mount used by the server instance. (This is where it comes in handy that you learned not to put logs on disk earlier in this chapter.) By repaving all your instances, you not only erase your server and application but also any possible malicious software placed on the instance, perhaps as part of an ongoing APT attack.

Repaving server instances can be difficult if you're running on bare-metal servers, but if you're using VMs, you can do this even if you're not using a PaaS. If you're running containers, it becomes even easier to spin up a new instance from a base image. If you can, consider repaving both the containers and the host running the containers. The application deployed must also be a completely fresh instance, so don't reuse any application state from a previous instance.

Containers and virtual machines

A *virtual machine* is a software representation of hardware. It's an emulation of a specific set of hardware that lets you put a separating layer between an operating system (OS) and the underlying hardware. That way, you can run multiple VMs on a single physical machine, usually with full separation between them, and each VM can pretend to have different hardware and run different operating systems.

A *container*, on the other hand, is a virtualization on the OS level, rather than a full virtualization of the hardware. This reduces the overhead of consumed resources compared to virtual machines, because each container doesn't need a full hardware emulation. Instead, multiple containers can share the kernel of the host OS. This is an advantage containers have over virtual machines, but, at the same time, it's also a disadvantage and puts limitations on the container. For example, you can't run a container dependent on a kernel that's different from that of the host OS. This is why you'll have trouble running a container with Windows on *nix, or a *nix container on a *nix host with a different kernel.

It's a common practice to run containers on virtualized machines. Because both are virtualizations, these are perfect tools for repaving servers and applications.

10.7.4 Repair

Repair vulnerable software as soon as possible after a patch is available. This goes for both operating systems and applications. What this means is that as soon as a patch is available, you start the process of rolling out the new software into production. When you do this, you don't incrementally apply the patch to an existing server; instead, you create a new known good state and then repave the server and application instances from the new state.

Again, this might sound like an incredibly difficult thing to do, but it's not if your platform and applications are designed for it. All the tools and technologies needed to do this are already available and widely adopted, so there's nothing stopping you from doing so. To give you an idea of what's needed, if you're not running in a cloud environment, you probably need to at least be running virtual servers, and it'll be even easier if you're using containers (although it's not necessary). If you're running on a cloud platform, you should already have all the tools at your disposal.

> **NOTE** Think of repairing as a variant of repaving. If you've got repaving down, it's not that different to start repairing.

You should also apply the repair concept to your own software. When there's a new version of your application ready to be released, it should be deployed as soon as possible. You should make new versions available as often as you can. If you're familiar with continuous delivery and continuous deployment, you might already be applying the repair concept on your own applications, even if you don't know it.

The reason for repairing as often as you can is that for every new version of the software, something will have changed. If you're constantly changing your software, an attacker constantly needs to find new ways to break it. Say you have a vulnerability in your software that you're unaware of. If you rarely change your software, the vulnerability remains for a long time, allowing for an APT to continue to do its job. But if you're continuously making small changes to your software and deploying it often, you might remove the vulnerability—again, without knowing it.

Don't forget to also repair your application any time a new security patch for a third-party dependency you use becomes available. To keep track of vulnerable dependencies efficiently, you should make it part of your delivery pipeline (go back to chapter 8 for tips on how to leverage your delivery pipeline for security).

In order to deploy new versions of operating systems and applications soon after a patch is available without causing downtime, your applications need to adhere to the twelve-factor app methodology and be cloud-native. Your processes and procedures for releasing updates also need to be streamlined. If they aren't, you'll most likely struggle to smoothly repair servers and applications.

Setting up everything needed to start applying the three R's is a lot easier if you're running on a cloud platform, whether it's a public cloud or a PaaS hosted in-house. But even if you're running on dedicated servers, you can still make the three R's a reality with tools already available to you. It all starts by creating applications that are cloud-native and follow the twelve-factor app methodology. Then you can learn from the design ideas used when architecting for the cloud and apply them in your own environment to reap the same benefits.

If you're working with existing applications and can't start from scratch, a step-by-step process of slowly transforming your applications toward the twelve factors is usually a viable approach. When working with existing IT systems, the biggest challenge is often coming to terms with a completely new way of handling enterprise security.

Summary

- The twelve-factor app and cloud-native concepts can be used to increase the security of applications and systems.
- You should run your application as stateless processes that can be started or decommissioned for any occasion.
- Any result of processing should be stored to a backing service, such as a database, log service, or distributed cache.
- Separating code and configuration is the key to allowing deployment to multiple environments without rebuilding the application.
- Sensitive data should never be stored in resource files, because it can be accessed even after the application has terminated.
- Configuration that changes with the environment should be part of the environment.
- Administration tasks are important and should be part of the solution; they should be run as processes on the node.
- Logging shouldn't be done to a local file on disk, because it yields several security issues.
- Using a centralized logging service yields several security benefits, regardless of whether you're running an application in the cloud or on-premise.
- Service discovery can increase security by improving availability and promoting an ever-changing system.
- Applying the concept of the three R's—rotate, repave, and repair—significantly improves many aspects of security. Designing your applications for the cloud is a prerequisite for doing this.

Intermission: An insurance policy for free

11

This chapter covers

- A broken system where no parts were broken
- Context mapping to understand what's going on
- Risk of myopic views of microservices

So far, we've covered lots of different ways to use design to make software more secure. We've collected designs from different areas, like cloud architecture, Domain-Driven Design (DDD), and reactive systems, where security wasn't the original focus. The nice thing is that all these designs can be used in ways that increase security as a beneficial side effect. All in all, we've covered a lot of ground, and we'll soon turn to applying these fundamentals to some different scenarios, such as legacy systems and microservices architectures. But before doing that, let's take a quick break and look at how a system of systems can break without any specific part being broken. We'll do that by examining a case study of a real-life system.

If you're in a hurry, you can safely skip this chapter. Otherwise, hang on, it's a fun story with some interesting details. This is a real-life story about how an insurance company came to give away policies without payment. It's also about how that disaster could have been avoided.

Like many companies today, the company in question decided to split its monolithic system into several smaller parts, changing the architecture to more of a

278

microservices style. Splitting the system was probably the right thing to do at the time, but some subtle yet important points were missed when the systems were developed separately. During this development, the meaning of the term *payment* shifted slightly, and separate teams came to interpret it in different ways. In the end, some systems thought the company had been paid the premium, when it had not.

One way to avoid this disaster would have been to model the different contexts more consciously and make the effort to draw out the context map in combination with active refactoring to more precise models. To make this happen, it's important to bring together experts early on from all the adjacent domains and have them discover subtle issues together. This becomes even more important when developing a microservices architecture, where a fragmented understanding can have severe consequences.

We'll take a brief look at a possible solution here and dive more deeply into these topics in later chapters (especially chapter 12 on legacy code and chapter 13 on the microservices architecture). This story serves as an introduction to those ideas, however.

Let's start with the story of a good old-fashioned, brick-and-mortar insurance company and how it began its digital journey. The name and location of the company have been withheld for obvious reasons, and the details of the court case have been changed so that it can't be traced.

11.1 Over-the-counter insurance policies

We'll start at the beginning. The insurance company has been in business for quite some time. Historically, its main business has been providing insurance policies for real estate (housing as well as business) and cars. The company has always worked locally with a branch office in every city in the part of the state where it conducts business. All business is done over the counter. When a new customer signs up for a policy, they sign a document at the office and pay over the counter, and the company mails a policy letter proving a valid policy. Likewise, when a customer renews an insurance contract, they show up at the office and pay over the counter, and a policy renewal letter is mailed. In recent years, the back-office system has started using a print-and-mail service so the personnel at the branches don't need to worry about printing and mailing. The system automatically mails the policy letter as soon as the payment is registered (figure 11.1).

Figure 11.1 When a payment is made, the insurance system mails a new policy letter.

Under the hood, the system couples a `Payment` with a new `PolicyPeriod`, which is what triggers a new mailing. This is all part of one codebase, developed and deployed as a monolith—but that's soon to change. If you were to make a context map at this point, it'd look something like figure 11.2.

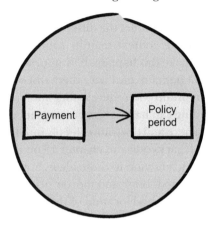

Figure 11.2   **A context map showing the one single context of the monolith**

Granted, this isn't much of a map right now, but we'll see how it evolves as our story unfolds.

11.2 Separating services

The team that develops the system grows over time. Many different policy plans need to be supported, and more are being added at regular intervals. At the same time, there's a lot of functionality around finance: keeping track of payments from customers, reimbursements, payments to partners, such as car repair shops, and so on. Even though the team has grown, they feel overwhelmed by the amount of functionality to develop and support. Because of this, it's decided to split the team and the system into two parts: one system for finance and one system for policies.

The finance team will keep track of payments, handle contracts with partners, and deal with reimbursements. The policy team will concentrate on the ever-increasing plenitude of policy variations. In this way, each smaller team will be better able to focus on its domain. If you draw the context map again now, you'll see that it's slightly more interesting than before the separation (figure 11.3).

The transition to separate the monolith into two systems goes pretty smoothly, perhaps because everybody is still familiar with the full domain and pretty clear about what's a `Payment` and what's a `PolicyPeriod`. But that's also soon to change.

These systems depend on each other in many ways. One of the main connections is that when a `Payment` is made in the finance system, that event is reported to the policy system, which reacts by creating a new `PolicyPeriod` and, subsequently, automatically prints and mails a policy letter. It's clear that the policy system reacts when the finance system registers a payment. The policy system is aware of `Payment` as a concept, but the team doesn't need to understand the intricacies of how such a payment is made.

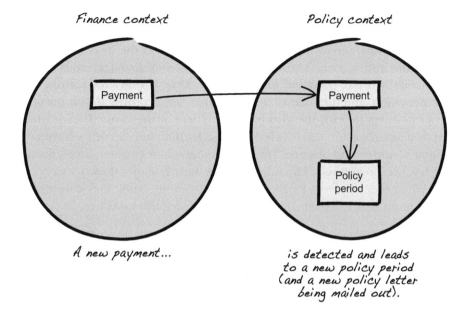

Figure 11.3 Payment for an insurance policy, across the two domains of finance and policy

As time goes by, the teams drift further and further apart. Keeping track of different financial flows seems to be work enough in and of itself, especially with the company signing new partner programs with both car repair shops and craftspeople, such as plumbers and carpenters. Keeping track of unusual policies is also a full-time occupation, with salespeople inventing combo deals and rebates to attract and keep customers. The two teams spend less and less time together and get less and less insight into each other's domains. On a few occasions, they even get hostile when one of the teams changes some event that the other subscribes to and breaks the other team's code. Still, things work out. But that's also soon to change.

11.3 A new payment type

The organization continues to grow, and there are now two product managers: one for the policy system and the team working on it and one for the finance system and the team working on that. Each of the product managers governs their own backlog, and they communicate little. Management takes the lack of communication as a good sign—obviously, it has managed to cut the development organization into parts that can work independently of each other. But now a new payment type is introduced, and a fatal mistake is made.

At the top of the finance team's backlog is a story to allow a new way of paying through bank giro instead of cash over the counter. *Bank giro* is a method of transferring money where the customer instructs their bank to transfer funds from one of their accounts to the insurance company without writing a check. The customer doesn't even need to know the insurance company's bank account number; instead, they use a special bank giro number. The insurance company can restructure its bank accounts or even change to a different bank without the customers needing to know or care.[1]

The businesspeople at the insurance company settle the deal with the bank that provides the giro service. The finance system product manager adds a story called "implement bank giro payment" high on the backlog. Within a few sprints, it's time for implementation, and the finance development team is provided with documentation on how to integrate with the giro payment system at the bank. They learn that with giro payments, there are three different messages that they can retrieve from the bank: Payment, Confirm, and Bounce. The documentation for Payment states that a giro payment has been registered. The finance team starts fetching these messages from the bank. When they receive a Payment message from the bank, they consider it to be a Payment in the finance system. Figure 11.4 shows what this looks like.

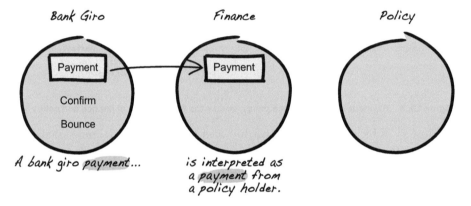

Figure 11.4   A Payment message arrives from the bank and is interpreted as a Payment by the finance system.

It seems logical that a payment is a payment, but it's crucial to pay attention to context, as the teams will find out. Doing system integration by matching strings to each other is a dangerous practice. Just as an order in the military isn't the same as an order in a warehouse, the finance team will eventually realize that something that's a payment in one context shouldn't automatically be interpreted as a payment in another context. But to be honest, the documentation doesn't help much (table 11.1), unless you already know the ins and outs of a bank giro transfer.

The finance team is careful not to disturb the integration point with the policy system. As we mentioned, there were some debacles when one team broke the other team's system. The finance team takes care to send Payment messages to the policy team in the same way as before.

---

[1] You can read more details on bank giro transfers at https://www.investopedia.com/terms/b/bankgirotransfer.asp.

Table 11.1 Bank giro payment process

Message	Documentation	Spontaneous interpretation	What it means
Payment	Giro payment has been registered	OK, payment is ready.	No money has been transferred yet; we've registered that we'll try to transfer it.
Confirm	Confirmation of payment processing	Oh? OK, whatever.	Money has been transferred.
Bounce	Confirmation still pending, will try again	No worries...	Failed to transfer money; if remaining attempts are zero, the failure is permanent.

In their system, the policy team continues to listen for Payment messages from finance. When they receive such a message, they create a corresponding `PolicyPeriod`, which triggers a new policy letter being mailed to the purchaser. They don't know whether it's a cash payment or a bank giro payment—and that's the beauty of it, isn't it? They can't know and don't need to know—separation of concerns in action. But there's a catch. If you now draw the context map again, as shown in figure 11.5, you'll see all three contexts and how they have been mapped to each other: the external bank context, the finance context, and the policy context.

You might be familiar with both the bank giro domain and the insurance domain. In that case, you'll see the subtle mistake that was made. A bank giro `Payment` from the external bank is mapped to a `Payment` of the internal finance system, which is then mapped to a `PolicyPeriod`. It seems natural enough—a payment is a payment. But due to two subtleties, one in the insurance domain and one in the bank giro domain, this approach isn't sound.

The subtlety in the insurance domain is that insurance policies aren't like most goods. If you buy a necklace, a seller might agree to get paid later. If you don't pay on

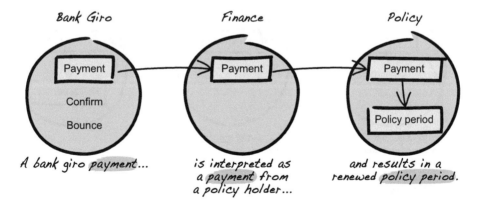

Figure 11.5 Mapping of a bank giro payment through the three domains: bank, finance, and policy

Figure 11.6   For some goods, it makes sense to take them back if payment isn't made; for others, not so much.

time, the seller can cancel the purchase and request to have the necklace back. This is customer trade practice. But for some goods, it doesn't work (figure 11.6).

An insurance policy is a kind of good where it doesn't work to cancel the purchase if the buyer doesn't pay. The buyer will have already enjoyed the benefit of the policy in the meantime; you can't take it back. Selling an insurance policy is like selling a lottery ticket; the seller must ensure the buyer pays for the ticket before the drawing, because few would afterward bother to pay for a ticket that turned out to be a loser. In the same way, who'd pay for a car insurance policy after a period when there were no accidents?

An insurance company (or a lottery ticket seller) could accept payment from a trustworthy, recurring customer in the form of an outstanding debt—a bond, debenture, or similar. In doing so, it would be trusting the customer to clear the debt later. But most insurance companies, including the one in our story, require customers to pay the money before the policy goes into effect. This leads to the second subtlety, the one in the bank giro domain, where a payment isn't a payment (see figure 11.7).

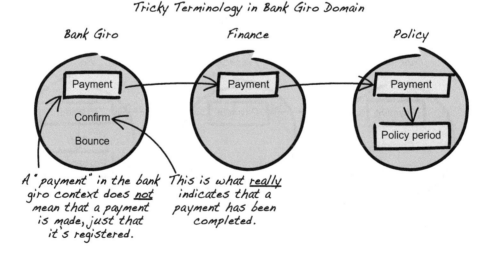

Figure 11.7   A bank giro payment isn't what you expect it to be.

As you might recall, the Payment message from the bank means a giro payment has been registered, but this doesn't mean that the money has been transferred. In bank giro lingo, it signals that a request for the payment has been made, and it'll be processed at the appropriate time (for example, during the coming night's large batch-job window). When the money is transferred, the bank giro payment is said to be complete and can be confirmed (hence the message Confirm). If the transfer can't be completed, perhaps because of lack of funds in the paying account, the giro payment is said to have bounced and will typically be retried a couple of times (hence the message Bounce).

You'll soon see how these two subtleties together can make for a disastrous combination—a customer who enjoys the protection of a car insurance policy before paying for it. But in our story, the finance and policy teams, the policy holders, and the company at large are still in ignorant bliss about future events. The company rolls out this new payment method.

11.4   *A crashed car, a late payment, and a court case*

Existing customers start using the hassle-free payment method, and new customers sign on. Things go fine until one day when a customer makes a claim on his car insurance policy. To provide evidence, the customer shows an insurance letter that was mailed to him (figure 11.8). That letter has an extended date to cover a new period. The problem is, he didn't pay his fee for this period.

What had happened was that the bank giro payment was registered in due order. But on the payment date, the customer didn't have sufficient funds in his account, so the bank giro withdrawal was rejected. During the following week, there were a few follow-up attempts, but as there were never enough funds, the payment was never completed. Still, the policy system sent him a policy renewal letter. Happy not to pay, the customer let this continue month after month. Well, that's until he crashed his car. Then the customer hurried to pay the outstanding debt, after the fact. What happened wasn't anything strange. The system worked as designed.

For customers who choose to pay by bank giro, when a policy comes up for renewal, the finance system issues a new payment request, which is sent to the customer's bank. On receiving this request, the bank sends a Payment message back to the finance system. The finance system treats this in the same way as a cash payment over the counter because they are conceptualized as the same thing. When it receives the Payment

Figure 11.8   A customer with a valid policy letter

message, it sends it on to the policy system, which reacts by prolonging the policy period and sending out a renewal letter to the policy holder.

The interesting thing is what *didn't* happen. Because there weren't sufficient funds in the policy holder's account, there never was a transfer and never a Confirm message. But because the finance system only listened for Payment messages, the missing Confirm went unnoticed. What happened was that the bank system issued a `Bounce` `{remaining_attempts: 3}` message, saying that it wasn't able to do the transfer but would try again later, three more times. The finance system could safely ignore those messages until there was a `Bounce{remaining_attempts: 0}` message, meaning that the bank had finally given up on its attempts to draw money from the customer's account.

When the insurance company first started accepting giro payments, the bounce-and-give-up scenario was completely ignored. There were other (but cumbersome) manual processes in place that would catch these cases. Later, the finance system was developed to detect these situations and put the customers on a watch list. The company then contacted the defaulting customers, starting with mailing out a reminder. Unfortunately, the functionality to do this was seen as a pure financial issue. The policy system never learned about this final `Bounce` and continued to believe the customers had paid.

And here you see the glitch. Even though we use the word *payment* for both things, a bank giro payment isn't the same as a cash over-the-counter payment. In the latter case, the insurance company gets the money in its possession immediately. But in the former case, the insurance company doesn't get the money until the giro payment is processed by the bank. If there's no money in the account after three retries, then no money is transferred, and the insurance company won't get paid, but the policy system will nevertheless have sent out a new policy letter.

The company claimed that the owner of the crashed car wasn't entitled to compensation—he hadn't paid his bill on time. The policy letter that was sent was due to a bug in the system. And paying the fee after a crash didn't count as a valid payment; it was clearly an attempt to try to cover himself. Although the customer had finally made a payment after the incident, this didn't entitle him to backdated coverage for the period during which he had not paid for the policy. On the other hand, the car owner claimed that he had a valid policy letter on the day of the crash, and that he had fulfilled his monetary duties by paying. Neither party would budge, so the case finally ended up in court.

In the trial, the judge ruled in favor of the policy holder. He interpreted the policy renewal letter as proof that the company had accepted a continued agreement: if the payment hadn't yet been made in full, then the company had clearly accepted payment in the form of an outstanding debt. Legally, the company was bound by the issued policy letter.

We can only speculate how the judge would have interpreted the situation otherwise, but it stands to reason that had there not been a renewal letter, then the company could've argued that it didn't accept an outstanding debt as a payment. Most probably the ruling would have gone in favor of the company instead. The essence here is that the way the company did business de facto defined how its intentions were interpreted legally (figure 11.9).

Figure 11.9 What a system does can be interpreted as what it's intended to do.

Even if the conceptualization that put bank giro and cash payments on par was a mistake, it was the way the company did business and, therefore, was interpreted as intentional. The court didn't care whether issuing the policy letter was a bug, a mistake, or a bad business decision. The company had acted as if it treated a bank giro payment (order) as a cash payment, and it needed to stand by that.

11.5 Understanding what went wrong

This situation, where the company hands out policies when it shouldn't, is clearly a bug. But where is that bug located? In fact, going back to the individual systems, none of them does anything that's unreasonable according to its domain. The bank giro system does what it should—arguably, it has some strange namings, but what domain doesn't? We might claim that the finance system contains a bug because it takes something that's not a completed money transfer (a bank giro payment) and considers it to be a payment from a customer. From a strict financial domain perspective, this is perfectly reasonable. Payments can be made in many forms, and cash is only one of them; in many contexts, it's normal to accept a payment in the form of an IOU (I owe you) note or some other outstanding debt. The policy system also does exactly what it should. It detects a policy payment and reacts by issuing a new policy.

It's hard to claim that the bug is in any one of the system integrations (for example, the integration between the external bank and the finance system). A registered but uncompleted bank giro payment can certainly be interpreted as the customer having declared the intention to pay, and the company, having accepted this, being in debt until the money is transferred. It takes gathering our collective understanding of the subtleties, looking at all three domains at the same time, to see that this situation isn't sound.

11.6 Seeing the entire picture

Avoiding this situation would have required collaboration and communication between people with expertise in all three domains: bank giro transfer, finance, and insurance policies. Let's take a closer look at what went wrong and what could have been done differently. How could we have ensured those people talked to each other, sooner (preferable) or later?

The focus on not breaking the technical dependencies was clearly a hampering factor. It encouraged the finance team to reuse the same technical construct, `Payment`, even though its meaning had diverged: the word *payment* had come to mean both immediate payment over the counter and a payment request sent to the bank for clearance. But in their unwillingness to disturb the policy team, the finance team continued to use the term *payment* for both cases. The sad part is that this is exactly what messed things up for the policy team, because to them, the two types of payment weren't the same. To the policy team, immediate payment over the counter was a sound foundation for issuing a policy renewal letter, but a payment request sent to the bank for clearance wasn't.

What should have been done instead? The obvious answer is that the finance team should have listened for the bank giro message Confirm instead of Payment. The Confirm message marks that a transaction has been completed, which is what the insurance company regards as a sound foundation for issuing a policy. But, how would that happen? What would have caused the finance team to do a different mapping?

Let's play out a different scenario. Suppose you're the project manager or technical lead in the finance team at the time the new payment option is introduced. You decide to guide the team in implementing it using deliberate context mapping. You stop to think about what the team thus far has called a payment. The concept was specific enough when cash payments were the only payments that existed, but now that you're about to add giro payments, this is no longer the case.

After some discussion with your team, you muster up the courage to refactor the domain and call the original type of `Payment` a `CashPayment` instead, because that's what it is. In the best interest of both worlds, you make a note that you need to talk about this with the policy team that sits downstream, and who'll need to handle the name change. And if you forget, or if it doesn't occur to you to talk to the policy team, perhaps you don't know that they listen for that specific Payment message? After you refactor `Payment` to `CashPayment` and deploy the change to production, it'll only be a matter of time until someone from the policy team approaches you and asks what has happened to their expected Payment messages. If nothing else, this will cause a discussion to happen; now you'll have to rely on your diplomatic skills! Jokes aside, it's not desirable to break a technical dependency. But if that's what it takes to ensure that a crucial domain discussion happens, then it's worth it.

Back to the story: now that your team has renamed `Payment` to `CashPayment`, you can draw the context map of the finance domain and the neighboring domains that it's about to integrate with: bank giro and policy. The map will look like figure 11.10.

Looking at the map, you can consider what should be mapped to what. It's pretty obvious that there's nothing in the finance domain that a bank giro payment can be mapped to—a `CashPayment` certainly doesn't suit. There's the temptation to abstract `CashPayment` to something that could accommodate a bank giro payment as well. But you fight that urge because it's much better to first gain a deeper insight and then do the abstractions than it is to make a premature abstraction that might be less insightful.

Preferring to be specific first, you add a new type to the finance domain, `Giro-Payment`. But you're still stuck on what it should map to. The `Payment` in the bank giro

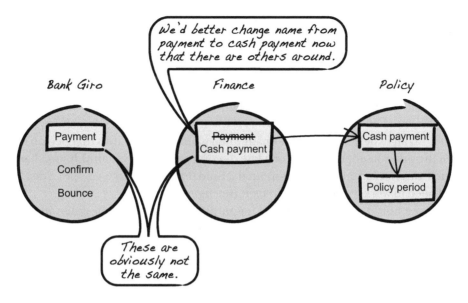

Figure 11.10 A map of the three domains after renaming `Payment` to `CashPayment`

domain certainly looks like a good candidate, but you have limited insight into the subtleties of bank giro payments and risk jumping to conclusions.

TIP Start by being specific, solve the domain problem, and then do abstraction when you have deep insight.

You now feel that you have moved as far as you can on your own. Your context map looks like figure 11.11, but you can't make the mapping between the bank giro concepts and your newly created `GiroPayment`.

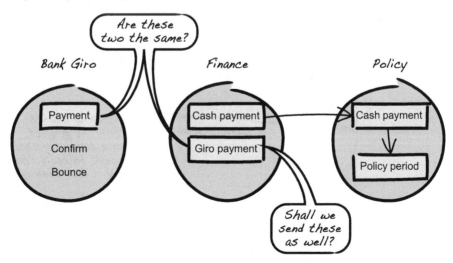

Figure 11.11 A map of the three domains with the newly created `GiroPayment`. What should it map to?

You decide it's time to meet with experts in all the affected fields. You invite domain experts from the policy team and from the finance department (or the bank), one of whom is knowledgeable about bank giro payments, to a small workshop. What you're looking for at this time is the deliberate discovery of how the external bank giro domain maps to your finance domain, taking the policy domain into account. This isn't a trivial thing, and therefore you deliberately set the stage to support these discoveries.

The sound of a deliberate discovery is when an expert in one domain says "Oh, OK, I get it" to an expert in another domain when gaining insight into that person's domain. On the other hand, the sound of a late discovery might be "Aaahhhh, no, that can't be true!" uttered by someone who spotted a fundamental mistake close to a deadline and will need to work day and night to fix it (see figure 11.12).[2]

To see how deliberate discovery might play out, consider the following hypothetical conversation between the policy expert, Polly; Ann from finance; and Bahnk, who really knows banking systems.

"What happens when we get a new payment?" asks policy expert Polly.

"Well, I guess we get a payment through giro," says Ann from finance.

"That's when we get a Payment message from the bank?" Polly enquires.

"Yep, that's when a payment is registered," says Bahnk, who's the expert on the bank systems.

"OK, so we have the money, and we can issue a new policy letter," Polly concludes.

"Wait. I didn't say we have the money," Bahnk protests.

"Yes, you did," Ann challenges, perplexed.

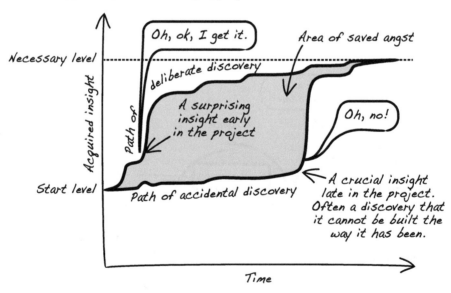

Figure 11.12   The difference between early deliberate discovery and late ignorant discovery

---

[2]   Credit to Dan North for making this distinction between early deliberate discovery and late accidental discovery. Read his article "Introducing Deliberate Discovery" at https://dannorth.net/2010/08/30/introducing-deliberate-discovery/.

"No, I said the payment was registered, not that it's confirmed," Bahnk explains.

"Does that mean we haven't got the money?" Polly wonders out loud.

"Right. The bank has just registered the request to make a payment; the money hasn't been transferred yet. It'll probably transfer at the next nightly batch run if there are sufficient funds in the sending account," Bahnk clarifies.

"Oh, but that shouldn't be a problem," says Ann from finance. "It means that the customer will owe us money until the money is transferred. It's still a transfer of assets. It will do."

"No, it won't!" Polly protests vividly, airing her policy expertise. "We can't start a policy until we are really paid-paid, not just promise-to-pay-paid."

"In that case, it's the Confirm message you should wait for," says Bahnk.

"Oh, OK, I get it," concludes Ann, who has learned something subtle about the interaction between the domains of bank giro and insurance policies.

During this meeting, you manage to facilitate a deliberate discovery about how the domains should map to each other. The new domain mapping will look like figure 11.13.

At this point, you've developed a deep knowledge about the business. You understand that for a policy to be renewed, there needs to be confirmation that the money has been transferred. You are now ready to define your abstractions—something you earlier decided to defer until you had a better understanding. One option might be to add a new abstraction, `PolicyPayment`, which is created when the finance system has received a payment for a new policy period. For a `CashPayment`, this happens immediately because you know the amount has been paid in full over the counter. For a `GiroPayment`, it occurs only when the finance system receives a Confirm message from the bank indicating that the payment has been completed. The policy system would then listen for this new message type instead of the old Payment messages, and create a new `PolicyPeriod` when it receives a `PolicyPayment` message.

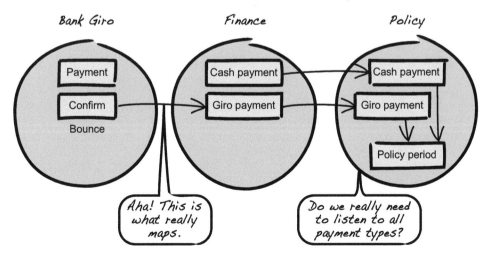

Figure 11.13   A map of the three domains with complete mappings

The key takeaway from this story is that none of these systems were broken if you looked at each domain in isolation. But the holistic effect was that a subtle mistake was introduced—a mistake that had serious consequences and at a different scale could have become catastrophic. The remedy is to not rely on expertise about a single system or a single domain when you want to ensure security. Instead, bring together experts from all the adjacent domains to gain a rich understanding.

11.7 *A note on microservices architecture*

Finally, we'd like to set this story in the context of a microservices architecture. In this story, there were only three systems involved. In a microservices architecture, there might be several hundred systems, each a service and each a domain. Many times we've seen the microservices architecture sold with the promise that when you need to make changes, you can do so surgically within one single service. Often this is coupled with the promise that if the service is maintained by a team, that team doesn't need to disturb (talk to) any other team. We think that this is a dangerous misrepresentation!

Don't misunderstand us. We're not opposed to using microservices; in fact, we think it's a good idea. We're opposed to the misconception that you can safely make myopic changes to a single service without taking the holistic picture into account. Thankfully, you seldom need to take all the services into account, but we definitely recommend that you always have a look at the neighboring services when you make a change.

Summary

- Do deliberate discovery early to get deep insights into subtle aspects of the domain.
- Start specific, then abstract later.
- Collect expertise from all adjacent domains.
- Refactor names if they change semantics, especially if they change semantics outside the bounded context.

Part 3

Applying the fundamentals

In the previous part, you learned about the fundamentals of secure by design. The tools and mindset certainly allow you to craft secure software, but, for some reason, applying this in legacy code is something many find challenging. Where should you start? What should you look for, or which strategy should you use? This is exactly what we'll address in this part.

The focus will therefore be a bit different than in previous parts. We won't explain security problems in depth, but rather focus on how legacy code can be improved using what you've learned so far in this book. We'll start by looking at common problems found in monolithic architectures and then progress to microservices, which pose their own unique set of security challenges. Then we'll finish this part with some last words about why you still need to think about security, before we let you go on your journey towards a world of more secure software.

FO 617 4127

Guidance in legacy code

12

This chapter covers

- How to deal with ambiguous parameters
- Security issues caused by logging
- How DRY is about ideas, rather than text
- Absence of negative tests as a warning sign
- Introducing domain primitives in legacy code

Once you've grokked the fundamentals of the secure by design approach, you can start applying the concepts when writing code. This is usually easier when you're doing greenfield development, but you'll most likely spend a lot of time working on *legacy codebases*—codebases that weren't created with a secure by design mindset. When working on such codebases, it can be difficult to know how to apply the concepts you've learned in this book and where to start.

In this chapter, you'll learn how to identify some problems and pitfalls that we've found are common in legacy codebases. Some of them are easy to spot, and others are more subtle. We also provide you with tips and advice on how to rectify them. Some issues require more effort than others, so you need to choose your approach based on your situation. Hopefully this chapter will provide you with enough guidance to make that choice easier.

295

You'll start by learning why ambiguous parameters in methods and constructors are a common source of security flaws. Then you'll learn what to look out for when logging and why defensive code constructs are problematic. We then show you how seemingly well-designed code can have subtle issues that cause security issues. At the end of this chapter, you'll learn about some mistakes that are commonly made when introducing domain primitives in legacy code and what to watch out for when you start implementing domain primitives.

12.1   *Determining where to apply domain primitives in legacy code*

In chapter 5, you learned about the concept of domain primitives and how they exist if and only if they are valid. This characteristic enabled you to apply domain primitives in several situations to either enable stronger security or completely remove the possibility of an attack—but there's a catch to all of this. Most agree that using domain primitives makes sense and is an intuitive design pattern, but to satisfy the invariant of validity, you must also identify the context in which the domain primitive applies. Otherwise, you won't be able to decide which domain rules to use, making it impossible to reject invalid data—this is a common pitfall when introducing domain primitives in legacy code.

To illustrate, picture the worst possible scenario: a homogeneous mass of code where strings, integers, and other generic data types are passed around. The only way to know what the developer's intentions are is to look at variable names, method signatures, and class hierarchies, but sometimes not even that makes it clear. All in all, the codebase is a mess that would benefit from using domain primitives—but where do you start?

Because the concept of domain primitives is easy to grasp, many start by wrapping generic types such as integers and strings in explicit data types, but doing so often ends up being a mistake. As we'll elaborate further in section 12.8, a domain primitive must encompass a conceptual whole, and wrapping generic data types only results in an explicit type system, not in the design that you want. Instead, what you should do is to start by identifying a bounded context and the semantic boundary, because this is where you'll start creating your domain primitives.

> **TIP** Start by identifying a bounded context and the semantic boundary, because this is where you should introduce domain primitives.

In chapter 3, we talked about bounded contexts and how a domain model captures the semantics of the ubiquitous language within a context. As part of this, you also learned that the semantic boundary can be implicit and hard to see in code, but it can be identified by testing the semantics of the domain model. As soon as the semantics of a term or concept change, the model breaks, which means that a semantic boundary is found.

   A good starting point when identifying a bounded context is therefore to group concepts that belong together. A common pattern is to use a package or a module for your classes and methods, but how you organize them doesn't matter. What's important is that all concepts that share the same semantic model should be grouped together. For example, if there's a method with the signature

```
public void cancelReservation(final String reservationId)
```

then every class or method that uses a `reservationId` or operates on a `Reservation` object must share the same understanding of what they mean, or it could result in misunderstandings and bugs. But a discrepancy in semantics isn't only a source of errors, it's also an indicator that the concept should be moved out of that grouping, which sometimes is a painful experience because it requires heavy redesign.

   Grouping concepts that belong together is only the first step toward creating a bounded context. The next step is to introduce domain primitives to express the semantic boundary. But this is also when things could go seriously wrong unless you're careful, so let's proceed by investigating how you deal with ambiguous parameter lists.

12.2 *Ambiguous parameter lists*

One easily recognizable design flaw in code is ambiguous parameter lists in methods and constructors. An example of such a method is shown in the following listing, where the `shipItems` method takes two integers and two addresses as input parameters.

Listing 12.1   Method with ambiguous parameter list

```
public void shipItems(int itemId, int quantity,
                      Address billing, Address to) {
  // ...
}

public class Address {
  private final String street;
  private final int number;
  private final String zipCode;

  public Address(final String street, final int number,
                 final String zipCode) {
    this.street = street;
    this.number = number;
    this.zipCode = zipCode;
  }

  // ...
}
```

The parameters itemId and quantity are of the primitive type int.

The billing address and shipping address are of the same composite type, Address.

In chapter 5, you learned that ambiguous parameters are common sources of security issues for a couple of reasons. One problem is that generic types lack the level of input validation that you should strive for to create robust code. Another is that it's common to accidentally swap the parameters with each other. We've kept the ship-Items method fairly short to make it concise as an example, but you might encounter parameter lists much longer than this. If you have a method with 20-plus parameters, all of type String, it's hard not to mess up the order. When you see this type of code construct, you should see it as an opportunity to change your code to be more secure.

As you can see in listing 12.2, it's easy to get the parameters mixed up when calling the shipItems method. Both itemId and quantity are of the primitive type int, and accidentally swapping them when calling the method is a mistake that can go unnoticed. The billing address and the shipping address are both complex types that look like domain objects. But they're of the same type, and there's nothing preventing you from making the mistake of mixing them up.

Listing 12.2   Accidentally swapping parameters

```
int idOfItemToBuy = 78549;
int quantity = 67;
Address billingAddress = new Address("Office St", 42, "94 102");
Address shippingAddress = new Address("Factory Rd", 2, "94 129");

service.shipItems(quantity, idOfItemToBuy,
                  shippingAddress, billingAddress);
```

The item ID and the quantity are mixed up, resulting in too many items of the wrong kind being sent.

The shipping and billing addresses are swapped, resulting in goods being sent to the wrong place.

Accidentally swapping any of these parameters can have severe side effects. For example, sending 78,549 packages of an item with ID 67 is different from sending 67 packages of an item with ID 78549. It's also highly unlikely that a company's finance department would appreciate having a handful of pallets of industrial grease dumped at its entrance, while the factory gets an invoice in its mailbox.

The solution for ambiguous parameter lists is to replace all of the parameters, or as many as you can, with domain primitives (see chapter 5) or secure entities (see chapters 5, 6, and 7). By doing so, you'll not only make the parameters unambiguous but also make the code more secure, as you learned in chapters 5–7. The way you go about doing this refactoring depends on the codebase at hand and how much time is available.

In this section, you'll learn three different approaches and when they're a good fit and a less good fit. The approaches we'll discuss, together with a summary of their pros and cons, are shown in table 12.1. It's worth noting that these approaches are also applicable when trying to introduce domain primitives in general, not only when replacing ambiguous parameters; for example, after you've identified a context boundary using the tips in section 12.1.

Table 12.1 Approaches to dealing with ambiguous parameter lists

Approach	Pros	Cons
Direct approach—Replace all ambiguous parameters at once	■ Solves everything right away ■ Works well with smaller codebases and few developers ■ Can be performed quickly if codebase is of reasonable size	■ Too much refactoring in large codebases ■ Not well suited if data quality is a big issue ■ Best performed by a single developer
Discovery approach—Find and fix the problems before changing the API	■ Works well if data quality is poor ■ Works with larger codebases and multiple teams	■ Takes a long time to complete ■ May not be able to keep up with a fast-changing codebase
New API approach—Create a new API and then gradually refactor away the old API	■ Allows for incremental refactoring ■ Works well with both small and large codebases ■ Works with multiple developers and teams	■ If data quality is an issue, combine it with the discovery approach

What about builders?

We often get asked if using the builder pattern can solve the issues with ambiguous parameters. We believe it's not so much a solution to the security issues but rather a band-aid. Using the builder pattern partially solves the problem with accidental swapping, because the builder makes it a bit easier to see that you're passing in the right argument. It's still entirely possible to swap parameters of the same type, and you're not getting the benefits of exact invariants and crisp definitions that you get by using domain primitives. The builder pattern is definitely useful for other purposes, especially upholding advanced constraints on creation, which we discussed in section 6.2.6.

12.2.1 The direct approach

The direct approach is to first introduce domain primitives and secure entities to replace all ambiguous parameters. After that, you perform the change and alter the method signature, typically one parameter at a time.

Listing 12.3 shows how the `shipItems` method looks with the parameters replaced with domain primitives. As soon as you do the swap, you'll most likely run into everything from compilation errors to test failures. You tackle this by solving one issue at a time. Once you have fixed all the problems and can build the application, you can deploy it to a test environment and let it process data. Because you've introduced domain primitives with more strict validation, bad data that used to flow through your system is now going to be rejected. Therefore, you need to monitor it for any errors that can pop up.

Listing 12.3   The direct approach: replace all at once

```
public void shipItems(final ItemId itemId,
                      final Quantity quantity,
                      final BillingAddress billing,
                      final ShippingAddress to) {
  // ...
}
```

> Replaces all parameters with either domain primitives or secure entities

---

An advantage of the direct approach is that it solves everything right away. When you're finished with the refactoring, there's no more work to be done. This approach is typically well suited for smaller codebases owned by a single team, where it tends to be the fastest approach. It's also worth noting that you don't have to refactor the code behind the method API immediately; instead, you can choose to gradually refactor it.

If the codebase is large, then this might not be a viable solution, because it can leave the code in a broken state for a long period of time before you manage to fix all the errors—it becomes a big-bang refactoring exercise. Even if you manage to fix all compilation errors and failing tests, it can take a while before you've ironed out possible runtime errors caused by poor data quality. Also, if the changes affect more than one team, it can be difficult or impossible to sync the work, and it needs to happen simultaneously.

You should also be aware that introducing domain types with strict invariants that reject bad data can lead to heated discussions about how domain primitives break the code instead of improving it. In those situations, it's important to remember that domain primitives and secure entities didn't create the problem. The bad data was already there, and what you should do is address the data quality at the source.

12.2.2 The discovery approach

Another approach is one we like to call the discovery approach. As the name implies, the tactic of this approach is to introduce domain primitives and secure entities behind the public API without changing the API. After you've done that, you'll discover and fix possible problems before swapping and replacing the ambiguous parameters. This approach is especially good if data quality is a big issue.

An example of how to apply the discovery approach on the shipItems method is shown in listing 12.4. You keep the method signature as is, and for each ambiguous parameter, you try to create the corresponding domain primitive. For the integer value itemId, you try to create a domain primitive ItemId; for the generically typed billing address, you try to create a domain primitive called BillingAddress; and so on. For each domain primitive you instantiate, you catch and log any exceptions that can occur. When you're done, you can start running your test suites and even deploy the code to production. Monitor the logs for errors and address the problems as they occur. Analyze each exception to find the root cause and fix the problem.

Listing 12.4 The discovery approach: fix the problems first

```java
public void shipItems(final int itemId, final int quantity,
                      final Address billing, final Address to) {
    tryCreateItemId(itemId);
    tryCreateQuantity(quantity);
    tryCreateBillingAddress(billing);
    tryCreateShippingAddress(to);

    // ...
}
```

For each ambiguous parameter, try to create the corresponding domain primitive.

```java
private void tryCreateItemId(final int itemId) {
    try {
        new ItemId(itemId);
    } catch (final Exception e) {
        logError("Error while creating ItemId", e);
    }
}
```

Log errors that occur while creating the domain primitives.

```java
private void tryCreateQuantity(final int quantity) {
    try {
        new Quantity(quantity);
    } catch (final Exception e) {
        logError("Error while creating Quantity", e);
    }
}
```

```java
// other tryCreate methods...

import static org.apache.commons.lang3.Validate.isTrue;

public class ItemId {
    private final int value;
```

An example of one of the domain primitives created

```java
    public ItemId(final int value) {
        isTrue(value > 0, "An item id must be greater than 0");
        this.value = value;
    }

    public int value() {
        return value;
    }

    // domain operations, equals(), hashcode(), toString(), and so on
}

// other domain primitives...
```

Remember that the purpose of the `tryCreate` methods isn't to prevent bad data from entering, but to discover it. Common sources for errors include bad data at runtime and invalid stubs or mocks used in tests. Once you feel confident that you've fixed the majority of issues, you can start replacing the parameters the same way as with the direct approach.

The discovery approach works well if data quality is a major problem and you want to avoid disruption. If the domain rules you're introducing with domain primitives and secure entities are so strict (albeit correct) that a lot of the data you're processing fails to meet those rules, then a defensive approach like this is a good choice. It also works well on both small and large codebases.

The downside of the discovery approach is it'll take longer to perform the transition to the new API. You first need to introduce the creation of secure domain types, then monitor logs for a period of time, and then address data quality problems. It isn't until all these steps are done that you can make the API change. Another challenge is when active development is occurring while you're performing the transition. New code can be written using the old API, adding to the technical debt on one side while you're trying to clean up the data on the other side. If a fast-moving codebase is a challenge, then you might want to combine this approach with the approach you'll learn about next— the new API approach.

12.2.3 *The new API approach*

The third and last approach we'll discuss is called the new API approach. The core idea in this approach is to create a new API alongside the existing one, as shown in listing 12.5. This new API only uses domain primitives and secure entities but still provides the same functionality. You ensure that the functionality is the same, either by delegating to the old API or by first extracting the logic from the old API and then reusing the extracted logic in the new API. Once the new API is in place, you can gradually refactor calling code to use the new API instead. Eventually all references to the old API will be gone, and you can delete it.

Listing 12.5   The new API approach: incremental refactoring

```
import static org.apache.commons.lang3.Validate.notNull;

public void shipItems(final ItemId itemId,          ◄──┐  New method with only
                      final Quantity quantity,         │  domain primitives or secure
                      final BillingAddress billing,    │  entities as parameters
                      final ShippingAddress to) {
    notNull(itemId);
    notNull(quantity);
    notNull(billing);
    notNull(to);                                    ┌─── The new method delegates to
                                                    │    the old method to ensure the
    shipItems(itemId.value(), quantity.value(),  ◄──┘    same functionality.
            billing.address(), to.address());
}
                                                    ┌─── The old method is marked
@Deprecated                                         │    as deprecated but
public void shipItems(int itemId, int quantity,     │    remains as long as
                      Address billing, Address to) { ◄── there are references to it.
    // ...
}
```

This approach has several advantages. One is that it lets you do the transition to the new hardened API in small steps. Because you refactor one part of the codebase at a time, you get smaller commits and fewer data issues to deal with. Another is that because of the gradual refactoring, it also works well when dealing with large code-bases or multiple teams. But if data quality is an issue, you'll still need to use the ideas from the discovery approach you learned about earlier.

You've now learned that ambiguous parameter lists are a common source of security problems. You've also looked at three different approaches for dealing with the problem once you've found it. When replacing generic parameters with domain primitives and secure entities, it's common that you'll expose issues with poor data quality. If this is the case, you might need to fix those problems first before you can completely introduce the new strict types in your API.

12.3 Logging unchecked strings

In chapter 10, we talked about the importance of using a centralized logging service instead of writing to a file on disk. Changing the logging strategy in legacy code sounds like a big operation at first, but often it's enough to replace the backend of the logging framework with one that sends data across the network instead of writing to a file on disk. This could, in fact, be done in a seamless fashion, but, unfortunately, that only takes you halfway from a secure logging perspective. What you still need to do is ensure that unchecked strings never get logged—which is addressed using domain primitives—because this can open up potential security vulnerabilities, such as data leakage and injection attacks.

When bringing this up, we often hear that most logging frameworks only accept strings, and avoiding strings isn't an option. We certainly agree, but there's a big difference between not logging strings and logging unchecked strings. Unchecked strings are, in fact, the root cause of many attack vectors and should be avoided at all cost. Unfortunately, not many realize this, and the mistake is often repeated over and over again regardless of experience level. Let's dive into an example and learn what to look for in a codebase so you don't make the same mistake.

12.3.1 Identifying logging of unchecked strings

The problem of logging unchecked strings isn't restricted to only legacy code. It can appear in any codebase, regardless of quality. The problem is often hidden in plain sight, and what you need to look for is the logging of unverified `String` objects (for example, logging of user input or data from another system). In the following listing, you see an example where an unchecked string is logged. The `fetch` method is part of a table reservation service in a restaurant system that lets you fetch table reservations by ID.

Listing 12.6 Logging of unchecked input when fetching a table reservation

```
public TableReservation fetch(final String reservationId) {
    logger.info("Fetching table reservation: " +
                                reservationId);
    // fetch table reservation logic
    return tableReservation;
}
```

> ◄── Logging of an unchecked reservation ID that could contain anything

It's not important why the reservation ID is logged. What's important is that the input argument is logged without being checked. Even though a reservation ID has strict domain rules (for example, it must start with a hash sign followed by seven digits), the developer decided to represent it as a `String`. This means that even though you expect it to be a valid reservation ID, an attacker could inject anything that matches the rules of a `String` object, which literally could be anything (for example, 100 million characters or a script). Another serious issue is the possibility of a second-order injection attack, as we discussed in chapter 9 when talking about handling bad data. If there's a weakness in the log parsing tool, an attacker could exploit it by injecting a malicious string that pretends to be a reservation ID and have it written to the logs—not good!

WARNING Never log unchecked user input, because it opens up the risk of second-order injection attacks.

The solution is to use a domain primitive instead of a `String` object, because it lets you control the input instead of the attacker having control. But, as you learned in section 12.2, how you introduce domain primitives in an API could cause a whole set of new problems, and choosing a strategy that doesn't cause too much fuss is recommended.

12.3.2 Identifying implicit data leakage

Another issue related to logging unchecked strings is leakage of sensitive data in logs due to an evolving domain model. This problem is somewhat hard to recognize unless you know what to look for, so let's turn back to our previous example, but with a slight modification, as seen in the following listing. What's been added is the logic for fetching the corresponding table reservation from a repository and a log statement, where the internal data of the matching reservation object is serialized as a `String` before it's written to the logs.

Listing 12.7 Serializing the table reservation object as a `String`

```
public TableReservation fetch(final String reservationId) {
    logger.info("Fetching table reservation: " + reservationId);
    final TableReservation tableReservation =
            repository.reservation(reservationId);
    logger.info("Received " + tableReservation);
    return tableReservation;
}
```

> ── Fetches a table reservation from the repository
>
> ◄── Implicitly serializes the table reservation object as a String before being written to the log

Logging a table reservation can seem harmless because it only contains data such as the table number, reservation ID, number of guests, and time slot. But what if the domain model evolves? For example, imagine that someone decides to include member information in a reservation to allow for better service. Then the `TableReservation` object suddenly contains sensitive data (for example, name, contact information, and membership number) that implicitly leaks when logging a reservation. But keeping track of how data is consumed in a large system is close to impossible, so how do you prevent this from happening?

As it turns out, preventing implicit data leakage is hard, but detecting it isn't that difficult. In chapter 5, we discussed how to deal with sensitive values and the read-once object pattern. This pattern lets you decide how many times a value is allowed to be read, and if this limit is exceeded, a contract violation occurs. That way, you only need to identify sensitive data in your system and model it as such to prevent it from being read more often than you allow, as would be the case when doing an unknown log operation.

> **TIP** Always limit the number of times a sensitive value can be accessed in your code. That way, you'll be able to detect unintentional access.

But there's another subtle problem in the statement `logger.info("Received " + tableReservation)`. Concatenating the string `"Received "` with the `tableReservation` object using the `+` operator creates an implicit call to the `toString` method of `tableReservation`, which allows it to be represented as a `String` object. This operation is more or less harmless if you haven't overridden the `toString` method in `java.lang.Object`, because it only results in a string containing the class name and an unsigned hexadecimal representation of the hash code. But `toString` is frequently overridden because it's an easy way to debug the contents of an object.

To avoid updating `toString` every time a field is added or modified, many choose to use reflection to dynamically extract all the data. This implies that sensitive data can implicitly leak through the `toString` implementation. You should, therefore, never rely on `toString` when logging. What you should do is use explicit accessor methods for data that you want to log, because then new fields never end up in logs by accident.

> **TIP** Always use explicit accessor methods for data that you want to log. Otherwise, new fields can end up in logs by accident.

Logging unchecked strings is certainly problematic, but avoiding it isn't that hard if you put some thought into it. Another issue that often appears in legacy code is defensive code constructs—so let's proceed and see how you can deal with this in an efficient way.

12.4 *Defensive code constructs*

To make your system stable and robust is indeed an honorable thing, and chapter 9 was devoted to this quest. A well-designed system should never crash with a `NullPointerException`. But we often see code riddled with `!= null` checks, even deep in the code where it wouldn't be sensible that a `null` value should show up at all. Repeated checks of null, of formats, or of boundary conditions isn't good design in itself. Rather, it's an expression that one piece of the code dare not trust the design of the rest of the code, so it feels the need to recheck just in case. Instead of having clear contracts of what the parts can expect from each other, the code becomes riddled with defensive code constructs of unclear purpose.

The problem here is twofold. First, the code becomes convoluted, hard-to-read, and bloated because of unnecessary repetition—also making it hard to refactor. This is bad in itself, but it leads to a second problem. When such code is maintained over time, it risks becoming incoherent. And code with incoherent checks is a great opportunity for attackers to exploit in creative ways. One way to turn this around is to clarify the contracts between different parts of the code (as described in chapter 4) and introduce appropriate domain primitives (as described in chapter 5).

12.4.1 Code that doesn't trust itself

Let's start by looking more closely at some code that doesn't trust itself. The code in listing 12.8 is taken from an online bookstore, where the ShoppingService adds books to an Order using the public method addToOrder. The public method has several private helper methods, such as putInCartAsNew and isAlreadyInCart. Note the prevailing checks of non-null and of formats, even deep inside the private methods. Take a particular look at the numerous checks inside isAlreadyInCart at the bottom of the Order class. Also note the irony of ShoppingService, which checks the format of isbn before sending it as an argument in order.addBook(isbn, qty). Although the format check is done, that check isn't trusted by the code inside Order. Compare this with the use of domain primitives, where you can rely on the fact that the value wrapped in an ISBN domain primitive adheres to the format rules for ISBNs.

Listing 12.8   Code with repeated non-null and format checks

```
class ShoppingService {

    public void addToOrder(String orderId, String isbn, int qty) {
        Order order = orderservice.find(orderId);
        if (isbn.matches("[0-9]{9}[0-9X]")) {      ◀─────┐ Checks format before
            order.addBook(isbn, qty);                    │ calling public method
        }
    }
}


class Order {
    private Set<OrderLine> items;

    public void addBook(String isbn, int qty) {   ┌─ Checks isbn on entering
        if (isbn != null && !isbn.isEmpty()    ◀──┘   the public method
            && !isAlreadyInCart(isbn)) {
          putInCartAsNew(isbn, qty);
        } else {
          addToLine(isbn, qty);
        }
```

```
    }

    private void putInCartAsNew(String isbn, int quantity) {
        if (isbn != null && isbn.matches("[0-9]{9}[0-9X]")) {
            items.add(new OrderLine(isbn, quantity));
        }
    }

    private void addToLine(String isbn, int quantity) { ... }

    private boolean isAlreadyInCart(String isbn) {
        boolean result = false;
        for (OrderLine item : items) {
            String itemISBN = item.isbn();
            if (itemISBN != null
                    && isbn != null
                    && isbn.matches("[0-9]{9}[0-9X]")) {
                if (itemISBN.equals(isbn)) {
                    result = true;
                }
            }
        }
        return result;
    }
    // other methods
}
```

How can itemISBN be null when it comes from an OrderItem?

Another deep check of isbn format

At first glance, it might seem wise to ensure that isbn is not null before matching it against a regexp (regular expression). You don't want a NullPointerException to be thrown arbitrarily, do you? The problem is that these kinds of checks don't make the code much safer or more robust—they make it harder to understand.

The code seems to distrust itself; it's not sure what rules are in play. Is it OK to send in an isbn that is null? If so, how should the code handle it? If not, has anyone stopped it before? It does make sense that the public method addBooks checks the input thoroughly, and it certainly ensures no null value or empty string enters the code. But it doesn't check the format:

```
isbn.matches("[0-9]{9}[0-9X]")
```

That particular check is instead done in other places. The following two methods obviously don't trust the null checks in addBook and repeat them, even deep in loops:

```
private void putInCartAsNew(String isbn, int quantity)
```

```
private boolean isAlreadyInCart(String isbn)
```

On the other hand, the same methods don't repeat the check !isbn.isEmpty(). It's fundamentally unclear what promises each part of the code can rely on from other parts of the code.

This is a condensed example, but it's not uncommon to find if (value != null) checks deep down in the code, sometimes in the middle of methods with several hundred lines. In the defense of the programmers who wrote that extra null check, their ambition was probably to ensure the program wouldn't crash. And, in many cases, those extra checks are put in place because the program has crashed with a `NullPointer-Exception` at that specific point. But here (in listing 12.8), instead of clarifying the design to ensure that `null` wouldn't show up, a simple `if` was patched as a band-aid over the spot.

Another problem with this code is the coping strategy. In this example, if the code finds an `item.isbn()` that doesn't follow the required format, it reacts by doing nothing! The code doesn't stop executing, throw an exception, or even report the fault through logging. It ignores the situation. Of course, in the long run, this leads to nothing ever getting corrected, and the data continues to be riddled with bad stuff. To make things worse, these kinds of sprinkled-out checks don't just bloat the code, they also get in the way of doing refactorings that would let the code state its functionality in a more concise way.

12.4.2 *Contracts and domain primitives to the rescue*

Instead of plastering `null` checks all over the code to protect it from `null` data, you should ensure that data is not `null`. In the same way, to avoid format checks being repeated, you want to encapsulate that such a check has already been done. The tools for this are contracts (as described in section 4.2) and domain primitives (as described in chapter 5).

Going back to our example from listing 12.8, there are two domain primitive types, `ISBN` and `Quantity`, that become part of the interface for `Order`. We're not going to describe the transformation in full because that was done in chapter 5, but will roughly sketch out the differences. When `ShoppingService` calls `Order`, it needs first to create the corresponding domain primitive objects to pass to the `addToOrder` method, as shown in the following listing. The code calling the `Order` object takes on the burden of validation by creating domain primitive objects.

Listing 12.9   Calling the `Order` object

```
public void addToOrder(String orderId, String isbn, int qty) {
    Order order = orderservice.find(orderId);
    order.addBook(new ISBN(isbn), new Quantity(qty));
}
```

When the `Order.addBook` receives `ISBN` and `Quantity`, the values are well wrapped, and you can rely on them having been properly checked. There's no need to do the same check again. The `Order` ensures it isn't sent `null` values, as seen in the next listing.

Listing 12.10   `Order` only upholds the contract `notNull` for the arguments

```
public void addBook(ISBN isbn, Quantity qty) {
    notNull(isbn);
    notNull(qty);
    if (!isAlreadyInCart(isbn)) {
        putInCartAsNew(isbn, qty);
    } else{
        addToLine(isbn, qty);
    }
}
```

With validated domain primitive objects coming in as arguments, there's no longer any need for `Order` to revalidate the format of the ISBN, for example. Also, by checking for `notNull` in the public method `addBook`, you avoid the need to repeat `null` checks in the private methods, such as `putInCartAsNew` and `isAlreadyInCart`. Take a look at the latter after cleanup in the following code listing. You'll see that the updated `isAlreadyInCart` method trusts that format checks are ensured by the design.

Listing 12.11   Updated `isAlreadyInCart`

```
private boolean isAlreadyInCart(ISBN isbn) {
    boolean result = false;
    for (OrderLine item : items) {
        if (item.isbn().equals(isbn)) {
            result = true;
        }
    }
    return result;
}
```

With all the confusing rechecks gone, it's much more obvious what the code does. You also can see ways to make it simpler. The `if` statement inside the `for-each` can be replaced with

```
result = result || item.isbn().equals(isbn)
```

Now it's clear that you sieve through the list to see if any of the `items` match the ISBN searched for, as seen in the following listing. If any existing `item` matches the searched-for ISBN, then it's already in the cart. Obviously, this can be done more smoothly with the Stream API.

Listing 12.12   Searching for the ISBN

```
private boolean isAlreadyInCart(final ISBN isbn) {
    return items.stream().anyMatch(item -> item.isbn().equals(isbn));
}
```

The design flaw to watch out for is deep checks of `null`, format, or ranges. What it hides is that the code isn't designed in such a way that it can trust itself. Also, the messy code can hamper clarifying refactorings. Introducing appropriate contracts and domain primitives is a way to get to a better state.

12.4.3   *Overlenient use of Optional*

There's a modern variant of this design flaw when working with optional data types, such as `Optional<T>` in Java. Instead of having data lying around as `null` values, those values are transformed to `Optional.EMPTY`. If there sometimes are missing addresses, the address field of an order might be written as `Optional<Address>`, although an order must have an address in the long run. When it's time to use the data, the flaw shows up by taking a detour using `Optional.map`.

Compare how `anAddr` and `perhapsAddr` are treated in listing 12.13. The code for `perhapsAddr` becomes much more convoluted. Instead of asking for the zip code using the method `zip`, it takes a detour using the method `map`, which is a higher-order function that accepts the function `Address::zip` as an argument and applies that function to each `Optional<Address>` in the stream, which is one in this case. This is a cumbersome detour to get one zip code out of one address just to take into account that the address might be missing.

Listing 12.13   Taking account for `Optional.EMPTY` gives convoluted code

```
Address anAddr;
Optional<Address> perhapsAddr;

Zip anZip = anAddr.zip();
Optional<Zip> perhapsZip = perhapsAddr.map(Address::zip);
```

Watch out for `Optional<Address>` in cases where the address is mandatory and the use of `Optional` carries no domain insight but is a cover-up for the code not trusting the rest of the design. Whether they're old-school repetitions of `null` and format checks or new-school overuse of `Optional`, defensive code constructs are a clear signal that something isn't right with the code. These parts of the code are a great place to start your quality and security work by applying contracts and domain primitives.

We've covered three problems that often show up in legacy code: ambiguous parameter lists, logging unchecked strings, and defensive code constructs. We'll now turn to three other problems that are somewhat subtler. These are situations where good design principles have been applied, but in a way that is incomplete or slightly beside the point. At first sight, these applications might even look good, but upon closer inspection, you realize that there are problems nevertheless. Let's start with how the design principle *Don't Repeat Yourself* (DRY) can be misapplied.

12.5   *DRY misapplied—not focusing on ideas, but on text*

The design principle Don't Repeat Yourself (DRY) was coined by Andy Hunt and Dave Thomas in their seminal book, *The Pragmatic Programmer*.[1] It states that when we capture our knowledge into code, we shouldn't repeat the same codification in several places.

> *Every piece of knowledge must have a single, unambiguous, authoritative representation within a system.*

Unfortunately, the principle of DRY has often been misunderstood as applying not to knowledge and ideas, but to the code *as text*. Programmers search their codebases for *repeated text* and try to get rid of the duplication. This misconception is enhanced by the helpful tools of modern IDEs that can automatically identify duplicated code

---

[1]   Andrew Hunt and David Thomas, *The Pragmatic Programmer: From Journeyman to Master* (Addison-Wesley Professional, 1999).

and even suggest automatic transforms that remove the duplication. Those tools are an excellent help when applying DRY correctly, but at the same time a speedy road to dependency hell if misapplied.

It's definitely true that duplicated text often is due to a duplication of ideas. And certainly, you can use "look for duplicated text" as a quick test to find DRY violations. (Note that we are using the word *test* in the sense of a medical test that checks for indicators of a disease, not a system development unit test or similar.) But "look for duplicated text" isn't a fault-free test. There are both false positives and false negatives: *false positives* look like repetition but aren't; *false negatives* don't look like repetition but are. False positives might lead you to link together parts of the code that aren't related, creating unnecessary dependencies. A false negative, on the other hand, risks inconsistent functionality evolving, raising the risk of security vulnerabilities.

12.5.1 A false positive that shouldn't be DRY'd away

In listing 12.14, you see part of the constructor for a class representing a delivery of books that's sent from an online bookstore to a customer, so naturally it contains both the order number and the zip code. A zip code is a five-digit string, and that happens to be the format for the order number as well.

> **Listing 12.14 No repetition of knowledge, although same regexp used twice**

```
BookDelivery(String ordernumber, String recipient,
             String streetaddress, String zipcode) {

    this.ordernumber = notNull(ordernumber);
    matchesPattern(ordernumber, "[0-9]{5}");      ◄── Regexp representing one thing:
    this.zipcode = notNull(zipcode);                   format of order numbers
    matchesPattern(zipcode, "[0-9]{5}");          ◄── Regexp representing something
    ...                                                else: format of zip codes
}
```

It might look as if you're repeating yourselves, because the same regexp occurs twice. But you aren't repeating yourselves in the sense of DRY, because those two regexps encode different pieces of knowledge: the knowledge about what order numbers look like and the knowledge about what zip codes look like. The occurrence of the same regexp is coincidental.

12.5.2 The problem of collecting repeated pieces of code

The problem starts when someone thinks, "There are two regexps that look the same; this is repetition and a violation of DRY," and then sets out to fix it by refactoring those two unrelated regexps to some common technical construct, such as a utility method. Those methods often end up as static methods in classes named `Util` and are then collected in packages named `util`, `common`, or `misc`. Needless to say, virtually every piece of code in the rest of the codebase will have a dependency on that `common` or `util` library. That might be acceptable briefly as a temporary state during cleanup, but it's certainly not desirable as a long-term solution.

> **TIP**   A Util class might be a handy place to collect small domain-logical helper methods, but it shouldn't be the end state, rather a temporary resting place on the road to further refactorings instead.

The problem escalates when you then start separating the codebase into different parts, perhaps into microservices. Microservices should be standalone. It's reasonable to have a small amount of dependencies to some common concepts, but here there's a massive dependency to a large util package from all the other parts. Now, whenever anything changes in any part of the humongous util package, everything needs to be recompiled and redeployed. You don't have a system of independent microservices, you have a tightly coupled distributed monolith dependency hell.

12.5.3   *The good DRY*

Instead of packing things because the pieces of code look the same, you should focus on what knowledge is captured. In our example, you'll note that we have two separate but primitive domain concepts: the concept of zip codes and the concept of order numbers. Those make two fine domain primitives: ZipCode and OrderNumber, respectively. Each of their constructors will have a regexp check that, code-wise, will look the same, but that's OK. If they're unrelated, then leave them apart. The obvious thought experiment is, "If we change the format of order numbers, will the format of zip codes then change accordingly?"

> **TIP**   Let unrelated things move independently. Repeated code in unrelated concepts is fine and not a violation of DRY.

12.5.4   *A false negative*

A false negative shows up the other way around: when the code doesn't look like a repetition, but really is. Look at listing 12.15 and note how there are two ways to check that a string is a zip code. One way uses a regexp to check the format; the other checks that the string has length five and parses to an integer.

> **NOTE**   Look out for small pieces of code that have the same purpose but are written differently.

Listing 12.15   Expressing the same idea in two different ways

```
if((input.length() == 5)          ◄──────   A string of length five that correctly
    && Integer.parseInt(input) > 0) {         parses as an integer
    ...
}

if(zipcodeSender.matches("[0-9]{5}")) {   ◄──────
    ...
}                                              A string of five digits, from 0 to 9
```

These two code snippets need not be in the same method, nor even in the same class. One of them might be a helper method for `CustomerSettingsService` and the other in the middle of a method 400 lines long; `LogisticPlanningsService`, for example. These pieces of code might be written at completely different times, and the programmer writing the first expression might even have quit before the programmer writing the second expression started on the project.

No text is repeated, and it won't be found by a duplication tool. Nevertheless, these snippets are a violation of DRY because they encode the same knowledge—the understanding of what a zip code looks like. Remember, "Every piece of knowledge must have a single... representation." Unfortunately, it's hard to spot this kind of repetition.

The problem with having two different encodings of the same knowledge is when things change. You might remember to change these two places, but there might easily be 37 other places that also encode the same knowledge. Probably, you'll remember (or find) 35 at most. The changes might also be small, but several are needed for consistency, so one or a few might easily be missed.

Official zip code formats don't change often, but a format for an order number might. In an order number, you might first restrict what the first digit might be; then you allow a trailing letter; then you restrict those that start with an odd digit to have some special meaning; and so on. And in each of these updates, you miss a few of the code sites, but not the same few every time. After a while, you have a lot of inconsistency in your business rules, and inconsistency is what attackers love.

Fortunately, the remedy is easy. Create appropriate domain primitives that capture formatting. If you have no obvious domain primitive to start with, then start turning all these snippets into small helper methods that you collect into some utility class. In one of our projects, we managed to get over 200 methods into such a class, which was a gold mine for creating domain primitives. As mentioned earlier, these kinds of utility classes are nothing you want in the long run, but as a temporary step they can be valuable. Now let's move on to another subtle issue; one where things look fine because we have domain types, but they lack sufficient validation.

12.6   *Insufficient validation in domain types*

Sometimes you'll find yourself working on a codebase with a well-designed domain model that has important concepts represented as explicit types, maybe even as value objects and entities.[2] The type of code we're talking about is typically well structured and easy to read, but there might be some lurking design flaws that can lead to security vulnerabilities.

One such flaw you should learn to spot is when there's insufficient domain validation of the data encapsulated by the domain types. This means that there's either no validation at all, or the validation that's performed is insufficient from a domain perspective. In chapters 4 to 7, you learned why strict domain validation is important for mitigating security flaws. When you spot domain types like this, you should seize the opportunity to improve them.

---

[2]   Go back to chapter 3 for a primer on basic concepts in Domain-Driven Design (DDD).

To illustrate this, listing 12.16 shows an example of a value object, `Quantity`, that's missing relevant domain validation. The value object validates the input data for not being `null`, and it's even immutable. But from a business domain perspective, a quantity is more precise in its definition than just being an integer. In our imaginary business domain, it's defined as an integer between 1 and 500.

Listing 12.16   A domain type with insufficient validation

```java
import static org.apache.commons.lang3.Validate.notNull;

public final class Quantity {

    private final Integer value;

    public Quantity(final Integer value) {
        this.value = notNull(value);
    }

    public int value() {
        return value;
    }

    // ...

}
```

If you apply what you learned about domain primitives in chapter 5 and enforce all the domain rules you know about a quantity in the constructor, the `Quantity` class ends up looking something like the following listing.[3] You have now taken a well-defined value object and increased the overall security by turning it into a domain primitive.

Listing 12.17   `Quantity` turned into a domain primitive

```java
import static org.apache.commons.lang3.Validate.inclusiveBetween;

public final class Quantity {

    private static final int MIN_VALUE = 1;
    private static final int MAX_VALUE = 500;

    private final int value;

    public Quantity(final int value) {
        inclusiveBetween(MIN_VALUE, MAX_VALUE, value);
        this.value = value;
    }

    public int value() {
```

---

[3] If you don't already know the domain rules in your business domain, then you should discover them together with the domain experts. Go back to chapter 3 for how to develop a deep understanding of your domain.

```
      return value;
   }

   // ...

}
```

You can use the same approach when it comes to entities. Make it a habit to always look closer when you see domain types with insufficient validation. Most likely, you'll find an opportunity to make your code more secure by design and, at the same time, deepen your domain knowledge through collaboration with the domain experts.

12.7 *Only testing the good enough*

When writing tests, developers tend to focus on two things: that the production code follows the intended behavior and that a safety net is established to prevent bugs from slipping through. Because of this, many use tests as documentation to learn how a system behaves when given a certain input and how the implementation supports different business requirements—but this isn't the only thing that tests reveal. They also show where the weak spots are in the code, which could be exploited by an attacker.

In chapter 8, you learned about how to secure your code using tests. Many times, developers stop writing tests after creating normal and boundary tests because they capture intended behavior and establish a safety net that's good enough. But as you know by now, to promote security in depth, you also need to test with invalid and extreme input, because it pushes your code to the limit.[4] Unfortunately, not many developers think of this when writing tests. Studying how code is tested is therefore a clever way to detect potential security weaknesses.

To illustrate this, we'll revisit the code example from section 12.3, but this time, we'll shift focus and analyze potential security weaknesses that can be exploited by looking at how the code is tested.

In listing 12.18, you see the table reservation method that allows you to fetch table reservations by ID. As you've learned, the reservation ID should be implemented as a domain primitive, but we've kept it as a `String` because this is how code tends to look before applying the secure by design mindset.

Listing 12.18   A table reservation is fetched by ID

```
public TableReservation fetch(final String reservationId) {
    logger.info("Fetching table reservation: " + reservationId);
    final TableReservation tableReservation =
            repository.reservation(reservationId);      ◄──┐  The table reservation is fetched
    logger.info("Received " + tableReservation);           │  from the repository by ID.
    return tableReservation;
}
```

---

[4]   Go back to chapter 8 if you need a refresher on the concept of normal, boundary, invalid, and extreme input testing.

Let's analyze this from a secure testing perspective. Because many weaknesses are flushed out using invalid and extreme input, you should look for tests that exercise this kind of data. If there aren't any, then there's a high probability that the code will break if provided such input. For example, the table reservation ID is represented as a `String`, which means that you could inject any input that satisfies the rules of a `String`, such as 100 million random characters. Obviously, this isn't a valid reservation ID and might seem absurd to test, but that's not the point. The point is, if the code can't handle this type of input efficiently, then an attacker could craft an exploit that potentially affects the overall availability of the system. Consider what happens to the log implementation if it receives extreme input, or how input of 100 million characters would affect the search algorithm in the database. It probably would break things. The solution is to use a domain primitive—say, `ReservationId`—to reject any input that doesn't satisfy the domain rules.

But using domain primitives can lull you into a false sense of security, unless you're careful. The design of a domain primitive certainly takes care of invalid input, but there's no guarantee that it protects against failures and unexpected behavior caused by a dependency. You should, therefore, also look for tests that exercise failure scenarios even if the input is valid; otherwise, you might end up with implicit weaknesses caused by your dependencies. For example, if the table reservation repository is backed up by a Mongo database, then a `MongoExecutionTimeoutException` could be thrown, regardless of whether the reservation ID is correct or not. This means that it's necessary to provide proper exception handling (as you learned in chapter 9) to avoid sensitive data leaking out.

Up to this point, you've learned how to identify several potential security problems in legacy code (for example, ambiguous parameter lists, logging of unchecked strings, and defensive code constructs) that seem to benefit from using domain primitives. But, unless you're careful, applying them incorrectly could create a whole set of new problems. Let's see what happens if you end up creating partial domain primitives.

12.8 *Partial domain primitives*

Another pitfall when creating domain primitives is to not encompass a complete conceptual whole. When designing domain primitives, it's a good idea to keep them as small as possible—perhaps only wrapping a value in a thin shell of domain terminology. But sometimes that wrap can be too small. When not enough information is captured in the domain primitive, there's a possibility of it being used in the wrong context. This might constitute a security risk.

Let's look at an example: using a monetary amount with the wrong currency. Imagine you have an online bookstore, and most of your book suppliers are situated in the United States and are paid in U.S. dollars. How do you represent the prices you pay? Most currencies have a unit and subunit: the U.S. dollar is divided into 100 cents, the Mexican peso into 100 centavos, and the Swedish krona into 100 öre. Monetary amounts look like real numbers, such as 12.56 or 5.04, but they're not.

No double money

Never represent money using a `double`, because 1/100th can't be represented exactly using powers of 2. The only cent values that can be represented exactly are 25¢, 50¢, and 75¢. All others will result in rounding errors that sooner or later will come back and bite you. There are other options.

One option is the Java SDK class `BigDecimal`, which is designed to represent decimal values exactly and is a much better option than `double`. Unfortunately, its API is somewhat of an acquired taste.

Another option is to represent dollar and cent values as two integers, splitting a dollar into cents when necessary and collecting cents to dollars when there are enough of them.

A third interesting option is to represent each amount as the amount in cents, a single `long`. In this way, a dollar is represented by `100`, and $12.54 is represented as `1254`. When you display the amount, you show it as dollars and cents, not the internal number-of-cents representation.

Floating-point language primitives like `float` and `double` are for representing real numbers, like physical measurements of length or weight. Don't use them for decimal values like dollars and cents.

Whatever representation you use for amount (`BigDecimal`, two `int`s, a single `long`, or anything else), you realize that you shouldn't have that representation floating around in the code. You need to form a domain primitive. What about `Amount`? It seems like a good idea, even if we'll shortly show you that it's too small.

You form a domain primitive `Amount` using some internal representation. On the outside, it has methods for adding (`public Amount add(Amount other)`), comparing (`public boolean isGreaterThan(Amount other)`), and perhaps splitting an amount into a number of piles (`public Amount[] split(int piles)`)—the latter ensuring that no cent is lost if $10 is split three ways.

12.8.1 Implicit, contextual currency

What we've unfortunately not taken into account yet is the concept of currency. Remember that most of your suppliers trade in U.S. dollars? That's most, not all. There has to be a currency somewhere. Right now, it's obviously implicit—by looking at a supplier, you can figure out what currency to use. Each supplier will be paid in the currency of its respective country: U.S. suppliers in U.S. dollars, the few French suppliers in euros, and the odd Slovenian suppliers in Slovenian tolars. If you want to know the total sum of your trade with a specific supplier, you can sum it up as shown in the following listing.

Listing 12.19 Summing up the purchase orders for a specific supplier

```
List<PurchaseOrder> purchases =
        procurementService.purchases(supplier);
Amount total = purchases.stream().
        map(PurchaseOrder::price).
        reduce(Amount.ZERO, Amount::add);
```

All purchase orders

Gets the prices

Adds them up using the add method in
Amount, starting with ZERO

The pitfall here is that the information about currency is contextual—you have to keep track of it outside the handling of monetary amounts. In this example, because a supplier is linked to a country that's linked to a currency, the linking of implicit, contextual information worked out fine. But that's not always the case.

12.8.2 *A U.S. dollar is not a Slovenian tolar*

Most suppliers are paid in U.S. dollars, but not all. And the code has to be aware of that fact. Imagine that this takes place in an organization where developers and business-people are strictly separated into different departments and never meet, and where all communication is mandated to go via business analysts and project managers. Yes, we know that sounds bizarre, but bear with us for the sake of the example.

Suppose a developer gets the task to sum up the value of all purchases for all suppliers. The developer might not know about the odd non-U.S. suppliers, and so might write code like that in the following listing. Notice how the method add is used in the same way as when summing purchase orders for a single supplier.

Listing 12.20 Summing up the purchase orders for all suppliers

```
List<PurchaseOrder> purchases =
        procurementService.allPurchases();
Amount sum = purchases.stream().
        map(PurchaseOrder::price).
        reduce(Amount.ZERO, Amount::add);
```

All purchases, all suppliers

Adding up the amounts, even
if different currencies

The design deficiency here is that the developer has summed up all the amounts. The result is something that's almost correct, because a U.S. dollar is approximately as much as a euro, and the purchases in tolars are so few that they disappear in the mass. But it isn't correct.

The problem is that it doesn't make sense to add 10 U.S. dollars and 15 euros. (Well, both are monetary values, so it might make some sense, but it won't add up to 25 of anything sensible.) The class Amount isn't aware of the difference between 10 U.S. dollars and 10 euros because currency is a concept that's implicitly understood, not explicitly stated. You should either convert one of those values to the other or say, "Can't add different sorts of money." But the class Amount isn't designed to capture that domain subtlety.

This discrepancy between explicit and implicit usually shows up when the implicit concept is suddenly explicitly needed, often in the case of interacting with external representations. In the following listing, you see this happening when trying to initialize a payment at a bank, which suddenly requires a currency. The currency is then fetched from a central service that keeps track of which supplier is in which country and, therefore, uses appropriate currency.

Listing 12.21   Sending off a payment to a bank, fetching currency out of thin air

```
public void payPurchase(PurchaseOrder po) {
    Account account = po.supplier().account();          Amount is part of the purchase order.
    Amount amount = po.price();
    Currency curr =                                      Currency is fetched as an
        supplierservice.currencyFor(po.supplier());      afterthought at the last moment.
    bankservice.initializePayment(account, amount, curr);
}
```

This code works because a supplier is bound to a country, and a country is bound to a currency. But that connection is contextual—the currency information is transmitted out-of-band with respect to the amount to be paid.

> **TIP** Stay alert and keep an eye open for contextual information that's transmitted out-of-band; it might be what's needed to make a domain primitive that wraps a conceptual whole.

Things get even worse when Slovenia decides to leave the tolar behind and start using euros instead. This happened in 2007, and the code in listing 12.21 is roughly what we found at one of our clients. Suddenly Slovenian suppliers didn't have one well-defined currency, but two different ones, depending on the transaction date. A supplier with a purchase order for 100,000 tolars signed in late 2006 would probably get paid in early 2007, but at that point, the code

```
supplierservice.currencyFor(po.supplier())
```

would no longer return tolars but euros instead. The supplier would instead be paid 100,000 euros, a significantly larger sum. Fortunately, our client realized this in time and was able to take precautions, but it caused a significant amount of extra work.

12.8.3 *Encompassing a conceptual whole*

If Amount isn't enough, what concept would be big enough to form a conceptual whole? If you wrap both the amount and the currency, you get a concept you might call Money. The PurchaseOrder wouldn't have had an amount only and simply relied on implicit currency information. Rather, it'd have the currency explicitly embedded in the price in the form of a Money object.

The code for paying a supplier using Money would look like the following listing. Notice that po.price() no longer returns an Amount, but a Money object that contains the currency. The currency information is no longer obtained out-of-band but from the purchase order itself.

Listing 12.22   Fetching currency and amount from the same conceptual whole

```
public void payPurchase(PurchaseOrder po) {          Amount is part of the purchase order.
    Account account = po.supplier().account();
    Amount amount = po.price().amount();             Currency is fetched from the
    Currency curr = po.price().currency();           same source as amount.
    bankservice.initializePayment(account, amount, curr);
}
```

When the currency and the amount travel together in Money, they form a conceptual
whole and make up a neat domain primitive. This also fixes another issue.

Recall the broken code for summing up all purchase orders for all suppliers in
listing 12.20. The mistake was to add U.S. dollars, tolars, and euros without discrim-
ination. Using Money as a domain primitive, as seen in the following listing, that
wouldn't be possible. The add method in Money checks that the two amounts to be
added refer to the same currency.

Listing 12.23   Summing up the purchase orders for a specific supplier

```
class Money {
    public static final Money ZERO = ...
    private Amount amount;
    private Currency currency;

    public Money add(Money other) {            Checks that you're not trying
        isTrue(this.currency                   to add different currencies
                .equals(other.currency));
        ...
    }
}

        List<PurchaseOrder> purchases =
                procurementService.allPurchases();
        Money sum = purchases.stream().           Breaks with exception when trying
            map(PurchaseOrder::price).            to add tolar purchase order to U.S.
            reduce(Money.ZERO, Money::add);       dollar purchase order
}
```

> **NOTE**   When designing your domain primitives, ensure that they encompass
> an entire conceptual whole.

In this chapter, we've covered some situations that you might encounter during your
work with making designs more secure. We've looked at some sources for potential
security weaknesses in the code—ambiguous parameter lists, logging of unchecked
strings, and defensive code constructs—and what you can do about them. We've also
looked at situations where things are better, and the code might look fine at first glance,
but where there are hidden issues if you think more deeply about it: the principle of
DRY misapplied, insufficient validation in domain types, and only positive tests. Finally,

we've covered two pitfalls where things are hard to get right when starting out: where to apply domain primitives and the risk of creating domain primitives that are partial.

These tricks also apply well in traditional codebases and are a great way to get started. But what about a system with a microservice architecture? What can be done, and what should you think about? That's the topic of the next chapter.

Summary

- Introducing domain primitives should be done at the semantic boundary of your context.
- Ambiguous parameters in APIs are a common source of security bugs.
- You should be on the lookout for ambiguous parameters when reading code and address them using the direct approach, the discovery approach, or the new API approach.
- Never log unchecked user input, because it opens up the risk of second-order injection attacks.
- Limit the number of times a sensitive value can be accessed, because it allows you to detect unintentional access.
- Use explicit accessor methods for data that you want to log. Otherwise, new fields can end up in logs by accident.
- Because defensive code constructs can be harmful, clarify them using contracts and domain primitives.
- The DRY (Don't Repeat Yourself) principle is about repeated representation of knowledge, not about repeated text.
- Trying to reduce repeated text that isn't repeated knowledge can cause unnecessary dependencies.
- Failing to reduce repeated knowledge because the text differs can cause vulnerable inconsistencies.
- Tests reveal possible weaknesses in your code, and you should look for invalid and extreme input tests.
- Ensure that your domain primitives encompass an entire conceptual whole.
- Be on the lookout for domain types lacking proper validation and address them with domain primitives and secure entities.

Guidance on microservices

This chapter covers

- How to design secure APIs for microservices
- Sensitive data in a microservice architecture
- Integrity of log data
- Traceability across services and systems
- A domain-oriented logging API

In chapter 12, we looked at challenges in legacy code that often appear in monolithic architectures and how to apply secure by design fundamentals. In this chapter, we'll focus on microservices, an architectural style that has grown in popularity in recent years. The topic is too large to cover fully in a single chapter, but we've selected an interesting set of challenges that are essential from a security standpoint. For example, you'll learn how to deal with sensitive data across services, and why it's important to design service APIs that enforce invariants. In addition, we'll revisit logging one more time and explore challenges like traceability of transactions across services and systems, how to avoid tampering of log data, and how to ensure confidentiality using a domain-oriented logger API. But before we dive into the world of microservices, let's establish what a microservice is.

13.1 *What's a microservice?*

Microservice architecture is an architectural style of building systems that has become popular as an alternative to and a reaction against the monolithic style. Monolithic systems are built as a single logical unit. They can consist of various technical parts, such as an application, a server, and a database, but those parts depend logically on each other, both during development and at runtime. If any of them are down, the system doesn't work. Similarly, any nontrivial change will likely affect several if not most of the parts and needs to be deployed simultaneously to work properly.

There's no single, authoritative definition of microservice architecture. Still, there's some common understanding about what the term means, as we can see by looking at the following quotes from Martin Fowler and Chris Richardson, respectively. Most people agree that microservice architecture describes a style of structuring the system around loosely dependent, relatively small, business-oriented services, each executing in its own runtime environment.

> *[T]he microservice architectural style is an approach to developing a single application as a suite of small services, each running in its own process and communicating with lightweight mechanisms, often an HTTP resource API. These services are built around business capabilities and independently deployable by fully automated deployment machinery.*
>
> —*Martin Fowler, https://www.martinfowler.com/articles/microservices.html*

> *Microservices—also known as the microservice architecture—is an architectural style that structures an application as a collection of loosely coupled services, which implement business capabilities. The microservice architecture enables the continuous delivery/ deployment of large, complex applications.*
>
> —*Chris Richardson, https://microservices.io*

A complete description of the microservice architecture style is beyond the scope of our security-focused discussion, but we certainly recommend reading up on it. These two websites are good places to start, together with Chris Richardson's book, *Microservices Patterns* (Manning, 2018), and Sam Newman's book, *Building Microservices* (O'Reilly, 2015). Executed well, it's a style that can return huge benefits.

A distributed monolith

Unfortunately, we've seen several examples of systems that were believed to be designed in the microservice style but that had severe shortcomings. One example was a previous monolith that had been split into seven separate services, running as separate processes. The trouble was that they all needed to be up and running for anything to work. If one of them went down, none of the others could do their jobs. Also, it was impossible to restart only one of them, because all seven services had to be started in a particular order. Needless to say, any isolated update was a complete impossibility. Even if the system was thought to be built as microservices, it certainly didn't match the architectural style, apart from superficial aspects.

Let's briefly sketch out three aspects of microservices that we think are important but that are, unfortunately, often overlooked: independent runtimes, independent update capability, and being designed for down.

13.1.1 Independent runtimes

A microservice should run in its own runtime, independent of the other services. A *runtime* in this sense could be a process, a container, a machine of its own, or some other way to separate the services from each other. That the runtimes are independent also means that there should be no dependencies of the type *this one has to start before that one*, and services shouldn't make assumptions about the particulars of other services. For example, if you need to move one of your services from one machine to another, you should be able to do so without the other services malfunctioning or ceasing to work completely. Although there are several ways of achieving this goal, following the advice on cloud-native concepts and the twelve-factor app methodology that we covered in chapter 10 provides a good starting point (in particular, see sections 10.2, 10.3, and 10.6).

13.1.2 Independent updates

Having independent runtimes makes it possible to take down a service and restart it without restarting the rest of the system. This ability is a prerequisite for independent updates. But it's not enough to be able to restart the service—you have to be able to do it with updated functionality.

A change in functionality should be isolated to a few services at most. The ideal case is that you only need to touch one single service for a functional update. But it makes sense that if you extend the functionality one service provides, then you'll most probably want to change some of the calling code in another service to make that change usable and valuable—and that's perfectly fine. What you want to avoid is a change that ripples from one service to the next, then over to a third, and so on. A huge help in this is orienting each service around a business domain. We've touched on this in earlier chapters (for example, in sections 3.3 and 3.4), and in this chapter, we'll elaborate on it further. (See section 13.2.)

13.1.3 Designed for down

With independent runtimes and independent updates, it's normal for one service to be up while another is down. To work well in this situation, a service needs to be designed both so that it behaves well when the other service is down and it recovers to normal operation when the other service is up again. The service isn't only designed for the happy case when every service is up, but also designed for when services it depends on are down. The techniques that we covered in chapter 9, especially the use of bulkheading to contain a failure and circuit breakers to avoid domino failures, will take you a long way towards this goal.

A neat trick when developing is to start with implementing what the service should do in case a service it depends on is down. This is easier if each service is designed as a bounded context of a business domain. Even if the other service isn't available, you can try to make the best of the situation in the context you're in. Another powerful approach is to design your architecture as event-driven, where the services communicate by passing messages. In that case, the services pull incoming messages from a queue or topic at their own discretion, so the sender makes no assumption about whether the receiver is up or down.

Now that we've looked at some characteristics of microservices, let's look at how to design such services. We'll start with designing each service so that it captures a model in a bounded context.

13.2 *Each service is a bounded context*

A common challenge when designing microservices is figuring out how to split functionality between different services. Whether feature X should go in service Y or service Z isn't always an easy question to answer, and it's one you shouldn't answer in haste. Slicing the feature set incorrectly can lead to multiple architectural challenges. One is that instead of independent services, you might end up with a distributed monolith, leading to the overhead of managing multiple services but without the benefit of them being independent. Cramming too much functionality into a single service is another challenge, because then you're working with a monolith again. A good way to tell if your microservices are inappropriately sliced is when you're experiencing testing difficulties or witnessing tight dependencies between different development teams that, in theory, should be independent.

You can design microservices in many ways, but we believe a good design principle is to think of each service as a bounded context.[1] Doing so provides several benefits:

- If you treat each service as a bounded context with an API that faces the rest of the world, you can use the various design principles and tools you've learned in this book to build more secure services.
- It'll help you decide where a certain feature belongs, because it's easier to reason about the home of the feature when you're thinking in terms of bounded contexts instead of technical services or APIs. This helps you with the challenge of slicing the feature set.

Our experience is that designing microservices this way leads to better defined APIs, less complex dependency graphs between services, and, most importantly, more secure services. When you think of each microservice as its own bounded context, it'll become clear that each service has different concepts and semantics, even if some concepts might share the same names (such as customer or user). With that understanding, you most likely won't miss that you need to perform explicit translations when you're moving across services. Each time you translate between different bounded contexts, you'll use techniques learned in part 2 of this book to improve security. For example,

---

[1] Go back to chapter 3 if you need a refresher on the concept of bounded contexts in Domain-Driven Design (DDD) and how to identify context boundaries.

you can use domain primitives and secure entities to enforce invariants in the receiving service. You can also make sure to handle exceptions in a secure way so that bad data doesn't lead to security issues. And it's more likely that you'll spot the (sometimes subtle) semantic differences between services that can lead to security problems. Let's take a look at three cases that we've found are common and that we think you should pay some extra attention to when designing microservices: API design, splitting monoliths, and evolving services.

13.2.1 *The importance of designing your API*

Designing the public API of a microservice is probably one of the most important steps of building microservices, but unfortunately, it's commonly overlooked. Each service should be treated as a bounded context, and the public API is its interface to the rest of the world. In chapter 5, we talked about how to use domain primitives to harden your APIs and the importance of not exposing your internal domain publicly. You should also apply those concepts when designing the API of your microservice to make it more secure.

Another important aspect of API design is that you should only expose domain operations. If the API only exposes domain operations, the service can enforce invariants and maintain valid states. This, as you learned in part 2, is an essential part of building secure systems. Don't fall for the temptation of exposing inner details of your domain or the underlying technology you happen to be using—free for anyone to perform operations on. A service isn't just a bunch of CRUD (create, read, update, and delete) operations; it provides important business functionality, and only that functionality should be exposed.

The following listing shows a customer management API designed in two different ways. The API is described as an interface because it's a concise way of expressing an API. The implementation doesn't matter, because the focus of this discussion is API design.

Listing 13.1   Designing the API: CRUD operations versus domain operations

```
public interface CustomerManagementApiV1 {          ◄──── CRUD-style API

    void setCustomerActivated(CustomerId id, boolean activated);

    boolean isActivated(CustomerId id);

}
                                                    API with only domain
                                                    operations exposed
public interface CustomerManagementApiV2 {          ◄────

    void addLegalAgreement(CustomerId id, AgreementId agreementId);

    void addConfirmedPayment(ConfirmedPaymentId confirmedPaymentId);

    boolean isActivated(CustomerId id);

}
```

The purpose of the customer management API is to provide the functionality of activating a customer. In this particular system, a customer is considered activated once a legal agreement has been signed and an initial payment has been confirmed. What's interesting is how the two different versions, `CustomerManagementApiV1` and `CustomerManagementApiV2`, handle how a customer becomes activated.

In the first version of the API, two methods, `setCustomerActivated(CustomerId, boolean)` and `isActivated(CustomerId)`, are exposed. This might seem like a flexible solution, because anyone that wants to can activate a customer and check if a customer is activated. The problem with this design is that the service owns the concept of a customer and the definition of an activated customer, but the way the API is designed, it's unable to uphold the invariants for it (having a signed legal agreement and a confirmed payment). There might also be other invariants for when a customer should be deactivated, which the service also is unable to enforce.

In the second, redesigned version, the API no longer exposes a method to directly mark a customer as activated. Instead, it exposes two other methods: `addLegalAgreement (CustomerId, AgreementId)` and `addConfirmedPayment(ConfirmedPaymentId)`. Other services that handle legal agreements or payments can call these methods to notify the customer service when a legal agreement is signed or when a payment has been confirmed. The `isActivated(CustomerId)` method only returns `true` if both a legal agreement and a payment for the customer exist.

TIP Services that only expose domain operations in the API can enforce invariants and maintain a valid state.

Only exposing domain operations in the API means the service is now in full control of maintaining a valid state and upholding all applicable invariants, which is a cornerstone for building secure systems. Because the service now owns all operations related to activating a customer, this design also makes it possible to add more prerequisites without changing any client code. The following listing shows a third version of the API, where a new requirement has been added for a customer to be activated: a customer service representative must have made a welcoming call to the new customer.

Listing 13.2   Introducing a new requirement in the API

```
public interface CustomerManagementApiV3 {

    void addLegalAgreement(CustomerId id, AgreementId agreementId);

    void addConfirmedPayment(ConfirmedPaymentId confirmedPaymentId);

    void welcomeCallPerformed(CustomerId id);          ◄─── Adds notification method for
                                                            the new requirement to the API
    boolean isActivated(CustomerId id);          ◄───
                                                     Returns true only if all three
}                                                    preconditions are satisfied
```

To implement the new requirement, all you need to do is add a third method, `welcome-CallPerformed(CustomerId)`, that notifies the customer service that the call has been made and makes sure the `isActivated(CustomerId)` method also checks for the new requirement before returning `true`. There's no need to make changes to all other services calling the `isActivated` method, because the logic for determining whether a customer is activated or not is now owned by the customer service. This would have been impossible to do with an anemic CRUD API like the one you saw in listing 13.1.

13.2.2 *Splitting monoliths*

Often, you'll find yourself in a situation where you're splitting a monolith into multiple smaller services. This might be because you're refactoring an existing system toward a microservice architecture, or perhaps because you started with a microservice that has grown too big and needs to be split. The tricky part can be to figure out where to split the monolith. If you identify the semantic boundaries in your monolith (as you learned in section 12.1), you can then use those boundaries to split the monolith into smaller microservices, each with a well-designed API.

In terms of API design, one thing to watch out for when splitting a monolith is that you must also discover and enforce the translation between the different contexts—contexts that are now in different microservices. Because the context boundaries you discovered were most likely hidden in the monolith, there's not going to be any existing translation in the code. When you're creating your microservice, possibly by extracting existing code from the monolith, it's easy to forget to add explicit translations between the contexts.

> **TIP** Make sure to discover and enforce translation between the different contexts when splitting a monolith, using explicit translation between services.

Always be wary when making calls across services and make it a habit to add explicit translation to and from the context you're talking to. A good way of doing this is by thinking carefully about the semantics and using code constructs like domain primitives. As soon as you receive incoming data in your API, immediately validate it, interpret the semantics, and create domain primitives from it. Doing this will take you a good way toward creating APIs that are hardened by design. To give you an example, let's go back to section 12.1 and this method:

```
public void cancelReservation(final String reservationId)
```

Say you've found that this method is part of a context boundary, and you want to split the monolith at this point to create a new microservice. A good first step before extracting the code to the new service is to introduce a domain primitive for the reservation ID. This way, you'll enforce explicit translation to and from the bounded context. Once you have that in place, you can go ahead and extract the code to the new microservice.

13.2.3 *Semantics and evolving services*

If you already have a microservice architecture, you should pay extra attention as services evolve, especially when there are semantic changes in the APIs. The reason for this is that subtle changes in semantics can lead to security issues if appropriate changes aren't also made in the translation between the different bounded contexts; in other words, broken context mappings can cause security problems.

The story in chapter 11, where evolving APIs led to insurance policies being given away for free, is a perfect example of how evolving microservices can cause serious trouble. Context mapping, taking nearby microservices into account, and thinking carefully about how to evolve semantics in the APIs are some effective ways of handling evolving services in a safe way.

When you evolve microservices and either introduce new concepts, change existing ones, or in other ways change the semantics, always try to avoid redefining existing terminology. If you feel an existing term has changed in meaning, then replace it with a new term and remove the old one. Another approach is to leave the old term unchanged and instead introduce a new term that'll let your domain model express the new meaning.

> **TIP** Avoid redefining existing terminology when semantics change. Introduce new terms that let you express the new semantics.

Changes in semantics are something that usually requires some degree of domain modeling and context mapping to get right.[2] Sometimes the changes in semantics can lead to a change of context boundaries, and, because each service is a bounded context, the change of boundaries leads to a change in the microservices you have. New services get created or existing ones get merged as a result of evolving semantics. Remember that even if you're using various secure code constructs in your APIs, you still need to invest time in the *soft* parts of API design in order to avoid security pitfalls like the one you saw in chapter 11.

Now you know that API design is an important aspect of microservice architectures (not only from a security perspective) and that putting time into it is an investment that'll pay off in many ways—improved security being one of them. In the next section, you'll learn about some pitfalls when sending data between different services.

13.3 *Sensitive data across services*

When thinking about security in any architecture, it's important to ask yourself what data is sensitive. In a microservice architecture, it's easier to make mistakes because the architectural style encourages developers to work by looking at one service at a time, and, when doing so, it becomes harder to keep track of cross-cutting concerns like security. In particular, to ensure that sensitive data is handled well, you need to see the

---

[2] You can always go back to chapter 3 on how to identify context boundaries and how to use context maps to understand how contexts interact.

entire picture. For a start, let's elaborate a bit on the classic security attributes in the context of a microservice architecture.

13.3.1   *CIA-T in a microservice architecture*

Information security classically focuses on the security triad of *CIA*: confidentiality (keeping things secret), integrity (ensuring things don't change in bad ways), and availability (keeping things…well, available when needed). Sometimes traceability (knowing who changed what) is added to this triad, creating the acronym *CIA-T*. In chapter 1, we elaborated a little on these concepts under the section on security features and security concerns.

The microservice architecture doesn't help us when addressing cross-cutting concerns like security concerns. In the same way that you can't rely on a single service to provide fast response times (because the bottleneck might be elsewhere), you can't look at a single service to ensure security (because the weakness might be elsewhere). On the contrary, most security concerns become harder to satisfy because a microservice architecture consists of more connected parts—more places and connections where things could go wrong.

Ensuring *confidentiality* gets trickier because a request for data might travel from component to component. In many microservice architectures, the identity of the original requester is lost by the time the request finally arrives at the end component. The situation doesn't get easier when the request is done (in part) asynchronously, for example, via message queues. To keep track of this, you need some token to be passed with the request, and when a request reaches a service, the service needs to check whether the requester is authorized. Security frameworks like OAuth 2.0 can help because they are built to provide such tokens. For example, in OAuth 2.0, the first request is given a token (the JSON Web Token, or JWT) based on the caller. The JWT is carried along with the downstream requests, and each service that processes the request can consult the authorization server to see if it should be allowed.

When guaranteeing *integrity* across multiple services, two things are important. The first is that every piece of information should have an authoritative source, typically a specific service where the data lives. Unfortunately, often data is copied from one place to the next, aggregated, and copied further. Instead of copying it, go directly to the source as often as possible. The second important thing is that the data hasn't been tampered with. Here, classical cryptography can help by providing some sort of checksum or signature to ensure integrity.

For *availability*, a microservice architecture needs to ensure that a service is responding or that some sensible value can be used if the service is down; for example, a cached value from a previous call or a sensible default. In chapter 9, we discussed circuit breakers and other tools that are useful to design for availability.

Ensuring *traceability* also becomes more complicated in a microservice environment. As with confidentiality, you need to be able to track the original requester, but you also need to be able to correlate different calls to different services to see the bigger pattern of who accessed what. The term *auditability* is sometimes used as a synonym for traceability. Later, in this chapter, we'll elaborate on how this property can be achieved through well-structured logging. CIA-T is a great way to reason about security, but what do we mean by sensitive data?

13.3.2 Thinking "sensitive"

Often *sensitive* is confused with confidential or classified. Sometimes this is indeed the case; for example, personal data like health records is considered sensitive and should be kept confidential. But the term *sensitive* is broader than that.

Take the license plate number of your car. Is that sensitive? It's surely not confidential, as it's on public display. But take the plate number and combine it with a geolocation and a timestamp, and suddenly there's information on where you were at a certain point in time—information that you might want to stay confidential. The challenge becomes even greater in a microservice architecture, where data travels from service to service and from context to context. (Remember the discussion about each service being a bounded context earlier in this chapter.)

Let's look at another example. A hotel room number such as 4711 isn't something that's confidential in and of itself. But who is staying in room 4711 on a certain night certainly is. After the guest has checked out, there's nothing confidential about the room number any longer, and the hotel goes into the regular housekeeping routine of cleaning, replenishing the minibar, and so on. This isn't security-sensitive. But suppose during housekeeping, a coat is found and is marked "found in room 4711" and placed in the lost-and-found. When the guest shows up to claim the coat, you suddenly have a connection between that customer and the room again—something that should be confidential. You can see that when moving in and out of different contexts, the same data (the room number) might merit being confidential or not.

The requirement for confidentiality isn't an absolute but something that depends on context. That's why you reason about sensitive data—data that could have security concerns. In this case, we looked at confidentiality, but a similar line of reasoning could apply to data that has integrity or availability concerns. A similar situation arises when a service is an aggregator of data. Such services are sometimes underestimated because they create no new data and therefore can't be more sensitive than their parts. This is a mistake. If you add together several different pieces of data, there might arise a complete picture that says a lot more than the parts did individually. This is basically the way any intelligence agency works, so you should pay attention to those harmless aggregating services in your architecture.

To us, sensitive is a marker that indicates we should pay attention to security concerns to stop us from focusing on one service at a time. What is sensitive or not is something that needs to be understood by considering the entire system.

To identify sensitive data, you can ask yourself the following questions:

- Should this data be confidential in another context?
- Does the data require a high degree of integrity or availability in another context? How about traceability?
- If combined with data from other services, could this data be sensitive? (Recall the example of the license plate number together with a time and geolocation.)

While thinking about this, you need to have the entire range of services in scope. Unfortunately, cross-cutting concerns like security can't be addressed by myopically looking at one or a few services at a time, any more than issues of response time or capacity can be solved by a single service.

Passing data over the wire

In a microservice architecture, data is more exposed. In a monolith, you might have everything encapsulated inside one single process, and data is passed by method calls from one piece of code to another. In a microservice architecture, you'll pass information between parts over a network connection—most probably HTTP or some message-passing protocol. This raises the question of how protected your network is.

- Are the network messages routed over an open network that is part of the internet and publicly available?
- Are they routed inside a closed subnet?
- How big is the risk, and what happens if the firewall is compromised?

You might need to protect the data in transit with TLS/SSL. Perhaps client certificates are needed. Perhaps you need authorization based on the user, and you need to dive into OAuth. This is the realm of classical network security, and unfortunately, we haven't yet found any design-based pieces of advice that can help. We do recommend you get a book on network security.

Now let's move over to the tricky field of ensuring traceability in a microservice architecture—the call for structured logging from multiple sources.

13.4 *Logging in microservices*

We've brought up logging several times in previous chapters and analyzed how it impacts the overall security of an application. For example, in chapter 10, we discussed the importance of avoiding logging to a file on disk, and in chapter 12, we talked about the danger of logging unchecked strings. The key takeaway is that logging contains lots of hidden complexity, and things can go seriously wrong if done naively; for example, logging could open up the risk of second-order injection attacks or implicitly cause leakage of sensitive data due to an evolving domain model. Although this has been discussed extensively in this book, there's one more aspect of logging we need to cover before closing the topic: the importance of traceability and how to ensure the integrity and confidentiality of log data.

13.4.1 Integrity of aggregated log data

In a monolithic architecture, you tend to get away with using remote login to access log data on a server when needed. In chapter 10, you learned that logging shouldn't be done to a local disk, but rather to an external logging system. This might have seemed like overengineering at the time, but when using microservices, it definitely starts to make sense. If you run multiple instances of a service that scale dynamically and use the same logging strategy as with a monolith, you never know which instance contains the log data you need, because a transaction could span multiple instances, depending on load. This means that log data will be scattered throughout the system, and to get a complete picture of what has happened, you need to aggregate data—but fetching it manually quickly becomes a painful experience.

Aggregating log data from multiple services is therefore preferably done through an automatic process—but there's a catch. To effectively aggregate data, you need to store it in a normalized, structured format (for example, as JSON), which means it needs to be transformed somewhere in the logging process. Consequently, it's common to find solutions where each service logs data in natural language and later transforms it into a structured format using a common external normalization step before passing it to the logging system (as illustrated in figure 13.1).

The upside to this, ironically, is also its downside. By having a normalization step, you encourage a design with great flexibility in terms of logging, but it opens up logging of unchecked strings as well—and that's a security concern! It's also common that normalization is implemented using a temporal state on the local disk, which is problematic because it complicates the repavement phase of the three R's of enterprise security (which we talked about in chapter 10). The third issue is less obvious and involves integrity of data during the normalization step.

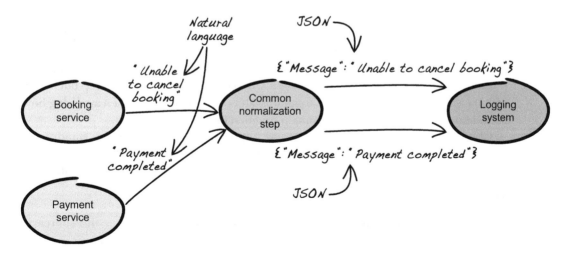

Figure 13.1   Log data is transformed into JSON in an external normalization step.

When normalizing data, you restructure it into a key-value format that, by definition, is a modification of its original form—but does that violate the integrity of the data? Not necessarily; you only need to ensure the data hasn't changed in an unauthorized way. In theory, this should be simple, but in practice, it's hard, because validating the transformation logic from natural language to a structured format isn't trivial and is something you probably want to avoid. Another solution is to therefore structure data in each service before passing it to the logging system, as illustrated in figure 13.2. This way, you avoid using third-party normalization software.

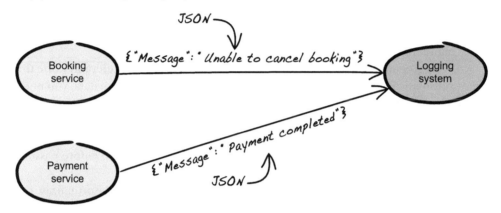

Figure 13.2   Log data is structured into JSON before being passed to the logging system.

The downside to this approach is that every microservice needs to implement explicit normalization logic, which adds complexity, but avoiding third-party dependencies also reduces complexity, so it probably evens out in the long run. Two other aspects are also interesting from a security perspective. First, by explicitly normalizing log data in each service, it becomes possible to digitally sign each payload using a cryptographic hash function (for example, SHA-256) before passing it to the logging system. This implies that the integrity of log data can be verified explicitly in the logging system, and you know it hasn't been tampered with. Second, normalization is often tightly coupled with categorization of data, which requires extensive domain knowledge (especially when you're dealing with sensitive data). The natural place for this isn't in a common normalization step but rather within each service. We'll talk more about this later on in this chapter when analyzing how confidentiality is achieved using a domain-oriented logger API.

Choosing the right logging strategy is important from an integrity standpoint, regardless of whether you have a monolith or microservice—but that's not all that matters when it comes to logging. The next topic to consider is traceability in log data.

13.4.2   Traceability in log data

When logging in a monolithic architecture, the presumption is that the source is always the same. Unfortunately, this simplification is no longer valid when using microservices because you might need to identify which particular service instance took part in a transaction. For example, consider two payment services, A and B, where A has version 1.0 and B has version 1.1. The services use semantic versioning, which means that service B contains some additional functionality compared to A but is fully backward compatible with version 1.0. The only problem is that service B contains a bug that causes a rounding error that doesn't exist in service A, and consequently, several financial transactions fail in production. At this point, you want to be able to tell whether service A or service B was used in a transaction—but if the logs don't contain enough traceability, it becomes a guessing game.

Semantic versioning

The semantic versioning specification was created by Tom Preston-Werner, the inventor of Gravatars and cofounder of GitHub. His idea was to create a simple set of rules and requirements that dictates how version numbers should be used in an ecosystem of software. Although there are many special cases to consider and the list of rules is extensive, here's the gist of it to help you understand the essence of semantic versioning:

- Software using semantic versioning must declare a public API. This API must define a version of the form X.Y.Z, where X is the major version, Y is the minor version, and Z is the patch version.
- Once a version has been released, the contents of that version must not change. If modification is needed, then a new version must be released.
- A change in major version means that incompatible changes have been introduced to the public API.
- A change in minor version means that changes have been made in a backward-compatible manner.
- A change in patch version means that only backward-compatible bug fixes have been introduced.

For further information about semantic versioning, visit https://semver.org.

The solution to the payment service problem is to add traceability to your system, but there's some hidden complexity to consider. For example

- A service must be uniquely identifiable by its name, version number, and instance ID.
- A transaction must be traceable across systems.

Let's see why this is important.

UNIQUELY IDENTIFYING A SERVICE

In a microservice architecture, you'll often choose to follow the rules of semantic versioning for your service APIs. This means it should be safe to invoke any service within the same major version range because all versions are backward compatible. But when it comes to traceability, you can't make this assumption, because even if a version is fully backward compatible, there might be differences (bugs or unintended behavior) that distinguish one service from another. It might even be the case that instances with the same version number behave differently because of installment issues or because they've been compromised. Being able to uniquely identify a service is therefore important from a security standpoint. A common way to achieve this is to add the service name, version number, and a unique instance ID to each log statement.

> **NOTE** Make sure to add the service name, version number, and a unique instance ID in your digital signature of a log statement. Otherwise, you can't tell if the origin of the data has been tampered with.

IDENTIFYING TRANSACTIONS ACROSS SYSTEMS

Uniquely identifying a service certainly allows you to achieve traceability on a micro level, but transactions seldom interact with one system alone. Instead, they span across multiple systems, and to fully support traceability, you also need to identify which services and external systems take part in a transaction. One way to do this is to use a tracing system, such as Dapper by Google[3] or Magpie by Microsoft,[4] but it might be overkill if you only need to identify which services and systems participated in a transaction. What you need to do is ensure that each transaction has a unique identifier and that it's shared between services and external systems, as illustrated in figure 13.3.

Every time system A initiates a transaction in system B, it needs to provide a unique trace ID that identifies the transaction in system A. System B appends this ID to a newly created, (probabilistically) unique, 64-bit integer and uses this as the trace ID. This lets you identify all services in B that took part in the transaction initiated by A. System B then passes the trace ID to system C, and a new ID is created in a similar fashion. This way, you can easily identify all services that participated in a transaction spanning several systems.

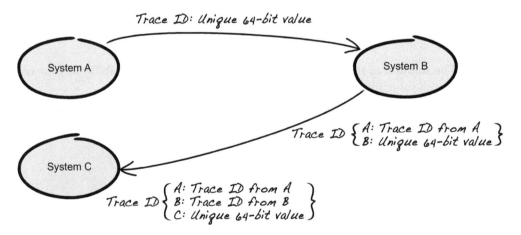

Figure 13.3   The unique trace ID is shared between systems A, B, and C.

---

[3]   Benjamin H. Sigelman, et al., "Dapper, a Large-Scale Distributed Systems Tracing Infrastructure." Google Technical Report dapper-2010-1, April 2010.

[4]   Paul Barham, et al., "Magpie: Online Modelling and Performance-Aware Systems," Microsoft Research Ltd., May 2003.

13.4.3 *Confidentiality through a domain-oriented logger API*

In chapter 10, we talked about confidentiality and how to ensure only authorized consumers get access to data. The solution proposed was to separate log data into different categories (for example, Audit, Behavior, and Error) and restrict access to each category, but doing this in practice requires some additional thought.

Logging data with different logging levels, like DEBUG, INFO, and FATAL (provided by a logging framework), is a common design pattern used in many systems. At first glance, it might seem as if this could solve the confidentiality problem in chapter 10, but unfortunately, logging levels tend to focus on response actions rather than confidentiality of data. For example, if you see a log statement marked as INFO, you tend not to worry, but if there's a statement marked as FATAL, you'll probably respond instantly—regardless of whether the data is confidential or not. Another more business-oriented example is that of a bank withdrawal, where sensitive information such as account number, amount, and timestamp needs to be logged. In a design using logging levels, this might be categorized as INFO because it's nothing out of the ordinary, but that level is also used for nonsensitive data such as average processing time. This diversity implies that all log entries marked as INFO must have restricted access because they can contain sensitive information—a confidentiality problem you don't want.

A better solution, based on our experience, is to treat logging as a separate view of the system that needs explicit design, similar to what you'd do for a user interface. How data is presented on the web, on mobile devices, or in some other consumer context must always be well designed, because otherwise you'll get a bad user experience. The same applies to logging, but with the difference that the consumer isn't your normal user. Instead, it's an automated analysis tool, developer, or some other party interested in how the system behaves. This means that structure and categorization of data need to be considered, but so does sensitive information.

How to classify information as sensitive or not is therefore an important part of your system design. But how to do this in practice isn't a trivial task, because the classification depends on context and is an overall business concern. This implies that classification of data requires extensive business domain knowledge and should be part of your service design, not something you delegate to a third-party application. To illustrate, we'll use an example from the hospitality domain.

Consider a web-based hotel system that handles everything a hotel needs to keep its business running from day to day: from bookings to housekeeping to financial transactions. The system is designed on a microservice platform, where each service defines a bounded context—but what's interesting from a logging perspective is how services address the confidentiality problem using a logger with domain-oriented API. In listing 13.3, you see the cancellation logic of the booking service, where domain-oriented actions such as `cancelBooking`, `bookingCanceled`, and `bookingCancellationFailed` are expressed in the logger API. These actions are customized for this context only and are achieved by wrapping the raw logger implementation with a cancel booking interface.

Listing 13.3 Cancel booking logic using a logger with a domain-oriented API

```
import static org.apache.commons.lang3.Validate.notNull;

public Result cancel(final BookingId bookingId, final User user) {
    notNull(bookingId);
    notNull(user);
                                                         Logs that the booking is
                                                         about to be canceled
    logger.cancelBooking(bookingId, user);

    final Result result = bookingsRepository.cancel(bookingId);
                                                         Logs that the booking
    if (result.isBookingCanceled()) {                    has been canceled
        logger.bookingCanceled(bookingId, user);
    } else {                                             Logs that the cancel booking
        logger.bookingCancellationFailed(                operation has failed
                     bookingId, result, user);
    }
    return result;
}
```

The main upside to the logger API is that it guides developers in what data they need in each step of the process. This certainly minimizes the risk of logging incorrect data, but it also separates data in terms of confidentiality—so let's pop the hood of the booking-CancellationFailed method to see how it's implemented.

The bookingCancellationFailed method in listing 13.4 is interfacing directly with the raw logger API, where the log method only accepts String objects. This implies that the logger doesn't care about what data it logs, just that it meets the requirements of a String. Categorizing data must therefore be made explicitly before invoking the log method, because the logger won't make that distinction.

Listing 13.4 Logging categorized data to the logging system

```
import static org.apache.commons.lang3.Validate.notNull;
                                                         Logger that interfaces
                                                         with the logging system
private final Logger logger ...

public void bookingCancellationFailed(final BookingId id,
                                      final Result result,
                                      final User user) {
    notNull(id);
    notNull(result);          Sends audit data to the logging system
    notNull(user);
                                                         Sends behavior data to
    logger.log(auditData(id, result, user));             the logging system
    logger.log(behaviorData(result));
                                  Sends error data to
    if (result.isError()) {       the logging system
        logger.log(errorData(result));
    }
}
```

Only accepting strings in the logger API does indeed make sense because how you distinguish between audit, behavior, and error data is specific to your domain. In listing 13.5, you see the `auditData` method, which translates audit data into JSON, represented as a `String`. The map contains an explicit entry for the audit category. This shouldn't be necessary because this is audit data by definition, but it allows the logging system to detect invalid data on an endpoint (such as audit data sent to the behavior log endpoint) or to separate data based on category if the same endpoint is used for all categories. The `status` field in the `Result` object indicates why the booking couldn't be canceled (for example, because the guest has already checked out).

Listing 13.5 Method that extracts audit data to be logged as JSON

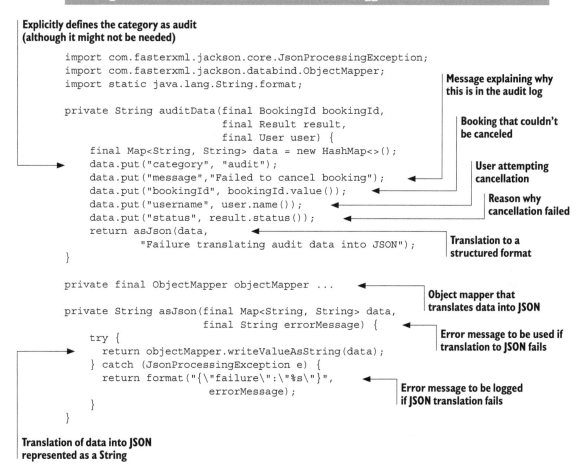

```
import com.fasterxml.jackson.core.JsonProcessingException;
import com.fasterxml.jackson.databind.ObjectMapper;
import static java.lang.String.format;

private String auditData(final BookingId bookingId,
                         final Result result,
                         final User user) {
    final Map<String, String> data = new HashMap<>();
    data.put("category", "audit");
    data.put("message","Failed to cancel booking");
    data.put("bookingId", bookingId.value());
    data.put("username", user.name());
    data.put("status", result.status());
    return asJson(data,
           "Failure translating audit data into JSON");
}

private final ObjectMapper objectMapper ...

private String asJson(final Map<String, String> data,
                      final String errorMessage) {
    try {
      return objectMapper.writeValueAsString(data);
    } catch (JsonProcessingException e) {
      return format("{\"failure\":\"%s\"}",
                    errorMessage);
    }
}
```

Explicitly defines the category as audit (although it might not be needed)

Message explaining why this is in the audit log

Booking that couldn't be canceled

User attempting cancellation

Reason why cancellation failed

Translation to a structured format

Object mapper that translates data into JSON

Error message to be used if translation to JSON fails

Error message to be logged if JSON translation fails

Translation of data into JSON represented as a String

Behavior and error data are extracted in similar fashion, but with the exception of sensitive data. Only the audit category is allowed to contain confidential or sensitive information. This might require special attention in other categories when extracting data; for example, when dealing with error data from a stack trace. Some frameworks or libraries choose to include the input that caused the exception in the stack trace message. This means that you could end up with information like an account number or Social Security number in the error log if an exception is thrown during the parsing process. Consequently, you want to exclude the stack trace message from the error log; otherwise, you might need to place it under restrictive access similar to the audit log.

Categorizing data this way certainly enables you to meet the confidentiality requirements, but one question still remains: should you store everything in the same log and have different views (audit, behavior, and error) or have one log per category? Both strategies seem to facilitate confidentiality, but there's a subtle difference in security to consider. Let's explore both alternatives.

Assume you choose to store everything in the same master log and have different views with restricted access. Then the log would contain intermixed JSON entries, as illustrated in the following listing.

> Listing 13.6 **Master log with intermixed JSON entries**

```
{
  "category":"audit",
  "message":"Failed to cancel booking",
  "bookingId":"#67qTMBqT96",
  "username":"jane.doe01@example.com",
  "status":"Already checked out"
}
{
  "category":"behavior",
  "message":"Failed to cancel booking",
  "status":"Already checked out"
}
```

The upside to this is that the solution is fairly easy to reason about and to implement in code. You only need to categorize data in each service and store it in the master log. Aggregation of data into a view is then a product of your access rights; for example, audit data and error data could be shown in the same view if you're granted access to both.

But this flexibility also results in a drawback that makes the solution unviable. By storing everything in the same master log and allowing categories to be intermixed, you open up the possibility of leaking sensitive data in a view, hence violating the confidentiality requirement. For example, audit data can accidentally become intermixed in a view with behavioral data. Even though this is highly unlikely, you need to ensure this never happens every time a view is generated, which adds significant complexity to the solution. As a side note, depending on what domain your system operates in, the logging system might need to comply with various data protection regulations (for example, the GDPR in the European Union), and violating confidentiality could then become a costly experience.

> **WARNING** Never intermix sensitive and nonsensitive data in the same log, because it can lead to accidental information leakage in a view.

A better alternative is to categorize data in the same way, but have each category stored as separate log streams. This has the benefit of making log data separated by design, which in turn reduces the risk of accidental leakage between categories in an aggregated view, but there's another upside to this as well. By favoring a design that enables log separation, you also open up the possibility of storing audit logs in a separate system with strict access control and traceability. This certainly seems to increase the complexity when accessing data, but the cost is justifiable when seeing it from a security perspective. For example, because audit logs could carry sensitive information, you must ensure they never end up in the wrong hands. This implies that strict access control and traceability are needed; otherwise, you don't know how sensitive data has been consumed.

The life cycle of audit data is also important from a security standpoint. When a system is decommissioned, you tend not to care about logs anymore; except for audit logs, because there might be legal requirements that demand audit data be persisted for a long time (for example, financial transactions). Treating audit logs with care and storing them in a separate system is therefore a good strategy, both from a security and operational perspective.

You have now read about how to deal with sensitive data in a microservice architecture, how to design your APIs, and what complexity logging brings from a security standpoint. We've nearly reached the end of our journey toward making software secure by design. In the next and final chapter, we'll talk about techniques that you should use in combination with what you've learned in this book. For example, we'll discuss why it's still important to run security penetration tests from time to time, and why explicitly thinking about security is necessary.

Summary

- A good microservice should have an independent runtime, allow independent updates, and be designed for other services being down.
- Treating each microservice as a bounded context helps you design more secure APIs.
- Secure design principles such as domain primitives and context mapping are also applicable when designing microservice APIs.
- In order to avoid common security pitfalls, only expose domain operations in APIs, use explicit context mapping between services, and pay extra attention to evolving APIs.
- It's important to analyze confidentiality, integrity, availability, and traceability (CIA-T) across all services.
- Identify data that's sensitive and possibly needs to be secured across services.
- The integrity of log data is important from a security standpoint.
- Normalization and categorization of log data requires extensive domain knowledge and should be part of the service design.

- A service must be uniquely identifiable by its name, version number, and instance ID.
- A transaction must be traceable across systems.
- Using a logger with a domain-oriented API facilitates a design that considers the confidentiality of log data.
- Don't intermix sensitive and nonsensitive data in the same log, because that can lead to accidental information leakage.

14

A final word: Don't forget about security!

This chapter covers
- Code security reviews
- Vulnerabilities in a large-scale tech stack
- Running security penetration tests from time to time
- Following security breaches and attack vectors
- Incident handling and the team's role

By now, you've been with us throughout the course of a pretty long book. We've spent much time talking about how to not think about security, but still get security anyway. Surprising as it might seem, we'd like to close this book by talking about how important it is to think about security. We started this book by noting a few things:

- Developers find it difficult and distracting to explicitly think about security while coding.
- Developers like and find it natural to think about design while coding.
- Many security problems arise from *bugs*, misbehaving code that happens to open up security vulnerabilities.
- Good design reduces bugs; some designs prevent some kinds of bugs, while other designs prevent other bugs.

In our approach, we suggest thinking more about design, thereby gaining security as a side benefit. In this book, we've presented a collection of designs that, in our experience, work well to counter weak security, making the code *secure by design*. Even if you use all the design patterns in this book and come up with a few yourself, there's still a need for explicitly thinking about security. The secure by design approach certainly reduces a lot of the cumbersome security work, but there'll still be aspects that are best addressed by explicit security work.

A detailed account of security practices is outside the scope of this book, but it wouldn't do to completely leave out a discussion of some things that we've found are pretty effective in lowering the security risk. These things are close to the development work that you do by yourself or with your team and have a positive impact on security, compared to the effort required. And that's what this chapter is about. Unfortunately, a detailed account would fill a book in and of itself. We'll keep our discussion brief and focus on the *what* and *why*, rather than digging into the details of *how* to do it.

Not that long ago, there was a deep divide between coders and testers. That divide has now been bridged, and we think of both coding and testing as natural parts of development. We have testers together with coders on our development team, and we perform testing during the run of a sprint, not as a separate phase after. In the same way, the historical divide between developers and operations has been bridged in many organizations with the advent of the DevOps culture, where teams work with both development and operational aspects in mind. Extending the idea of DevOps, we'd like the whole team to embrace the security aspects of their products and services as well. Most probably, there'll still be external security experts, but we'd like to sketch out how to get your existing team to become more self-supporting when it comes to security.

With security, there are no guarantees, and following the practices in this chapter won't get you 100% secure. But the secure by design approach takes you most of the way, and the tips here will get you close to where you need to be. Let's start with something close to the code and related to something you hopefully already do to some degree: code security reviews.

14.1 Conduct code security reviews

Code reviews are an effective way to get feedback on solutions, find possible design flaws, and spread knowledge about the codebase. If you aren't already conducting code reviews, we recommend you try it.

The exact format of the code review (what to focus on, which people should participate, and so on) depends on your specific needs, and there are many resources available to guide you in getting started. Just as regular code reviews are beneficial for the software development process, in both the short and the long run, code security reviews are equally beneficial, especially from a security perspective.

> **TIP** Use recurrent code security reviews to enhance the security of your code and to share knowledge. Make them a natural part of your development process.

Code security reviews are much like regular code reviews, but with the purpose of reviewing the security properties of the code. A code security review helps you find possible security flaws, share knowledge of how to design secure code, and improve the overall design. Because a code security review is, by definition, performed after the code has been written, it complements all the other techniques and tools you use to make your software secure, including the ones you've learned in this book. Keep in mind that there's no reason to wait until the entire application is finished before conducting code reviews. Instead, it's usually more beneficial to perform code reviews continuously and often while developing your code.

There's more than one way of doing a code security review. You can, for example, choose to focus primarily on the overall design of the code, while paying extra attention to things like the implementation or absence of secure code constructs. This approach works well with the concepts in this book. Another option could be to focus on more explicit security aspects, such as the choice of hash algorithms and encodings or how HTTP headers are used. You could also use a combination of different approaches. Which approach you choose depends largely on what type of application you're building and the dynamics of your team and organization. Pick an approach you feel comfortable with and then evaluate, refine, and experiment. Eventually, you'll find a way that suits your specific needs.

14.1.1 *What to include in a code security review*

If you're unsure what to include in a security review, an approach that can be helpful is to use a checklist as a guide. Write down a list of things you want to include in the review, then each person performing the review can check off the items they complete. If all items in the list have been checked, you know you've at least achieved a baseline.

The following list is an example of how a checklist for code security reviews might look. We've tried to include items with different perspectives to inspire you about what to include in your own checklist.

- Is proper encoding used when sending/receiving data in the web application?
- Are security-related HTTP headers used properly?
- What measures have been taken to mitigate cross-site scripting attacks?
- Are the invariants checked in domain primitives strict enough?
- Are automated security tests executed as part of the delivery pipeline?
- How often are passwords rotated in the system?
- How often are certificates rotated in the system?
- How is sensitive data prevented from accidentally being written to logs?
- How are passwords protected and stored?
- Are the encryption schemes used suitable for the data being protected?
- Are all queries to the database parameterized?
- Is security monitoring performed and is there a process for dealing with detected incidents?

Remember that this is just an example of what to include in a checklist. There's no be-all, end-all checklist for us to present. When creating your own list, you should focus on including the things that are most important and beneficial for you. It might also be that you start out with a long list to make sure you cover everything, and after a while, you remove items that are nonissues, making the list more concise and relevant for your particular team.

14.1.2 Whom to include in a code security review

Another aspect to think about is which people should take part in the code security review. Should you only involve people within the team, or should you also include people from outside the team? We think it's good to include both because they'll bring slightly different perspectives when performing the review. Outside developers, testers, architects, or product owners will all have slightly different views on security, and it can all be valuable input.

One thing to watch out for is that because people from outside the team can bring such different feedback, it might become difficult to keep the review focused and efficient. If that's the case, you can try to split the process up and conduct two separate reviews: one with team members only and one with external reviewers. Experiment and find out what works best for you.

14.2 Keep track of your stack

In chapter 8, you learned how to use your delivery pipeline to automatically check for vulnerabilities in third-party dependencies. Whenever a vulnerability is found, you can stop the pipeline; the issue then needs to be addressed before the pipeline can be continued or restarted. Chapter 10 talked about the three R's of enterprise security (rotate, repave, repair) and taught you to repair vulnerable software as soon as possible after a patch is available. The concept of repairing should also be employed when pushing out new versions of your application caused by an update of a vulnerable dependency.

Managing security issues in delivery pipelines and getting security patches out into production quickly is fairly straightforward when dealing with a moderate number of applications. If you operate at a large scale and have hundreds or thousands of applications, you need a strategy for efficiently handling monitoring and management of vulnerabilities in your tech stack. Otherwise, you'll soon find yourself with more information than you can handle. Some aspects you need to consider are how to aggregate information and how to prioritize work.

14.2.1 Aggregating information

Once you have the tooling to automatically find security vulnerabilities (as discussed in chapter 8), you need to figure out a way to aggregate all that information to create an overarching view of your tech stack. A number of tools can perform such aggregation, both open source and proprietary.[1] Keep in mind that if an issue found in an application can be handled directly by the team responsible for that application, it's usually easier to work with the detailed information generated for that specific application, rather than working with an aggregated view.

> **TIP** Overarching views of security vulnerabilities are essential when operating at large scale. Invest in tooling for aggregating and working with large amounts of information across the company.

Being able to work with aggregated views of information is necessary when dealing with issues that need to be addressed at a company level. Aggregated views are also an indispensable tool for any type of high-level reporting. Setting up the tools and infrastructure to make it effortless and automatic to get a bird's-eye view of vulnerabilities in your tech stack is a worthwhile investment. As with many other things, it's usually a good idea to start small and move to more complex tooling as you grow.

14.2.2 *Prioritizing work*

When you operate at scale, there'll probably always be multiple known vulnerabilities at any point in time. Most likely, you won't have the time to address them all at once, so you need to prioritize.

> **TIP** Set up a process for how to prioritize and distribute work when vulnerabilities are discovered. Doing this beforehand will save you headaches later on.

As early as possible, figure out a process for dealing with vulnerabilities. Decide how to prioritize vulnerabilities against each other and against other development activities. You also need to decide who should perform the work of fixing a vulnerability and how to prioritize the work against other types of development activities. Thinking through a process or strategy for dealing with prioritization might seem like overkill, but security work usually competes with regular development work. Having a clear strategy for how to balance security work against other work can help speed up the process, as well as avoiding potential heated discussions and possible hurt feelings.

The process doesn't need to be complex and rigid. Sometimes it's more appropriate to have a lightweight and adaptable process, if that fits your way of working better. The takeaway is that it's better to have thought about how to handle vulnerabilities before they happen.

14.3 *Run security penetration tests*

As you've learned by reading this book, security weaknesses can reside anywhere in a system; for example, in the deployment pipeline, in the operating system, or in the application code itself. Consequently, many choose to run security penetration tests

---

[1] The OWASP Dependency-Track project (https://dependencytrack.org) is an example of an open source tool that can aggregate vulnerability reports for multiple applications.

DJ 940 0817

(*pen tests*) to identify weaknesses such as injection flaws, sensitive data leakage, or broken access control.

You might have wondered whether the secure by design approach renders pen tests obsolete, because good design should have taken care of all the security problems. This certainly is an appealing thought, but good design isn't a substitute for pen tests. In fact, the idea of using secure by design as an argument to cut pen tests out of the loop reveals an underlying misconception about the purpose of pen tests.

Many believe pen tests should be used to prove whether a system is hackable or not, but that's not their purpose. The main objective is to help developers build and design the best possible software without security flaws. Regardless of what design principles you follow, running pen tests from time to time is a good practice to challenge your design and prevent security bugs from slipping through.

14.3.1 *Challenging your design*

When designing software, you always end up making trade-offs. These could be in anything from how you interact with legacy systems to how you design your service APIs, or whether domain primitives are used or not. Regardless, there's always a chance that your design contains flaws you might have missed or that overall domain evolution has caused exploitable microlesions in your code, similar to what you learned in chapter 12, where you learned how sensitive data leaked through logging caused by an evolving domain model.

Effective pen testing should therefore include the technical aspects of a system (such as authentication mechanism and certificates), as well as focusing on the business rules of a domain. This is because security weaknesses can be caused by a combination of design flaws and valid business operations.

> **TIP** Run pen tests on a regular basis to detect exploitable microlesions in your design caused by evolving domain models and new business features.

In general, business rules are meant to be used with good intentions. For example, if you make a table reservation at a restaurant, you intend to show up. But if the same reservation rules are used together with a too generous cancellation policy (for example, cancellation without charge), then it's possible for someone with malicious intent to craft a denial-of-service attack, as we talked about in chapter 8. Although this might seem unlikely, there are, in fact, lots of businesses suffering from this without even realizing it. This is because logs and monitoring show normal usage and nothing is out of the ordinary, except that financial reports might indicate a drop in revenue or market share. Understanding how to attack a system using business rules is therefore an important part of system design and something you should encourage in a pen test. Unfortunately, not many pen testers realize this because they're not trained in exploiting domain rules, but our experience is that pen tests that include this are far more efficient at identifying weaknesses in a system than tests only focusing on technical aspects.

14.3.2 *Learning from your mistakes*

Challenging your design using pen tests is certainly important, but there's another side to running these tests on a regular basis. Every time you receive feedback from a pen test team (this could be in a formal report or just when talking by the coffee machine), you have the opportunity to see it as a learning experience. It doesn't matter how big the findings are; what's important is that you see it as a chance to improve your design and not as criticism of what you've built. Our experience is that security flaws often can be addressed as normal bugs, which means it should be possible to add tests in your delivery pipeline that fail if you ever introduce the same problem again. This makes your system robust and secure over time.

Another aspect of pen test feedback is the chance to discuss it within your team and learn from your mistakes. Unfortunately, not many organizations reason this way: they think security flaws should be kept secret and be handled by as few individuals as possible. This means that most developers don't get a chance to address security flaws or learn why certain design choices open up exploitable weaknesses. Analyzing results together is therefore a good opportunity to raise overall security awareness, as well as a chance for developers to learn how to address security in code. Also, if you don't run pen tests on a regular basis, there's often lots of ceremony associated with a test, similar to what you get when only releasing to production a few times a year. By discussing results within your team and seeing it as a chance to learn, you reduce overall anxiety about finding serious flaws or that someone has made a mistake.

14.3.3 *How often should you run a pen test?*

A question that often comes up when discussing pen testing is whether there's a best practice to follow regarding how often you should run a test. The short answer is no, because it all depends on the current situation and context. But from our experience, a good interval tends to be as often as you think it brings value to your design. For example, if you've added several new business features, changed your external APIs, or integrated with a new system, then it's probably a good idea to run a pen test, but there's no best practice dictating this. Instead, let the current situation and context determine whether it makes sense to run a pen test or not, like in context-driven testing, where the current situation and context guide you in choosing a testing strategy. This might seem more complex than just coming up with a fixed schedule, but our experience is that this lets you establish a good rhythm that makes pen testing a natural part of your design process.

Context-driven testing (CDT)

The context-driven approach was initially developed by James Bach, Brian Marick, Bret Pettichord, and Cem Kaner in 2001. The essence of CDT is that testing practices completely depend on the current situation and context in which an application resides. For example, if you have two applications, one of which has strict regulatory requirements and one where only time-to-market matters, then the testing practices will completely

(continued)

differ between them. A bug slipping through in the first application can lead to serious consequences; whereas in the other, you need to release a patch.

The school of CDT considers good software testing as a challenging intellectual process that depends on the current situation and context rather than a set of best practices to be followed when choosing testing objectives and techniques. The seven basic principles of context-driven testing follow:

- The value of any practice depends on its context.
- There are good practices in context, but there are no best practices.
- People working together are the most important part of any project's context.
- Projects unfold over time in ways that are often not predictable.
- The product is a solution. If the problem isn't solved, the product doesn't work.
- Good software testing is a challenging intellectual process.
- Only through judgment and skill, exercised cooperatively throughout the entire project, are you able to do the right things at the right times to effectively test your products.

For more information on CDT, see http://context-driven-testing.com.

14.3.4   *Using bug bounty programs as continuous pen testing*

One issue with pen testing is that it's often carried out during a limited period of time. This opens up the possibility of sophisticated vulnerabilities going undetected, which makes it difficult to trust the pen test report—how do you know if you've tested enough? There's no way to know, but the use of bug bounty programs or vulnerability reward programs allows you to increase your confidence by simulating a continuous, never-ending pen test. There are, however, significant differences between bug bounty programs and pen tests.

A pen test is normally conducted by a highly trained pen test team, whereas a bug bounty program can be seen as a challenge to the community to find weaknesses in a system. The length of the challenge can vary, but it's not uncommon to have programs running without an end date, which makes them similar to eternal pen tests. Anyone can join the program and take on the challenge, as long as they follow certain rules— for example, you can't interrupt normal usage or damage user data, because all testing is carried out in production. Findings are then usually rewarded by a monetary amount that varies by severity level. For example, identifying a way to extract credit card numbers or personal data is probably worth a lot more than spotting a misconfigured HTTP header or cookie. It's also important to follow the rules of disclosure, because many companies don't want vulnerabilities to be publicly announced before having a chance to address them.

As you probably agree, the idea behind bug bounty programs certainly makes sense, but one thing many forget is that running such a program requires a great deal from an organization. For example, you need to handle enrollment, provide feedback, and properly document how to reproduce a problem. You also need a mechanism to assess the value of a finding:

- How serious is it?
- How much is it worth?
- How soon do you need to address it?

All these questions need answers before you can start a bug bounty program. Because of this, we recommend that you don't fire up a challenge without properly analyzing what it requires of your company. A good starting point might be to look at existing programs to get an idea of what they entail from an organizational point of view. For example, look at *Hack the Pentagon* by the U.S. Department of Defense or at a program hosted by the Open Bug Bounty Community. This way, you might be able to take inspiration from someone else's rule book and learn what it'll mean for your organization.

> **WARNING** Make sure you understand what it means to run a bug bounty program before you announce a challenge.

Using pen tests to improve your design and make software robust over time is definitely a good idea. But reacting to the result of a pen test can be reacting too late, because the field of security is constantly changing. This brings us to the next topic: why it's important to study the field of security.

14.4 Study the field of security

Security is a field in constant motion: new vulnerabilities, attack vectors, and data breaches are discovered at a pace that makes it hard to keep up as a developer. As you know, addressing security issues with proper design is an efficient way to achieve implicit security benefits, but this doesn't mean you can forget about security as a field. In fact, learning about the latest security breaches and attack vectors is as important as studying new web frameworks or programming languages. Unfortunately, not many developers realize this, probably because they're interested in building software rather than breaking it, which makes it important for security to be a natural part of development.

14.4.1 Everyone needs a basic understanding about security

Over the years, we've seen many organizations that treat security as a separate activity that doesn't fall within the normal development process. This division is unfortunate because it makes it difficult to promote security in depth. Luckily, the secure by design mindset mitigates this to some extent, but to make security part of your daily work, you also need to ensure everyone has a basic understanding of security. For example, when developing a web application and onboarding a new team member, you could make learning about the OWASP Top 10 a requirement.[2] This way, it becomes natural to

---

[2] See https://www.owasp.org/index.php/Top_10-2017_Top_10.

talk about new findings and how to address weaknesses like SQL injection or cross-site scripting in your codebase.

Learning how to exploit weaknesses in a system is also important to gain a deeper understanding about security as a whole. Our experience is that many developers never get the chance to attack a system, which might explain why sometimes it's difficult for developers to see weaknesses in their designs. To mitigate this, we've seen several examples where organizations encourage developers and other team members to attend basic pen test training. This can be overkill, but developers often get a real eye-opener about the consequences of designing insecure software—and that's worth a lot. In addition, learning more about pen testing and understanding its purpose makes it easier to establish a culture where pen tests are seen as a vital part of the development process.

14.4.2 *Making security a source of inspiration*

In figure 14.1, you see an illustration of how input from various security sources (for example, conferences, meetups, and blog posts) is used together with knowledge from other domains to inspire solutions that address security problems by design. As it turns out, this strategy has been one of our main drivers to find new patterns that address security problems by design.

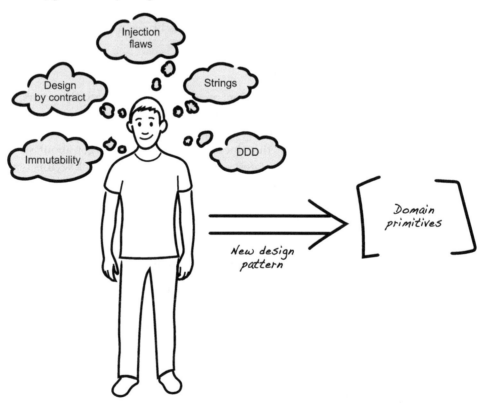

Figure 14.1   Combining knowledge from different sources yields new solutions.

For example, think about the general problem of an injection attack. The reason why it's possible to trick an application is because the type of the input argument is too generic: if it's a `String`, then it can be anything! The classic way to address this is to apply input validation, but it doesn't solve the problem completely because it brings up the issues of separating data and validation logic, plus the need for defensive code constructs. This made us combine knowledge from Domain-Driven Design, functional programming, and Design by Contract to establish the design pattern called *domain primitives* (see chapter 5). Attending conferences and meetups and reading about the latest findings in the security industry are therefore important activities in learning more about how to develop secure software.

14.5 *Develop a security incident mechanism*

Whether we like it or not, security incidents happen. When they do, someone will have to clean up the mess—that's what a security incident mechanism is all about. Let's discuss what needs to be done, and how you and your team are involved.

First, it pays to reason that the development team should be involved when there are security incidents, because no one better knows the intricate details of how the system might behave or misbehave. Some organizations have separate units for handling security incidents. In those cases, it's important that the security incident unit closely cooperate with the developers, as well as with operations people.

Preferably, security issues should be as instinctive a part of the development team's work as operational aspects are. Cooperation and cross-pollination between development and operations has made DevOps something that feels natural today. We hope that security will merge into that in the same way—that we'll see SecDevOps as an in-team practice for a lot of things and a heartfelt cooperation between development teams and specialists.

Distinguishing between incident handling and problem resolution

Security processes often distinguish between incident handling and problem resolution. This is a distinction that's in no way unique to these processes, but it's also found in more general frameworks for software management.

- *Incident handling* is what you do when there is a security incident; for example, when data is leaked or someone has hacked their way into your system. What can you do to stop the attack and limit the damage?
- *Problem resolution* is what you do to address the underlying problem that made the incident possible. What were the weaknesses that were exploited? What can you do about them?

Keeping these two apart helps keep an organization from panicking when under attack and aids in focusing on those things that are most important to be done at the time.

14.5.1 *Incident handling*

Your system is under attack. Someone is stealing the data out of the database. Should someone do something? Certainly! That's why you need incident handling. The question is rather in what way the team should be involved and why.

The development and operations team (or teams) are those with the best insights into the details of how the system works. In our experience, you get the best results from incident handling when developers are directly involved in the process. During an attack, you typically want to find out:

- What channel are the attackers using to get access to the system? How can you shut that channel? For example, you might be able to cut a database connection or shut a port.
- What further assets (databases, infrastructure, and so on) are at risk? What can the attackers do with the assets they have gained access to? For example, can they elevate their privileges on the machine or use credentials they've obtained to reach a new machine?
- What data did the attackers get access to—customer records, financial information?
- Can you limit the amount of data the attacker has access to? For example, you might empty a database while leaving it open, giving the attacker the impression that they've gotten all there is to get.
- Can you limit the value of the data; for example, by mixing it with false data?
- Can you limit the damage of the data loss; for example, by notifying or warning customers, partners, agencies, or the public?

The development team gives deep and important insights when considering these and similar questions. The most important task at hand is to stop the bleeding, but stopping the attack doesn't mean the incident is over. Investigation and damage control are part of handling the incident, so you should also capture forensic evidence to be used after the fact. During a security incident, you should focus on what needs to be done to handle the immediate situation, but later on, you can dig deeper to fix the underlying problems.

The rest of the organization must be prepared too. A security incident is by its nature unplanned and gets the highest priority. No one can assume that the team will continue to work as planned at the same time as they're saving the business assets of the company. No stakeholder should complain that their favorite feature was delayed because the team was preoccupied with a security incident.

14.5.2 *Problem resolution*

When the emergency phase of the incident is over, it's time to resolve the underlying problem. *Problem resolution* is the work that's done to understand why the incident occurred and to fix it so that it can't happen again (or at least make it more unlikely). The questions the team asks itself during problem resolution are slightly different:

- What vulnerability did the attacker exploit? For example, was there a bug in the code or a weakness in a library that was used?
- Were there several vulnerabilities that, when taken together, made the attack possible? For example, one machine with a weakness might have been protected by another mechanism until a vulnerability was found in the other mechanism.
- How could the attacker have gained information about the existence of the vulnerabilities? For example, they got information about the infrastructure because of exceptions carrying unnecessary details being exported to the caller.
- How did the vulnerabilities end up in the code? For example, a vulnerability in a third-party library might have gone unnoticed, so the version wasn't patched.

Problem resolution should cover both product and process. It should fix the problem in the product (for example, patching a broken version of a third-party library), but it should also address the problem in the process (for example, reasoning around why the team didn't know the version was broken and how they could have avoided the situation by patching earlier).

The work of resolving the problem differs a little from incident handling. In incident handling, the situation is most often drop everything else. Even if it's not all hands on deck, for those that are involved, there's nothing more important. In problem resolution, this isn't always the case. Once you've identified what the problem is, it's back to assigning priorities. For every feature you normally develop, there's a business value that motivates it. That value might be the mitigation of a risk. The same goes for problem resolution; you spend effort on mitigating a risk and securing a business asset, but the value of that effort must be weighed against all other efforts that could be expended instead. You're back to good old-fashioned priorities.

Exactly how problem resolution gets prioritized in the backlog is outside the scope of our discussion. The backlog might reside in a digital tool or be represented by sticky notes on a physical wall. Regardless, this is where the problem resolution goes—into the backlog to compete with everything else.

We are aware of the problem that not all product owners have a broad view of the product and the priorities around it. Too many product owners are stakeholders who only see one perspective—often, what's directly facing the customer or the user. A good product owner should balance features and quality work, ensuring capabilities such as response time, capacity, and security. We all know that security has a hard time getting to the top of the priorities list, but at least a backlog item that's about fixing a security problem that has already caused an incident has a somewhat better chance of getting to the top.

14.5.3 *Resilience, Wolff's law, and antifragility*

Earlier in this book, we talked about the resilience of software systems; for example, how a system that loses its connection to the database recovers by polling and reconnecting. After a while, the system is healed and is back to its normal operation as if the disturbance hadn't occurred. This is a desirable system property, but with security, you'll want to take it one step further.

We'd like to see systems that not only resume normal operation after an attack but actually grow stronger after recovering from one. That kind of phenomenon is nothing new to humanity; in medicine, it's well known and goes under the name *Wolff's law*. The nineteenth-century German surgeon Julius Wolff studied how the bones of his patients adapted to mechanical load by growing stronger. Later, Henry Gassett Davis did similar studies on soft tissues, like muscles and ligaments. Just as muscles and bones grow stronger when they're put under load, we'd like our systems to grow stronger when put under attack.

Even if it would be cool to have software that automatically adapted to and evolved after attacks, this isn't what we're after. We need to change what we mean by system, moving away from the computer science sense to what it means in system theory; we need to zoom out a little and talk about the system that consists of the software, the production environment, and the team developing the software.

> **System theory**
>
> *System theory* studies how a system of connected parts reacts to external input and how the parts react to each other, where the parts can be man-made or natural (even human). Often such systems display interesting emergent behaviors. For example, think of a queue of cars at a stoplight. When the light turns green, each driver waits until the car in front of them has moved enough to give them a comfortable safety margin and then starts driving. Seen from the side, it looks like there is a wave going through the queue, starting at the stoplight and traversing back through the queue.
>
> Taking a system theory view of a software system under attack, we'd probably view the software as one part, the attacker as another part, and the development team as a third part. Thereafter, we'd look at how those parts affect and react to one another.

Unfortunately, many systems grow weaker after attacks, when problem resolution consists of making a quick patch (as small as possible) before the team goes back to developing the next story from the backlog. The system over time becomes a patchwork of inconsistent design and becomes more vulnerable to attacks. But with insightful product ownership that also takes security seriously, the team and the system have the potential to improve after attacks. If each attack is met with incident handling, a postmortem analysis, learning, and structured problem resolution of both the product and the processes, it's possible for a system to follow Wolff's law and grow stronger when attacked. In 2012, Nassim Taleb coined the term *antifragile* to describe this phenomenon in the field of software development.[3]

---

[3] Nassim Nicholas Taleb, *Antifragile: Things That Gain from Disorder* (Random House, 2012).

One specific example of how the system grows stronger is through the security code review checklist that we mentioned earlier. The power of checklists has been proven by professionals in many fields. For example, the World Health Organization's Surgical Safety Checklist was shown to reduce complications by 40%,[4] and aviation preflight checklists have been used to improve safety since the 1930s. If you're interested, take a deeper look in *The Checklist Manifesto: How to Get Things Right* by Atul Gawande (Henry Holt, 2009). By adding carefully crafted checks to your list, you're using this power.

The tragedy of penetration tests and going antifragile

Security penetration tests provide valuable information about the vulnerabilities of your system. But the true value of the information depends on how the information is used as feedback to improve the product and the process. The results of security penetration tests can be in different formats: some more helpful with recommendations, some less helpful. The minimum is a list of what vulnerabilities were found and, often, how they could be exploited. For example, such a report might contain the following:

```
Quantity field in order form vulnerable with SQL Injection.
Attack vector `'OR 1=1--` gives access to all data in database.
```

The development team can react to this kind of information on three (or four) different levels:

- *Level 0: Ignore the report completely.* Do nothing. Obviously, this leads to no benefits, neither short-term nor long-term. The product is released with all the flaws.
- *Level 1: Fix what is explicitly mentioned.* The report is interpreted as a list of bugs that are to be fixed. This provides some short-term effect on the product, at least fewer of the obvious flaws. But there might be more vulnerabilities of the same kind. Also, the same kind of mistakes will probably be repeated in the next release.
- *Level 2: Find similar bugs.* The report is treated as a set of examples. The development team searches for similar weaknesses, perhaps by devising some grep commands and running them. There's a good short-term benefit for the product. If the grep commands are included in the build pipeline, there'll also be some small long-term benefit as well.
- *Level 3: Systemic learning.* The report is treated as a pointer for learning. Apart from fixing and searching for similar bugs, the team also engages in understanding how vulnerabilities could happen. One way is running a themed retrospective with the security penetration test report as underlying data.[*] The insights are included in code review checklists and build pipeline steps and become part of the everyday work of the team.

Clearly, level 0 (ignore) is a complete waste of time and effort. Level 1 (fix) is not much better: it's a good fix, but security penetration testing is such a time- and effort-consuming activity that testers often only have the time to find *some* weakness of each kind, not *all*

---

[*] The Queens of Retrospectives, Esther Derby and Diana Larsen, recommend themed retrospectives at regular intervals. Read their *Agile Retrospectives: Making Good Teams Great* (Pragmatic Bookshelf, 2006) for excellent advice on how to do good retrospectives.

---

[4] Haynes, A., et al., "A Surgical Safety Checklist to Reduce Morbidity and Mortality in a Global Population," *New England Journal of Medicine* 360 (2009): 491-499.

(continued)

of them. So, fixing just the reported problem provides a poor payoff for the efforts. And the payoff is only short-term, not long-term at all.

At level 2 (find and fix similar), you at least get some substantial value worth the money. You can be pretty sure that the product has a certain level of quality; there are no (or few) security weaknesses left of the kind that has been found. But the payoff is still mainly short-term. At level 3 (learning), you're actually improving the system, both product and process, in a way that is antifragile. This is where you get both the short-term and long-term benefits.

For security testers, the most saddening scenario is when a report is completely ignored. But a close second is when the organization fixes exactly the weaknesses that were reported and nothing else. Of course, what these specialists want is to be part of a genuine learning process where everybody improves.

Making systems grow stronger when attacked is hard, but not impossible. The aviation industry through structured learning has increased the security of air travel by over a thousandfold.[5] Their methods are not rocket science: structured incident investigations and reports that are shared within the profession—an impressive case of group learning. Structural engineers have done similarly with the design of elevators.

If the engineering branch of computer science is immature in any regard with respect to other disciplines, it's in our lack of structured learning and sharing with our peers. But there's hope. The OWASP Builders' community focuses on shared learning on security among software builders, and you can do a lot for your system with your peers on your team.[6]

Summary

- You should use code security reviews as a recurring part of your secure software development process.
- As your technology stack grows, it becomes important to invest in tooling that provides quick access to information about security vulnerabilities across the entire stack.
- It can be beneficial to proactively set up a strategy for dealing with security vulnerabilities as part of your regular development cycle.
- Pen tests can be used to challenge your design and detect microlesions caused by evolving domain models.
- Feedback from a pen test should be used as an opportunity to learn from your mistakes.

---

[5] Annual deaths per billion passenger miles have dropped from 200 in the 1930s to 0.1 in the 2010s.

[6] For more on this community, see https://www.owasp.org/index.php/Builders.

- Bug bounty programs can be used to simulate a continuous, never-ending pen test, but bug bounty programs are complex and require a great deal from an organization.
- It's important to study the field of security.
- Knowledge from different domains can be used to solve security problems.
- Incident handling and problem resolution have different focuses.
- Incident handling needs to involve the whole team.
- The security incident mechanism should focus on learning to become more resistant to attack.

index